W9-BLE-017

Also by John T. Kirk

THE IMPECUNIOUS COLLECTOR'S GUIDE
TO AMERICAN ANTIQUES

[1975]

AMERICAN CHAIRS:
QUEEN ANNE AND CHIPPENDALE

[1972]

EARLY AMERICAN FURNITURE

[1970]

CONNECTICUT FURNITURE,
SEVENTEENTH AND EIGHTEENTH CENTURIES

[1967]

AMERICAN FURNITURE & THE BRITISH TRADITION TO 1830

¶ The Dependence and Independence of American Craftsmen

¶ The Sources of American Furniture Design and Construction in British and Continental Practices

¶ The Tradition of Painted Furniture in Europe and America

¶ The Emergence of an American Aesthetic

AMERICAN FURNITURE & THE BRITISH TRADITION TO 1830

John T. Kirk

Alfred · A · Knopf / New York

1 9  *8 2*

THIS IS A BORZOI BOOK
PUBLISHED BY ALFRED A. KNOPF, INC.

Published in the United States by Alfred A. Knopf, Inc., New York, and
simultaneously in Canada by Random House of Canada Limited, Toronto.
Distributed by Random House, Inc., New York.
Portions of this book are based on articles originally published in *Antiques*.
Library of Congress Cataloging in Publication Data
Kirk, John T. / American furniture and the British tradition to 1830.
Includes index.
1. Furniture—United States—English influences. 2. Furniture, Colonial—
United States. 3. Furniture, Early American—United States. 4. Furniture—
England—History. I. Title.
NK2406.K55 749.214 82-15201
ISBN 0-394-40038-0 AACR2
Manufactured in the United States of America
FIRST EDITION

To

Trevor John Fairbrother

Contents

Issues Relating British to American Furniture

Visual Survey of British & American Furniture

Preface

The study of American furniture—as of American art in general—began with the pioneer work of collectors and dealers, who sought to order the material they loved and longed to possess or sell. Their scholarly concerns were automatically overlaid by national chauvinism, genealogical studies, and investment economics. Not only was the initial approach to the material antiquarian and chauvinistic, but in most cases its public display in period rooms and historic houses betrayed the late colonial revival taste of those who loved and cared for it. Although there were important exceptions, few authors and fewer teachers worked free of this conditioning—a stultifying heritage that has until recently skewed much of the work on American art. Fortunately, many of the new generation of scholars are largely outside these pressures; but objectivity must still be a conscious act, for the marketplace remains the material's natural domain. Indeed, when evaluating the aesthetic or cultural role of a $200,000 chair, teapot, painting, or building—whether for sale, privately owned, or part of a public institution where the donor is still active—it can be difficult to avoid non-scholarly issues.

That there is now a greater detachment and a richer understanding of American art results from the past forty years of conferences, seminars, exhibitions, and writings on the American arts. The major collector-donors who formed the institutional collections are no longer on the scene, and graduate programs are providing a pool of scholars trained to ask harder questions. Unfortunately, most graduate students must find employment not in universities and colleges, where objectivity is reinforced, but in museums and historical agencies, where the acquisition of objects from present and potential donors remains a prime concern.

In the third quarter of the twentieth century scholars working with American art made greater use of documents: diaries, accounts, inventories, newspapers, census records, and family, religious, and oral histories. Valuable contributions emerged, and the methods paved the way for interdisciplinary studies; but the documentary approach constricted understanding of the subject matter. Not only did these documents blind most researchers to an international perspective, they generally deflected attention from other arts occurring in the same locality, and from the *undocumented* work of the very artists and craftsmen under study.

Although the training now is more sophisticated, many of those who deal with American art still lack a rich understanding of European artifacts. They find it hard to take seriously objects created in Europe, and do not place what they study in the crosswinds of world art. In 1980, it was possible for some to claim of a New England tea table: "These severe New England interpretations of the Queen Anne style are often truer to the oriental inspiration of the designs than their English counterparts."[1] Yet a study of British tables—figure 1272, for example—shows that they *are* the chronological and stylistic link between the Oriental and New England forms.

Despite the remaining problems, a dramatic advance in our understanding of American art has taken place during the past decade. When in 1967 I selected the pieces and wrote the catalogue for the exhibition *Connecticut Furniture: Seventeenth and Eighteenth Centuries* (Wadsworth Atheneum, Hartford, Connecticut), it still seemed logical to do sweeping shows of a large region's furniture. An overview was necessary at the time; but recent, more specialized exhibitions have built sounder understandings of the art of some localities. Two such helpful exhibitions and catalogues have been *New London County Furniture: 1640–1840* (1974), and *Plain & Elegant, Rich & Common: Documented New Hampshire Furniture, 1750–1850* (1979).[2] The former provides a concentrated understanding of the New London region. The latter sidestepped the issue of quality and exhibited and published a group of documented pieces that provide a rationale for regional attribution.

In 1970 it seemed necessary to write *Early Amer-*

ican Furniture, for I felt it important to help people *look* at American furniture in order to see what causes quality and weakness in design, as well as to raise the issue of types of furniture—high style to rustic—so that an object would be judged in relationship to its peers. Now, in the early 1980s, I include very little design analysis, for words seem less significant than the visual juxtaposition of similar objects made in disparate areas.

The struggle to establish regional differences that was addressed in *American Chairs: Queen Anne and Chippendale* (1972) resulted in statements now generally accepted: for example, that there are three basic forms of pierced splats in Philadelphia. Today, broader surveys of construction and motifs, such as a study of neo-classical card tables, are being assisted by computer-analyzed data. And the similarity of regional products seems as important as their differences.

Part of the growing honesty and insight found in the study of American objects in the last decade has arisen from the less stereotyped work of a group of interdisciplinary scholars from anthropology, archaeology, cultural geography, folk studies, and cultural and social history. Funding from such sources as the National Endowment for the Humanities has reinforced this shift, because they ask cultural agencies to provide the meaning of an object for the general public. With the new designation "material culture" (not a discipline, but a term denoting the entire range of artifacts), the focus is on the complete man-made place. This new use of material includes a rapidly expanding interest on the part of art historians, historians, and "material culturalists" in placing American art and cultural developments within a broader context—for example, provincial England—so that the New World is viewed as an extension of the Old. At the same time, many scholars are discerning unique or indigenous American expressions at the vernacular or regional level.

The deliverance of American art from the old, narrow approach is a happy one for both the art historian and the objects, as it makes all American material embraceable. About 80 per cent of the body of early material never had great aesthetic merit (and much of the remainder has been diminished by "restorers"), yet art historians were expected to take all of it seriously. With the "material culture" designation, even the second- and third-rate items can inform cultural statements. At its best, this catholicity allows all disciplines to add insights to a network of perceptions that benefits everyone. At the same time it frees historians of American art from the responsibility of finding aesthetically significant everything made in this country—a request not normally made of their colleagues who study other developed cultures. This will be dangerous if the art historians take the opportunity to ignore the less aesthetic work and thereby screen themselves from new insights. Equally likely, and perhaps more disastrous, is the prospect that the interdisciplinary scholars will want to free material culture from aesthetic judgments and thus eliminate one factor of its being. Others propose to ignore the high style or academic and confine their sample to the vernacular. This again will hamper our understanding, for we can surely benefit most from a correct perception of everything made and used during a particular period.

In practical terms this two-pronged advance—placement of American art within a world, and particularly a European, context, and its use to understand America's cultural and social development—should produce articles, books, and exhibitions that reveal more clearly the American product and what produced and surrounded it. An awareness of how much the American-made piece depends on its sources ensures the perception of how it differs from its prototypes and therefore an understanding of its true nature. And as an indicator of cultural developments and social patterns, the artifact should correct the historian's all-too-prevalent dependence on written sources, allowing in turn a fuller perception of the American experience.

A concentrated interest on the part of scholars in understanding American art within a European context is surprisingly recent, as a brief review of some of the literature and exhibitions shows. In a 1916 Metropolitan Museum of Art *Bulletin,* it was noted that the greatest colonial portrait painter, John Singleton Copley, had based his portrait of Mrs. Jerathmael Bowers (now identified as Mrs. Joseph Sherburne) on a mezzotint after the museum's recently acquired portrait of Lady Caroline Russell by Joshua Reynolds.[3] In 1945 an exhibition, "Old and New England," organized by Gordon Washburn at the Museum of Art, Rhode Island School of Design, focused on the relationship of American and English high-style and court paintings. Between 1944 and 1949 Waldron Phoenix Belknap, Jr., sought print sources for a diverse group of colonial portraits, including those by Copley, and his findings were published after his death, in part in 1955, more fully in 1959. That major colonial artists could depend on prints for their sitters' poses and clothing, rather than showing personal items and home environments, shocked a generation of scholars who had assumed that to be fully great and American the artist must be free of European contamination. In 1952 Alice Ford, in *Edward Hicks, Painter of the Peaceable Kingdom*, demonstrated that even a vernacular artist in rural Pennsylvania depended on prints for the form of animals, waterfalls, houses, trees, and the arrangement of people—placed individually or in groups. Several American scholars went to Europe in 1957 to find paintings closer to American examples than were then known. As with furniture, published European paintings were generally by the better-known artists, and, like court furniture, the attitudes differed from the American. These scholars found in England—and on the continent—paintings that closely resembled colonial works. Upon her return, Anna Wells Rutledge in "Fact and Fancy: Portraits from the Provinces" amusingly placed statements made about Americanness under European examples employing similar techniques.[4]

Daniel Robbins disturbed many in the folk art field when in 1976 he suggested in "Folk Sculpture without Folk" that folk pieces rarely emerged *ex nihilo*. Rather, the makers were part of the normal process of art history, and diligent work would reveal more high art sources for folk forms. The idea of sources existing for folk art remains anathema to many. John Michael Vlach, ignoring the natural dependencies of most artistic expressions, and feeling that the use of sources abrogates all originality, wrote in 1981: "To speak of Hicks as an original painter is obviously pointless."[5] A recent article by Trevor J. Fairbrother places Copley's borrowings within the context of English studio practices and focuses on what was new about Copley's work.[6] At present, exhibitions and books on the parallel European and American arts are in the planning stage, and a clear understanding of both the dependence and independence of American artistic expressions should emerge during the next decade.

Organization

The initial plan for this book was to divide the illustrations equally, alternating American and European examples to allow continuing visual contrasts. But as I began to sort the British photographs, it became apparent that a greater percentage of European work should be used because scholars of American furniture would already be familiar with related American examples; as in publishing an archive, this was an opportunity to make unknown British material available. Figures 8 through 54 are strictly paired English and American pieces. Throughout the rest of the book there is usually at least one American example among each form and pattern.

The body of illustrations is preceded by nine essays. The first is a general discussion of the nature of artistic dependence. The second shows a series of paired English and American pieces, mostly furniture; establishes the closeness that existed; and examines the distribution of motifs over various crafts and styles. An essay on a series of Gillows designs for dining tables focuses on the availability at one shop during one period of many styles and degrees of sophistication; it demonstrates the customer's role in the final product. The essays on painted furniture and carving are used to review the larger issues of American dependence, the question of style lag, and the impact of continental pieces on English and American design. These are followed by a series of short essays on particular features, such as retracted claws and through tenons, once seen as signaling an American origin. The two final essays deal with the type of furniture that was *not* made in America, allowing a discussion of great English work; and then the particular achievement of the American aesthetic is singled out.

In the essay section, bold type is used for the main reference to an object, serving to direct the reader to the corresponding text, and no separate caption is used.

The arrangement of the book's second half, the Visual Survey, is by form, and within each form, by style. The classifications have been kept large, and are generally without subgroups that would make it harder to find related material. Where appropriate, objects within each designation are grouped as they relate to particular American regional expressions. For example, in Chippendale chairs, those that resemble Massachusetts chairs are put together, then the groups proceed down the coast. To keep like designs together, such regional variations are not adhered to when visual similarities suggest a different order. Woods are mentioned when they are known.

In presenting the comparisons central to this study between English and American work, it is possible that I am reinforcing the all-too-prevalent chauvinistic attitude that American furniture is aesthetically superior to what was made in England. Often it is so when comparing *similar* English and American material, but such pieces are not among the best English work. Proper attention to the extraordinary qualities of the court and Palladian pieces should eliminate this prejudice. I have included a few continental pieces where they inform this study; a detailed survey of parallel continental work is still needed.

The task of assembling so many revealing examples beyond what I could manage to see personally necessitated acquiring photographs where they could be obtained: from museums, dealers, and auction houses. Often the furniture itself was no longer available; these pictures were scrutinized for stylistic aberrations that suggest later repairs or out-of-period work. Under ideal circumstances, I would not publish a piece unless I had seen it. But in this case, had I limited myself to available pieces, the years I spent in Britain would have produced a smaller collection of images and I would have been forced to neglect important photographic collections.

Dating

Often I have dated furniture later, or given a longer than customary span of possible manufacture. The many dated pieces included—not least the drawings by the Gillows firm—make this necessary. For example, the Gillows papers show drawings of chests-on-chests with plain styling as a regular feature in the 1790s (figures 567 and 568); the 1793 drawing of a turned "Queen Anne" foot (figure 1255) proves the use of this form until the end of the eighteenth century. Similarly, the Philadelphia 1766 drawing by Samuel Mickle of a solid-splat chair (figure 839) helps date a related group of chairs in the second half of the eighteenth century. Examples of English furniture that suggest a new dating scheme are the seventeenth-century-style pieces dated in the eighteenth century. These extended date blocks take into account the longevity of many of the simpler expressions, but they are not stretched to include the unusually retardataire or revival objects such as an 1816 table with Marlborough legs and feet (figure 1387). Rather, the dates cover the period of a form's popularity even when it overlaps with other available styles. (See the list of dated pieces on page 391.)

Note that unless it is appropriately part of the text, the date of an object (given in parentheses) follows the first mention of the piece or its number. Secondary woods, also in parentheses, follow the primary wood.

Acknowledgments

A Fulbright Fellowship enabled me to spend the academic year 1963–4 in England pursuing those characteristics thought to be unique to American furniture. The late Delves Molesworth, then Keeper of Furniture and Woodwork at the Victoria and Albert Museum, upon being convinced that it might be possible to regionalize English furniture, persuaded the Fulbright office to increase my stipend to allow travel throughout England for six months. The resulting visits to approximately three historic houses, museums, and antique shops each day provided the beginnings of this book. Derek Shrub introduced me to the qualities of both English and continental furniture, and refined my understanding of design by insisting that the superior expressions were the only legitimate concern of art historians. He will appreciate those pieces in Chapter 8 most.

Jane Garrett, friend and editor, secured funding from the John Anson Kittredge Foundation, then headed by Walter Whitehill, to make possible a brief return to England in 1973. The trip was to ascertain whether sufficient advances had been made in understanding English regional types for another year's work there to be profitable. The National Endowment for the Humanities subsequently funded my stay for the academic year 1974–5. During that period, Peter Thornton provided easy access to the furniture at the Victoria and Albert Museum in London. John Hardy tirelessly assisted my research into the museum's vast collection of photographs of English furniture, and he has since provided helpful information. Derek Shrub reviewed stacks of photographs and directed me to examples of English painted furniture. He and Delves Molesworth took me to the Langley Marish Parish Church, in Buckinghamshire, which became central in the discussion of England's use of paint. Finally, the National Endowment for the Humanities, through a further grant, funded a leave of absence from Boston University, allowing the preparation of this manuscript; the Scholars Program at Winterthur Museum provided two weeks with that museum's research collections; and an anonymous grant assisted with production costs.

Over many years Israel Sack, Inc., has been generous with photographs and advice. Ruth Bacon and the late Roger Bacon assisted my quest to understand vernacular forms. Sotheby-Parke-Bernet permitted me to select an array of photographs from their London files; David Stockwell, Inc., and Benjamin Ginsburg Antiquary provided photographs and advice. Heidi Katz produced prints from my often inadequate negatives. Henry Glassie, the late Charles Montgomery, and Philip J. Greven, Jr., assisted with grant proposals and Daniel Robbins rewrote one of the proposals and discussed parts of the manuscript. I am indebted to Anthony Wells-Cole for reviewing and correcting the places of origin assigned to the early oak pieces.

In preparing the manuscript, I have been assisted by Richard Albright, Hope Alswang, Peter Benes, Edgar M. Bingham, Jr., Richard Cheek, Lillian Blankley Cogan, Michael Conforti, Wendy A. Cooper, Abbott Lowell Cummings, Deborah Ducoff-Barone, Allison Eckhardt, Nancy Goyne Evans, Dean F. Failey, Jonathan L. Fairbanks, Anne Farnam, Kathy Foster, Donald R. Friary, Beatrice Garvan, Christopher G. Gilbert, Benjamin Ginsburg, Henry Glassie, Wallace B. Gusler, Morrison H. Heckscher, Danny Hingston, Graham S. Hood, Frank L. Horton, William N. Hosley, Jr., Kevin Jenness, Patricia E. Kane, Karen Keane, Elizabeth D. Kirk, Nina Fletcher Little, Vincent F. Luti, Thomas S. Michie, Florence Montgomery, Sarah Nichols, Jane Nylander, Richard Nylander, Dianne H. Pilgrim, Jules D. Prown, Bradford Rauschenberg, Lewis Rockwell, Bill Reider, Albert Sack, Robert Blair St. George, Frances Gruber Safford, Robert W. Skinner, Frank H. Sommer, David Stockwell, John A. H. Sweeney, Neville Thompson, Robert F. Trent, Linda Wesselman, and Richard W. Withington.

The late Benno M. Forman was a corrective influence on my work; his willingness to share his amazing knowledge of documentary sources and his humanity enriched all those who knew him. He was particularly helpful in preparing the chapter on painted furniture when parts of it first appeared as articles in *Antiques*. As the citations in the Notes attest, I am indebted to him to a greater extent than I can here acknowledge. I am grateful to Wendell Garrett for allowing me to rework as Chapter 4 articles from *Antiques* and for making available the color separations that were prepared for them. For their work on the completed manuscript and their transformation of it into a handsome book, I am grateful to many at Knopf, and especially to Bob Gottlieb, Jane Garrett, Nancy Clements, Ann Adelman, Betty Anderson, Cynthia Krupat, and Dennis Dwyer. I am also continually indebted to my parents, Elizabeth H. Kirk and Samuel E. Kirk, for providing a varied education.

This book is dedicated to Trevor Fairbrother, who assisted in the various stages of its preparation, from photography in England to editing several drafts. His ability to recognize visual relationships between disparate objects and his sensibility to form and quality have greatly enhanced this work. Among many discoveries, he found the Oriental claw and ball feet seen as figures 302 and 303, and recognized the relationship between the profile mask in figure 108 and that on the Great Bed of Ware in figure 241. Without his assistance, the present diversity and depth of understanding would not have been possible.

Map of England

USING OLD COUNTY DESIGNATIONS

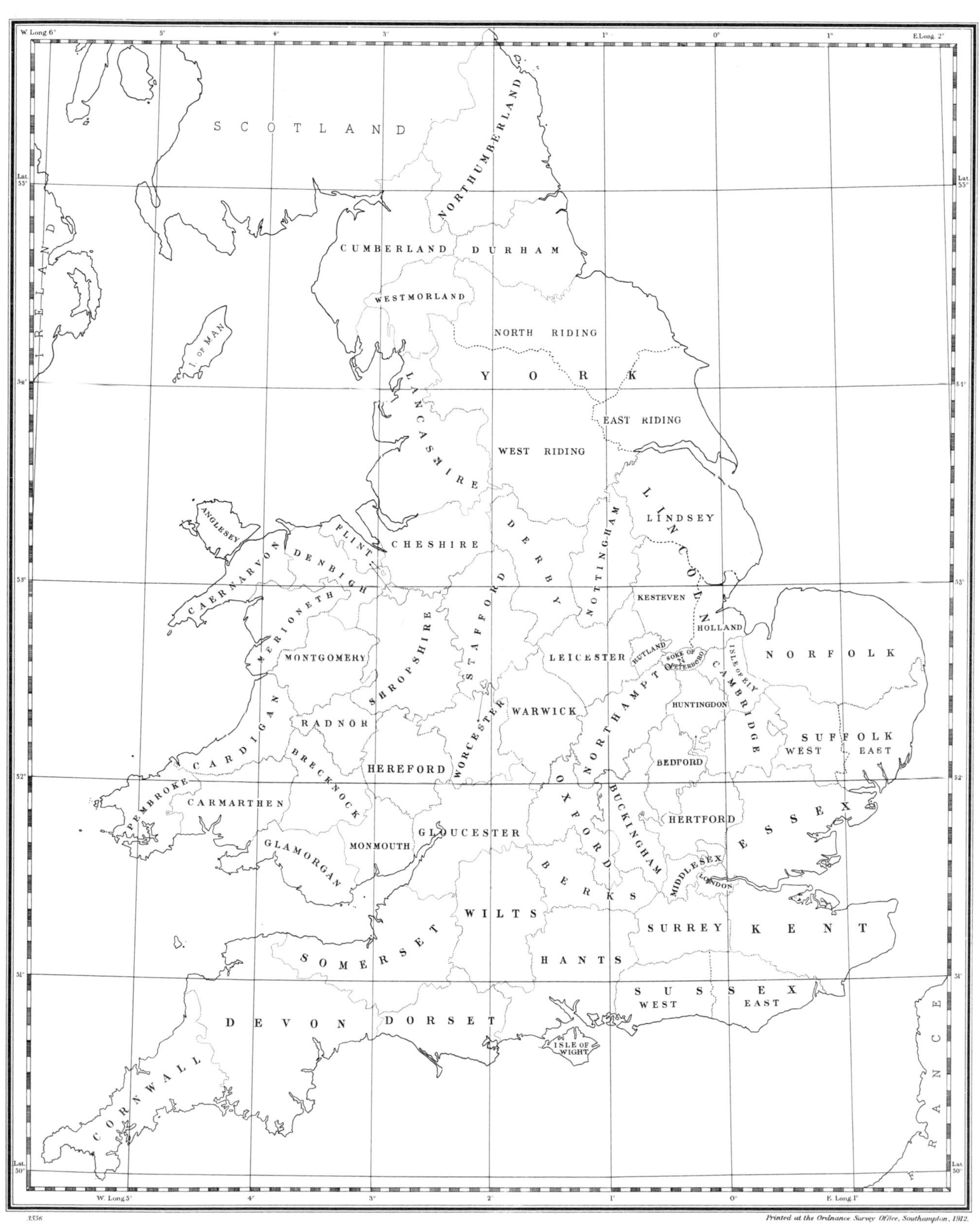

Reigns of the English Monarchs

HENRY VIII	1509–47
EDWARD VI	1547–53
MARY I	1553–58
ELIZABETH I	1558–1603
JAMES I	1603–25
CHARLES I	1625–49
[COMMONWEALTH	1649–60]
CHARLES II	1660–85
JAMES II	1685–89
WILLIAM III & MARY II	1689–94
WILLIAM III	1694–1702
ANNE	1702–14
GEORGE I	1714–27
GEORGE II	1727–60
GEORGE III	1760–1820

Issues Relating British to American Furniture

1

Dependence & Levels of Sophistication

Dependence and Independence

Until the more thoroughly international styles of the later nineteenth century, American designs were derived from European models. During the period of this study the main, but not the exclusive, influence was from Britain, particularly England and Ireland. The presentation here of 1,500 illustrations of similar British and American pieces should facilitate a study of the development of American furniture while also suggesting answers to the larger questions of cultural dependence and independence.

The European photographs were collected during two years spent in Britain hunting for every design and constructional feature then thought to be uniquely American. The purpose was not to diminish the importance of the American experience. Rather, by demonstrating the nature of the dependence and seeing how European designs were interpreted, it would then be possible to isolate what was distinctive about the American statement.

In part, this is a study of provincialism: the struggle between the emulation of a more developed distant culture and the simultaneous satisfaction with local and personal values. It is the nature of cultural hierarchies that a place which is perceived as culturally superior in one relationship may, in another, be culturally dependent. While the colonists looked to Britain for guidance, England looked in turn to the continent, where Italy, Germany, France, and The Netherlands provided aesthetic inspiration and standards. Indeed, there is a dearth of artistic greatness in surviving British furniture made before the 1660 restoration of the Stuart monarchy, which brought both artists and a richer vision of aesthetic excellence from the continent to England.

The London chest of drawers with doors in figure 1 is dated 1653. It neatly arranges a series of squares, octagons, triangles, circles, and paired applied split-spindles in the English late Renaissance, mannerist style. Focal areas are enriched with inlaid designs of mother-of-pearl. (Related pieces are shown as figures 467 through 475.) Although this is an important English example, it does not reach the aesthetic level of developed Dutch, French, German, or Italian furniture. The upper and lower sections are too similar; there is not sufficient building of majesty from floor to cornice. (The feet are not original.) In contrast, the 1642 drawing by the Dutch designer Crispin de Passe II, figure 2 (detailing alternative designs at the right and left), has greater upward thrust and scale as well as clarity of parts. This creates a more sophisticated design, and therefore a superior presence.

England was dependent on the continent, and it should not surprise us that the colonists, although

1

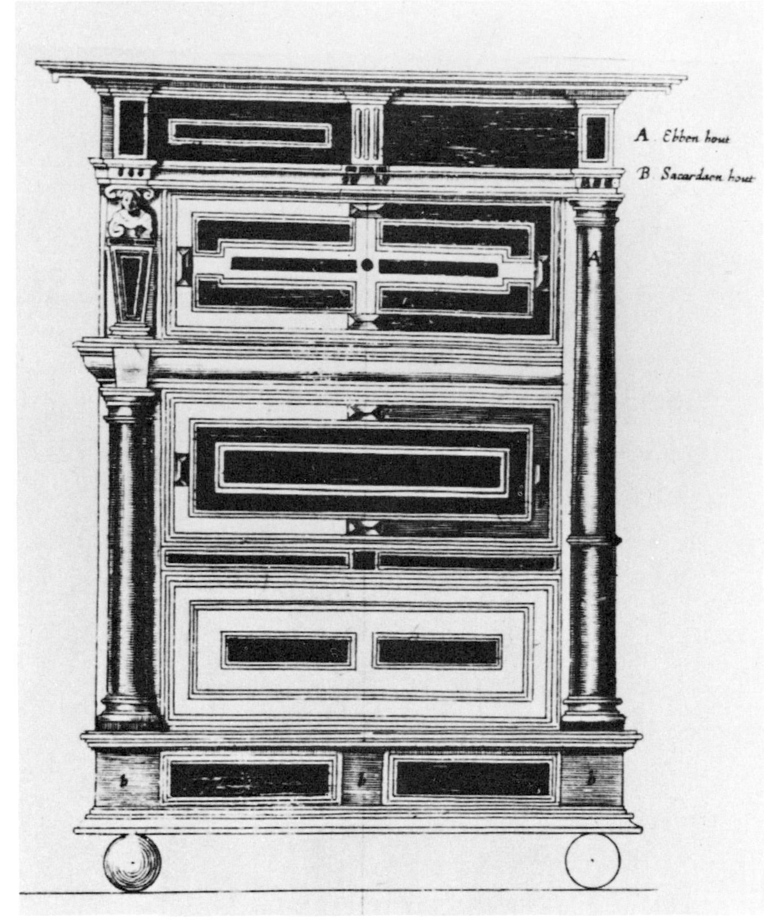

2

wishing to change their religious and political patterns, would continue to look to Europe for cultural, social, and aesthetic guidance. There is no evidence that once established on new shores anyone thought of aesthetic freedom or saw it as an opportunity to make new aesthetic choices. Rather, to the extent that prevailing conditions allowed, the first colonists set about making their homes like those they had left behind. That these conditions, which included the distance from England, should set in motion immediate cultural, social, and aesthetic changes was part of what would lessen the dependence on European furniture designs. Differences began early in the colonial period and are observable in the work of most eighteenth-century artisans.

To a great degree growing differences must have been conscious, at least among the more culturally developed makers. One of the finest groups of designer-makers of the third quarter of the eighteenth century is linked together by furniture historians as the Goddard and Townsend school of cabinet makers, of Newport, Rhode Island. These men, sidestepping London fashions, often produced unique sculptural forms that equal the best made in Europe. When the rococo style, with its leafy, playful lines (figures 7 and 56), dominated developed English work, Newport used a pulsating baroque rhythm that played void against projecting masses and smooth surfaces against richly patterned shells (figure 3). This mahogany desk and bookcase was made for John Brown of Providence, between 1770 and 1790. (The secondary woods are: tulip poplar, chestnut, and white pine.) It is true that this was not wholly a Newport development in that it looked to continental forms such as those depicted in the design for a desk and bookcase by J. G. König of Augsburg, Germany (figure 4), published about 1740–50. The engraving elaborates its baroque form with rococo-style veneers and leafage; the central niche of the upper case, and the flanking positive verticals, are capped with shells; the sides are framed with pilasters. Panels are delineated under the side scrolls of the pediment. On contemporary pieces of German furniture, such pediment panels may be executed

3

4

by letting decorative veneers into the surrounding plain veneer, or they may be raised above the adjacent surface. On upper cases that do not reach a great height, these raised panels may be the fronts of drawers.

The Newport piece lacks rococo leafage and the mass (made of light mahogany) is held by engaged fluted quarter columns, cornice, and finials of dark mahogany. The pediment plaques, which are shaped like the edges of the drawers below, carry blocking and are thus sufficiently bold to bring the upward tripartite thrust of the main blocking to the central finial and flanking rosettes. (The stylistic origins of the block-front form are further discussed in Chapter 7.)

Although general precepts for the Newport expression are discernible, its manner of handling form, surface, and decoration was original, and included a conscious rejection of the prevailing London rococo style. It is fairly certain that John Goddard (1723–1785), who was central to this school of workers, owned a copy of the third edition (1762) of Thomas Chippendale's design book *The Gentleman & Cabinet-Maker's Director,* first published in 1754. This copy—now in the Museum of Fine Arts, Boston—has a detailed history of having belonged to him, and was signed twice by his son Thomas Goddard (1765–1858), who along with his brother Stephen inherited their father's shop and tools.[1]

Chippendale's publication distributed London rococo taste throughout Europe and a few areas of the New World. David Roentgen, based in Germany, borrowed from it, and a copy of the French edition may have belonged to Catherine the Great.[2] While great designers were inspired by the *Director,* more dependent cultural centers such as Charleston, South Carolina, in a provincial desire to be an extension of London, embraced it as a means of securing "correct" London taste. By contrast, the best Newport cabinetworkers rejected such adherence, consciously risked independence, and because of their superior abilities achieved a new, important artistic statement. At the vernacu-

5

lar level, the furniture often associated with the Gaines family has equal importance as an American achievement (see figures 22 and 391).

Levels of Sophistication

Pieces made in a given center would result from the abilities, technical and artistic, of the makers, and from the aesthetic taste and financial commitments of the purchasers. In developed style centers, patrons were able to choose various levels of sophistication from a variety of makers. Fashionable London homes might contain elaborate pieces that directly reflected the prevailing style in the important rooms but would use simpler pieces in the lesser places. These varying degrees of enrichment could come from the same or different shops. Outside London, which was never too distant in such a relatively small country, pretentious patrons could be supplied with elaborate and plain pieces by one or more of the London shops. For example, Chippendale provided for Sir Rowland Winn, owner of Nostell Priory in West Yorkshire, a plain, straight-leg drop-leaf table with matching chairs (1766); an elaborately veneered and carved mahogany clothes-press (1767); and a simple oak chest of drawers (1768). (The mahogany clothes-press and oak chest of drawers went to Nostell Priory; the table and chairs may have been used in Sir Rowland's London house, although they are now at Nostell.)[3] The Nostell Priory chair seen in figure 57 was based on plate 12 in the 1754 *Director* (figure 56) and probably came from Chippendale's shop.

In the provinces it was possible to use rural makers trained to execute the current high style, but usually the pieces lacked the highest level of artistic line. The mid-century English chair (figure 5), stamped by the maker Samuel Sharp of Norwich, Norfolk (made freeman in 1737, will filed in 1761), is typical of stylish work produced in a rural center. (The back feet are not original.) The Gillows firm of Lancaster, in the northwest, made furniture for houses throughout England and had an outlet in London.[4] Fortunately for modern scholars, the firm kept elaborate records of what was sold. In detailing each item, it usually listed the purchaser, the costs of materials and labor, and provided a sketch of the piece. Chapter 3 reviews a group of these drawings, demonstrating that it was possible at any moment to purchase a variety of interpretations of each form with greater or lesser amounts of enrichment in imported or local woods.

English and Irish high-style furniture dominates this book, running parallel to the American high-style work made for a similarly successful merchant class. In England, for each successive style there was a grand version for aristocratic settings. Such furniture was richly patterned and detailed, and usually the work of makers with more refined cabinetmaking skills and aesthetic judgment. These court-level pieces relate to the American products only in being part of the same sequence stylistically. Thus the cane chair seen as figures 41 and 356 is of the same style as the Massachusetts bannister-back chair in figure 750, but its grandiloquence removes any common ground on which to meet the American piece. Court-level work is included here when it informs our understanding of the English work that did affect American furniture designs, and when it clarifies England's artistic qualities.

During the 1720s and 1730s, another type of English furniture emerged that had little to do with the general stylistic development of the first sixty years of the eighteenth century. In those years, London high-style and court furniture shifted from the graceful lines of early Queen Anne design (figure 369) to the frenzied movement of the rococo (figure 365). Although this was a gradual development, the names of the prevailing monarch were assigned by later scholars to designate the succeeding phases: Queen Anne, 1702–14, George I, 1714–27, George II, 1727–60; the dominating name of Chippendale usurps the last stage, under the first years of George III (1760–1820). Separate from this high-style and court development was furniture more appropriate to eighteenth-century Palladian magnificence. Designers such as William Kent drew upon architectural and decorative arts details from ancient and Renaissance Italy to create furniture suitable for settings enshrining classical ideals. This stance, which has little visual relationship with upper middle-class furniture of the eighteenth century, only rarely conditioned American design (for a rare instance, see figures 359 and 360). At least as grand as court work, such furniture did not relate in either scale or elaboration to even the most ornate American rooms, and in terms of cost would have been prohibitive. When, however, an American artist like John Singleton Copley wished to create splendid settings for local sitters, he felt free to borrow Palladian details from mezzotint engravings after English portraits.[5] Palladian-style furniture is included in Chapter 8, on What America Did Not Do.

Vernacular furniture was more widely used than high-style work, whether urban or rural. These pieces might employ features from the prevailing high-style taste, and generally reflected it in proportions and shaping; but more often than not they continued details considered obsolete by people of higher fashion. For example, figure **6** shows a wainscot chair dated 1742, a time when rococo designs were popular in elite London (for a detail of the back, see figure 298); in contrast, the design seen in figure **7** is dated 1746 and appeared as plate 5 in Henry Copland's *New Book of Ornaments,* published in London in the same year. And the wainscot chair with "Chippendale" crest rail in figure 299 is dated [17]85, twenty-five years after Robert Adam began designing buildings and furnishings in the neo-classical style. These vernacular or locally oriented pieces satisfied, and in many instances were preferred by, those who prized consistency over change. (Some writers place furniture along with other objects made and enjoyed by communal folk under "folk art," but exclude from this designation individual expressions when the artist stands outside the communal norm.[6] It is my belief that this makes the designation "folk art" too restrictive. Therefore, I have used the term "vernacular" to encompass all non-elite work.)

In doing the research for this book, I was particularly concerned to find examples of British vernacular furniture to see how it used or rejected

6

7

high-style ideas, and whether the American work derived its ideas from similar English furniture or drew primarily from American high-style forms. Also, I was interested in establishing the existence of an English tradition of painted furniture, and vernacular examples then seemed the most likely participants in this approach to surfaces. However, it proved difficult to find examples or even photographs of vernacular work, for it is seldom handled by dealers, auction houses, or museums that photograph their furniture. Groups of vernacular pieces are discussed in Chapters 4, 5, 6, 7, 9, and the Conclusion, and others are scattered throughout the book.

8

9

10

2

Similarity of Designs, Role of Wood Identification & Ubiquity of Motifs

The closeness of European and American pieces can be astonishing. During the mid-1950s there were rumors of a chest found in Ottery St. Mary, Devon—in the southwest of England—with carved motifs like those used on the "Dennis" group in New England.[1] Even more surprising, the chest had a polychrome finish that linked it firmly to pieces made in eastern Massachusetts. The chest (figure 8) has been fully researched by several scholars and indeed, when paired with the Dennis/Searle pieces, such as figure 9, and both with another Devon chest, figure 10, the relationship is obvious. The stiles and rails display carved, intertwined, foliated S scrolls, most of the panels have flower and leaf designs, with a large ring or stylized partial urn holding the base of the stems. (Rings linking floral stems and vines were common mannerist devices: see figures 196 and 202.)

The similarity of the carved designs surprised scholars, but the use of bright red paint with blue accents on an English piece astonished them. English painted pieces were then seen as rare exceptions, not as part of England's furniture tradition. The Ottery St. Mary chest also helped alter an assumption about American work. It had been accepted that such English pieces were made early in the seventeenth century and that seventeenth-century American work lagged stylistically behind furniture made in England by twenty to forty years. This painted English chest is dated 1671 on the top rail of the left end (and could have been made as late as 1700); the New England example was made between 1670 and 1710. The three chests are of oak, except for the top and bottom of the American piece, which are pine, a wood not normally used this way in England. (These chests are discussed in greater detail in Chapter 4.)

The chair-tables in figures 11 and 12 differ in their arrangement of stretchers. The English example (figure 11) is of oak, and was made during the second half of the seventeenth century. The top has narrow boards, a custom prevalent in England, where wide lumber was scarce. The New England piece (figure 12) was probably made during the last quarter of the seventeenth century and uses white oak where the lingering tradition of its superior strength over other woods made it seem logical: for the stretchers and seat rails (a similar logic conditioned where oak was used in the Boston chair seen in figure 682). The posts of figure 12 are of soft maple, which turns to crisp shapes unmarred by open grain; the top and seat are pine. Although England did use pine, or deal, in America it was readily available in enormous widths—a factor, as we will see in Chapter 9, that immediately began to alter American designs from their English counterparts. (Because of shrinkage, the top of the American piece, which was made of wide boards, now appears to be of narrow members. The feet are restored with an inappropriate straight-edge lower section.)

11

12

13

14

The caned arm chairs in figures **13** and **14** were once published side by side as American, and probably of New England origin.[2] But recent microanalysis of the woods has shown the one in figure 13 (1710–30) to be of European walnut, and that in figure 14 (1720–40) to be of American maple and beech. Accurate microanalysis—the examination of wood cells—is a welcome recent tool in the study of furniture.[3] When the wood is American, it probably indicates an American origin. However, one of the reasons for establishing the colonies was to provide England with timber, and American woods are found in English furniture. The accounting for a chest of drawers and a pillar table in the Gillows drawings, figures 449 and 1434, indicates that they were made in part of American oak. And another table, made in 1803, is recorded on page 1728 of the Gillows Estimate Book as having legs of American oak.

Figure **15** (1720–35) mixes American and English woods. It has American black walnut as the primary timber and a seat rail of the English white oak group. The presence of English wood suggests England as the source of the chair, for exportation was normally from colony to mother country. However, there are records of planks of English wood being sent to America: in 1716/17, walnut worth £20. 16s. 8d. and plank oak worth £59. 13s. 4d. were sent from England to Maryland.[4] A visual analysis of figure 15, and a comparison with the English chairs in figures **16** and 1148, suggest that it is an English chair, primarily because of the tight, vertical line, particularly of the front legs.

Sometimes a mixture of English and American woods results from changes made soon after the piece was first finished. The early eighteenth-century looking glass in figure **17** (1700–35) has an American white pine crest, while the rectangular frame is of English spruce. This mixture seems

15

16

not to have occurred at the time of manufacture, for the painted tortoiseshell–like design on the frame has a finer pattern, and now a slightly different color, from the painted decoration on the crest. Probably the lower part was imported with the glass, and the beautifully drawn crest (which has great age) was added upon arrival in the colonies.

Some pieces of American and English furniture used wood that was not indigenous to either country. England imported wood from the continent before and after settling America, and both imported exotic woods from other lands. The 1780–1810 stand, figure **18**, is entirely of mahogany. Its location in England may suggest that it was made there, but many pieces of American furniture have been found in England. In the eighteenth century Tories leaving the colonies for England, Canada, and other countries because of Revolutionary fervor took with them a number of pieces, and others were exported for sale. During the ensuing years pieces have continued to go abroad as owners moved them to new homes. The line of the pillar and the legs of this stand seems English, but as the parts are of mediocre design it is difficult to be certain. Plain objects of inferior line are often difficult to regionalize on stylistic grounds.

The tables (1740–90) in figures **19** and **20** with slender cabriole legs and complexly shaped skirts are made of cherry. The first, which is English, has a simpler top and flatter feet and may come from East Anglia, where such shaping and the use of cherry are known. (It probably once had knee brackets.) The American table, with white pine as a secondary wood, is one of a group from

17

18

19

20

central Connecticut that have beautifully shaped legs and actively moving skirts and tops.

The English beech chair (1725–60) in figure **21** has features in common with chairs often associated with the furniture makers in the Gaines family of Ipswich, Massachusetts, and Portsmouth, New Hampshire; for example, the exquisite maple chair painted black, figure **22** (1725–60). The splat of this New England chair is a version of the splat in the chair that follows.

21

22

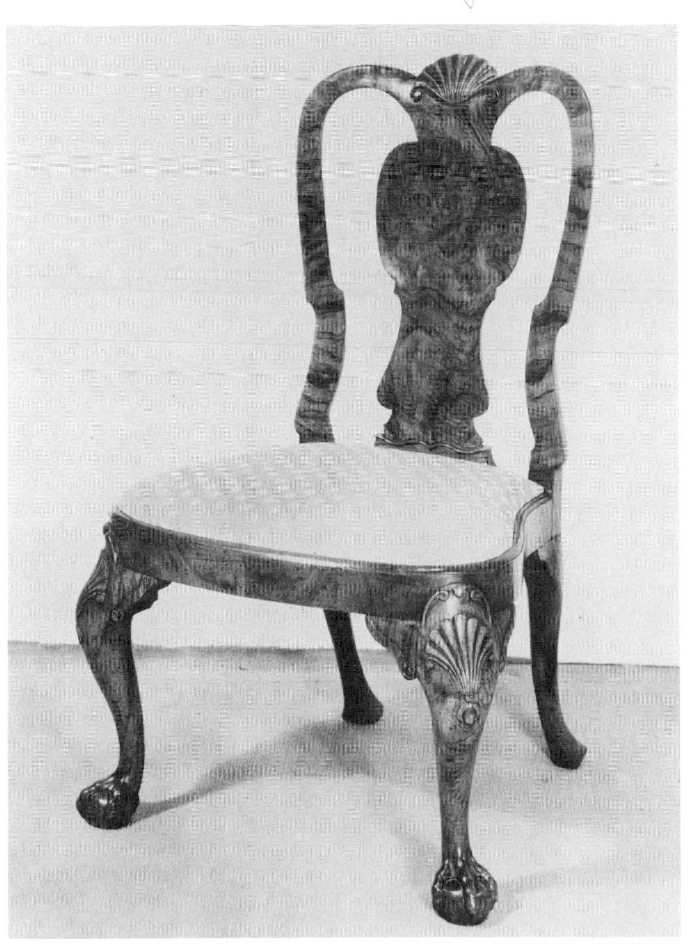

23

24

25

26

The English high-style early George II chair (1725–40), figure **23**, has veneer on the seat rail, splat, and back posts above the seat. The New York chair of walnut (maple), figure **24** (1730–60), has a veneered splat. This form of crest rail and knee shells also appeared in Rhode Island. The shaping of the shoe with paired reverse curves seems, in America, to be confined to New York.[5]

The English gaming table (1750–85), figure **25**, was made of mahogany (oak, pine) and the skirt rail is veneered. (The top seems to have been planed down, eliminating the depression for a recessed cloth covering.) The New York table (1750–90) of mahogany (white oak, white pine, red gum), figure **26**, has asymmetrical knee carving of a pattern found also in Massachusetts and in England (see figures 894 and 895).

The English mahogany chest-on-chest, figure **27**, is similar in form, drawer arrangement, and its use of brasses to those in the Gillows papers dated 1786–92 (figures 566 through 568). The cornice has a crenellated or embattled molding (like dentils with hollow centers), and the drawers have cock-beaded edges. The Pennsylvania, probably Philadelphia, walnut (poplar) chest-on-chest (1765–95), figure **28**, has lipped drawers—a practice that preceded cock-beaded drawers stylistically, but continued to be used on many pieces after cock beading appeared.

The arm chairs (1785–1810), figures **29** and **30**,

27

28

29

30

31

32

have broad shield-shaped backs without a point at the base (as is found on figure 1056). The English chair (figure 29) has block rather than spade feet, and the fronts of its arm supports are molded like the face of the shield. The New York chair (figure 30), of mahogany (maple, ash, cherry), has spade feet, and back legs that do not curve out at the base—whereas such curving is found on many chairs made in Massachusetts.

Log furniture (figures **31** and **32**) has been accepted by many as a frontier necessity where a dearth of trained furniture makers made inventiveness essential. These pieces are, however, the products of a long tradition, which valued rugged appearance even when more elaborate designs were available. (The log chest in figure 410 reflects this attitude.) Figure 31, made of New England white pine, was found in New Hampshire. Carefully detailed, the line of the back, before breakage, was nicely drawn. There is no "style" feature to suggest a date, but the use of rectangular and round-headed nails to secure the seat indicates a date after 1850. The probably eighteenth-century Scandinavian (Danish or Swedish) chair, figure 32, has a raised band and rear brace, a traditional decorative feature rather than a functional device.

An American origin is often inferred on the basis of a single detail. Although Chapter 7 focuses on many of these features, two examples are sufficient to establish the possibility that such assertions can be misleading. Cabriole legs with turned feet and scroll-edged knees with lambrequin decoration are regularly assigned a Newport, Rhode Island, origin. The detail of a knee and leg in figure **33** is from an English chair, and figure **34** is part of a Newport, Rhode Island, chair. (The full English chair is shown as figure 812 and a related Newport chair as figure 814.) Trifid feet are associated with Philadelphia and related work: Southern and Connecticut examples that may derive inspiration from Philadelphia practices. The trifid feet in figures **35** and **36** are from an English or Irish stool and a Philadelphia chair, respectively. (The full British stool is seen as figure 1217; the base of its feet has been worn away.)

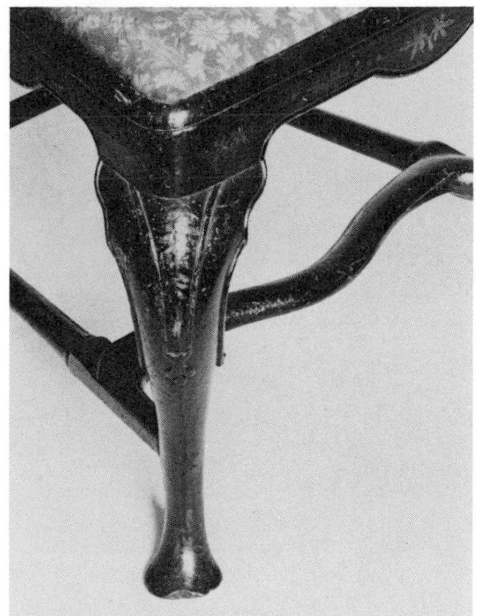

33

34

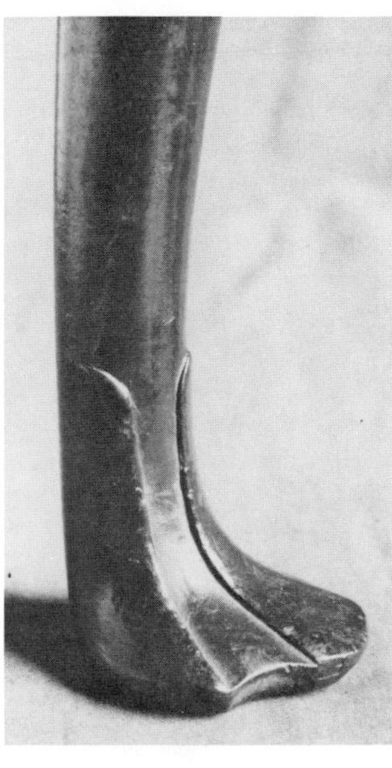

35

36

37

38

39

40

Distribution of Motifs

At any given moment, motifs and particular design features may be used by a variety of crafts and persist or be revived throughout the subsequent sequences of styles, although they will probably be modified to suit the prevailing aesthetic. Winged heads, which many Americanists associate primarily with gravestones, were a feature of ancient decoration and enriched a variety of forms over the ensuing centuries—sometimes with and sometimes without religious import. Winged heads appear on the mid-seventeenth-century font in the English priory church of St. Mary & St. Martin at Blyth, Nottinghamshire, figure **37**. The baroque classical styling is most apparent in the massiveness of the gadroons. These heads appear again in the spandrels of the late sixteenth-century inlaid chest in figure 113, and with less skill in the Mendlesham, Suffolk, pulpit made about 1600 (figure 167). A similar motif appears in the spandrels of a British 1650–75 embroidered picture (figure **38**), which depicts, at the right, Charles I kneeling in a chapel; another on the crest rail of the contemporary northern Netherlands chair, figure 669. The 1670s baroque-style plasterwork by Robert Bradbury and James Pettifer on the drawing room ceiling of Sudbury Hall, Derbyshire, includes the winged putto seen in figure **39**. An English oak bookstand and walnut cane chair, both made about 1680–90 (figures **40** and **41**), demonstrate the difference in quality existing at the same moment. The carving of the top of the stand is better than that on the Suffolk pulpit (figure 167); the base of the stand is cut to a tulip form flanked by hearts. The cane chair, influenced by continental work, is one of the greatest aesthetic achievements of late seventeenth-century English furniture. (The full chair is seen as figure 356.) The Henry Copland engraving of 1746 (figure 7) places a winged head on a rushing scroll.

This motif easily migrated to the New World. The silver flagon (detail seen in figure **42**) was made for the First Parish Church of Charlestown, Massachusetts, around 1720–30, by John Potwine, who moved from Boston to Connecticut at about this time. Polychrome winged heads (figure **43**)

41

42

43

44

45

46

47

48

appear in the spandrels of the architectural detailing of the Nichols-Wanton-Hunter House, built in Newport, Rhode Island, about 1750.

Other Crafts

There is still insufficient knowledge of the relationship between English and American gravestones. Henry Glassie, while studying the artifacts of Devon, England, photographed in Braunton a stone (figure **46**) made for John Haydon and his three sons, all of whom died in 1731, and Thomas How, who died in 1762. Glassie attributes this stone to John Berry of Muddiford, near Barnstaple. When this and slides of other Devon examples were shown to James Deetz, he saw a connection with Rhode Island stones. The stone in figure **44**, which is dated 1768, was for the Reverend Richard Round, and is in Burial Place Hill Cemetery, Rehoboth, Massachusetts, near Rhode Island. Here the leafage is rounder in profile than that on the Devon stone. That in figure **45**, dated 1771, was for Seth Carpenter and is in the South Attleboro, Massachusetts, Newell Cemetery.[6] Other New England stones have wings emerging from below the head. Resurrection trumpets, as seen on the Devon stone, appear on various American examples, but normally with a figure blowing a single trumpet.

The American silver teapot (1720–35), figure **47**, was made by Peter Van Dyck in New York. It is a superlative example of American craftsmanship, but has been all too readily praised as an instance of American dependence solely on line, as if that were sufficient to distinguish it from English or continental examples. In fact, it is close in both line and proportions to the slightly plainer 1718–19 teapot made in London by Richard Bayley (figure **48**; part of the top of the handle may be missing). The American pot appears slightly more vertical, possibly because of the angle of the photographs.

If we turn to English and American architecture, comparisons are perhaps more dangerous, for changes in exterior surfaces and interior arrangements appeared early. However, formal comparisons of visual mass and detailing are fair, and figures **49** and **50** show just such a relationship. Figure 49 is the rear view of Church Hall, in Broxted, Essex (about 1600), which was finished with rough-cast plaster. (The right bay is an earlier building.) Figure 50 is a nineteenth-century woodcut of the Bridgham House at Boston, Massachusetts, built 1670–71.[7]

American painting continues to be divorced

49

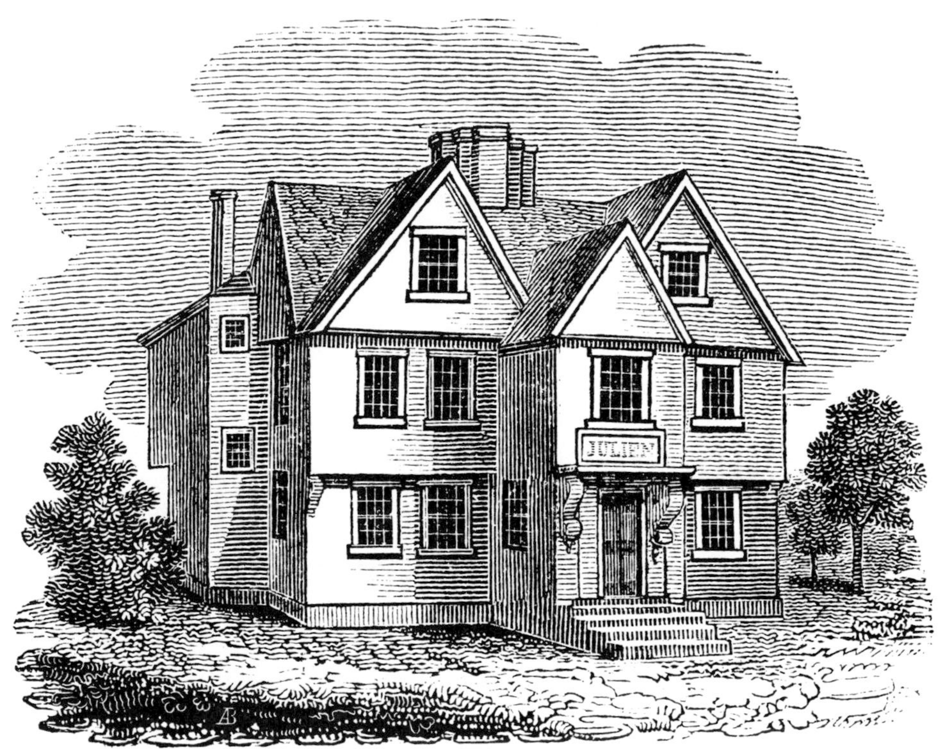

50

from similar English work. The Boston double portrait of Mrs. John Freake and her baby Mary (Mrs. Freake about 1670, baby Mary added about 1674–5[8]) in figure 51 will form an important part of the discussion of painted furniture in Chapter 4. The picture is placed here to stress the similarity of the mood and presentation of *Mrs. Freake* and such English portraits as that of Elizabeth Roberts in figure 52 (1650–75).

The juxtaposition of textiles in figures 53 and 54 demonstrates the type of print source research that has developed in the study of American art.[9] The probably English silk embroidery with watercolor on silk, figure 53, follows closely an engraving by Francesco Bartolozzi after a painting by Angelica Kauffmann, published in London in 1782. The American painting on velvet, figure 54, is entitled *Homage to Parents,* and was made by Elizabeth Bass Hinckley in 1820 while a pupil at Miss Farnham's Academy, in Boston, Massachusetts. It seems likely that both makers used the print, although it is possible that an English textile or painted version of the print made its way to American shores to serve as a model.

51

52

53

54

In the last quarter of the eighteenth century the utilization of printed sources was developing into a standard practice. Published sources had long been useful to colonial arts—architecture, painting, engravings on silver, furniture, and textiles. But only *after* the Revolution did they become a prominent factor, when they were part of the explosion in the field of the domestic arts, and professional establishments drew heavily upon them. Thus in furniture, for example, American eighteenth-century Chippendale-style chairs rarely drew direct inspiration from published sources (see the discussion in the Visual Survey above the entry for figure 844). But with the advent of George Hepplewhite's *The Cabinet-Maker and Upholsterer's Guide* (1788) and Thomas Sheraton's *The Cabinet-Maker and Upholsterer's Drawing-Book* (1791–94), published imagery had a direct and rapid impact. This is part of what makes it more difficult to regionalize post-Chippendale furniture.

Figure 55 shows a section of a bed hanging whose history in the scholarship of American textiles typifies the problems that may arise when the focus is on provenance rather than visual understanding. The set of hangings has blue and green wools on linen-cotton and is dated 1674 (there are also two initials, "A P," but their date is uncertain). They have been published as possibly American because of an assigned history and the linear quality and sparseness of their pattern, which was seen as appropriate to colonial Massachusetts rather than to England, where lusher work is expected. The history said they had been found in a linen bag hanging from a rafter—to keep them from rats—in a house on Cape Cod. However, a recent discussion with the last dealer involved led to an earlier dealer who reported that he had found them ". . . in Hatherleigh near Plymouth, Devon, England, in 1963."[10] A comparison with other examples of English work, which may have been part of relatively simple English households, places these hangings squarely within that phase of the English tradition.[11] The scholars who wrote about these curtains were hesitant to call them American, for there is nothing non-English about them, but the provenance caused some to see American characteristics in them. Found in Devon, near the origin of the chests in figures 8 and 10 and the gravestone in figure 46, these hangings could in fact have been made and used in similar houses in either the Old or the New World.

55

3

Variations Available: Interpretations & Customers

American furniture has been characterized by some English scholars as simplified English furniture, as though England were populated only by richly developed examples and America staggered in its wake with lesser versions. The first chapter reviewed the expressions that were available in England: Palladian, court, urban high style, rural high style, and vernacular. The following brief review of three English and two "foreign" versions of one published chair design exemplifies the range of interpretation and quality of execution that could be purchased from London and provincial shops producing high-style furniture. And the subsequent more extensive analysis of one form, the dining table, made by a single firm for over thirty years, demonstrates the gradual changes that occurred within one style (the neo-classical); how basic shapes and details persisted once invented; and how the final appearance of the product was affected by the customer's needs.

Influence of a Published Chippendale Engraving

The backs of the chairs in figures 57 through 61 all derive their form and detailing from a design published in plate 12 in the first edition of Chippendale's *The Gentleman & Cabinet-Maker's Director* in 1754, and in plates 13 and 14 of the third edition of 1762 (figure **56**). Probably the first chair (figure **57**) came from Chippendale's shop, for it is at Nostell Priory, a county seat for which this firm supplied a number of pieces. The back, except for the molding of the posts, is close to that of the drawing. It does, however, lack the published design's more intriguing play of forms and scale of parts. Whether for aesthetic reasons, because of economic pressures, or the fact that they were for the dining room where the legs would be obscured when in use, the legs do not follow either of those suggested by the design. (The right C-shape bracket is missing.)

The arm chair (figure **58**) might be from the Chippendale firm, for the back is sufficiently close to the published design to suggest this; but it is probably from another shop, which followed either the Chippendale design or a chair that had used the engraving. The form and carving of the cabriole legs are not particularly distinguished and might have been produced in a number of shops. The front feet are lathe-turned—an inexpensive method of shaping, employed on both urban and rural products until the end of the eighteenth century. (A 1793 sketch of "round toes" appears on page 977 of the Estimate Book of the Gillows firm; see figures 92 and 1255.)

The back of the chair in figure **59** is a flatter, more dispersed version of the Chippendale design,

56

57

59

60

58

61

with the line of the crest rail broken into smaller units. The shoe of this aesthetically uninteresting chair is inscribed: "6 pedestals for Mr. Chippendale's backs." This may mean that the maker purchased the splats, crest rail, and back posts from Chippendale's shop for insertion in his otherwise simple chairs (purchasing parts was a standard practice). But because of the lack of quality, it is more likely that the inscription means that the "pedestals" (shoes) were to go with splats based on Chippendale's designs, yet made in the same shop as the other parts of the chair.

The chair in figure **60** is a provincial expression of the Chippendale source. It may have been based directly on the published design, a chair based on the design, or the last of a succession of chairs descending from the engraving. It is one of several probably made in Baltimore, possibly by James Davidson, and is of mahogany. (The secondary woods of this example are replaced.)

The form of the tapering legs of the Irish chair, figure **61**, appears on various Chippendale designs, for example, at the right of plate 9 in the 1762 edition.

Forms and Degrees of Elaboration Available: Gillows Dining Tables

The Gillows firm, based in Lancaster, sold to customers throughout England and by 1769 had a branch in London. A review of one specific form recorded in their records between 1784 and 1817 provides an opportunity to examine the constancy of earlier details, to note the gradual stylistic evolution during this late Robert Adam–George Hepplewhite–Thomas Sheraton classical period, and to acknowledge the lack of standardization of proportions and details. (The date and page reference follow the first mention of each item, when it appears on the manuscript page or can be discerned from the adjacent pages. Often the illustration and its description appear on facing pages, both carrying the same page number.)

Sets of dining tables grew in popularity during the second half of the eighteenth century. Today

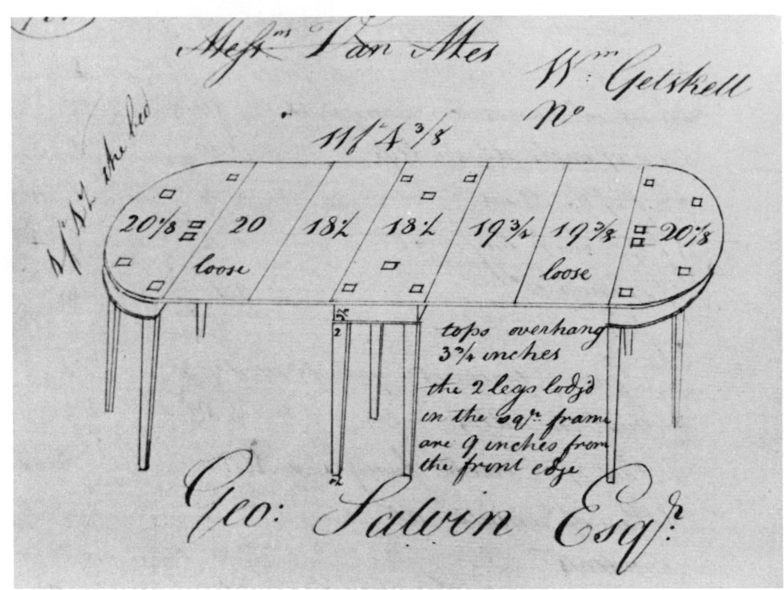
Wm Gelskell
loose
loose
tops overhang
3½ inches
the 2 legs lodg'd
in the sq^r^ frame
are 9 inches from
the front edge
Geo: Salvin Esqr

62

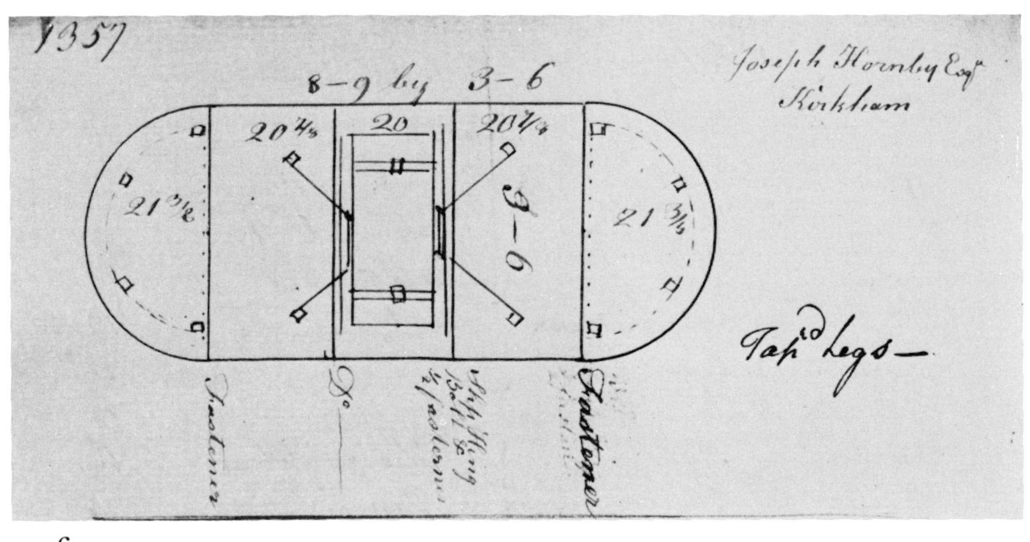
8–9 by 3–6
Joseph Hornby Esqr
Kirkham
Tap^d^ Legs—

63

64

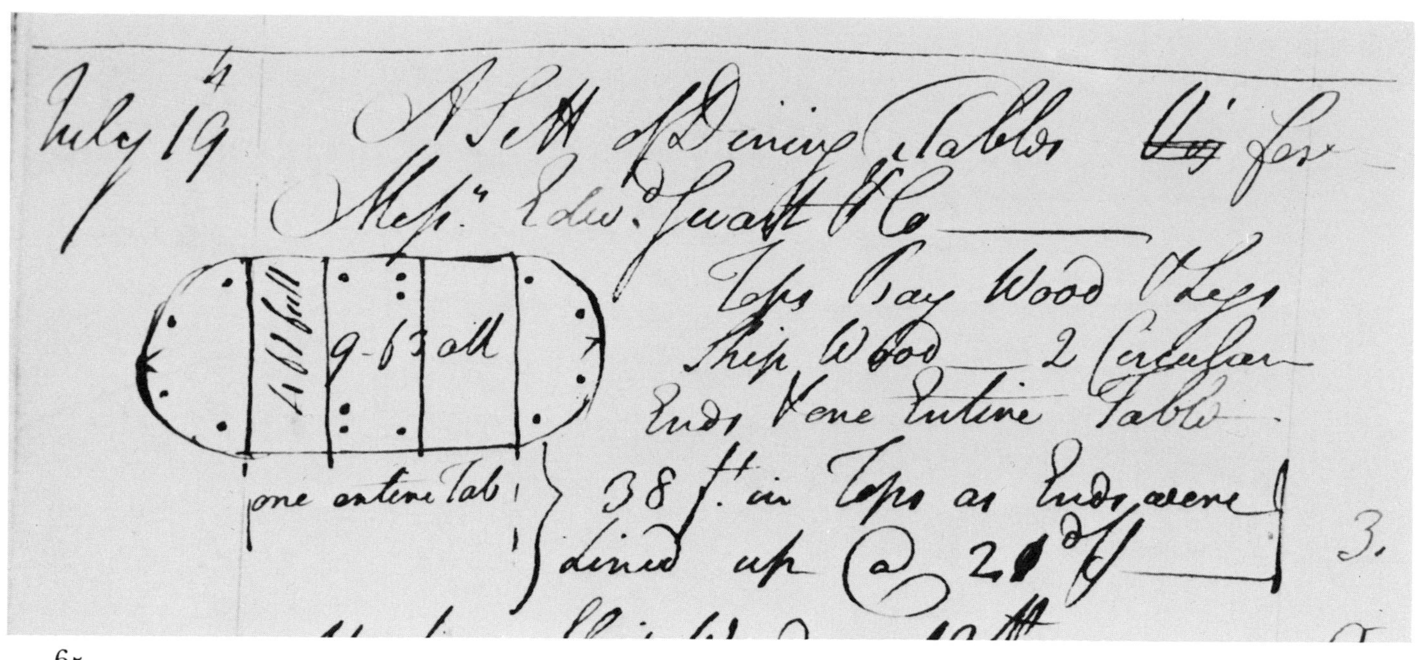

65

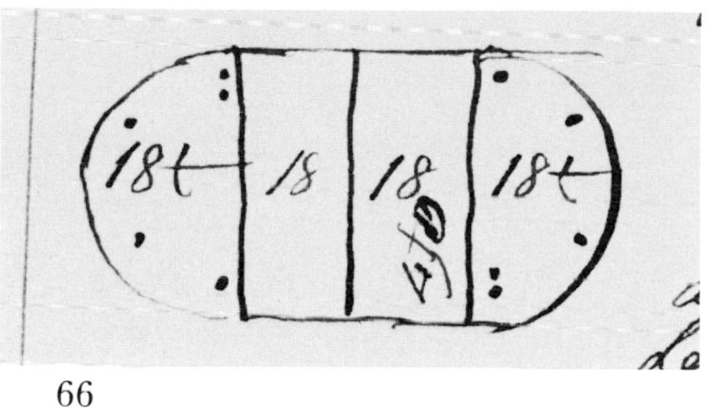

66

67

they are usually thought of as matching in form and decoration, and consisting of a central unit of one or more tables with drop leaves. It is also accepted that all the tables in a set match in width. Accompanying circular ends are known to have been made with or without drop leaves.

Figure **62** (October, 1791, p. 781) typifies the accepted understanding of the form. The central table of this mahogany set had two drop leaves, as did the circular end. Four square-tapered end legs on the center table swung out to support the leaves when open (they are not swung out in the drawing). This table also had a stationary leg placed further in at each end. A plan of how this worked is seen in figure **63** (June, 1797, p. 1357), which was listed as "A set of Oak Dining Tables"—a wood one might suppose to have been out of fashion on a developed form of this period. (It was recorded on page 1728 that in 1803 the legs of an oak dining table were of "American Oak.") Notes on the drawing in figure 63 indicate where the fasteners that lock the tables together were placed. The legs were "Tap[er]ed," and of square section.

When open, the drop leaves of the circular ends of figure 62 were supported by two swing legs in the center of their straight side. The circular ends of figure 63 had no leaves, and their four legs were stationary. A variation on leg arrangement, common on American tables, is found on figure **64** (July, 1784, p. 73). The central table is marked off as "one Entire Table." A total of sixteen tapered legs was designated by dots on the drawing. The swing legs were positioned near one of the corner legs (always at the right hand of anyone about to draw out a leg). Figure **65** (July, 1784, p. 76) shows "one entire Tab[le]" with legs in a similar arrangement, but the circular ends lacked leaves.

We might assume that a pair of ends with no center table had lost that middle section. But figure **66** (September, 1784, p. 107), called "A Sett of Mahogany Dining Tables," had only circular ends with leaves and swing legs. Figure **67**

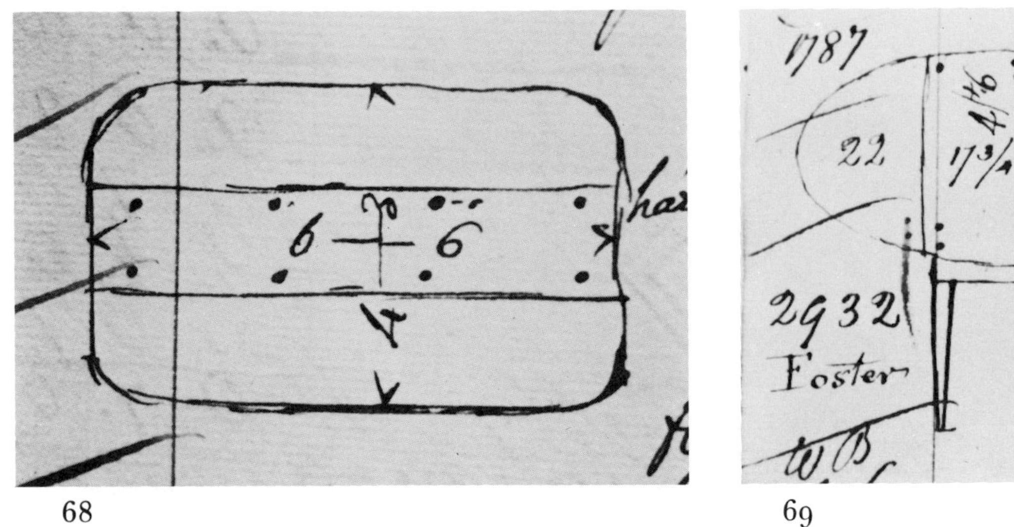

68 69

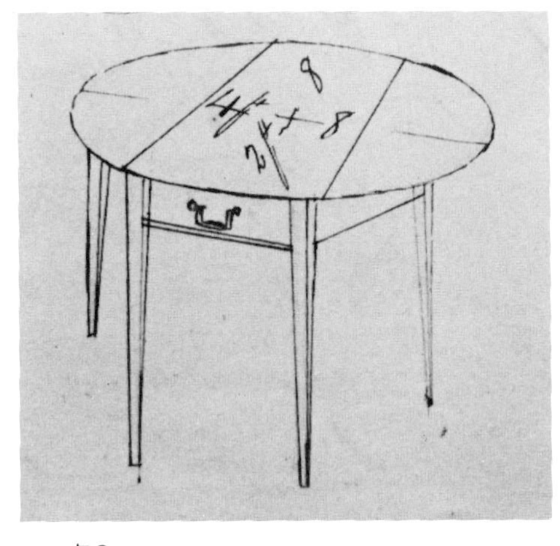

70

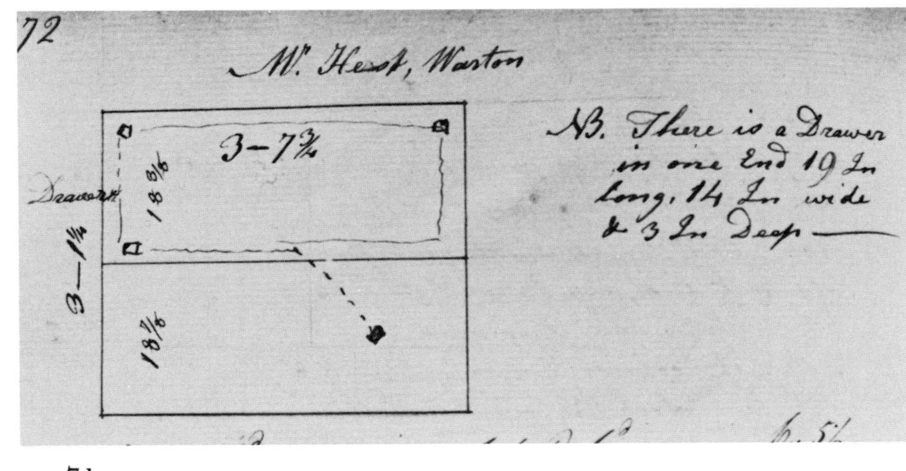

71

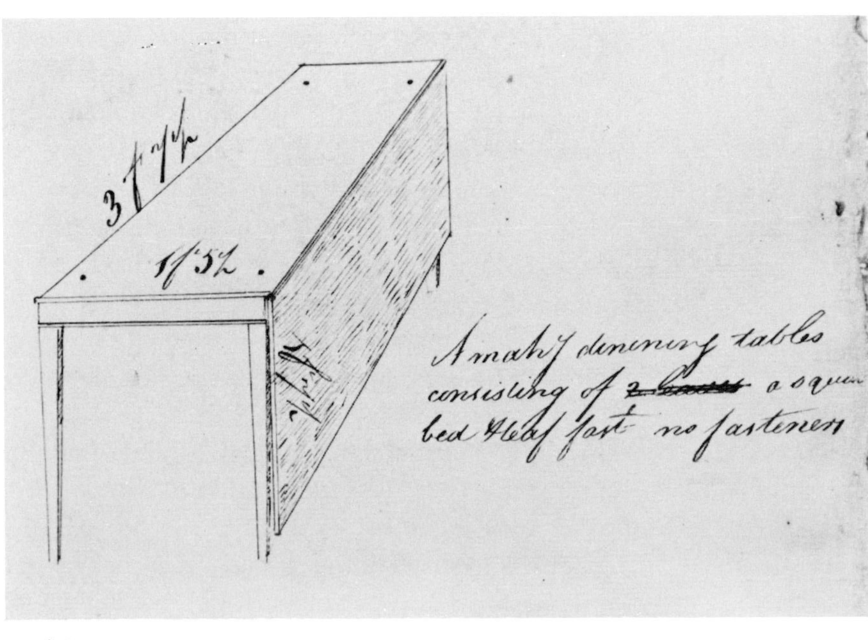

72

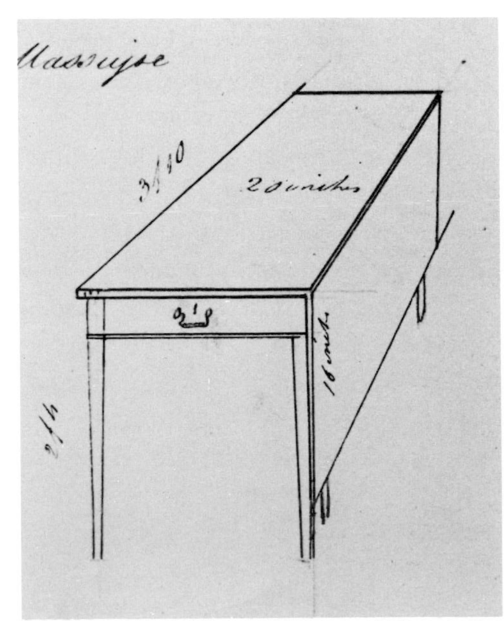

73

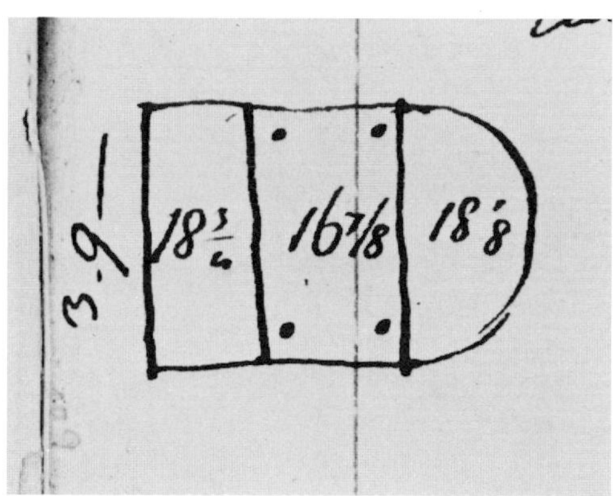

74

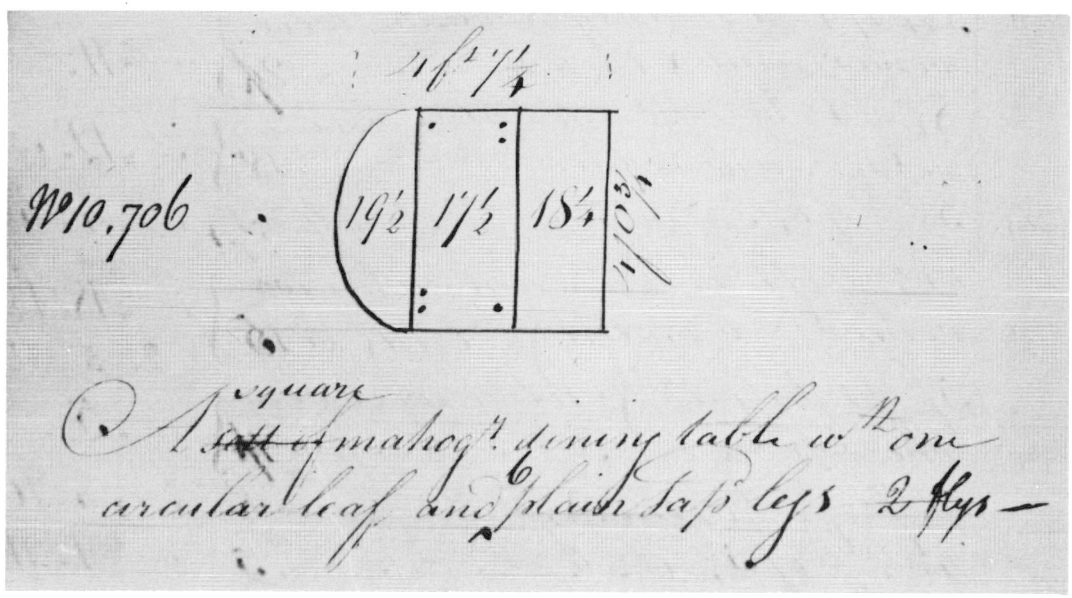

75

(October, 1784, p. 117), another "sett," had a total of eight fixed legs and the leaves were supported by a "fly," or bracket, which swung out from the straight side with no leg attached.

It was possible to purchase a long table made in one piece. Figure **68** (January, 1786, p. 291) was 4 feet 3 inches wide and 6 feet 6 inches long. The unusual length required eight legs and four pair of hinges. The rounded corners on the leaves are usually associated with the early years of the nineteenth century, as seen on figure 99.

A single oval table with drop leaves, figure **69** (1787, no month given, p. 503), was called "A very good Mahogany oval Din[in]g Table." Four and a half feet wide, it had four fixed and two swing tapered legs. (The artist first placed the dots indicating most of the legs on the leaves, then smeared them out when noticing the mistake, and replaced them correctly.) A similar dining table was available in oak with a drawer, figure **70** (June, 1802, p. 1690). The mahogany table with one leaf, figure **71** (August, 1797, p. 1372), was listed as "A Dining Table," and had a drawer in one end. Figure **72** (October, 1791, p. 791) is a perspective drawing of another single-leaf mahogany dining table. (The description of the table first included "2 leaves" but this was scratched out.) A similar table could be had in deal, for figure **73** (May, 1793, p. 974) was described as "A common deal dining table." The "fly rail" was of oak, and the drawer was fitted with a lock, an escutcheon, and "A Common handle."

Not all drop-leaf tables had similarly shaped leaves. Figure **74** (February, 1784, p. 23) had one round and one square leaf, supported by "fly" brackets. There were "4 Turned Legs." The feet may have been similar to those on figure 97 or as shown in figures 92 and 1255. Figure **75** (September, 1789, p. 522) was called "A square mahog[an]y dining table w[th] one circular leaf and 6 plain

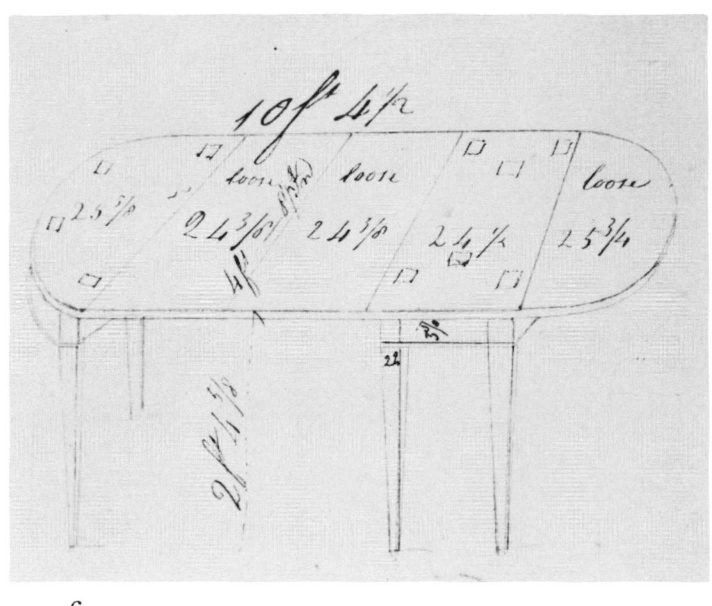

76

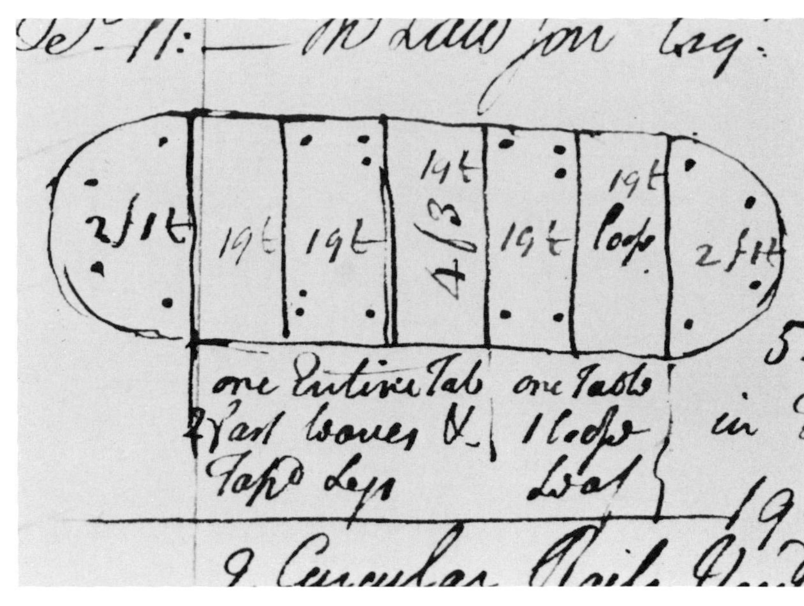

77

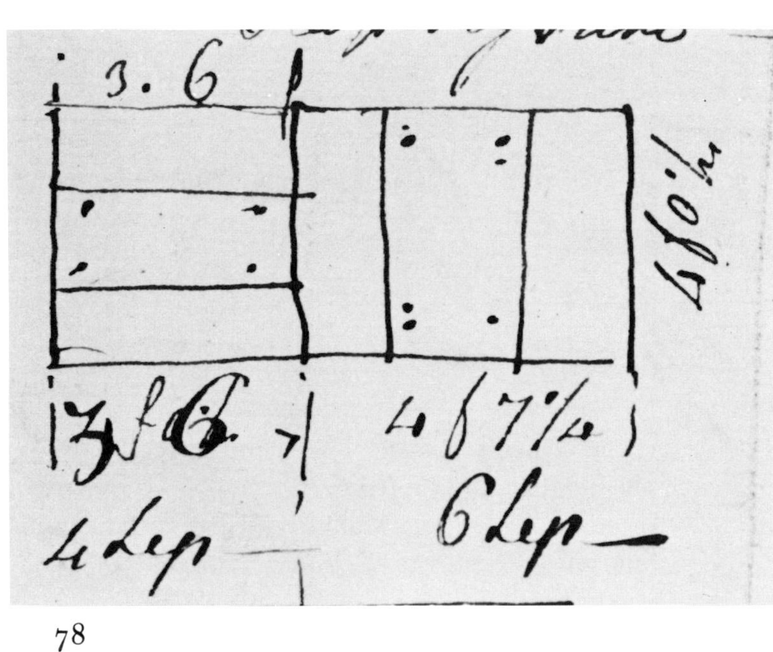

78

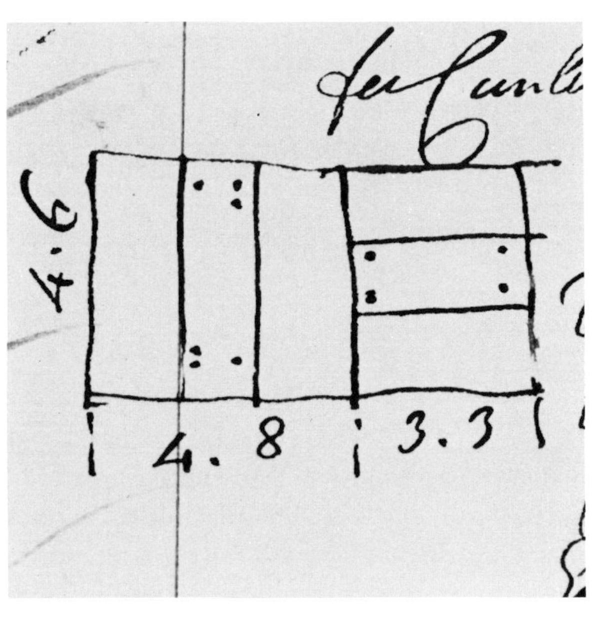

79

80

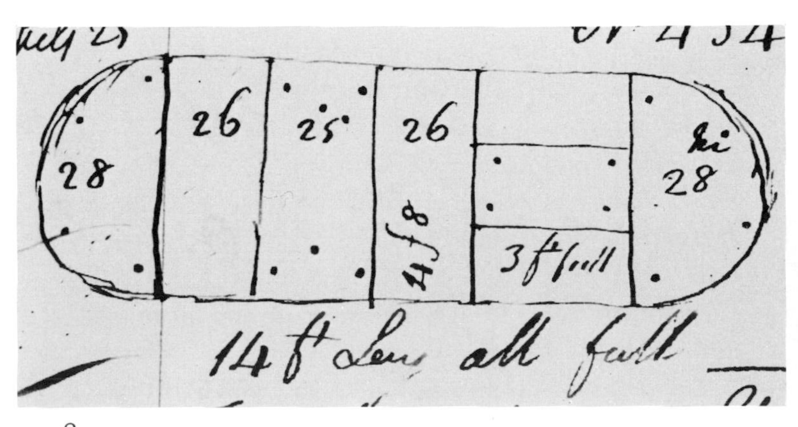

81

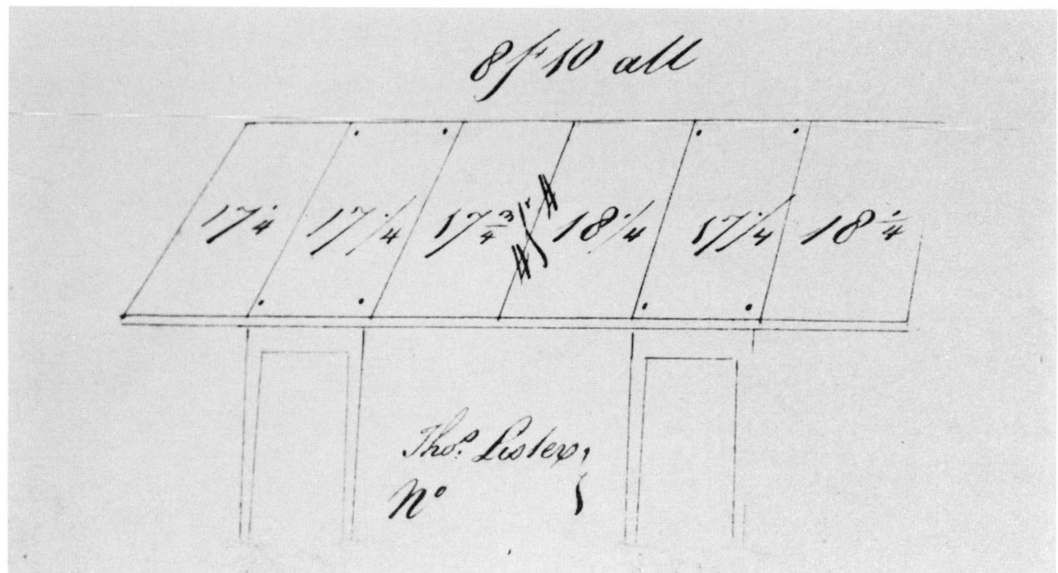

82

Tap[ered] legs." Figure **76** (October, 1790, p. 664) juxtaposed a drop-leaf table with one round and one rectangular leaf with one circular end table. Figure **77** (December, 1784, p. 136) comprised four units; the two different center tables are described on the drawing: "one Entire Tab[le]" with two leaves, and "One Table 1 loose Leaf." These had tapered legs.

It was figure **78** (January, 1784, p. 9) in these remarkable papers that initiated this study of dining tables, for it suddenly made evident the fact that sets of dining tables were not always of the same width. If such tables were found together today, it is unlikely that we would think of them as a pair. The width of the larger table is 4 feet and that of the smaller 3 feet 6 inches. Figure **79** (July, 1785, p. 216) had one table 4 feet 6 inches wide and one of 3 feet 3 inches. A comparison of the dimensions of figures 78 and 79 demonstrates the lack of standardization even for simple tables. Figure **80** (August, 1784, p. 101) had a center table with the leaves running lengthwise. Figure **81** (July, 1785, p. 212) had two center tables: the one with four legs has its leaves running lengthwise. The other center table had six legs. All eighteen legs were "tapered."

Almost identical tables might not match in size. Figure **82** (November, 1792, p. 839) was "2 Square mah[ogan]y dining tables." The leaves on the table at the right were both 18¼ inches wide. On the other table the left leaf was 17¼ inches, the right one 17¾ inches. Such tables might now be assumed to have had one set of leaves cut down after they left the shop. (Perhaps even more surprising is that one circular leaf on figure 69 was 22 inches wide while the other was only 20 inches.)

Tables used as one unit might have various constructions, and perhaps different decorative features, and they may have been of different styles. Figure **83** (January, 1788, pp. 214–15) depicts "Two Circular Ends of dining Tables to Join to old tables." Figure **84** (August, 1791, p. 760) consciously mixes two styles. The center table has tapered legs, the circular ends a turned "pillar" and "claws" (a term for legs jutting from the pillar, regardless of their form). The end tables of figure **85** (July, 1801, p. 1638), made at the beginning of the nineteenth century, use saber-shaped claws. (This shape began to appear in the last decade of the eighteenth century; see figure 1437.) The left circular end has a narrow leaf supported

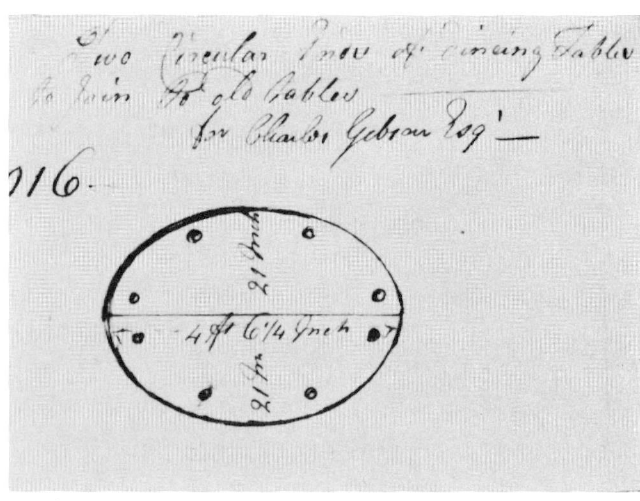

83

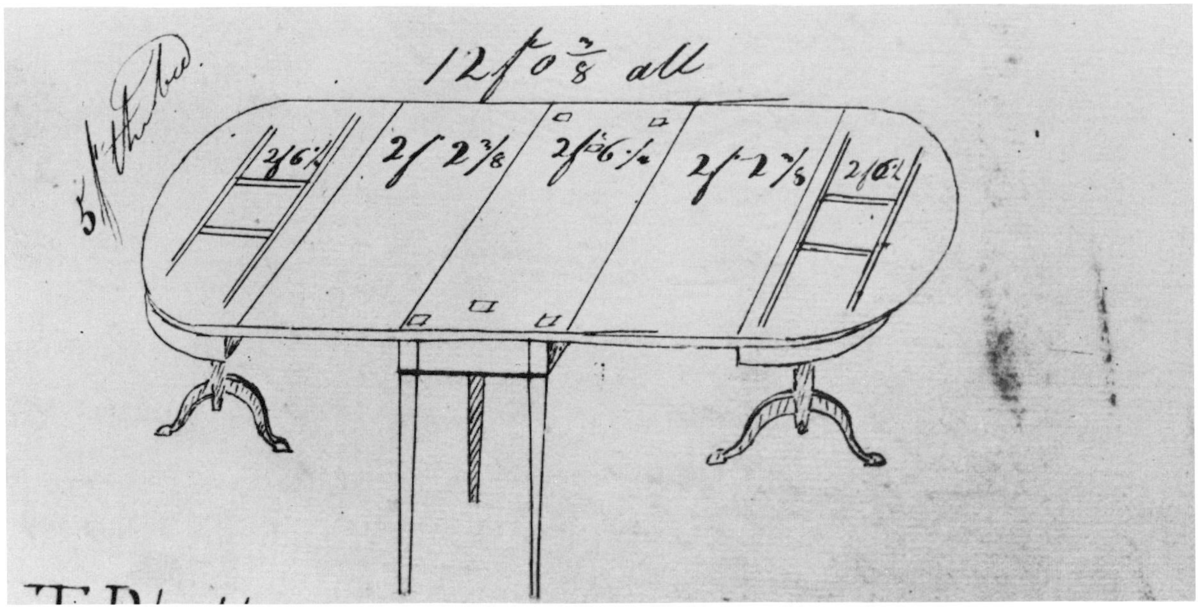
12 f 0 3/8 all
2 f 2 7/8
2 f 2 7/8

84

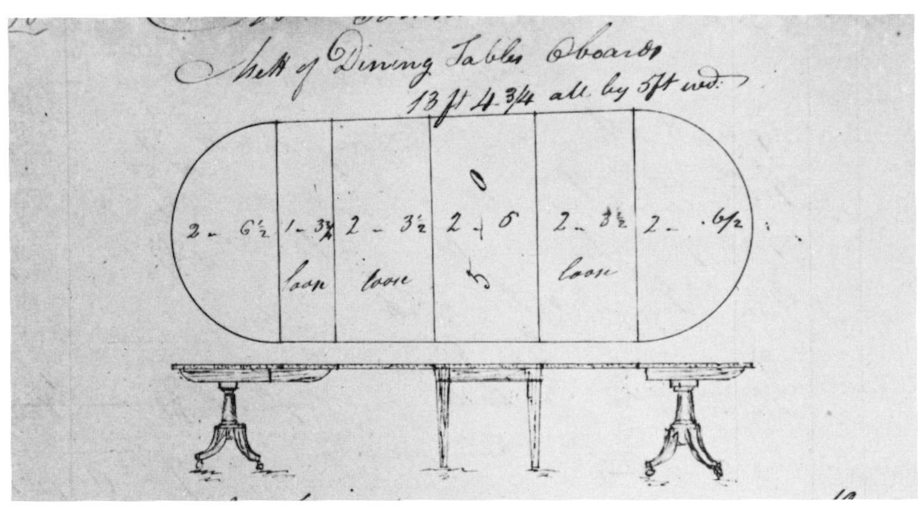
Sett of Dining Tables & boards
13 ft 4 3/4 all by 5ft wd.

85

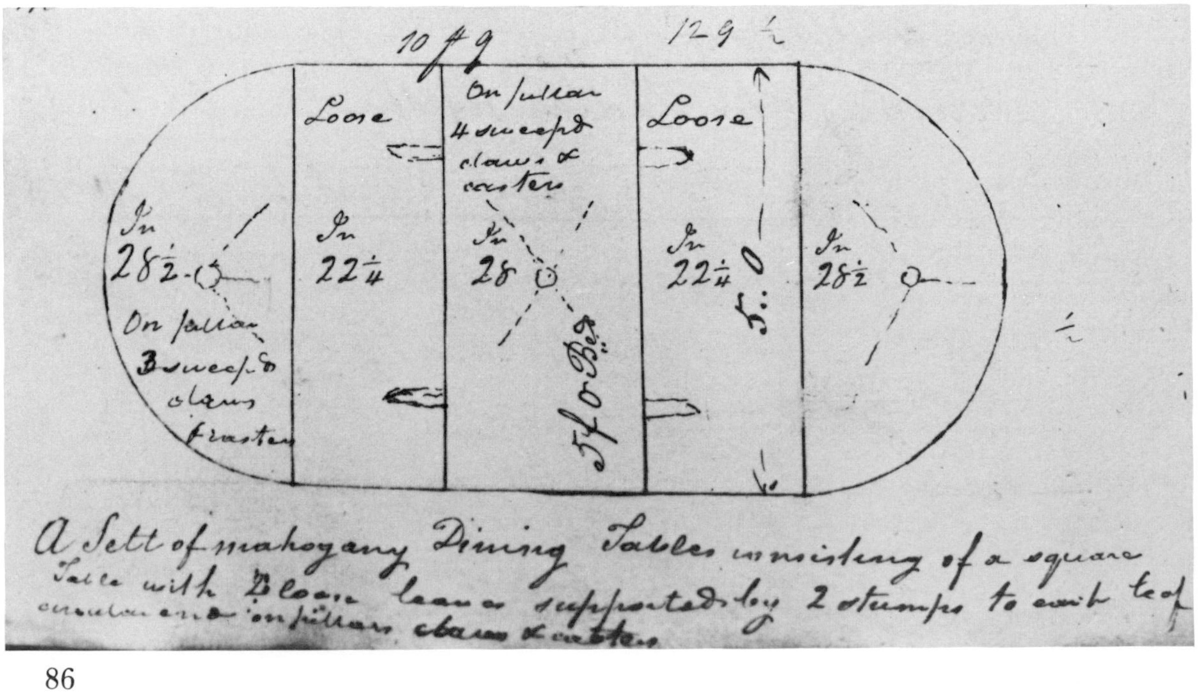

86

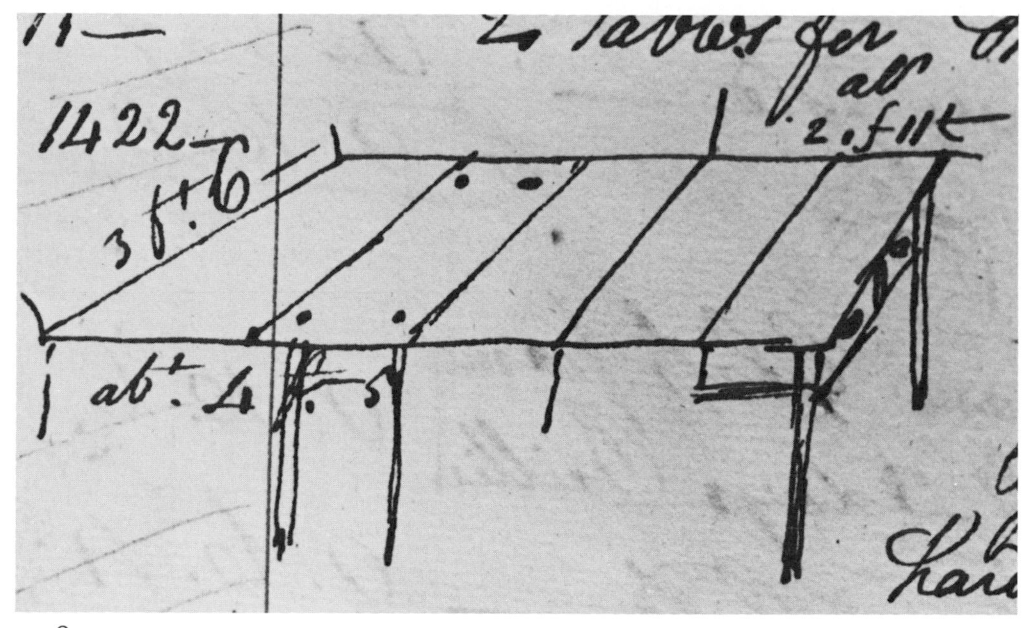

87

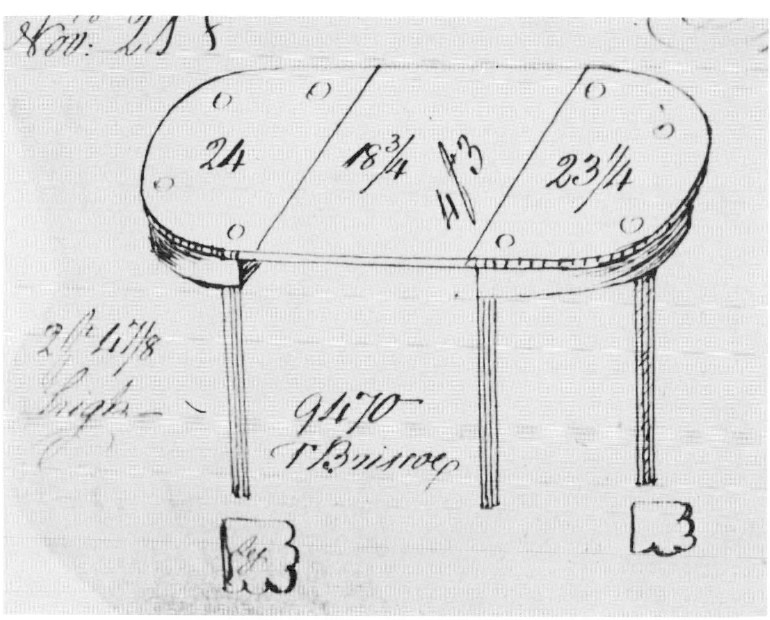

88

by two "stumps": brackets that swung from the straight rear rail. Their shape is seen in profile in this sketch and in plan on the center table of figure **86** (October, 1796, p. 1285). In the latter drawing, the circles in the circular ends and central board signify pillars. The central one had "4 sweep[e]d claws & casters," indicated by four lines radiating from the circular pillar. The end ones had "3 sweep[e]d claws & casters" designated by three radiating lines. Ten large brass casters with iron plates are listed for this set, along with iron plates for the bases of the three pillars.

This mixture of styles now surprises us. But more amazing to the modern sensibility is the mixture of a card table and drop-leaf table to make one large table, as in figure **87** (April, 1786, p. 329). The table at the left was called "The Din[in]g Table"; that on the right was described as "The other Table wth one leaf & 2 draws," with "Round Handles."

It is possible to discern a basic style sequence in the form of legs, but more interesting perhaps is how long each lingered once introduced. As the drawings to this point demonstrate, at any given moment several styles were available. Except for figure 91, the following ten illustrations are arranged chronologically. Figure **88** (November 21, 1788) had straight, reeded legs. (Similar legs ap-

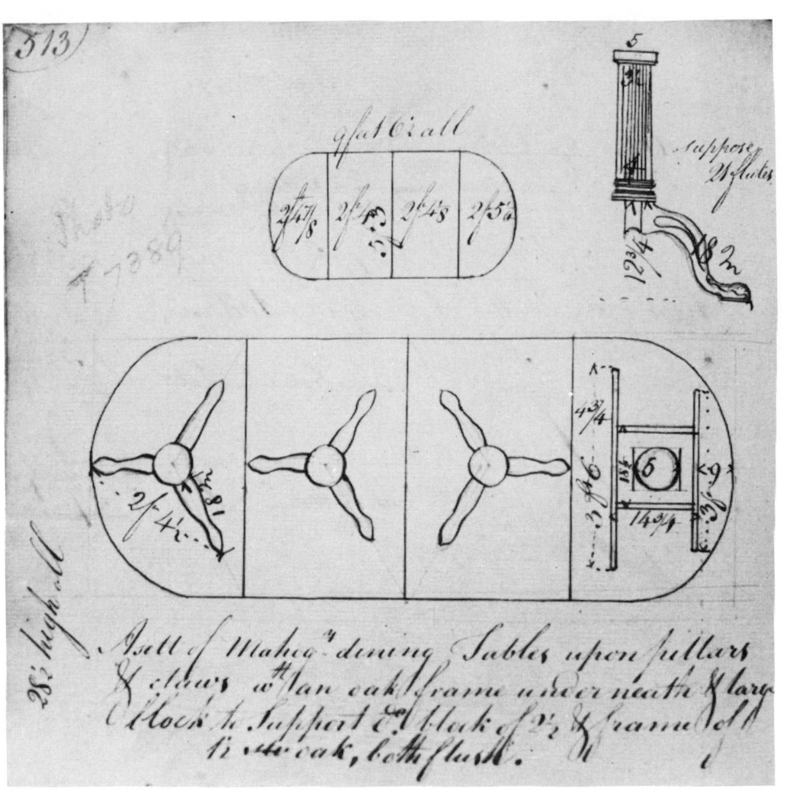

89

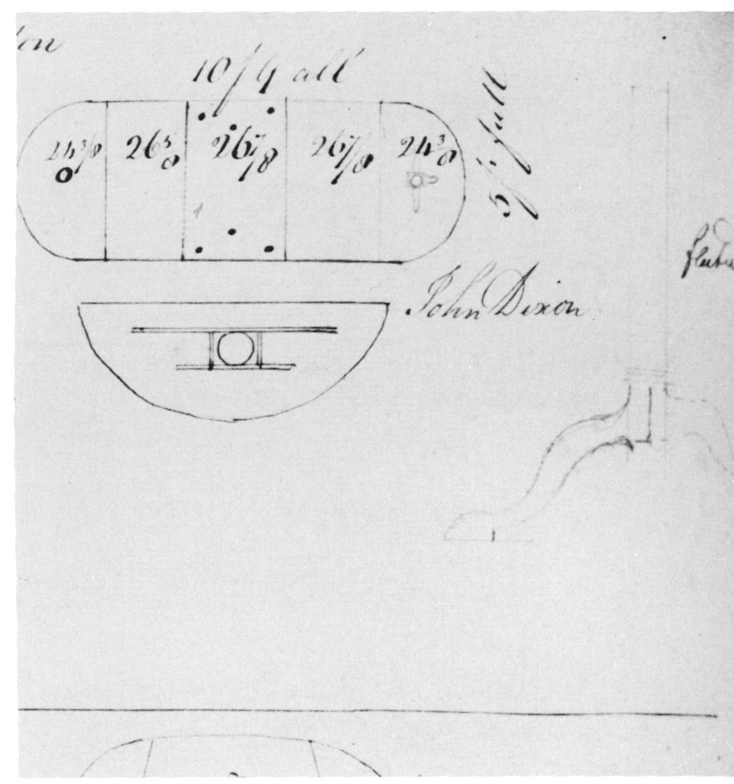

90

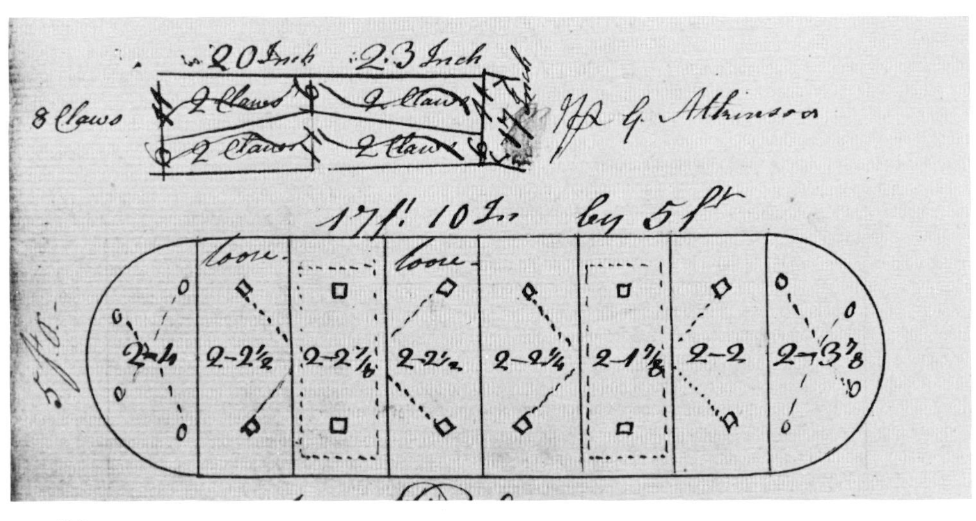

91

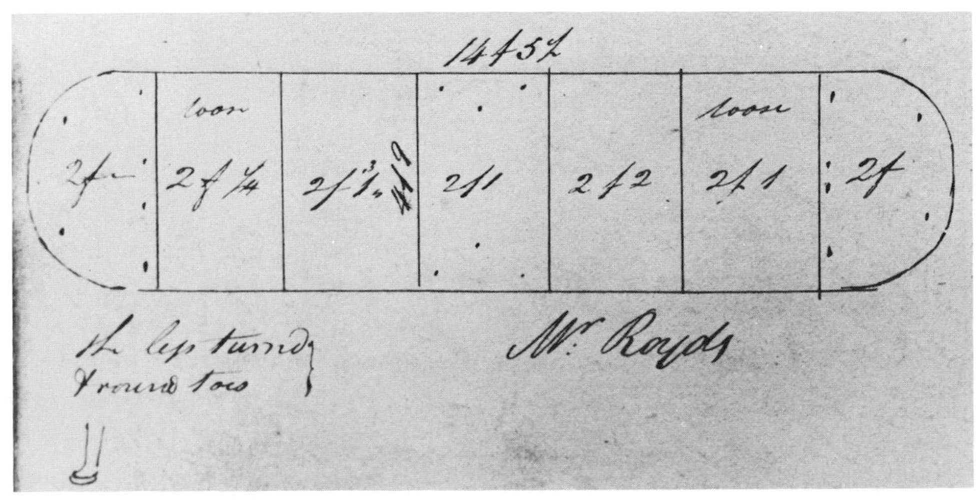

92

pear in the Gillows papers on an oval Pembroke table dated July, 1796, on p. 381.) All four units of figure **89** (July, 1789, p. 513) had pillars with three claws, and each pillar twenty-one flutes. The end pillars of figure **90** (April, 1790, p. 591) were also fluted. The center tables of figure **91** (March, 1797, p. 1330) had square-tapered legs, and circular ends with pillars, each supported by four claws. The form of the eight claws and how they were cut from a block of wood, using angled lines, was detailed above the table design.

Figure **92** (May, 1793, p. 977) had eighteen legs. Their description—"The legs turned & round toes"—was clarified by a sketch at the lower left of the page, showing part of a turned leg and an off-center turned foot (a detail is shown as figure 1255). This small drawing is of great importance as it documents the continuation, after about seventy years, of a form of foot that had proved inexpensive and attractive.

The legs of figure **93** (June, 1794, p. 1089) are pillars, each "on 4 large Claws," which curve down and out, and then continue down to brass casters. This movement is the opposite of that on figures 89 and 90. The table tops were held horizontal by brass snaps and could be turned vertical. Each of the three pillars on figure **94** (May, 1796, 1241) had "4 sweep[e]d moulded claws and casters." The

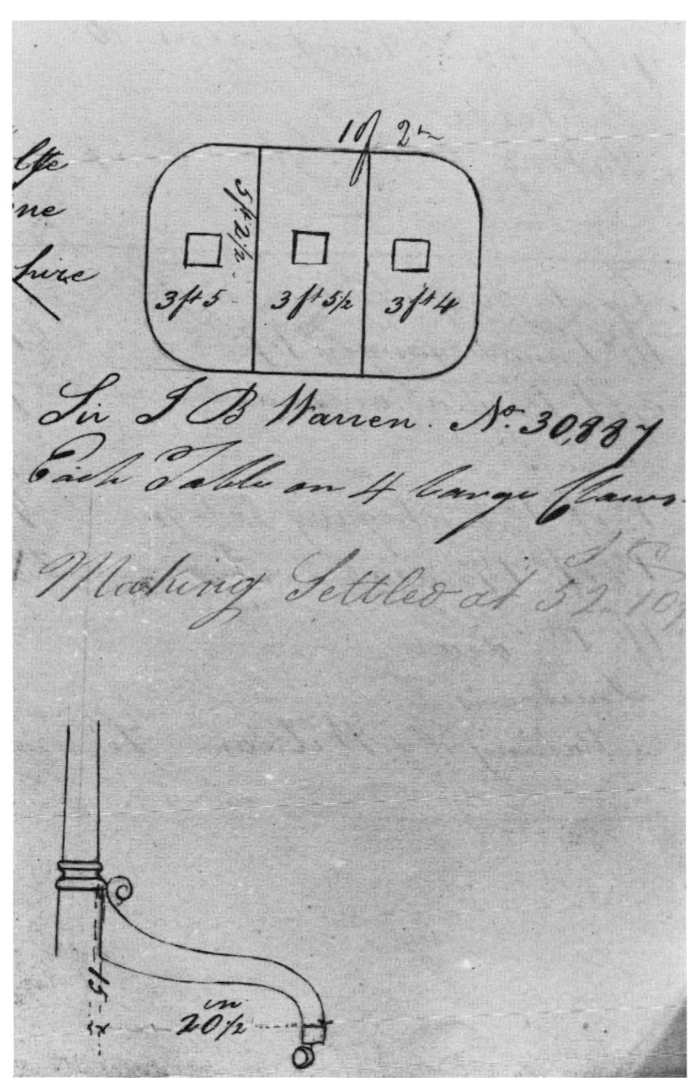

93

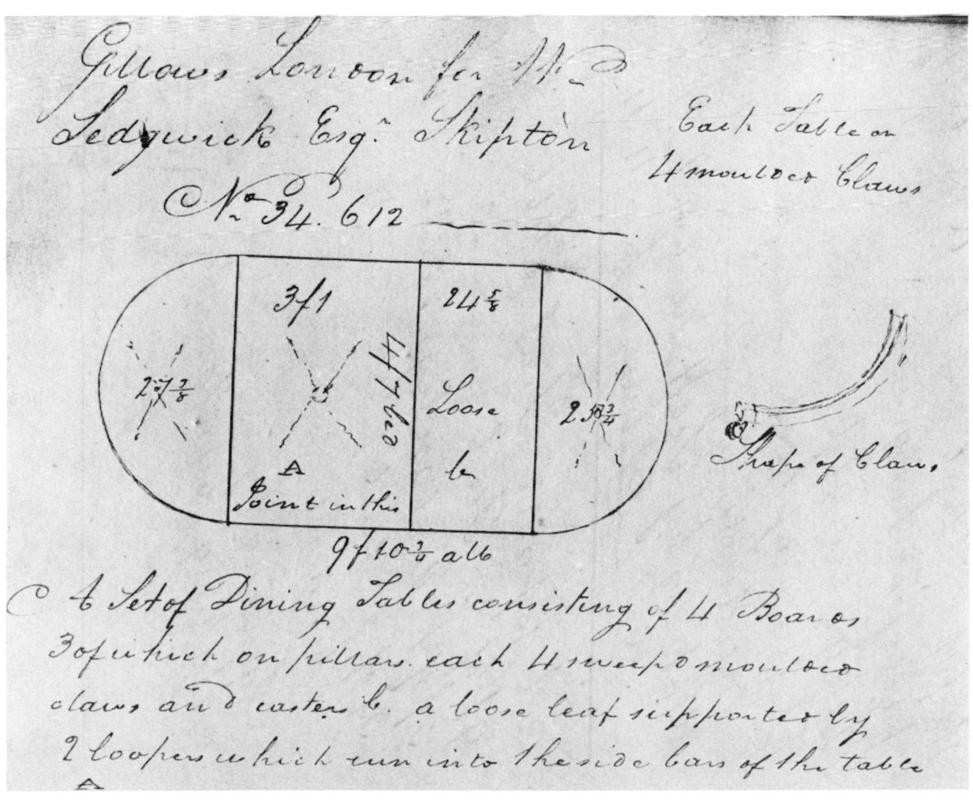

94

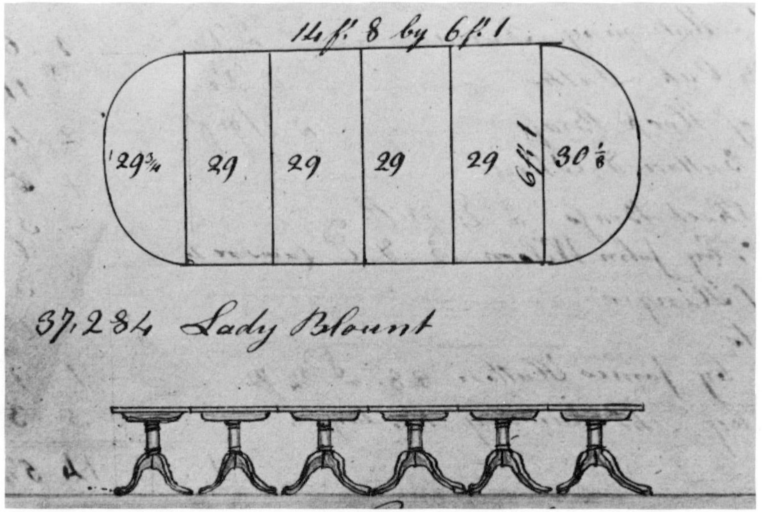
14 ft 8 by 6 ft 1
29¾
29
29
29
29
6 ft 1
30⅛
37,284 Lady Blount

95

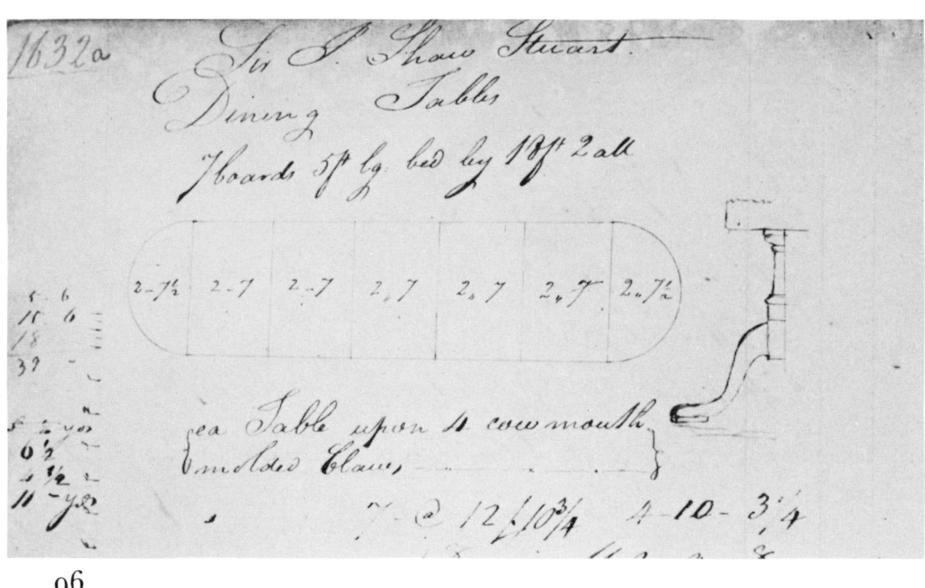
1632a
Sir J. Shaw Stuart.
Dining Tables
7 boards 5 ft lg. bed by 18 ft 2 all
2-7½
2-7
2-7
2-7
2-7
2-7
2-7½
ea Table upon 4 cow mouth molded Claws
7- @ 12/10¾
4-10-3¼

96

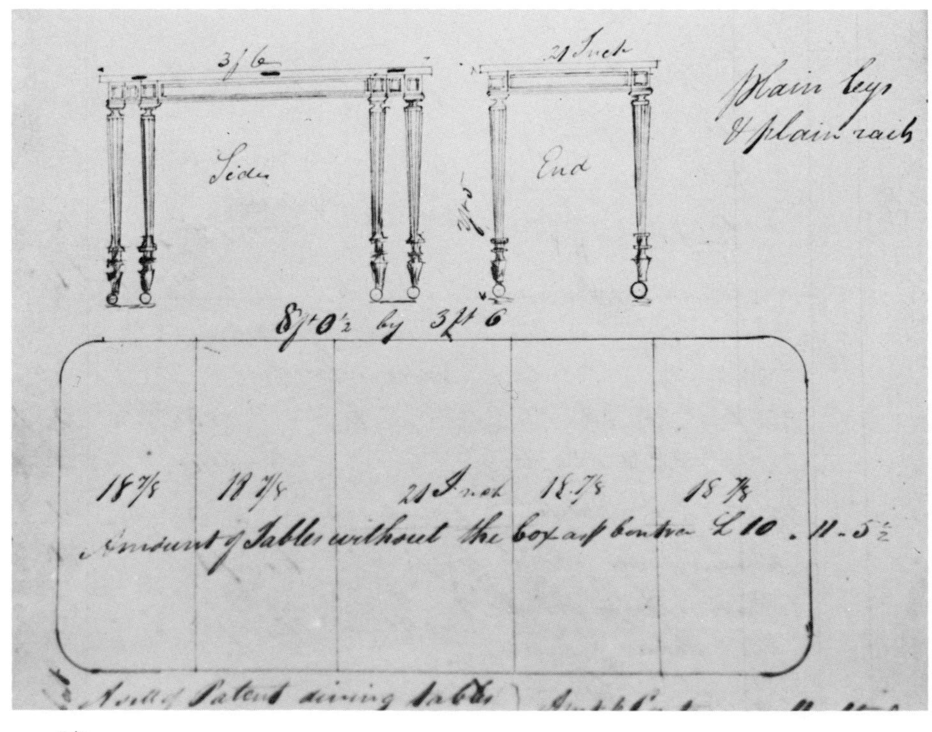
3/6
21 Inch
Plain legs & plain rails
Side
End
8 ft 0½ by 3 ft 6
18 7/8
18 7/8
21 Inch
18 7/8
18 7/8
Amount of Table without the box at centre £10 . 11-5½
A pair of Patent dining tables

97

loose leaf was "supported by 2 loopers [pulls] which run into the side bars of the table."

Every section of figure **95** (August, 1798, p. 1465) had its own pillar. There were "6 Iron Plates Bottom of the Pillars." All seven boards of figure **96** (May, 1801, p. 1632) had a pillar, and each was "upon 4 cow mouth [?] molded Claws." There were seven iron plates for the bases of the pillars.

"A Sett of Patent Dining tables," figure **97** (August, 1801, p. 1644), had circular ends, which drew on mahogany "sliders," and the table was accompanied by a storage box for the leaves. The thinness of the legs is surprising, for heavier turned legs had long been in fashion. Similarly slender legs also appeared on a 1826 Gillows drawing of a card table (p. 3473).

Although by 1817 changing fashions and advanced technology had resulted in new forms and construction, tables similar to those made a generation earlier were still being ordered, as for example, in figure **98** (October, 1816, p. 2032). Yet in the following year the firm made "A Sett [of] Imperial Dining Tables 33 feet by 6 feet," figure **99** (May, 1817, p. 2047). This had sixteen turned and reeded legs on "4 Setts conceal[e]d Casters." The accompanying "Rack for Tables leaves" was lined with green baize and finished with mahogany veneer.

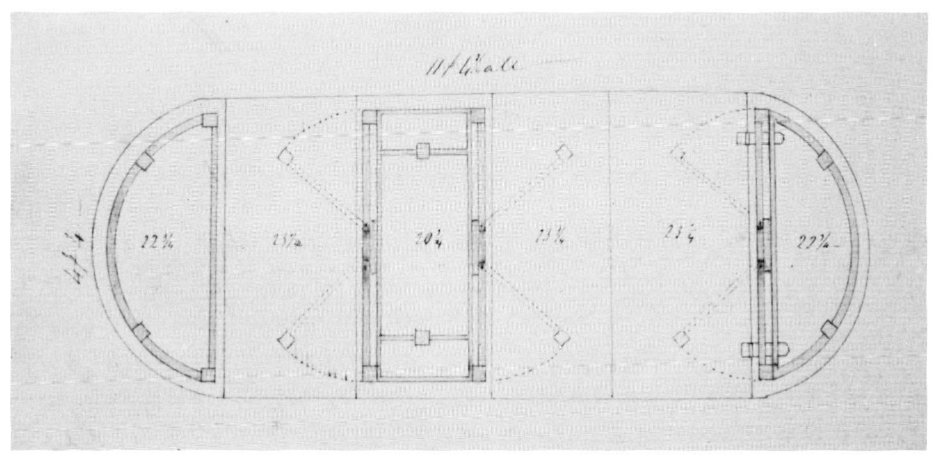

98

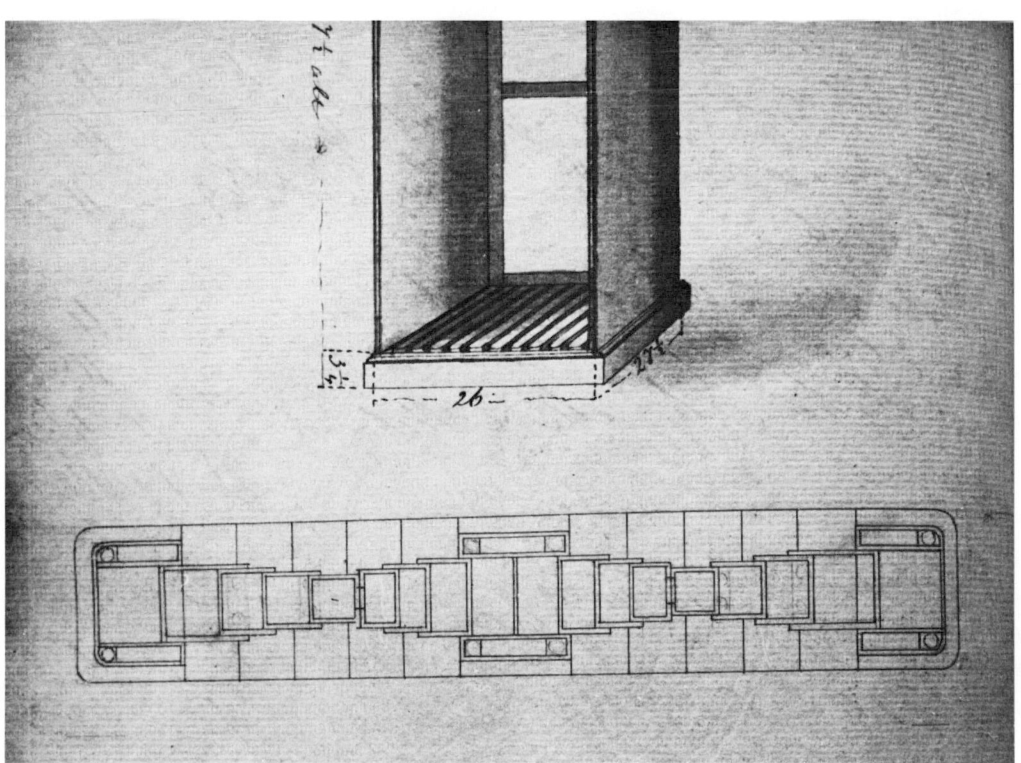

99

4

The Tradition of Painted Furniture

Medieval and Mannerist England

It is not difficult to establish that there was from early times a tradition of English painted furniture, and that it often made a major contribution to brightly colored settings. A review of early house inventories discloses painted pieces, and there are contemporary books in which authors advised on methods of painting furniture and room paneling. When these written records are combined with the early pieces of furniture that eluded "refinishers," a clear picture of this tradition emerges. The fact that this form of finish has so long been ignored has skewed our understanding of English furniture, for it was often part of high-style and court settings, and frequently present on vernacular furniture.

There is now a great scarcity of English painted furniture, in large part because the English have been collecting and stripping their early furniture much longer than we on this side of the Atlantic. Horace Walpole collected early turned chairs in the second quarter of the eighteenth century—I have a fantasy of his taking them to the shop of Thomas Chippendale in London to be "cleaned up." Clearly, much of the "refinishing" began in the 1830s with that aspect of the Gothic revival that favored an unpainted surface. It gained momentum from the early Victorian preference for the natural grain and color of wood, which was linked to a moral emphasis on cleanliness. The more recent American taste for knotty pine and shining maple has a different impetus, one that incorporates raw wood and other natural materials into the great romance of the rugged Pilgrim, the pioneer, and the frontier ethic. A similar and roughly contemporary English trend derives from nostalgia for the "merrie England" of the sixteenth century that never really existed; it delights in darkened wood, preferably oak, set against bright white plaster, and is perpetuated in "Tudorized" pubs. Another reason English painted furniture is scarce is that great quantities have been shipped here to be sold at a higher price as American work.

Paint was often a means of imitating expensive surfaces. Sometimes it provided only a general color, as when a piece was painted red-brown to imitate walnut or mahogany; but in other instances it clearly imitated the design and surface of complex patterns: exotic woods, complex veneers, inlays, lacquer work, marble, precious stones, textiles, and paneled walls.

The use of paint to suggest expensive surfaces has a long history. In the tomb of Tutankhamun there were pieces of furniture covered with gold and jewels, and others that suggested similar patterns in paint. Some were veneered with ivory and many were of wood painted white to imitate it. A few examples suggested ebony, sometimes with paint, sometimes with colored varnish. Certain furniture excavated at Pompeii parallels expensive items by the use of paint. More recently, Lambert Hitchcock and other early nineteenth-century workers would stencil onto mass-produced chairs images that were carved on the more expensive pieces by such makers as Duncan Phyfe. These motifs included eagles, cornucopiae, and leafage.

The practice of making available inexpensive versions of more elaborate objects was not confined to furniture. In eighteenth-century Europe there was a similar shift from weaving or embroidering a pattern into textiles to the less expensive process of printing it. To emulate as closely as possible the more expensive stitched product, the printed version often included a printed rendering of the stitches.[1] Yet another example of inexpensive substitutes is the trompe l'oeil printing of mid-nineteenth-century flat textiles to resemble expensive textiles gathered and festooned in the latest mode. The printed fabric could be tacked flat above windows or used as part of bed furnishings to suggest expensively draped swags.[2]

In ranging through the history of furniture, it is always helpful to turn to textiles for an understanding of how furniture once looked, since an unfaded textile can show much of the artistic temperament of its time. Indeed, until their mass production in the nineteenth century, textiles were often the most expensive feature of an object, the wooden portions serving largely as support for its display. Frequently the textiles in a house inventory were valued higher than the silver plate. When elaborately painted decoration appears on furniture, it often served as a substitute for textiles on the less visible or more vulnerable areas. An example of this is seen on figure 145, where (unlike figure 144) the lower frame was painted in imitation of the decorative textile above. In some instances early chests were covered with fabric, and at other times the surface painted to imitate it. The early fourteenth-century Italian *cassone* from Florence, figure **100**, is such an example. It was gessoed and painted with red and bright blue checkers, which were finished with painted scenes. This *cassone* is now displayed in the Victoria and Albert Museum near a late fourteenth-century German (Lower Saxony) tapestry of similar design.[3]

The Public Records Office in London has a collection of chests from the fourteenth through the eighteenth century that form a group of untouched painted pieces. Two of the earliest were housed, on November 10, 1361, in " 'a little red press' in the Great Treasury."[4] One formerly held the documents on the release and ransom of David Bruce, King David II of Scotland, who reigned from 1329 to 1371. It is made of oak and painted with a red ground. The top has a painted inscription that includes the date 1357, and the top and front have painted shields. The collection also

100

includes a traveling chest—known as a standard—possibly owned by Henry VII's mother, Lady Margaret Beaufort, who died in 1509. It is made of oak strengthened with iron straps and painted red-orange. The top is shaped like three facets of an octagon and covered with *cuir bouilli* (decorated leather soaked in oil and spirits to make it less permeable to water).[5]

Traveling chests often had tops shaped to drain off the rain and usually a protective covering, regularly of leather. Some surviving examples suggest that the leather was once dyed or painted in bright colors. Because aging has generally changed the original surface of these chests, their appearance in paintings and written descriptions of them are helpful in evoking how they once looked: "A great ship chest, bound with flat bars of iron of flanders work, covered with yellow leather" (1527);[6] "one London chest, covered with black leather, and banded with iron" (1596).[7] The color red is frequently found on leather. Often it was the remains of a stain used in the curing process; at other times it was red paint, perhaps in imitation of the stain.

Leather was also used as a base on more expensive objects, the upper part of the English harpsichord-organ of 1579 shown in figure 135 being one example. Decorated leather hangings, often painted, were used to cover walls like tapestries. In the 1670s the dining room of Ham House, near Richmond in Surrey, was hung with white and gold leather, and in 1702 a parlor in Dyrham Park, near Bristol in Gloucestershire, was hung with embossed, painted, and gilded leather representing fruit, flowers, and putti.[8]

Iron chests might also be painted, occasionally on a canvas covering. In 1836, Henry Shaw described a chest of this kind, which was dated 1532 and had a history of having once belonged to Sir Thomas More: "It is wrought iron the edges, studs and portions of the lock, gilt; and the space between covered with canvass, on which are painted imitations of fruite and flowers."[9] Such a decorative scheme could make the chest look as though it were covered with elegant fabric.

In England, medieval and Elizabethan written evidence is perhaps now more plentiful than contemporary examples of untouched painted furniture: "one painted table for cups" (1393);[10] "in the Great Chamber a coberd [cupboard] paynted with grene and a carpet ove[r] the Same" (1536);[11] "The rede coffer. whiche is w^{t}in my rede coffer att my bedde fette [foot of the bed]" (1538);[12] "In the hall of Stevyn Bodyrugton grocer. It [Item] a Colberd [cupboard] Joyned payntyed grene" (1547);[13] "a rede chist of wainscot" (1548);[14] "a bedsted painted grene with pillers" (c. 1555);[15] "a little paynted ambry wth II doors" (1564);[16] "A Joynt green chest, banded with iron" (1590).[17]

Sometimes the paint was finished with varnish, for in 1610 there was a piece "coulered redd and Varnished."[18] Paint could be used on inferior woods to suggest the more expensive walnut: "To the same [John Grene] for mending of 5 chairs that were broken the feet painted the colour of walnuttree" (1560–61).[19] And despite its expense, walnut, too, was sometimes painted to make the surface match the even more expensive textile hangings: "a fayre, riche, new, standing square bedsted of wallnuttree, all painted over with crimson, and silvered with roses" (1588).[20] The crimson and silver were probably to match similarly colored hangings.

Gothic architecture imposed its attenuated pointed arches and complex tracery on all late medieval England, and it has found continual expression since its first appearance, although not always as the dominant feature of each period's stylistic mode. The English coronation chair shown in figure **101** was given a polychrome finish when it was made by Master Walter of Durham, the king's *painter*, in 1300–1. "It was originally brightly painted, and later gessoed and gilt—during restoration seven layers of paint have been found."[21] (The lion base is not original.) Although unusual for its grandeur and role as a symbol of state, the chair was not special in its finish, for such coloring was standard on woodwork and furniture of this date (figure 411 was similarly painted).

The parish church of St. Edmund in Southwold, Suffolk, was begun about 1430 and finished about 1460.[22] The exterior is decorated with the contrasting colors of flint and ashlar freestone, arranged in a checkerboard pattern. An alternating band of the same materials surrounds the base of the church, and stone of various colors also enriches the south porch. But although the exterior is dramatic, it is the interior paint and gilding that inform our knowledge of English color over the centuries, because in the church there are three states of "Gothic" color: the first executed about 1500; the second in the mid-nineteenth century; and the third during the twentieth century. The two restorations sought to reproduce the quality of the original colors, but the different handling of color in each of the three states forces us to realize again that we can never perceive an earlier time without adding to it much of our own taste and limited understanding.

The screen in the church was completed about 1500 and has areas of gilded gesso and panels painted with representations of apostles and prophets (figure **102**). The major verticals and the main horizontal rail above these panels are molded and painted with lines of white, red, blue, and gold. Some parts are rendered more dramatic by diagonal striping or undulating lines of red and white or blue and white. Various gold flowers and blue cornflowers enrich these surfaces (figures **103** and **104**). The original brilliance of the screen is somewhat diminished by age, but probably much of its early force can be grasped when it is seen flooded by sunlight. Colors change with time, and artists have long been concerned whether their colors will do so. In the seventeenth century they were admonished not to use "Fading Colours, such as will not continue long in their Beauty, but turn to another colour."[23]

101

In this church there are a few other areas of original color. On the pier supporting the northern arches of the tower is a late fifteenth-century carved clock jack in the form of a man-at-arms with the original polychrome decoration (figure **105**). In 1937 a later coat of black paint was removed to reveal the original red and black of clothing and armor; only the gold accents needed to be retouched. The color on this figure—and on painted exterior figures from other English churches—raises the question whether the statues that filled the exterior niches of this church were also colored like its interior statue and the once polychromed statues of ancient Greece.

Part of the interior of the roof of St. Edmund's was repainted in the mid-nineteenth century to restore the original blue ground with gold stars accented by angels in gold, pink, and green (figure **106**). These later colors have a sentimental softness now recognized as characteristic of some nineteenth-century work.[24] The pulpit (figure **107**), part of the original woodwork of about 1500, was repainted in 1930. Its colors have a murky, romantic milkiness not unlike colonial Williamsburg colors of the same date. In 1839, probably before any overpainting, the pulpit was described as having "panels of vermilion and brown, decorated with black, white and gilt."[25]

A polychrome Gothic-tracery lectern in the church is a modern copy of the late fifteenth-century one at All Saints' Church, Pavement, near York. A huge, elaborately pierced, painted, and gilded cover for the font is a 1935 copy of the original one. The coloring of the lectern and font cover has a rather hard immediacy, as though attempting the clear, translucent brilliance of the colors applied in 1500.

Repainting, sometimes after repairs, is not a modern development: in London between 1558 and 1560, a payment was made "To the same [John Grene] for new painting and gilding of the same with silver and gold . . . and for making of one new Skotchion for the same with Letters of the Queen. . . ."[26] In the eighteenth century Thomas Chippendale repainted at least one Windsor chair olive green, for Sir William Robinson.[27]

Wear was not the only reason for altering painted surfaces. Some were defaced or destroyed by religious zealots. Writing of fifteenth-century stone fonts, Francis Bond noted in 1908:

> Many of the fonts of this period shew traces of rich colour. It was the custom, however, of the Post-Reformation churchwarden to whitewash the font or to daub it sky-blue, or to paint it to look like marble; at "restorations" this has been scraped away, and almost always the original painting with it. Remains of rich gilding and varied colouring may still be seen on the fonts of Brooke, East Dereham, Gresham, Loddon, New Walsingham and Great Witchingham, Norfolk; and at Gorleston, Westhall and Woodbridge, Suffolk.[28]

By 1575, continental influences had altered major segments of English work from the late medieval taste to a new classicism. This mannerist phase of the Renaissance style affected the imagery and design of painted decoration without quenching the love of color. It eliminated the running vine (surviving from antiquity through medieval times), which included loose, undulating leafy vines often augmented with fruit and flowers (as seen in paint on the moldings of figure 106 and on the carved chest in figure 194). What emerged was an academic emphasis, reflecting the mannerist phase of the Italian Renaissance. This new style or taste focused on architectonic panels and arches, and appeared in two guises. One joined the new architectonic detailing with the old tradition of vivid coloring, as seen on the chests in figures 8 and 9. The carved motifs on stiles and rails were now tightly arranged, foliated S scrolls and at times further restricted in their movement by alternating on them small areas of light and dark paint. The second expression, beginning about the same time, was a more academic mode and had a restricted palette, in which subtle variations of different wood tones and ebonized details play against the light color of oak (figure 109). A consciously restricted palette is best remembered in seventeenth-century paintings of Dutch interiors, where, in rigid formality, the use of somber brown furniture with black detailing contrasts with stark black and white floor tiles and the glowing colors of clothing, cushions, curtains, table carpets, and tapestries. This shift from late medieval color to the subtler variations of mannerist classicism was found by the mid-sixteenth century in major London-made furniture; but it would not significantly alter provincial work, either English or American, until the following century.

102

These two attitudes toward decoration—tightly organized bright colors and an ordered, subtle palette—coexisted, often within the same cultural and economic setting, allowing a wide range of painted and unpainted wood and painted plaster walls to be roughly contemporaneous. The move toward the new style began under Henry VIII, but there is little evidence of it in his early building. In 1529 he took over the building of Hampton Court, begun by Cardinal Wolsey in 1514. But despite the suggestion of classification in the rectilinear framework on some of the interior and exterior walls, it remained a late English Gothic palace. Nonsuch Palace, which Henry VIII began in 1538, introduced to England a French version of mannerism. Nonsuch was built by English workers in a fanciful late medieval style, but the interior details were executed, at least in part, by foreigners.[29] Although Nonsuch was destroyed about 1670, remaining fragments and drawings of its details reflect French mannerism. The draw-

103

104

105

106

107

108

109

ing shown in figure **108**, possibly a scheme for Nonsuch, is probably by Nicolas Belin, who worked at Fontainebleau under Francesco Primaticcio and perhaps under Rosso Fiorentino, who in turn had brought the mannerist style from Italy to the French court in 1530. Belin may have transferred from the service of Francis I to that of Henry VIII by 1532.[30] In any case, the drawing shows many of the motifs that were to become the vocabulary of the English mannerist style. In the upper right-hand corner half of the English coat of arms is edged with curling strapwork that resembles heavy leather, a dramatic type of strapwork developed in stucco by Rosso. Hermae, masks, panels, columns, arches, and cornices abound. The large-eared, bearded, and capped silhouette mask in the strapwork above the lion's tail resembles a figure on the famous Great Bed of Ware made about 1590 (figure 142). As Fontainebleau was the center from which inspiration flowed throughout parts of Europe, so Nonsuch, in a lesser way, affected urban and rural designs all over England.

About 1575, a room in this new taste was made for Sizergh Castle, Westmorland, on the border of the Lake District (figure **109**).[31] The master may have been English, for although this is not the work or design of a local, rural artisan, it lacks

110

111

the complexity of the great continental, particularly German, inlay work. The dominant color is that of oak. The light, foliated S scrolls are poplar, and the nearly black inlay in the panels is stained oak. In the upper part, black paint or stain was used to ebonize the channels of the fluted pilasters, the spandrels, and the center of the thin vertical panels that divide each pair of arches.

Also from the continent came a similar design attitude toward furniture, as exemplified by the German late sixteenth-century cupboard on stand in figure **110**, detailed in figure **111**. The large marquetry panel has a two-handled urn holding flowers with a central carnation; the flanking lower panels, and the ends of the drawer, have square trompe l'oeil strapwork designs; and the outer panels of the upper part have hermae supporting baskets, from which spring vines that undulate across the top and support birds. The quality of the best continental work was seldom equaled in England during this period, as a comparison of this cupboard and an inlaid English wainscot chair made about 1600 (figure **112**) shows. The lower panel of the chair has a central carnation growing from a mound flanked by scrolling vines supporting birds. (The crest rail may not be original.)

Paint was a means of securing such decoration

112

less expensively. The chests in figures **113** and **114** were made about 1575 to 1600, at approximately the same time as the Sizergh Castle room, the German cupboard, and the wainscot chair. The first chest is decorated with inlay and carving; the second employs a minimum of carving and an extensive use of paint, thus achieving the attraction possible through inlay and carving. The front of the chest in figure 113 has a strip of intarsia across the base and a double layer across the frieze. (Such decorative strips of patterned wood could be purchased from specialists. They often end without a logical design terminus, having been cut from a long piece for a given space.) The panels are inlaid with colored woods; the centers of the arches have masks. From their mouths flows undulating strapwork consisting in part of monsters. This strapwork terminates at the other ends as the necks of profile masks. The applied split-spindles resemble those found on other English and New England pieces, as discussed under figures 317 and 318. (Probably the feet are not original.) The second chest has panels painted in imitation of inlay, and the double arches use paint to simulate guilloche or cable carving, as appears on figure 425.

In addition to imitating inlay and carving, paint could imitate imported lacquer work. The early seventeenth-century cabinet with mother-of-pearl inlay, and painted decoration in gold and silver, figures **115–116**, features flower-filled urns on its trompe l'oeil panels. Running vines enhance the frames around the panels. The flower- and vine-filled urn on this and the preceding pieces was an ancient universal motif found in various media. It appeared on the sixth-century Byzantine ivory "Throne of Maximian"[32] and is prominent on the mid-seventeenth-century wool on cotton and linen twill-weave bed curtain, detailed in figure **117**. The repeated urns on the curtain hold flowers: a central heraldic rose, surrounded by a pansy, carnation, honeysuckle, borage, and tulips. The four other motifs are lilies, a daffodil, and a pomegranate. The decoration is

113

114

115

116

in braid, back, link, stem, and long and short stitches with speckling enrichment.[33] The interior face of the doors of the cabinet (figure 116) is painted to mannerist strapwork similar to that found on figures 108 and 109. The painted drawer fronts suggest inlay. The ground of the cabinet is black—a color associated with lacquer work and ebony.

The East India Company imported lacquered ware. In 1690 the company sold at East India House lacquered sticks for fans, brushes, trunks, "Escretors," bowls, cups, dishes, inlaid and non-inlaid tables, panels in frames painted and carved for rooms, and screens in frames.[34] Sometimes Oriental pieces—or fragments of them—were incorporated into English pieces (see figure 1454), and imitations of imported lacquer were achieved by smoothing the wood, filling the pores, and finishing the piece with paint or colored varnish.[35] These imitations could be enhanced through marbleizing or creating the effect of tortoiseshell with paint. Imported and domestic lacquer pieces remained an important subgroup of English furnishings well into the eighteenth century. The desire for ebony wood joined with lacquer to make black a fashionable color, as accounts record: "Itm one Chaire and a desk of wood painted lyke Ibony" (1581),[36] and: "To Thomas Grene for the timber-

117

118

119

120

121

122

work of one chair and one ebony painted desk" (1581–2).[37]

From 1600, the new mannerist taste for restricted units enriched with natural wood colors and ebonized accents grew in popularity. Colorful rooms glowing with vivid hues continued to be made, but the handling of patterns tended to reflect the revived sense of classical order and symmetry.

A series of wall treatments executed during the first quarter of the seventeenth century can help us to understand this phase of English decoration. First, Langley Marish Church, in Buckinghamshire, has striking examples of elaborate decoration. The library, added to the church by the Kederminster family about 1617, is focused around its fireplace, which is surmounted by a gigantic emblazoned boss flanked by engaged columns (figure **118**). Below the mantel shelf, mannerist panels decorated with grotesques alternate with masks. Above and below these are bands of trompe l'oeil strapwork scrolling (figure **119**).

The Renaissance word "grotesque" comes from decorations found in antique Roman grottoes, which inspired much Renaissance and mannerist decoration. The grottoes had been rooms in the Roman buildings, but were later buried by accumulated rubbish and found below ground level. Raphael popularized this type of decoration when he used it on the Vatican loggetta in 1519. The Italian majolica plate (figure **120**), made about 1530, plays with similar forms, patterns, and colors. Probably the walls in at least one room at Nonsuch Palace had painted grotesque decoration.[38] In the late seventeenth century Randle Holme described this type of enrichment: "Antique, or Antick Work, is a Work for delight sake, being a general or irregular composition of all manner of compartments of Men, Beasts, Birds, Flowers, Fruit, and such like, without either Rule or Reason."[39]

To return to Langley Marish Church, the main door of the library, the doors covering the bookshelves, and the walls, all contain panels painted with religious figures and trompe l'oeil mannerist-type scrolled cartouches (figures **121** and **122**). In the top row of panels are landscapes, some of which depict local buildings.

Immediately outside the library is a paneled screen (figure **123**), probably dating from between 1600 and 1625. It has large areas of latticework and

123

small panels of pierced Gothic tracery. The screen is painted in imitation of gray, purple, and blue marble. The trompe l'oeil bosses, the moldings around them, and the moldings around the panels of latticework are all marbleized a violet shade (figures **124** and **125**).

Marbleizing was a popular means of enriching the appearance of wood or plaster and could be accomplished in a number of ways. William Salmon, in 1701, recommended that when the background paint is still very wet, a thinned mixture of another color should be dripped on to make the large veins. After the background paint has dried somewhat and the other color will not spread so widely, more of the second color is dripped on and, with something like a feather, these smaller veins are broken to create the smallest veins. Within two or three days the piece should be varnished.[40]

Another method is later cited by George Smith, who in 1755 wrote:

> To marble upon Wood. Take the white of eggs, beat them up till you can write or draw therewith, then with a pencil or feather draw what veins you please upon the wood; after it is dry'd and harden'd for about two hours, take quick-lime, mix it well together with wine, and with a brush or pencil paint the wood all over; after it is thorough dry, rub it with a scrubbing brush off, so that both the lime and the whites of the eggs may come off together; then rub it with a linnen rag till it is smooth and fine; after which you may lay over a thin varnish, and you will have a fine marbled wood.

Smith also suggested still another means of marbleizing: mix plaster of Paris, quicklime, salt, oxblood, stones of different colors, and pieces of glass. Beat the ingredients into powder, add vinegar, beer, and sour milk, and brush the mixture onto the wood. When it has dried, smooth it with pumice and then leather and oil.[41]

References inform us that marbleizing appeared as a finish on many pieces of furniture, often using the same colors as on architectural woodwork. In 1661–2 the cabinetmaker Thomas Malin billed: "For an extraordinary Large Table fower foot[een] [14 feet] long & almost fower foot wide Marble Wood, inlayed. . . . For her Ma[ts] 2 Bedchamber & Closet at White Hall." He also billed for "two paire of Stands and two Tables of Marble Speckled wood" and for "one Marble coloured Table Violet Wood deliuered to M[r] Francis Rogers."[42]

Speckling was a means of enriching a painted or imitation lacquer finish by sprinkling it with

124

small, shiny, colored particles while it was still wet. William Salmon described some uses for speckles in 1701:

They are of divers sorts, as Golden, Silver, Copper, and many other colors, some finer, some courser, which are to be used according to the Fancy of the Artist, and as the nature of the matter may require: they are used on Mouldings, outsides and insides of Bowls, Cups, Boxes, Drawers, &c. . . . To lay Speckles on the drawing part of Japan Work, as on Flowers, Herbs, Trees, Fowls, Beasts, Rocks, Garments &c. . . . After a piece is painted or varnished, . . . before it is dry, put some of your Speckles into your Sieve [you make one by knocking the bottom out of a pill box and stretching an open-weave cloth over it], and gently shake the Sieve, over the Places you design, till they are all speckled according to your Intention.[43]

Textiles, and the surfaces of other crafts, are described as "speckled" (figure 117, for example). The dots were not always tiny: those on the Holme family triptych (detail, figure 160) are large red spots on a red ground.

Tapestries covered plaster walls or partially obscured rich paneling. The early seventeenth-century Mortlake tapestry at Haddon Hall, Derbyshire, shown in figure **126** has a top border of

125

126

strapwork with a central cartouche in which is a cabochon-shaped dark blue "jewel" with trompe l'oeil highlight. This parallels in weaving the effect of the trompe l'oeil bosses on the Langley Marish Church screen (figure 125) painted about the same date. The border of the tapestry has inner and outer trompe l'oeil moldings, so that the tapestry represents a gigantic frame enclosing a decorative panel.

Textiles made what were perhaps the most generous contributions of color to the settings for English furniture. Inventories of elegant houses refer to elaborate tapestries as part of important rooms. In the royal household accounts for 1674, among many other tapestries the following are listed: "Hero and Leandor," "Eneas," "seasons in small figures," "story of vulcan," "story of Jacobb," "Herculus very old," "the Tryumph of Caesar," "the Apostles," "the 12 months," "Kings of Assirria," "Bacchanalls," "story of the boys," "Landskipp with Potts of fruite in the Borders." Further textiles of equal richness include: "Blew figured velvett," "Crymson Damask Canopye," "[A] Large velvett Chaire of state trimed with silver and Gold fringe A Crimson velvett Cushion suitable to itt," "blew & Gold damask hangings paned & brodered with Stript velvett," "Screene of Crymson velvett," "Large Persian Carpett," "Turkey Carpett & 1 Green Cloth Carpitt," and, surprisingly, "white damask window Curtaines to draw up."[44] The last appeared in various inventories.

Painted and stained cloths, less expensive than tapestries, also decorated interior walls, as the inventories again record: "the curtryning that hangeth about the purse chambre, steynyd with Verdure [green vegetation] worke" (1486),[45] "in the grene chamber hangett aboute wth panted ares [arris] worke. in the red chamber hanget aboute wth red paynted worke. in on[e] of byest chambers ov[er] the gate hanget wth paynted work of yalowe [yellow] and redd" (1599),[46] "and also all the panted clouthes that are within my howse except the paynted clouth that hangeth . . ." (1573).[47] The textiles mentioned are "murray," "buckeram," and "fustyon."[48] Other hangings also enlivened the royal audience rooms: in one picture of Elizabeth I, the room is entirely hung with what seems to be cloth or leather with

127

painted floral decoration.[49] A portrait of Mary I shows her standing against a plain hanging with a fringed edge. The textile has creased rectangular folds, probably having been so formed by being smoothed in a press.[50] A similar pattern of creases is often seen on tablecloths in seventeenth-century paintings and engravings, such as those by Abraham Bosse. In the portrait of Mary I, the rectangles are larger and look like panels.

Plaster walls were often decoratively painted, although at times the fact was obscured by hangings. The black on white plaster panels, figure **127**, were discovered in Ipswich, Suffolk, and date from about 1600. Other plaster walls were more colorful, and in some instances made to appear as though they had been enriched with applied wood or marble. The wall to the left of the screen shown in figure 123 has a trompe l'oeil entablature with swags, triglyphs, and shields on the frieze, and dentils below it. The entablature is crowned with painted strapwork, echoing the wooden strapwork on the screen, and is supported by trompe l'oeil bracketed pilasters. Plaster walls were also made to appear paneled by using less expensive paint.

Figures 128 through 131 show flat plaster walls painted about 1600 in Cumberland Lodge, St. Helen's, near Ipswich, to simulate richly colored

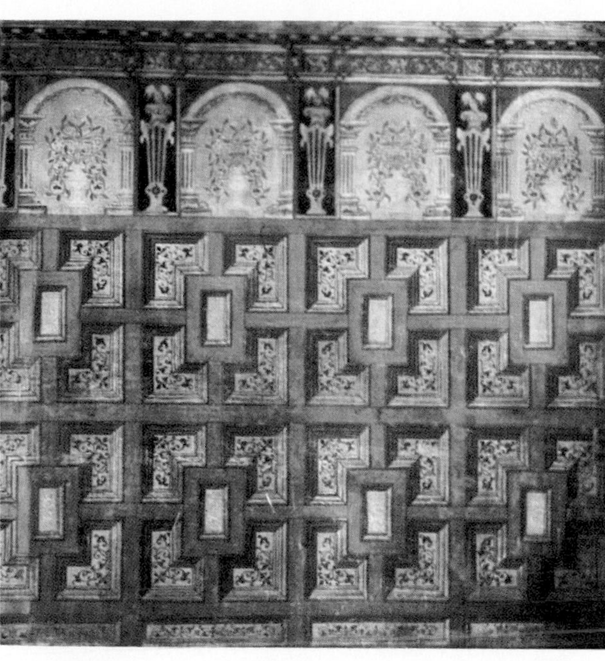

128

129

130

131

132

133

paneling. On the wall shown in figures **128** and **129**, green verticals and horizontals frame red moldings around panels decorated with black arabesques. (These trompe l'oeil inner-frame panels resemble the real panels seen in figure 109.) Above, hermae divide arches that frame flower-filled urns. The spandrels of the arches contain green leaves around a red flower. At the top an entire entablature is painted. The design is so realistically drawn that the "joints" of the green horizontal and vertical framing are "secured" by painted pins (figure 129).

The wall shown in figures **130** and **131** creates the illusion of panels decorated with mannerist strapwork cartouches, rather like the panels in the Langley Marish Church library (figure 122). In the center of each panel is a trompe l'oeil pyramidal boss. The beveled ends of the light-color moldings are delineated by black lines, and the "pins" that secure each "joint" of the frame are light-color dots (figure 131). However, unlike the painted pins shown in figure 129, these pins are incorrectly placed. They go through the line where the boards touch and not through what would be the mortise-and-tenon joints. A similarly decorated plaster wall, formerly found in Bennett's Castle Farm House, Dagenham, Essex, is dated 1618.[51]

So much unpainted paneling survives today that one might assume it was always unpainted. However, walls such as those shown in figures 128 through 131, which imitate painted paneling, would not have been made if real panels had not been similarly decorated. Indeed, the process of painting plaster to look like painted paneling was usual, for in the late seventeenth century Randle Holme found it a standard practice: "Seileing, is House Painting, where Plaister Wall are made to look like Wainscote, or outlandish Timber."[52] In 1701, in describing the painting of real wood paneling, the suggestion was that it needed fewer coats of paint than outside woodwork: "*But here note*, that Wainscotting, and other Painting within Doors, need not be done above twice over, with the last Color; tis only that Painting which is exposed to the Air and Weather, that requires so many times running over it."[53] Portraits of Elizabeth I often include decorated walls. Some have panels with highly developed mannerist grotesques, which may have been either painted or inlaid.[54]

The paneling in figures **132** and **133**, from

Hawstead Place near Bury St. Edmunds, was painted about 1600. Rather vernacular in its handling of landscape and floral imagery, it does not approach the level of high-style or court work but is like the decoration many future New Englanders would have known in England. The panels are edged by black paint applied to the stiles and rails (figure 133). Painted inscriptions and strapwork are found on some upper panels.

Today, linen-fold wainscoting is usually found unfinished, or at best varnished or waxed. The paneling from about 1600, figure **134**, bears several layers of paint, of which the bottom seems to be red. That the paint has not been stripped is surprising, for even Fred Roe, who wrote in 1902 in praise of early objects, was able to state:

> Not satisfied with ornamenting the wainscoting of their apartments with linen and other patterns, the effect was in many instances heightened by a lavish application of gold and colors. This would seem to be a very fair illustration of the phrase "guilding [sic] the lily," and though such as have remained so to our time are interesting from the fact of their being in an untouched state, their effect considered as a whole is less restful and pleasing than when the natural surface of the wood is retained. During their first freshness this exaggerated splendour must have been considerably more obvious.[55]

Such an attitude from one so aware of the importance of early material now astounds, if not horrifies, us and is part of what makes our search for untouched painted surfaces so difficult. The famous ceiling of the dining room at Haddon Hall in Derbyshire, finished about 1545, has black and red rectangles painted on the beams. Between them the flat plaster ceiling is painted to yellow and black squares around large "panels" containing Tudor roses and other heraldic emblems. The walls are covered with what are now natural oak panels, although they were in all probability once painted like the ceiling. The top row of panels has carved heraldic designs echoing the painted ones on the plaster ceiling. When cleaned, the walls retained their carved designs; to clean the ceiling would be to remove the decoration, and so the ceiling paint remains.

Painted furniture joined the colorful grandeur of these settings. The earliest known English harpsichord-organ (figure **135**) is an important

134

135

136

key to documenting mannerist decoration in English decorative arts. It is dated 1579, and signed by Ludowicus Theeuwes II, a Dutch virginal maker who was working in London by 1568.[56] The panels are painted to trompe l'oeil strapwork and scrolling in imitation of carved and painted panels. The decoration is unusual in combining illusionary painting with real projecting "jewels" or bosses. The instrument is a fine and elaborate piece by English standards, although contemporary Italian workers were capable of much more complex and refined work. The Victoria and Albert Museum also owns a spinet made in Milan in 1577 on which the strapwork patterns are of ivory inlaid into an ebony ground, and the applied "jewels" are 1,928 precious and semi-precious stones.[57] This comparison is made not to lessen the achievement of craftsmen in England, but to promote a broader understanding of two different communities engaged in cultural exchange. To some extent the relationship bears basic similarities to the exchange between rural seventeenth-century English and New England craftsmen and the most sophisticated ones in London.

Turning strong lights on the famous Great Bed of Ware, figure **136**, produces a surprising effect, for its vivid colors are normally shrouded in shadow.[58] The bed was owned by Sir Henry Fanshawe (b. 1569) of Ware Park, in Hertfordshire, and was first recorded in 1596 by a German traveler, Prince Ludwig of Anhalt-Köhten, who marveled that it was wide enough for four couples. It was sufficiently well known to be referred to by Sir Toby Belch in Shakespeare's *Twelfth Night*, and Lord Byron mentions it in *Don Juan*. By 1610 the bed was in an inn, where it eventually became the custom for occupants to carve their initials and the date, or to impress their seal in wax, on its frame; the earliest date is 1653.

The two main panels in the headboard (figure **137**) have scenes made with various colored woods in the manner of the so-called Nonsuch chests of about the same time, and around the panels are elaborate carvings realistically painted. The lion

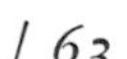

137

138

139

masks (figure **138**) are colored gold, resembling the example from a contemporary tapestry (figure **139**), and a basket of fruit supported by a herm (figure **140**) is as colorful as that on the same textile (figure **141**). The bearded mask (figure **142**) is like the silhouetted mask above the lion's tail shown in the mannerist drawing, figure 108. Below the hermae, masks with rings mark the center of strap-edge cartouches (figure **143**). The tester, or ceiling, of the bed is fitted with panels (figures 136 and 137). Some have flatly carved red roses enclosed by green leaves; others more three-dimensional red roses without leafage. Like a small contemporary room, the bed combines columns, carvings, inlay, and painted and unpainted areas, and, when properly dressed, it would have had rich, colorful textiles.

Many of the most aristocratic chairs in the sixteenth and early seventeenth centuries were upholstered to the floor and supplied with a deep cushion attached to the seat, in addition to a loose cushion that rested between the arms. Sometimes

140

141

142

143

a third cushion rested on the second, and if wide enough extended over the arms. As in figure **144** (1615–25), there was usually an accompanying footstool, and as seen in figures 676 through 678, important chairs were often flanked by a matching set of stools of seating height. (Another all-upholstered chair appears as figure 197.) The elaborate textile cost many times the price of the frame. In 1603, for the coronation of James I, eight chairs were made at the cost of £66. 6s. 6d. each. The price of the wood was £1, the labor 25 shillings, and the textile £64. 1s. od. The material was cloth of gold and crimson damask.[59] For the chair in figure **145** the cost was lowered by reducing the amount of fabric and painting a pattern on the exposed wooden legs. (Its present ancient covering hides the original loose cushion and the red velvet and silver lace upholstery.[60] The finials are missing.)

The early seventeenth-century arm chair shown in figure **146** has original red velvet on the back and arms, and there once was silver fringing. Where the chair was not covered with a textile, it was painted a similar red and damasked, or diapered, with gold (figure **147**). In the seventeenth century Randle Holme described diapering as "tracing or running over a work (when it is finished) with Damask Branches, and such like; it is the counterfeiting of Cloth of Gold, Silver, Damask, with either Branches, Flowers, or other antick devices, in what fashion is most pleasing; it is termed also Damasking."[61] Flowers painted over the red and gold (figures 147 and **148**) are colored much as they appear on contemporary textiles (figure **149**). On an arm chair that retains most of its original painted damask decoration (figure **150**), gold tracing was used to create stylized vines on the back posts and floral vines on the prominent front posts. According to tradition, it was originally used in Boughton House, Northamptonshire.

Figure **151** in Hardwick Hall, Derbyshire, is a couch of state (1625–30). These two-ended pieces were heavily cushioned and placed with a long side against a wall under a canopy, where they served as ceremonial couches.[62] The painted pattern on the ends (figure **152**) would have matched the textile on the cushions, which would have "upholstered" the undecorated areas. The pattern of the painted decoration suggests that the covering was similar to the mid-seventeenth-century

144

145

146

147

148

149

150

151

152

153

154

curtain seen in figure **153**. The flow of the vine loosened up during the latter half of the century, and when painted on the Taunton, Massachusetts, chest over drawer, dated 1736 (figure **154**), there was a freely scrolling line.

Another couch of state (1620–35), figures **155–156**, is in a sense a fragment, but it is an important one: it originally had two identical ends; the top rail of the remaining end has had its outer corners rounded (probably, as in figure 152, they projected beyond the corner stiles over applied brackets); the rails between the ends seem to be replacements. It is the paint on what remains of the couch of state that fascinates us. Peter Thornton has suggested that the paint on this couch—a soft green ground decorated with floral sprigs—matched the original textile, probably silk, covering the deep cushions.[63]

155

156

The inside of the Holme family triptych (figures **157–160**) depicts the family of Henry Holme, of Pall-Holme, near Kingston on Hull, Yorkshire. The fronts of the doors are paneled, painted, and dated. The upper part of the left door is inscribed: "W [?] H," and the right door: "WEE MUST [clock dial = DIE ALL] YET BY [CHRIST] LIVE ALL 1628." The framing around the panels is marbleized yellow, and the red panels are speckled. Paired arches at the top of each door are separated by flat, wooden, heart-shaped elements, pierced to arabesque designs and applied above split-spindles (figure 159). Similar decoration appears on the couch of state shown in figure 155 and the chest in figure 113. The heart shape is echoed closely, but on a different scale, on the seventeenth-century tulip cupboards made in the Wethersfield area of Connecticut (for example, that in figure 227). These are closer in size to those on the English shelves made about 1700 (figure 581). The applied split-spindles on the triptych are similar to those on certain chests and cupboards made in Connecticut and Massachusetts (see the discussion on figures 317 and 318 at page 123). The Holme family inside the triptych was a generation earlier and of higher economic station than Mrs. Freake and her baby Mary, seen in figure 51.

Color in New England

New England gives us a somewhat less disturbed picture of English rural practices than England itself, and we can now document that the seventeenth century in New England was visually one of the colorific periods in the history of design. Vivid colors and lively patterns were most prominently used by the well-to-do, for they were usually more expensive; but colors and patterns were enjoyed at all social and economic levels. There were in New England, as in England, sumptuary laws that defined the proper dress for each level of society and kept those with greater wealth and station more discernible by allowing them more color, more ornamentation, and greater freedom to create complex fashions. Sermons against elaboration, and court cases involving ostentation, are often cited as proof of Puritan simplicity. In fact the reverse is true, for the suits resulted from infringements of the laws by those who were to be restricted.

The double portrait of Mrs. Elizabeth Freake and her baby Mary, figure 51, was completed about 1674 and does not differ from other late

157

158

159

160

seventeenth-century Massachusetts portraits in including elegant details. Both figures are garbed in lace, and Mary is dressed in what may be a piece of the lemon-colored silk mentioned in the 1675 inventory of her father, John. Mrs. Freake also has a white necklace, a black bracelet, a gold thumb ring, sleeves gathered by red and black ribbons, and her skirt pulled back to show her embroidered red petticoat. She sits in a turkeywork chair with columnar-turned back posts. Posts of that shape are not known on an American-made chair of that style, which suggests that this and the other thirteen turkeywork chairs in the Freakes' house were imported from England. The bottom edge of the vividly colored turkeywork back panel has a multicolor fringe. The painting is of Puritan Bostonians of the class that had its portraits painted; Mrs. Freake and her child are dressed much like a mother and child of similar station and economic circumstances in England, whether Puritan or Church of England (figure 52). The painting shows only part of the richness that surrounded the Freakes. In the 1675 inventory of John Freake's Boston estate there are, besides the fourteen turkeywork chairs (possibly two arm chairs and twelve side chairs), many other expensive items, including three looking glasses, forty yards of lemon-colored silk, and, among the silver valued at the large sum of £68, two tankards, a saltcellar, a sugar box, a caudle cup with cover, a candlestick, a basin, twenty-four spoons, and eight forks. The entire estate was valued at £2,391 1s. 9d.—a high figure for seventeenth-century New England.[64]

Abbott Lowell Cummings has documented the use of color and pattern outside, and more particularly inside, seventeenth-century Massachusetts houses.[65] Common were color schemes in which interior wooden framing members were painted to contrast with whitewashed walls: black, vermilion, green, or red and yellow against white. Cummings also reports the use of tinted whitewash. Architectural details were sometimes dramatically emphasized: the shadow molding in whitewashed wall sheathing might be emphasized by black, and alternating black and red dentils cap the fireplace opening in the room from the Hart House of Ipswich, Massachusetts, now installed in the Metropolitan Museum of Art. Probably in the seventeenth century, certainly by the eighteenth, the walls themselves were often enriched by large areas of color, sometimes daubs of strong color dotting the whitewash. Among the many similarly decorated rooms, the upper entry of the William Boardman House in Saugus, Massachusetts, is famous for its diaper pattern of "sponge" dots. Some furniture was similarly decorated.[66]

The textiles used in the seventeenth century dramatically added color to a setting. A room might have window and bed curtains, cupboard cloths, chair coverings, and cushions of a matching and striking color: green was by far the most frequent, but red, yellow, and blue were often used. Although the colors usually matched, the material was not always the same: wool, cotton, and even matching colored leather could be part of a single scheme. In fact, the cloth varied from homespun to gold-fringed velvet. In a few rare instances, there were Oriental carpets on tables and cupboards.

Some Massachusetts walls were enriched with lively hangings, although very few have survived. At least one "Turkey Tapestry for room" is mentioned in an inventory, and would have been as vivid as the back of Mrs. Freake's chair. A set of seventeenth-century painted hangings may still have been in use in Boston in 1762.[67] Part of a large mid-seventeenth-century wall hanging of coarse linen with a block-printed and painted scene and used in Massachusetts does survive.[68] It is probably English, for the gentlemen on horseback resemble those in English woven tapestries of about 1650.

It is not surprising that much of the furniture in these lively settings was painted. Sometimes only certain details were picked out, but often the entire visible surface was sumptuously decorated (figure 9).[69]

Late seventeenth-century inventories of eastern Massachusetts households list painted furniture, such as a "rede chest" or "greene chist"; more intriguing are references to pieces of which we have no known examples, such as the ten "speckled chairs" listed, along with twelve turkeywork chairs, in Jacob Smith's Boston inventory of 1700, and the six "chaires guilded" listed in the Boston inventory of Mary Nash, also of 1700, along with six turkeywork chairs, four leather chairs, and six cane chairs.[70] American chairs with speckled decoration have not been found, nor is any example of an American gilded chair, or an English gilded chair used in America before the classical revival of the late eighteenth century, yet known. Perhaps such pieces will come to light; but it is more likely that they have not survived, or that they have had their surface removed through "refinishing." Probably a full understanding of the richness of early Massachusetts rooms will continue to elude us.

The present scarcity of American examples is largely attributable to the simultaneous existence in the late nineteenth century of four closely related trends: the beginnings of collecting early American objects; the early emphasis on collecting seventeenth-century oak furniture; the emergence of oak as a fashionable wood for new furniture that was praised for its tones and grain; and the strong desire—unfortunately still present among some collectors—to clean up a piece to make it "suitable" for use. These trends combined to make it seem natural that paint that had become shabby should be removed. Fortunately, there have always been some collectors aware of the visual, historic, and economic merit of original surfaces.

It has become traditional to see the difference between what was made in New England and in London—about a twenty- to forty-year hiatus—as a cultural lag, as though seventeenth-century colonial makers *chose* to be behind London. It is arguable if this is even possible, whether a maker can easily work in the style of the previous generation. In fact, the "lag" was the time it took stylish London designs to affect provincial work in England and the colonies. In short, what was made in America was basically like rural English work of the same date, providing that rural craftsmen or objects in the latest style continued migrating to the colonies.

There were, of course, exceptional cases in which London directly affected an American piece. The chest of drawers with doors shown in figure 467 is a rare example of mid-seventeenth-century London taste coming straight to mid-century Boston, with only minor simplifications. Because of its classical stance, it was once thought to date from the very late seventeenth century, after the demise of the carved and painted furniture tradition. However, Patricia Kane and Benno Forman have argued convincingly that the piece is too close to mid-century London work (figures 1 and 468 through 475) to be retardataire and that it must be contemporaneous with London work of 1640 to 1660, and have been made by a London-trained craftsman on his arrival in Boston.

As was pointed out in Chapter 2, one of the most important finds for scholars of American furniture has been the chest in figure 8, because of its similarity in carved decoration, painted surface, and date to New England chests such as that in figure 9. Until recently the American piece was assigned to the hand of Thomas Dennis, who worked in Portsmouth, New Hampshire, and later in Ipswich, Massachusetts. The attribution was based on a similarity of design to the Dennis family pieces: two wainscot chairs, a box with a drawer, two chests, and a tape loom, all of which descended in the family. Thomas Dennis, joiner, married the widow of William Searle, who had also been a joiner. The Searles had emigrated from Ottery St. Mary, Devon, where the chest shown in figure 8 resides, and it is part of a group of pieces that were made in that area (for another example, see figure 10). This suggests that Searle, not Dennis, brought this design to America; that Searle may have made at least some of the "Dennis family" pieces; and that they accompanied his widow when she married Thomas Dennis. Dennis probably used features from Searle's designs in his own work. While there are at present no certain solutions as to which pieces are by Dennis and which by Searle, the three chests (figures 8 through 10) most emphatically raise the question of dependence in American work.

The oak English chest (1630–60) at Boston, Lincolnshire, figure **161**, has red paint under a later coat of yellow. The top is paneled—a feature far more prevalent in England than America, where wide boards were easily obtainable. (A rare example of an American paneled top appears in figure 417.) With its simple band of carved lunettes on the top rail, the chest is less grand than figures 8 and 10 and is typical of many pieces made in England and the colonies, with little or no decoration, chiefly for reasons of economy. Later, in both England and America, hundreds of such examples were made more desirable to collectors by adding carving, inlay, or painted designs. In many cases the later enrichment was added openly as the taste for complex early pieces grew throughout the nineteenth and twentieth centuries. In other instances the additional decoration was in-

161

tended to increase the monetary value of the objects.

As in England, painted pieces and those displaying natural wood colors and ebonized details existed side by side. Figure 9 and figure **162**, dated [16]76, are roughly contemporary. The cabinet was made in Salem, Massachusetts, just five years after the Ottery St. Mary chest (figure 8). It is of red oak (a variety of oak thought not to have been exported), red cedar, and soft maple. The door is carved: "7 B 6 / T & S." (Related English and American cabinets appear as figures 575 through 579.)

Figures **163** and **164** dramatically convey two choices available in one American setting at the end of the seventeenth century. Both pieces were made in the Guilford-Milford area of Connecticut, and the similarity of the applied split-spindles on each suggests that these were by the same turner. The cupboard is a stylish piece, with deep mannerist paneling. It is of white oak, soft maple, chestnut, and American red cedar, and the parquetry is American black walnut (an early use of this wood in America). (The top, middle shelf, and base molding are new.) In contrast, the tulip wood and white oak board chest has simulated paneling on the front. In the manner of seventeenth-century drawer fronts (see figure 463), thin strips were applied to make it look like framed construction. (A few American and English chests combined a genuinely framed front with an otherwise board construction chest, as in figures 418 and 419.) On the chest in figure 164, red and black paint provided some of the color contrast also found on the cupboard. The chest of drawers in figure **165** was made in the Saybrook-Guilford area of Connecticut (1690–1710), and with the preceding cupboard and chest demonstrates the great range of elaborate statements available in one rural setting at the end of the century. Besides providing a contrast to the paneled cupboard and board chest, this extraordinary painted chest of drawers gives us an opportunity to look closely at the means through which decorative details were transferred to recently settled areas.

162

163

164

165

166

167

The drawers in the middle tiers of figure 165 use an earth mound and a two-handled cup, which holds a central carnation and flowing vine with birds. These may derive from inlaid, painted, or embroidered designs like those in figures 110 to 117, or from a book decoration. The latter seems unlikely since the use of color and the closeness to known English inlaid and painted pieces suggest a polychrome source. There may be a painted, inlaid, or embroidered source for the lower drawer design, but it was probably based on a black and white book ornament that appeared widely in America and England (figure **166**). This cut is taken from *The Orthodox Evangelist,* by John Norton (1606–63) of Ipswich, Massachusetts. Published in London in 1654, this became the first extensive theological treatise to emerge from New England.[71] The rose and thistle symbolized England and Scotland united under James I in 1603. The central fleur-de-lys dates to England's former claim to part of France, surrendered in 1559 by Elizabeth I when she relinquished the claim of sovereignty over Calais. The vines around the drawer edges, on the stiles and side panels of figure 165, are related to those inlaid and painted on figures 112 and 115. The profile faces spewing vines from the inner edge of the paired drawers in the top tier are part of a long decorative tradition that encompasses both Christian and non-Christian imagery. Early Christian ivories and European medieval church door surrounds abound with faces of humans and animals—full face or in profile—with vines emerging from the lips or neck (as on the arches of figure 113, and figure 200). Many of the illuminations in the Book of Kells show this device. Furthermore, the Tree of Jesse is particularly linked with this tradition, where the vine can emerge from mouth or loins.[72] In both the Old and New Testament the vine is a symbol of God's grace.

Figure **167** shows part of the pulpit at a church in Medlesham, Suffolk.[73] The church in Crowcombe, Somerset, has a sixteenth-century full-face mask with emerging vine.[74] The mouth of the dragons on the frieze, figure 253, hold floral and grape vines. The full-face and profile mask and vine, which were part of the early French mannerist ornamental vocabulary (flanking the columns in the upper left of figure 108), reappear at the end of the seventeenth century, as seen on the legs of figure 207.

The decorative scheme found on the Connecticut chest of drawers was perpetuated in the eighteenth century on such pieces as that in figure **168**. Related English furniture with equivalent painted decoration has not been discovered, but some high-style and court pieces with similar floral surfaces executed in marquetry are known (figure 538).

Germany provided designs to England (figure 110), and through immigrants directly to Pennsylvania. There is a close relationship between the inlay in the cupboard on stand in figure 110 and that in the top of the walnut (pine, tulip) Pennsylvania dressing table (figures **169** and **170**), dated 1724. The German and Pennsylvania handling of design differs from the English and Connecticut attitude. It is more linear and open in movement. Also, the German and Pennsylvania sensibility tends tightly to enclose the central unit, as with the heavy oval on the dressing-table top. The same distinction between English and German work is seen when comparing book ornaments from these countries.[75] Both the German cupboard on stand and the dressing table have grouped berries—in pairs in the German example and in threes on the dressing table. The complex cup turnings of the legs of the latter are possibly German inspired, while being similar in form to those of the cane chair in figure 711. Open flowing vines with birds continued to be part of the German-related Pennsylvania work well into the next century, as seen on the painted pine chest probably made in Centre County about 1810–30 (figure **171**).

While eastern Massachusetts developed within the general sequence of rural English work—from a choice of paint or contrasting wood tones to a greater use of the latter—one part of central Connecticut was experiencing what seems to be a shift in the opposite direction: it moved from molded paneling with ebonized turnings played against natural oak to all-over paint. Recognizing this seemingly regressive change is important if we are to understand the role paint has often played throughout the history of furniture. Rather than a shift from an old to a new style, this represents a shift from a more expensive to a less expensive means of decorating an object.

The late seventeenth-century chest over drawers from the Wethersfield-Hartford region of Connecticut, figure **172**, shows a rural use of the mannerist style: an emphasis on panels and turn-

168

169

170

171

ings, and a restricted palette with ebonized details.[76] The floral carving on this group is not composed of loose and flowing vines in the medieval taste, such as are found on "Hatfield" chests (figure 231); rather, it is tightly compressed, restricted, and balanced. The panels are contained within applied moldings, whereas on medieval pieces the moldings are run into the stiles and rails, not applied. Applied moldings were more expensive since they took more wood and were individually applied, but they helped to provide the clarity and sense of depth that were part of the new mannerist style.[77] The emphasis on panels also conditions the decoration of the drawers. The two long drawers below the chest section have moldings applied to their face to make them look like four paired drawers. These drawer panels were separated and flanked by applied, paired split-spindles (now mostly lost on the drawers and on some areas of the stiles). The black ebonizing paint emphasizes small areas: the turnings, the cut corners of the central panel on the chest and those of the simulated panels on the drawers, and the main horizontal moldings. The moldings

172

173

174

175

176

around the real and the simulated panels on the drawers were painted red, and the former were enriched by grouped black lines. (The form of the tulip on the outer panels is found on the legs of the table made in the north of England and seen in figures 295 and 296; a related Connecticut cupboard appears as figure 227.)

Similar chests continued to be made in Hartford County into the eighteenth century. However, about 1700 a version began to appear that continued to use applied moldings, but was more dependent on painted ornamentation. The chest over drawers dated 1704, figure **173**, lacks turnings and carving, and its panels are decorated with painted rings of interlaced tulips like the carved ones on the central panel of the chest shown in figure 172.[78] A year later there appeared a painted version, figure **174**, without even the heavy horizontal moldings above and below the drawer. Dated 1705/6, it has a patterned circle on its dated central panel (figure **175**) and large images on its outer panels (figure **176**) like the chest shown in figure 172. The circle in figure 175—a stylized compass design—encloses a series of arcs, while the corners are filled with stylized flowers.

With its rich, dramatic, yet subtle use of color, this is one of the greatest pieces of painted furniture; the flowers on the outer panels are particularly strong. The stiles and rails are decorated with small colored dots on a black ground. These are the painter's interpretation of "speckles" carried out in a flagrant and delightful manner. Staccato punctuation was not confined in America to furniture, but also appeared on contemporary silver, glass, and pottery, and is well known on New England textiles. In a listing of fabrics found in inventories of merchants in Suffolk County, Massachusetts, between 1660 and 1695, we find "speckled calico," "speckled linen," "speckled bed rugs," "speckled napkins," and "spotted coverlets."[79] Such texturing enlivened late seventeenth-century embroidery where, for example, the green ground of a leaf may be textured with an all-over diaper pattern of colored dots.

177

English Color after the Restoration

From the mid-seventeenth century there was a growing desire for furniture with the warm colors of natural wood other than oak, and these surfaces often incorporated elegantly patterned marquetry in the continental taste. The late seventeenth-century cabinet on stand, figure **177**, is entirely wrapped in floral decoration executed in a variety of woods and white- and green-stained horn. Like the formerly prevalent use of carving, paint, and textiles, the new technique of marquetry continued the tradition of enriching an entire surface. While natural wood was more fashionable, paint remained a means of achieving exotic wood colors in cheaper materials.

The late seventeenth-century provincial English portrait shown in figure **178** depicts Sir Thomas Ingram of Sheriff Hutton, North Yorkshire, sitting in an ebonized bannister-back arm chair. The chair, lacking the usual puffy cushion, provides pictorial evidence of the ebonizing noted in written records. The black and gold stool in figure **179** was made in England late in the seventeenth

178

179

180

century, and would originally have had a thick cushion.

By the beginning of the eighteenth century quieter surfaces were being juxtaposed against richly curving walnut forms, and by the mid-century there were complex designs in mahogany. While rich brown wood tones dominated, japanned pieces, such as that in figure 370, were part of the high-style milieu; and consciously fantastic pieces were made with contrasting colors, such as the black, red, and gold bed, figure 367, and the black and gold dressing commode, figure 329, both made for the fourth Duke of Beaufort for Badminton House, Gloucestershire, between 1752 and 1754. The candlestand, figure **180**, was made about 1760 of softwood colored in sections to resemble mahogany. It is very similar to a design dated 1756 by Thomas Johnson, published in an untitled book of designs by Johnson in London in 1758, and again in his *One Hundred and Fifty New Designs* in 1761.

The classical revival engendered by Robert Adam and others in the 1760s brought a radical shift in design and a new concern for bright colors.

These were often rendered in rather precious materials, such as patterned marbles, but paint again played a major role in creating stylish work. Adam drew heavily on antique patterns he had seen in Italy, including Raphael's Vatican grotesques, which had influenced the mannerist grotesques of the sixteenth century. In the "Etruscan Room" (1775–77) at Osterley Park, Middlesex (figure **181**), the furniture, ceiling, and walls are painted. The designs on the walls show the open organization of some grotesques during the 1760s and 1770s. (Another contemporary attitude toward such ornaments, also by Adam at Osterley Park, is seen as figure 210.) Missing from the room is a carpet that would have been a near repeat of the ceiling, completing the unity of the design.

At the vernacular level, and on consciously rudimentary pieces by such shops as the Gillows firm, paint never ceased to be one means of finishing furniture. Inexpensive woods needed to be sealed, and paint achieved this while also adding color. The eight pieces shown in figures 182 through 190 span about one hundred years, demonstrating the persistence of painted finishes on this type of furniture. The red-painted pine wing chair, figure **182**, has a bowed crest rail shape that suggests a date in the second half of the eighteenth century. Constructed of thick planks, it makes a strong provincial statement not unlike some rural Pennsylvania work. (A side view appears as figure 1169.) The pine child's chair (1750–1800), figure **183**, has the remains of a thin coat of red-brown paint. The small pine writing desk (1780–1810) in figure **184** was photographed on its back in order to show the bottom, for there the bright red paint is less damaged by age. Probably the rest of the desk has a protective coat of shellac or varnish, which has darkened with the passage of time.

The Gillows firm in 1787 charged 1 shilling for painting the oval deal table seen in figure **185**.[80] In 1792 the firm recorded on a single sheet, figure **186**, "A Painted deal nest of draws" (shown at the top) and "A Solid mahogany Wardrobe."[81] In 1793 they made the piece in figure **187**, described

181

182

183

184

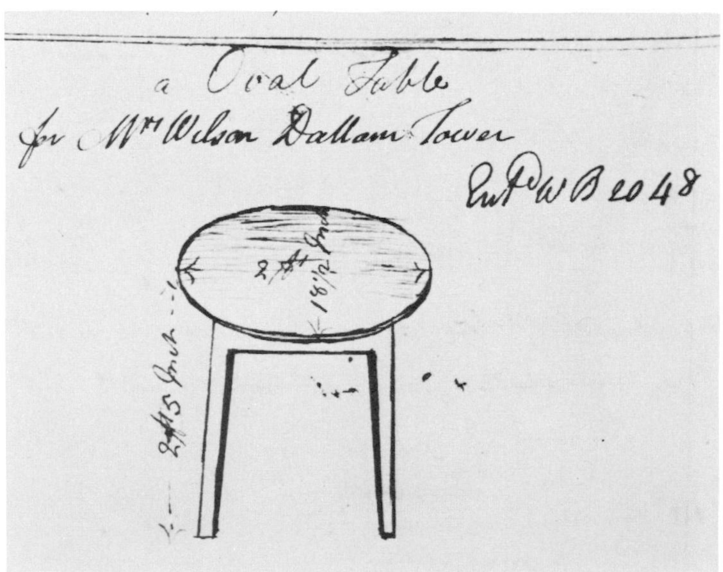

185

as "A whitewood Japand easy chair." "Painted black ground and stroked wth pink." The seat was "Rush bottom" and there was a cushion for the seat and another for the back.[82]

The vernacular pine cradle, figure **188**, has a mottled orange-red outside and a bright blue interior, very much in the manner of some New England, New York State, and Canadian furniture. A similar color scheme is used on the pine cradle shown in figures **189** and **190**, which is one of the best-documented pieces of English painted furniture. Its black zigzag decoration on the orange-red

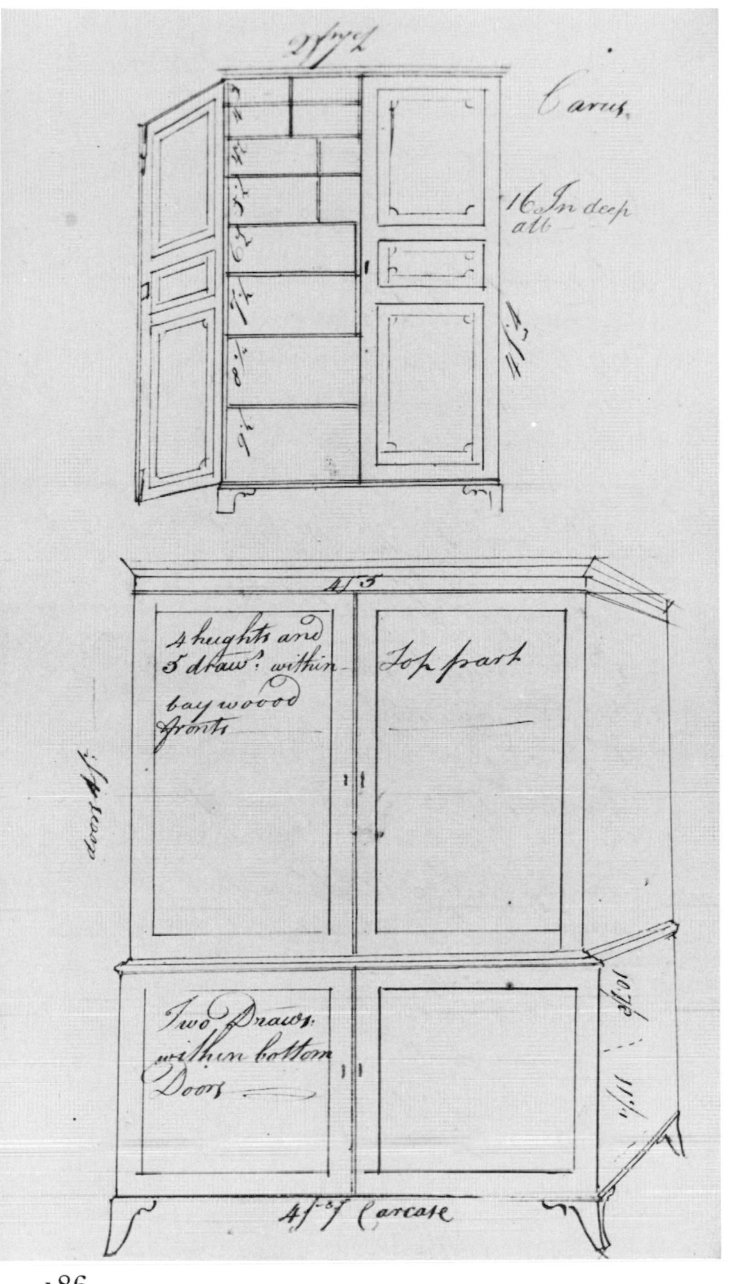

186

188

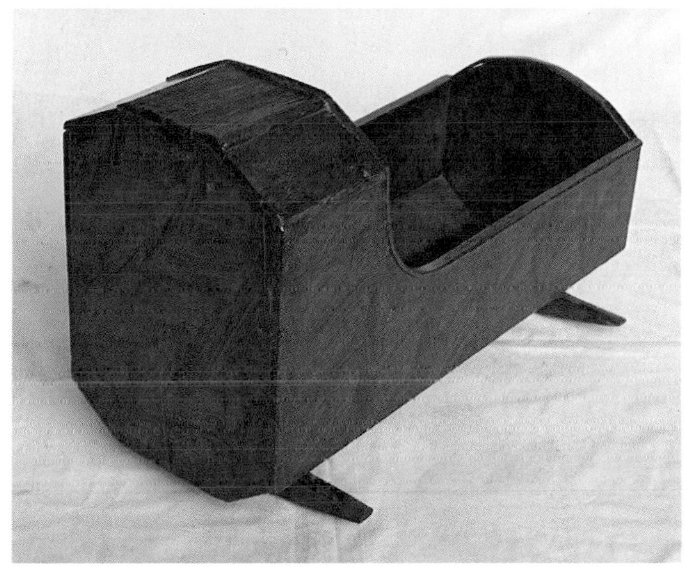

189

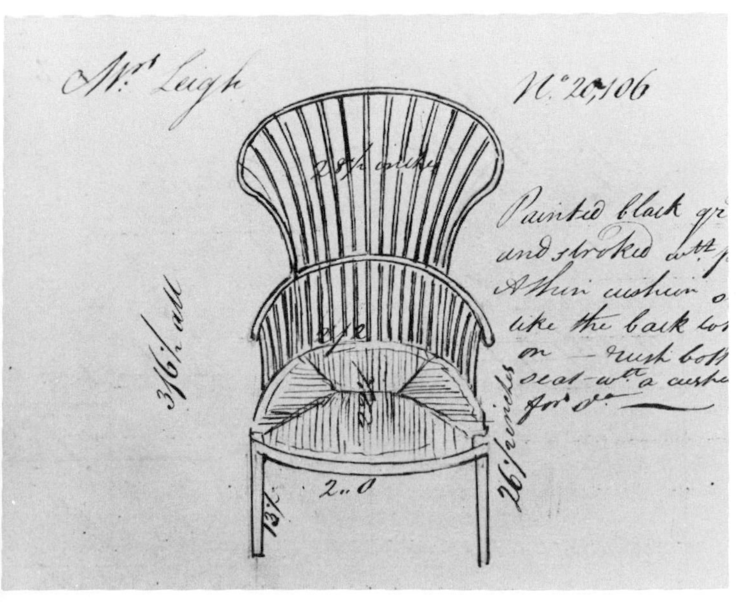

187

190

ground is similar to that on painted pieces made in Connecticut, Massachusetts, and Vermont in the eighteenth and early nineteenth centuries. This cradle could easily be sold as an important New England painted piece of an early date unless the subtle differences between English and American work are recognized. Fortunately, on the bottom, the decorator wrote: "Lilla Eliza / Wilner 1864 / Gunthorpe."[83]

In 1801, the Gillows firm made the piece in figure **191**. The drawing is headed: "2 Whitewood tables to be painted," although the cost list is headed: "A maple table." It, or they, had a limewood top and stretchers, maple legs, and rails of maple and deal. One Geo. Multan painted the table, but the customer was not charged for this.[84] With its fanciful play on Greek forms, this piece is part of the "Elegant fancy furniture" style that John and Hugh Finlay helped popularize in Baltimore, Maryland, early in the nineteenth century. Other consciously simple and high-style painted pieces by the Gillows firm appear throughout this book; for example, the Windsor chair, sofa, and chamber table in figures 1093, 1196, and 1426, respectively.

Late in the nineteenth century painted forms played a major role in the artist-craftsman movement led by William Morris, William Burges, and others, as they sought to move away from what they saw as the slick, stifled designs of mass-produced objects toward a direct and honest expression of their romantic ideals. The elaborately painted cabinet, figure **192**, was designed by William Burges for H. G. Yatman in 1858, and made by Harland and Fisher with panels painted by E. J. Poynter. It freely combines medieval and Renaissance details and figures depicting legends. The Arts and Crafts movement appealed to a special segment of society; to be fair, its furniture should be seen against a much larger group of pieces that were finished with clear varnish.

191

192

5

English & American Carving

English Stylistic Development: Classical Strapwork and the Baroque Line

The chests shown as figures **193** and **194** were made in the late fifteenth century, the first in Italy, the second in England, and together demonstrate the gulf that then existed between the arts of these two cultures. The Italian Renaissance *cassone,* part of the first classical revival period, employs an antique sarcophagus form covered with gilt gesso. With classical symmetry, a centrally placed coat of arms is flanked by repeating units: urns supporting griffins edged by S-scrolling floral vines. The entablature's staccato rhythm is formed by a dentilated frieze above a palmetted architrave. Although such detailing would later become part of English mannerism (figure 195), Palladian grandeur (figure 208), and the neo-classical styling of the late eighteenth century (figure 210), contemporary English furniture was still late medieval in its appearance. The feet of the English plank chest (which have been cut down) are formed of Gothic cusped arches. The spandrels are filled with leafage and topped by a band of squared "flowers" similar to those executed in gold on the Southwold screen of about 1500 (figure 103) and on the movable screen at Rufford Old Hall (figure 212). The back of the chest (shown in figure 194) is carved to a panel with running vines sprouting leaves, bunches of grapes, and a rose. (A similar late medieval vine was painted on the Southwold roof molding, figure 106.) The inner panel on the back reads "N: FARES."

As we saw in Chapter 4, the Renaissance style in its mannerist guise began to condition fashionable English items by 1540, over a century after the Renaissance began in Italy. The carved stone and oak chimney piece erected in the Old Palace at Bromley-by-Bow, Middlesex, in 1606 (figures **195** and **196**) is typical of developed English work of the period. The ornamentation is compartmentalized—vertically by columns, and horizontally by cornices; the arched niches for statues are edged by mannerist-style, pyramid-shaped rustication; the top edge is finished with "Elizabethan" strapwork similar to that in figure 123. The pulvinated frieze below the mantle shelf is decorated on a matted ground by straight and curved strapwork with griffin heads. This strapwork is divided into units by a series of vertical actions and the straps are linked by strap rings. A mannerist-style mask with a palmette headdress is centered above the frieze, and flanked by projecting panels carved to addorsed, ring-linked, foliated S scrolls. For Eng-

193

194

195

196

land at this time this chimney piece is a superior example; the leafage of the stone part is particularly well executed. As all contemporary arts show a similar sense of pattern, it is not surprising that the textile on the opulent chair (1615–25) seen in figure **197** has the same decorative features found on the oak pulvinated frieze (figure 196). Here the textile strapwork with leaves and ring linkage is applied to a red satin ground.

The English chest in figure **198** is inscribed: "THIS : IS. ESTHER • HOB • SONNE CHIST • 1637"; the Hobson family were tenant farmers on Lord Yarborough's estate in Lincolnshire. Like the chimney piece, it is stylistically advanced over the chest with meandering vine (figure 194). Its decoration is compartmentalized, with each set of motifs confined to the constructional unit it decorates. In part this is because the framed rather than broad construction provides naturally limiting units, but the parts were given different decorative schemes; only the muntins and top rail share contained running vines. The ground was richly matted with a punch. Although this carving is among the best English rural work, a comparison with a finer piece shows it to be rather mediocre by wider standards. The contemporary oak chest in figure **199** was, according to tradition, found in a Cornish farmhouse. It employs similar mannerist motifs, but it was executed by a craftsman superior to most English workers. He drew more sophisticated shapes and provides more intriguing spacing, confidently leaving uncovered the bottom rail and base of the legs.

197

The elm chest seen in figure **200** is from the south of England, perhaps Wiltshire. It is dated 1639—two years after that in figure 198—and although made of planks, it is divided into the decorative units that the new styling demanded. Bands of addorsed, foliated S scrolls with profile masks cover the bottom of the chest section, leafy dragons the top edge and ends. The resulting "panels" are focused by leaf-filled diamonds. Each decorative area is edged by a scalloped line. The boards that enclose the base of the chest and form the feet are inscribed, the front one reading: "16. THIS: CHEST . WAS : MAD : IN : THE. YEARE : OF. OVR. 39." The left end foot-board carries the name of the maker, James Griffin. Traces of color below the lock plate and on the ground of the panels suggest that the chest was once painted.

The Yorkshire oak cupboard, figure **201**, combines the decorative vocabulary that emerged from the late medieval period with the new compartmentalizing sensibility: the vines are rigidly placed as three bands flanking and dividing paired doors, which have four baluster-filled "panels." The remains of shaped inlay in the top and bottom rails of the front suggest that their now-recessed areas were once filled with foliated S-scroll inlay. The guilloche on the side of the cupboard has tightly enclosed flowers, possibly roses, and follows the movement of the front vines. The faceted "triglyphs" on the front stiles are part of the mannerist decorative scheme. Although similar pieces, such as the 1637 chest in figure 198, were executed early in the seventeenth century, others were made well into the next (see figure 6).

As the lining paper detailed in figure **202** demonstrates, floral strapwork also continued in the other arts. This example is glued into the chest section of a walnut (elm, oak) chest over drawers, and a related paper on the lid with the royal arms of Charles II dates both to about 1670. In this design, arabesques linked by rings divide the paper into circular areas filled by leaves, grapes, and various flowers, which include tulips, carnations, columbine, honeysuckle, and borage. The motifs

198

199

200

201

202

are textured, as though covered with embroidery stitches.

The triumphant return from exile of Charles II in 1660 began greater contact with the art available on the continent: his and ensuing courts embraced the freer, lusher, and more emotional baroque style. Lavish in movement, costly to execute, pulsating curves and swelling foliage dominated high-style and court work. One of the finest examples of this style is the upholstered wooden headboard in figure **203**, made for the first Earl of Melville about 1695. It plays opulently with husks, leafage, C scrolls, rosettes, cusped diamonds, and tassels. (The full bed appears as figure 354, and another detail as figure 355.) At a somewhat reduced level the late seventeenth-century oak and pine panel from a staircase balustrade seen in figure **204** entwines leafage, flowers, and fruit in a manner associated with the carver Grinling Gibbons (1648–1720). Although this example does not approach his exceptional standards of craftsmanship, it is finely handled. The symmetrically arranged late seventeenth-century oak panel in figure **205** is flatter in movement than the preceding examples, and can be more appropriately compared with the crest rail of a bannister-back chair made in the Boston, Massachusetts, area between 1700 and 1735 (figure **206**, seen in full as figure 750).

By the beginning of the eighteenth century, a new attitude in decorative strapwork developed on the continent. Figure **207** was made in Paris about 1700 in the style associated with the designer Jean Bérain (1638–1711). Here a delicate strapwork frame edges each panel and heavy strapwork supports the central figures. Elaborate forms are hung on the enclosing frame—such fantasies will lead naturally to rococo delights.[1] The cabriole legs with hoof feet have leafage edged by human masks in profile, which spew forth further leafage. (For a discussion of masks and leafage, see the text to figures 165 and 167, pages 72–74. The heavy brass moldings on the front and sides are later additions.)

English eighteenth-century furniture developed from the subtle use of line and enrichment under Queen Anne to the style associated with Thomas Chippendale, in which playful, naturalistic forms impinge on the lingering baroque structures. The exception to this general development was the furniture made during the second quarter of the

203

204

205

206

207

eighteenth century as part of the Palladian style associated with William Kent. The sarcophagus-shaped chest from Shobdon Court, Herefordshire (figures **208** and **209**), is an imposing and rather stern statement of respect for the majestic forms of the classical age. The decoration of the top makes an enlightening comparison with the mantle in figures 195–196, dating a century earlier. Although a relatively late expression, the mantle has the clarity of its Renaissance heritage, loosely reflecting the uplifting formality of triumphal arches, and the strapwork on the pulvinated frieze projects stoic symmetry. The decoration of the chest top, while using a classical or Renaissance vocabulary, expresses a hybrid mixture of styles: the bolder details, particularly the raised ends of the scrolls, recall the baroque; while the loose sweep of the curves looks to the exuberance of the

208

209

210

rococo. Fretwork, as seen in the band behind the hinges of the chest top, will by 1750 be tightly condensed in Chippendale's "gothick" and "Chinese" designs. (The gilt gesso on the top bears the cipher of William Bateman but is without a coronet, suggesting it was made before he became Viscount in 1725.)

With the work of Robert Adam and others who developed the neo-classical style in England, a widespread and fastidious use of classical strapwork supplanted the naturalistic imagery of the rococo. In 1758, Adam returned from studying antique, Renaissance, and mannerist decorations in Italy, and joined their formal, organizing ideals to the playfulness of the still-strong rococo spirit. In the 1760s and 1770s, he designed the rooms shown in figures **210** and 181 for Osterley Park. Unlike the openly spaced painted decoration of the "Etruscan Room," the plasterwork in the Eating Room, figure 210, lacks a strapwork frame and builds on a central axis: through griffin tails, husks, palmettes, and panels. (The Italian *cassone*, figure 193, has similar motifs.) By the end of the eighteenth century classical detailing would become ever more academic as designers drew closer to what they perceived as archaeologically correct designs.

Differences and Similarities in English and American Carving: Flat versus Rounded Carving; Foliated S Scrolls; the Rose

It has become customary to designate English carving as rounder in profile than that executed in America. The truth of this generalization depends on the examples chosen from each source; before moving to Chapter 6 (which studies a group of English vernacular furniture and a related group made in the Connecticut Valley), a brief review of similar English and American carving is necessary. The sequence of illustrations in figures 203 through 205 shows three high-style pieces of the late seventeenth century with differing degrees of flatness. That in figure 205, with the lowest relief, does exhibit more richness of form than is found on contemporary American furniture. This handling is, however, only one aspect of English carving, for flattened forms were always a possibility—sometimes as a stylistic statement, at other times the result of the maker's limitations. A review of two carved motifs prevalent in this book provides an opportunity to look at examples of flat English carving and to perceive the ubiquity of motifs.

The foliated S scroll is by now familiar, appearing on the Italian Renaissance *cassone* in figure 193, on the upper panels in the detail of the chimney piece in figure 196, on the chests in figures 8, 9 and 10, and with a relish of three-dimensional movement on either side of the caning on the chair in figures 41 and 356. Over a door opening of the rare, movable fifteenth-century screen at Rufford Old Hall (figures **211** and **212**) the carving is in considerable relief, but the motifs are relatively flat. On that in figure 211, some straps are lowered to allow others to pass over, but they do not twist to provide a full illusionistic sense of depth. The strapwork in figure **213** is part of a staircase made about 1600–20 in Valley Farm, Dedham, Buckinghamshire. This carving has no interruption of the two-plane (front and rear) surface. It is difficult to be certain whether this was a consciously flat statement or the result of a carver's limited skills, but on such a developed staircase the former is more likely.

The wainscot panel in figure **214**, made in East Anglia about 1600–20, has some surfaces cut at angles to make the strapwork seem to twist to differing levels. Here, too, it is hard to be certain whether the relative flatness was by choice or necessity. In figure **215**, the carving on the architrave and the pulvinated frieze just above the fireplace opening of an East Anglican mantle (1600–20) is relatively flat; but that on the frieze is more entwined, giving some suggestion of changing planes. Since the carver chose to keep the lower band flat while maneuvering the other in space, it seems certain that the flat one results from choice. The Yorkshire chest (1650–90), figure

211

214

212

215

213

216, freely combines round and flat carving with inlaid strips of alternating light and dark woods.

As two or more colors were mixed on marquetry pieces (see figures 480 and 481) to create striking illusions, some carved decoration on urban and rural pieces was flattened in response to such contrasting light and dark areas. The rather flat handling of the carving on the pulvinated shelf of the early walnut cupboard (1590–1610) made in or near London, figure **217**, integrates nicely with the inlay. (The back supports are replaced.) But on such later pieces as the cupboard in figure **218** (discussed in detail as figure 257), or figure 262, the light and dark contrasts of the carving are more clearly related to the late seventeenth-century marquetry and inlay aesthetic. The cupboard with drawers, figure **219**, was made in the Guilford area of Connecticut between 1650 and 1690. Probably the flatness of its two-plane carving results from the impact of inlaid work on East Anglican carving from which it drew inspiration. American examples display rounded forms and are discussed in Chapter 6.

216

218

217

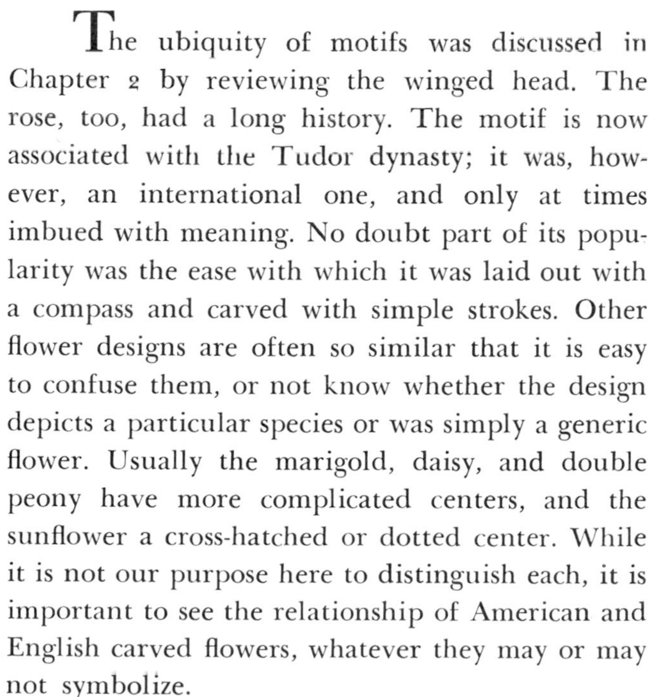

The ubiquity of motifs was discussed in Chapter 2 by reviewing the winged head. The rose, too, had a long history. The motif is now associated with the Tudor dynasty; it was, however, an international one, and only at times imbued with meaning. No doubt part of its popularity was the ease with which it was laid out with a compass and carved with simple strokes. Other flower designs are often so similar that it is easy to confuse them, or not know whether the design depicts a particular species or was simply a generic flower. Usually the marigold, daisy, and double peony have more complicated centers, and the sunflower a cross-hatched or dotted center. While it is not our purpose here to distinguish each, it is important to see the relationship of American and English carved flowers, whatever they may or may not symbolize.

Six English pieces—figures 220 through 226—demonstrate the diversity of British expressions. The six-piece candle mold from Dorset (four parts

219

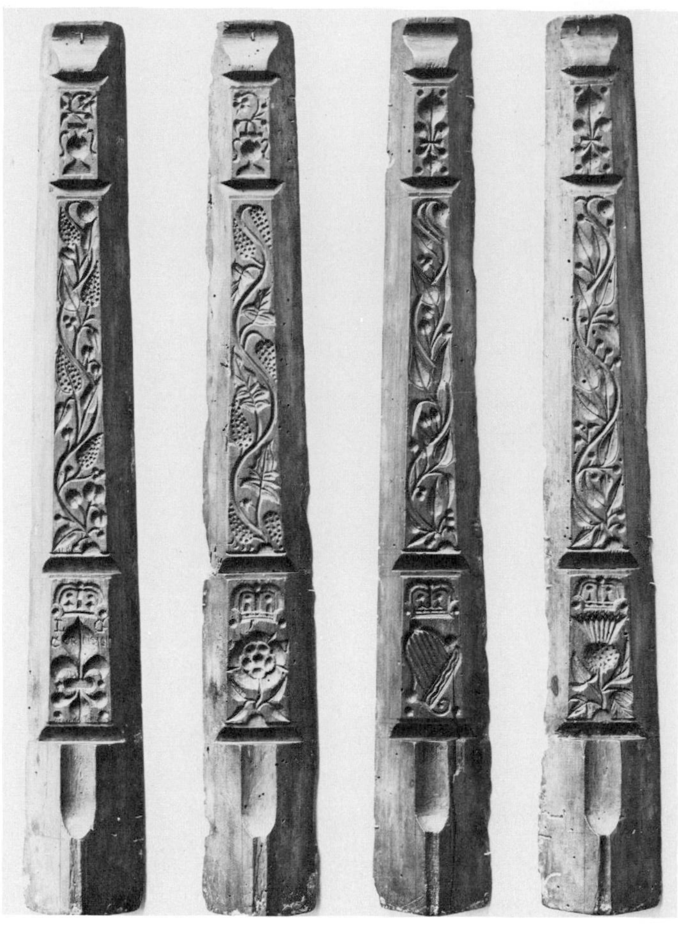

220

222

221

223

are shown), figure **220**, has running vines, urns, and the crowned rose of England, harp of Ireland, thistle of Scotland (suggesting a date after James I united England and Scotland in 1603), and fleur-de-lys of France (although Elizabeth gave up Calais, England's last claim to part of France, in 1559—a similar mixture of devices appears on the fireback in figure 195). In the candle mold, the motifs seem consciously symbolic; but symbols may easily lose their connotation and continue as decorative conceits long after they bear messages. For example, harps appeared as part of book decoration in seventeenth-century America, without didactic impact,[2] and the fleur-de-lys was used on many Connecticut pieces, perhaps without a specific connotation. The Connecticut cupboard, figure 227, has three roses on the central panel and paired thistles at the base of the lower side

224

225

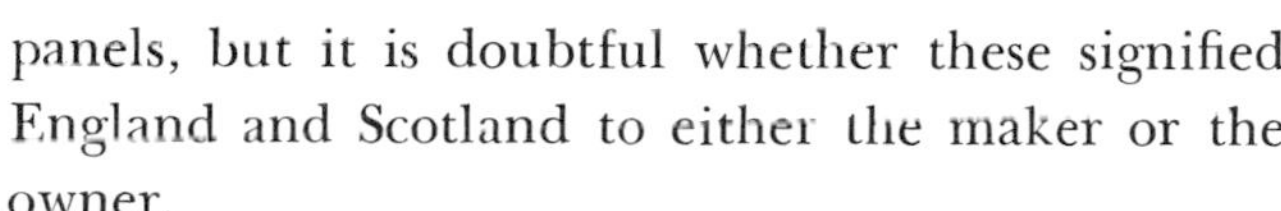

panels, but it is doubtful whether these signified England and Scotland to either the maker or the owner.

The piece in figure **221** was probably once a single strip of carved wood which was later cut to three sections. It is dated 1608, and according to tradition comes from Leire Church, near Lutterworth, Leicestershire, where it may have been part of a pew. The guilloche-enclosed flowers are not particularly distinguished. The piece's importance lies in its early date and in the variety of the compass-laid-out flowers. By contrast, the mid-seventeenth-century chair in figures **222** and **223** exhibits considerable sophistication. The matting of the ground behind the date on figure 221 was done with open spacing, while that on the chair is tighter and more intense. This could be a difference in style, period, or personal handling, rather than a difference in quality. The carving of the motifs on the chair is, however, finer in line and execution. The wainscot chair, figure **224**, was made about the same time as figure 222, probably in Derbyshire, and is dated 1649. The attitude of the design, particularly for the asymmetrical tulip on the crest rail and within the arch, is flat. It is not certain whether this flatness is intentional (as an echo of inlay), a desire to appear part of the locally accepted vernacular styling, or simply the work of a less skilled carver. The same question arises for the chair in figure **225**, which was probably made in Lincolnshire during the second half of the seventeenth century. The asymmetrical tulip on the panel, with dog-tooth petals, resembles similarly shaped and fluted tulips carved in Connecticut (see figures 227 and 294).

The English carved paneling in figure **226** has an array of carved compass work; fortunately it is dated, 1692—the same time at which pieces like that in figure **227** were being made and carved in the Wethersfield area of Connecticut.

According to tradition, the wainscot arm chair, figure **228**, was owned by John Winthrop, Jr. (1606–1676). Winthrop moved his center of activities from eastern Massachusetts to Connecticut in the 1640s, and he probably acquired the chair in Connecticut after the move. As on the Connecticut chair in figure 648, the front of the panel is raised, or fielded—a practice rarely used in England before about 1700. The handling of the flowers is like that on figure 221, from Leicestershire. A similar use of roses and cabling was favored in the Gloucestershire and Somerset areas of England, and arcaded fluting appeared in Dorset.

A related use of floral motifs can be found on textiles, tiles, silver, and other contemporary crafts in most Western countries. The lining paper, with large flowers and flower-filled two-handled urns, figure **229**, is in the chest of drawers seen in figures 462 and 463, made between 1660 and 1700.

226

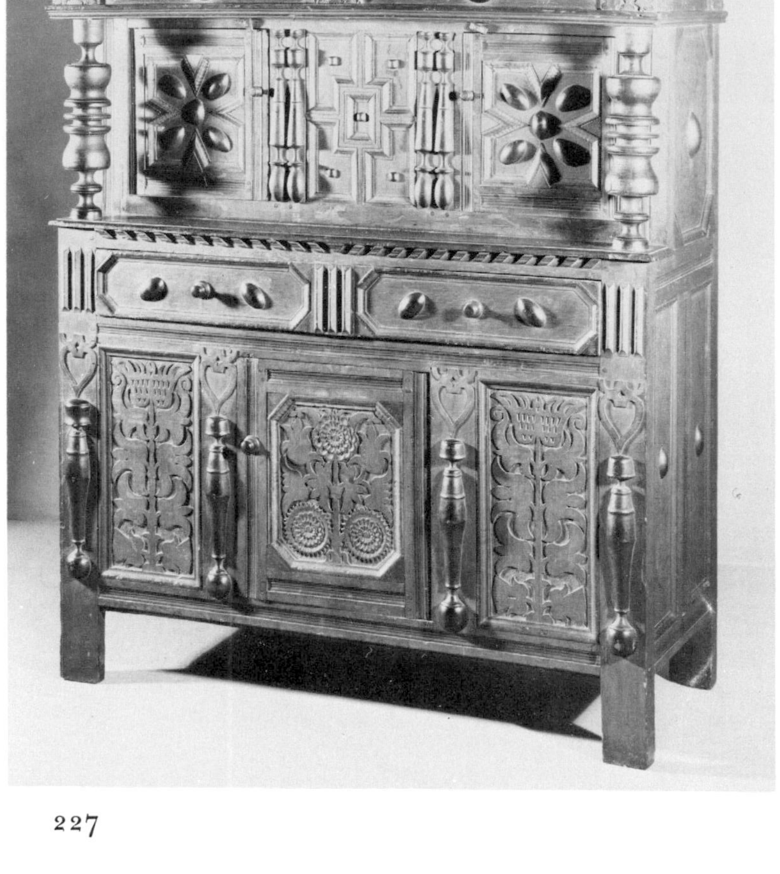

227

228

229

6

The "Hadley" Composite Motif & Through Chamfering

One of the most famous and cohesive forms of American furniture is loosely placed under the designation "Hadley chest." To review British pieces that contributed to the decorative scheme and unusual construction of these chests, it is necessary to study the vernacular furniture of one region in the north of England, to see variants possible within that region, and to learn how the special characteristics occurred—often in different guises—in other areas of that country.

The Connecticut chests have in common a composite motif, consisting of a scroll, tulip, and leaf. Many use a through-chamfered construction: beveling the edge of the verticals and horizontals that surround the panels. The known examples of related Connecticut Valley pieces number about 125, and were made in the area between Hartford, Connecticut, and Deerfield, Massachusetts, by a variety of men. Early scholars of American furniture assigned certain examples to particular makers, although recent scholarship by Patricia Kane and others has shown that none of the attributions remains tenable after the scrutiny of modern research.[1] Many of the chests, most with one or more drawers, divide into three groups. The first is rather circumspect, the second less so; the third divides into smaller subgroups, which need not be detailed here.[2]

The first group, which is in some ways the closest to English precedents, consists of five pieces that are similar in their handling of decoration and construction. They are represented here by figure **230**.[3] Standard to this group is the manner of detailing the Hadley composite motif. On the chest in figure 230, the scroll, tulip, and lobed-edge leaf are repeated ten times: four times on both the top rail and drawer, and twice in a vertical orientation on the central panel. The horizontal repeats are so similar in outline that a template must have been used in laying them out. On three of the five chests there is in addition a smooth-edge leaf, shaped like a teardrop, and a similar leaf appears on the central panel of figure 232. On the first group, the composite motif has punched work, which edges the stems of the leaves and dots other areas; chiseled lines mark the centers of scrolls, edge the tulips, and add veins to the leaves. Chip carving—crescent-shaped notches—provides further detailing to the leaves and tulip. The leaves are recessed either side of the midribs, which are rounded in profile. The rest of the composite motif is flat and the recessed ground is matted with punch work.

On four of the five chests there are panels with concentric half-circles with serrated edges; above them is a compass-designed, six-pointed star, and at the top a pinched tulip. A similar tulip appears on the center panel of figure 231 and the panels of figure 426. The central line formed by these units is flanked by the composite design of scroll, tulip, and lobed-edge leaf. The fifth chest in this group has full concentric circles with serrated edges,

230

231

232

similar to that in the central panel of figure 231, a member of the second group. Diamond-carved panels appear on three of the five chests. The panels of the first group are edged with applied moldings. The muntins of four of the chests have inlaid strips of alternating light and dark diagonals. These four chests have applied split-spindles,[4] and on three of the four the stiles are turned to shaped feet. (The fourth has had the lower section removed and probably originally had turned feet.)

All five chests have carved dates, which fall between 1699 and 1701, making them contemporary with related English examples. One has a running vine, as found on the second group. A sixth chest, which differs in many ways, has this group's interpretation of the composite motif carved across the top rail.[5] This first group is now generally designated the "Hartford type" because Irving W. Lyon found the figure 230 chest in that city, although the history of the piece does not support this nomenclature.[6]

On most of the second group—eleven chests in all—there is a running vine, as on the representative example, figure **231**. Some have stiles with turned feet. Inlay and applied split-spindles are *not* featured. Common to these chests, and to those in the third and largest group (represented by figure **232**), is the distinctive through-chamfered construction. The edges of the stiles, rails, and muntins surrounding the panels are beveled their entire length. The bevel is visible where it edges a panel and again on the stiles below the bottom rail: American examples are shown in figures 231, 232, and 399; English examples in figures 272 (dated 1703), 281, and 285 (dated 168?). The ends of the rails' muntins and drawers have extended bevels to cover the chamfering. The drawing, figure **233**, shows how this joint differed from the normal square-end butt joint. First, the chamfered line was planed onto the muntins and what would be the inner, front edge of the rails and stiles surrounding the panels. (The chamfered edge is not shown on the drawing of the rails.) A and C demonstrate the more standard joint; B and D the through-chamfered joint; E shows how the tenon end was formed: it did not entail more cutting than a normal tenon. The detail of a door in figure 249 shows the chamfered edge of the door stile covered by the extended bevel of the top rail. Similarly, in the detail figure 289, the side bracket of the back extends a bevel upward to cover that on the lower edge of the crest rail.

The center panels of the second group relate to the center panel of figure 230, although the central axis has at the base a broad tulip with serrated top edge below a stylized rose formed by a set of full concentric circles with serrated edges. (A similar "rose" appears on the Connecticut chest, figure 438; and the serrated shaping is like the chevron and beakhead ornaments found on Norman door and fireplace arches.) Above the rose is a squeezed tulip. A few pieces in this group are carved only on the panels; they lack through chamfering, and have shadow moldings on their stiles, rails, and drawers. These variations suggest the work of more than one maker for this group. This second group was designated by Clair Franklin Luther the "Hatfield type," and includes the chest with the notorious forged signature of Nicholas Disbrowe.

The third group, numbering about sixty-five chests, was made and decorated by a variety of hands. It is usually specified as the "Hadley type," although all the chests included in the three groups are sufficiently related to have this as their overall designation. The third group, represented by figures **232** and 399, has as unifying factors

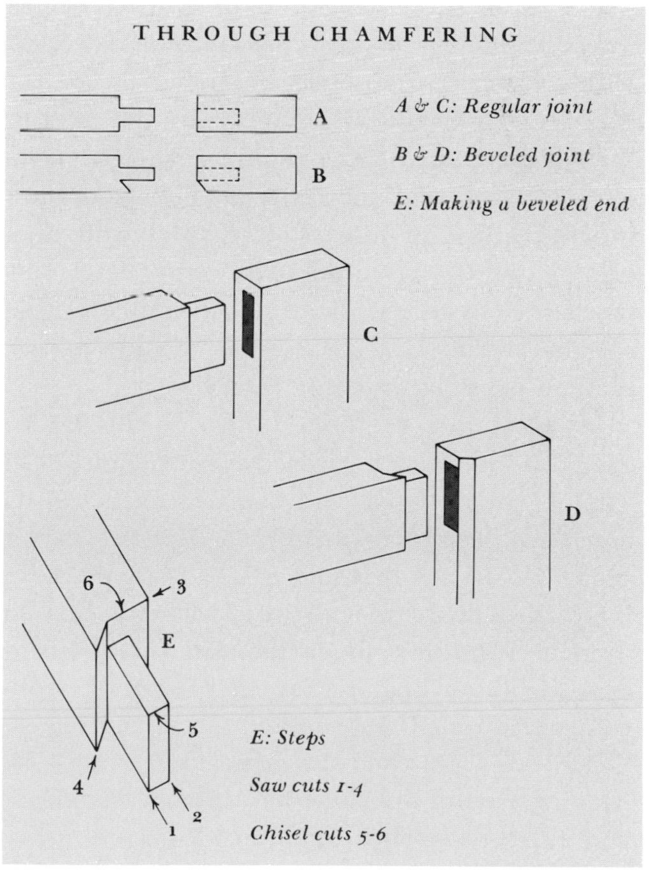

233

through chamfering and a consistent handling of the composite motif: the scroll, tulip, lobed-edge leaf, and smooth-edge leaf are flat, without any rounded forms. On a given piece, and some groups of pieces, the composite designs are so close in outline that a template must have been used. The center of the rails and drawers have diverse patterns creating a vertical line. On some chests limited space did not allow the completion of some of the composite motifs, and rather than adjusting to a smaller-scaled version, the leaf is abruptly cut off (as on the ends of the rails of figure 399). More chests from this group retain original paint surfaces. It is certain that carving often followed painting, for on many of those pieces with original finishes there is no paint in the recessed, or carved-out, areas. (Unfortunately, on a few repainted pieces, areas of the front surface have been left bare and paint placed in the recessed sections.) Since it is often possible to find original paint on the bevels covered when the chests were assembled,[7] it seems that for many in this group, the steps of manufacture were: shaping the wooden parts; painting the outer face of the parts; carving the design; assembling the chests.

The through-chamfered construction was not limited in New England to the central part of the Connecticut Valley but, like nearly all "distinctive" features, can be found in varying degrees wherever immigrants, or cross-cultural movement within America, transferred it. A few pieces with the distinctive beveling appear in the area of Plymouth, Massachusetts (figure 265). The wainscot chairs by William Searle or Thomas Dennis, probably made in Essex County, Massachusetts—using a tradition from the southwest of England—simulate it with chamfering that stops near the corners of the panel. (A similar shaping appears on the English chair, figure 657.)

My awareness of the presence of the Hadley composite motif and beveled construction on an English piece began with the discovery of the north Lancashire cupboard seen in figure 257, in storage at the Victoria and Albert Museum. Later I included this cupboard in a catalogue of Connecticut furniture[8] to demonstrate Connecticut's dependence on England for the pattern of scrolls, tulips with rounded stems, and lobed- and smooth-edge leaves enriched by chiseled veining. The framing around the panel has through chamfering and a flat, two-plane, undulating vine.

In seeking to establish the regional origins of this cupboard, it seemed logical that since the expression was rather tightly focused in New England, it would have been similarly localized in England. With research it gradually became clear that related motifs were most popular over the northern half of Lancashire and the western part of Yorkshire, and that the construction was more widely spread over Yorkshire, Lancashire, and Westmorland. Furthermore, as in Connecticut, this mode of decoration and construction was only one of several expressions available in those regions. While this group was concentrated in the northwest, the motifs and the construction did appear occasionally elsewhere in England.

It was fairly standard to chamfer the rail below a panel, even when leaving the other three enclosing members square. Perhaps the angled surface below proved less likely to collect dust. On occasions this bevel was continued behind a muntin, as on figure **234**. Before the mannerist taste for applied moldings, it was customary to decorate the unchamfered edges with a scratch molding, fading at each end (as at the top and right of figure 234). Therefore, when the piece was assembled, the molding did not need to join accurately at the corners. Since the muntin in figure 234 butts against rails, it has a completed edge molding. Another method of achieving neat corners was through chamfering: beveling entirely the edges of the rails and stiles, and to make the parts that joined them cover the bevels. The strap-paneled room in Towneley Hall, Burnley, Lancashire (figure **235**), is exceptional both in its use of a herringbone pattern and in the fact that all the main vertical and horizontal framing members have through-chamfered edges (figure **236**). The paneling is dated 1628, predating by about eighty years most of the dated English and American pieces of furniture with this construction.

The cupboard seen in figures **237–241** is dated 1693, making it contemporary with related American examples. The construction and decoration are like that of the 1705 cupboard (figure 247), which has a history of having come from a farmhouse in the Trough of Bowland in central Lancashire, near the Yorkshire border. This house still contains fixed woodwork with similar decoration.[9] The upper doors of the cupboard in figure

234

235

236

237 have applied moldings, the lower doors through chamfering. The carving of the upper doors (figure 239) consists of a central arch supporting flowers with a central, recessed heart shape. (Hearts appear on some of the Hadley chests and on a few English pieces, figure 40, for example, but they were more common on continental work.) The carving is augmented by tightly arranged punch work and crescent-shaped chip carving. The ground is densely matted.

Panels with similar decoration and applied moldings appear also on figures 242, 247, and 251. The latter two pieces have inlaid strips of diagonally arranged light and dark woods. This group of cupboards relates to the first group of Connecticut chests (figure 230) through the use of applied moldings, the decoration of the upper panels, the inlaid light and dark strips, the pattern and handling of the carved panels, and the use of dates. And one of the five pieces in the first Connecticut group has running vines with shapes nearly identical to those on figure 241.[10] The English cupboards are related to the second Connecticut group (figure 231) in the use of running vines, through chamfering, and panel decoration. The scalloping of the frames of the upper doors on figure 237 may be original; similar shaping is found on other English work (see figures 279, 284, and 291). (The scalloping along the top and the finials on figure 237 and the cornice on figure 242 are not

237

238

239

241

240

242

243

244

245

246

original.) The repeating serrated petals on the Connecticut chest, figure 231, make the carved bands appear scalloped.

The cupboard, figures **242–246**, is dated 1698, five years later than the preceding example, and the closeness of much of the decoration suggests that the same hand carved both. The upper door panels have a matted ground, central arc, crescent-shaped chip carving, and halfway down the sides of the panel C shapes protruding in from the edges. The tightly scrolling leafage on the upper panels of the lower doors is similar to that on figure 240, although on figure 242 there is a double line of scrolling vines. The frieze—with a heavily punch-matted ground—displays a more three-dimensionally carved leafy vine, accented by crescent-shaped chip carving. The stems of the leaves circle under the main vine to form crescents rather like those at the sides of the upper door panels.

The design on the lower panels of the bottom doors is related to that in the diamonds on the outer panels of the Connecticut chest seen in figure 230. The zigzag line in the molding, figure 245, is found in inlay on figure 287 and carved on figure 291. The applied moldings of the upper doors have carved details; the lower doors are through-chamfered. The ends (figure 246) have simulated through chamfering: the stop chamfering of the stiles is made to terminate in line with the bevel of the rail. This group of pieces uses on the upper-section door stops consisting of a diagonally placed strip of wood in the upper, inner corner of each opening. The corresponding door corner has its backing board cut away (as seen in figure 244) to close against it. The drawers in the earliest pieces are side-hung: the sunk fillets in the sides of the drawer run on projecting strips of wood (figure 245). (The cornice, bottom strip, and feet of this piece are not original.)

By the beginning of the eighteenth century the depth of the panels was being turned to face outward, and the projecting, or fielded, form played a role in the decorative scheme. The cupboard from the Trough of Bowland, shown in figures **247–250**, is dated 1705. The running line of the frieze combines a three-dimensional vine and rounded grapes with flat scrolling, flowers, and leaves. The leaves have rounded stems and midribs. The three-dimensional grapes and vine appear with flat flowers on the upper muntins. The variation possible in similar carved designs by one worker can be seen by comparing the vines on the rails above and below the upper door (figure 248): the upper rail has a flat vine; the lower vine is rounded. The decoration of the upper door panels relates this piece to the preceding two cupboards. The fronts of the corner posts—above the drops and below the recessed cupboard and mid-rails of the lower doors—have inlaid strips of diagonally oriented contrasting colors, like those found on the first group of Connecticut chests (figure 230). Inside the upper cupboard there is a shelf held on beautifully shaped brackets (figure 250). The lower doors have through chamfering, and the detail in figure 249 shows the bevel construction, where the top rail of the lower right door joins its left stile.

In America, a similar use of applied moldings on upper panels with cheaper run moldings around the low panels appeared on pew doors made by John Norman in 1659 for the first meeting house, Marblehead, Massachusetts, on Burial Hill.[11] The frequent use of simulated through chamfering on the sides of cupboards suggests that

247

it was among the cheapest means of enriching an edge. A chest from the same region as these cupboards, figure 216, uses about half the features found on them: flat and round carved vines; inlaid strips of diagonal colored woods. As on the upper part of the cupboards, the panels have applied moldings.

On the 1710 north Lancashire cupboard, figure **251**, the fielding is a prominent part of the decoration and the inlaid strips have more complex designs. The north Lancashire cupboard dated 1716, figure **252**, is perhaps carved by a different hand than the previous examples. The shaping of the vines is not a flowing, undulating line; rather, it consists of foliated S scrolls. It also differs in having the decoration on the upper doors oriented toward the central panel, which has a vertically pointing pattern. (The feet are not original.)

The three north Lancashire cupboards, figures 253 through 257, did possibly share the same carver. The upper door panels of the first (figures **253–255**) have at their base paired scrolls rounded in profile; these become various flowers, and the midribs of shaped-edge leaves with chiseled veins.

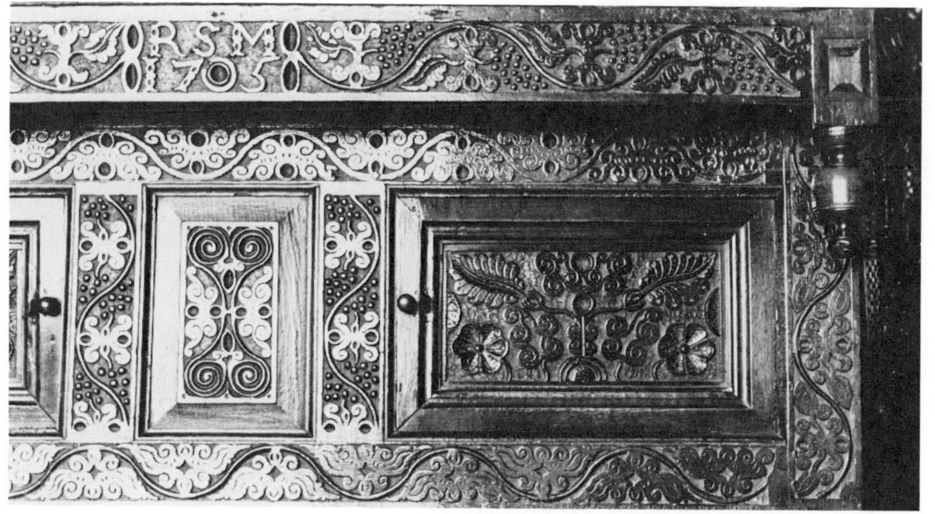

248

249

250

251

252

253

254

255

256

257

The surrounding frames use flat, conventionalized leaves, and flowers or grapes on an undulating vine. The upper panels of the lower doors (figure 255) have paired scrolls that become tulips and lobed- and smooth-edge leaves, with chiseled vines. Paired birds are feathered by crescent-shaped chip carving. The panels below have carved diamonds with leaf-carved centers and "flags" emerging from their points. Dragon forms spewing forth vines with grapes and flowers enhance the frieze.

Dragons or monsters were a popular motif in northwest England, appearing on many pieces made where Lancashire borders Westmorland to the north. The flowing leafage on either side of shells on the rail above the lower doors is baroque in movement and thus differs from the other carving. (The feet are not original.) The carving on the rail between the frieze and the upper doors relates this cupboard to the one that follows. The piece in figure **256**, built with fielded panels, was probably made in the first quarter of the eighteenth century. It was for hanging clothes, and has a storage area, like an open chest, below the door level. The small north Lancashire cupboard, figure **257**, was discussed earlier as the initial discovery with Hadley precedents; it appears also as figure 218.

The cupboard shown in figures **258–261** differs from those that precede it in the motifs and the use of full balusters rather than drops. (The shape of the present balusters seems wrong in movement; they may be the same date as the later feet.) The top rail has arcading filled with leaves; the diamonds of the upper doors are filled with leafage, flanked by deeply chiseled rosettes; the upper

258

259

260

261

muntins and the rails above the lower doors have foliated S scrolls on a matted ground; the upper panels of the lower doors contain large paired S scrolls, with straight rather than curving axes; and the panels below have diamonds with inlaid centers. Most of the shadow moldings on the doors and rails have chiseled wavy lines with star-punched accents (figures 260 and 261). Diamonds enclosing foliage formed of C shapes, as on the upper doors, are known as a design in Yorkshire (figures 275 through 280), but here it is more deeply cut and the S shapes on the lower door have an unfamiliar straightness. A straightness of line is found to the north, in Westmorland, but as part of more frenzied patterns (figure 267), and also in the south. However, the handling of all the shapes on figure 258 links it to similar work on a pulpit in Holy Trinity, Blythborough, Suffolk, in East Anglia.[12] There, too, appear flat diamonds without shaped profiles, as on these upper panels.

The carving of the Suffolk cupboard detailed in figures **262–264** is also like fixed woodwork found in East Anglia. Its flat execution, dominated by foliated S scrolls, is rich in form and movement, and the matted ground is deeply recessed. A similar handling of this motif is found on a Massachusetts chest, figure **265**, possibly made in Dedham or Medfield, by John Thurston, who was trained in

262

263

264

the Suffolk tradition and eventually settled first in Dedham, then Medfield.[13] The wavy carving of the upper central panel in figure 262 is like that on a chest possibly also made in Dedham by John Houghton, who was also trained in the Suffolk tradition.[14] Applied moldings edge the upper panels, while the lower doors and most of the rails and stiles surrounding all the doors are through-chamfered. (Through chamfering appears on a few pieces made in the Dedham-Medfield area of Massachusetts, as on figure 265.) The base has a shadow molding in the centers of the corner posts, muntins, and top and bottom rails (figure 263), which joins to form a continuous channel from part to part, creating a raised edge around the door openings. This feature has not been shown previously. The cupboard is also different in having applied split-spindles. On the sides the corner posts have stop chamfering, figure 264. (The boards on the top, the shelf, and the feet are not original.)

The furniture made in the northwest county of Westmorland usually has complexly arranged paneling, and the carving (generally limited to a few areas) is richly patterned, deep, and rounded in profile. These pieces may have a great sense of light and shadow. The Westmorland cupboard, figure **266**, is dated 1658. Except on the corner posts, through chamfering edges the horizontals and verticals framing the panels. The interweaving of the carving on the upper panels of another Westmorland cupboard, figure **267**, typifies the more extreme examples of this region. Here, through chamfering is employed as on the preceding cupboard.

The cupboard with pegs for hanging clothes, figures **268–270**, was probably made in Yorkshire. It has through chamfering in some areas, and in others this is simulated by carefully integrated stop chamfering. (See, for example, the top of the panels flanking the door, figure 269, where the rail is cut to a bevel only above the panel.) On the sides the chamfering is less integrated at the central muntin, figure 270 (the lower left corner seen in this illustration is a repair). The straight form of the S shapes on the rail above the door suggests the northwest of England, but the serrated line in the middle of the shadow molding on the muntin flanking the door (figure 269) is found on the Lancashire piece seen in figure 245. (The frieze section is removable and must be from another piece. The feet are not original.)

The mid-seventeenth-century Yorkshire or Lancashire cupboard in figure **271** has through-chamfered doors, applied moldings on the panels that face the lower storage area, and shadow moldings on stiles, muntins, and rails. (The cornice is probably a later addition.) The chest in figure **272** is dated 1703, and has a style of carving not previously seen, although it was made in Yorkshire. The motifs are familiar, but the action is frenzied. The pattern of the upper panels is like the late medieval painted and embroidered motifs seen on figures 152 and 153, and is related to those on the crest rail of figure 292.

The preceding cupboards show through chamfering to be a widespread, optional construction that was more readily used in the northwest of England, and that the Hadley composite motif was more confined geographically. Wainscot chairs demonstrate the same regional patterns. The chair, figure **273**, dated 1674, simulates

265

266

267

268

269

270

271

272

through chamfering around the panel. The shape of the crest rail and the pattern of carving assign it to where Yorkshire and Lancashire meet. Typical of that region is the scrolling of the crest rail. The outer scrolls and the adjacent, upward-slanting "buds" are a stylized echo of the spiraling snail forms known on Westmorland examples (see figures 297 and 298). The scooped-out line of the spiraling on figure 273 is matted with chisel marks. The decoration of the front rail is a quieter version of that found on the more complex arm chair, figure 274, from Yorkshire. The panel and crest rail of figure 273 have smooth-edge leaves that are more richly expressed than on Connecticut chests (figure 232) or the more rudimentary English cupboards (figures 243, 255, and 257), but are similar in using rounded stems that become the midribs of the leaves. In this more sophisticated carving, the marginal veins of the leaves are beautifully handled. (A chest carved by the same hand appears as figure 433.)

The richly carved, through-chamfered arm chair, figure 274, was, according to tradition, once at Thorpe Arch Hall, Yorkshire, and the actively scrolled crest rail gathered at the top by a ring is typical of that area. The back posts have long,

273

274

275

277

278

276

279

flowered leaves above and below the arms. (The probably replaced seat is dated 1682.)

The two through-chamfered arm chairs (figure **275** and a different chair, figure **276**) have typical Yorkshire crest rails, centrally placed diamonds containing leafage, and strips of diagonal light and dark inlay. The diamonds are enclosed in tripartite cross-hatched rings separated by fleur-de-lys. The back posts, above the arms, have gauge carving.

The Yorkshire chair, figure **277**, with ball-turned front posts, has leafage at the points of the diamonds, and on the back posts long flowered leaves continue from the seat to the crest rail. The lower rail of the back has an undulating leafy vine, and the front seat rail foliated S scrolls linked by rings. The bottom of that rail includes center and side brackets. The panels of figures **278** through 281, and the side chair, figure 664, have a variety of "flags" at the points of diamonds. In the detail of the Yorkshire chair, figure **279**, the recessed grooves of back posts show the remains of the diagonally patterned inlaid strips, and on the panel the laying-out lines made by a knife. (Similar lines appear on the chest detailed in figure 443.) These lines directed the placement of the compass to draw the semi-circular flags; the central marks left by the compass were covered by a star-shaped punch. Near the base of the crest is a row of scallops found on other examples from the same region. At the right only a fragment of the original brackets remains. The Yorkshire child's chair, figure **280**, is 38¾ inches high and 17⅞ inches wide without its missing feet.

The Yorkshire chest, figure **281**, has long leaves terminating in a flower and bud or acorn. The bottom rail employs ring-linked, foliated S scrolls. Parts of the flags and other motifs are picked out with paint. Through chamfering on the stiles continues to the floor.

Diamonds with tight scrolls forming paired circles at their points appear on a pew in Kirkly Malham, Yorkshire, dated 1631.[15] The bench in figure **282** combines paired circles with foliated S scrolls and flowers. (The seat is replaced in plywood.) That in figure **283** is without carving, but the through chamfering and shape of the arms relate it to the preceding example.

The arm chair, figure **284**, has scalloping on the lower edge of the typical Yorkshire crest rail. The tops of the arms are chip-carved and the panel

280

281

282

283

284

285

displays large, loosely moving, paired foliated S scrolls. (The ear brackets are missing.) The chest in figure **285** is probably by the same Yorkshire carver as figure 284. The foliated S scrolls are similar in outline, movement, and the use of drill-like circles enclosed by leafage. The edge of the motifs on the chest and at the center of the crest rail of the chair are bordered by a thin carved line, and their centers punched with a four-pointed "star." The through chamfering of the corner posts of the chest continues to the floor. It is partially dated, 168[?]. This may have been to allow the last digit to be added when the chest was purchased. (The early eighteenth-century Daniel Bliss House in Rehoboth, Massachusetts, has in the south face of its chimney a pottery plaque, about 8 inches square, in which the first two digits of 17[42?] were incised before firing; the last two were scratched in afterwards by a less skillful calligrapher, probably after purchase and now are difficult to read.)

The oak arm chair, figure **286**, broadens the use of through chamfering geographically further than figure 262, which demonstrated its East

286

287

288

289

290

291

Anglian usage. The low form of the crest rail, the presence of a "dentilated" front seat rail, arch, turned front posts, and the extensive use of guilloche detailing, all place it in the southwest, probably in Gloucestershire or Somerset, where through chamfering was only rarely used. (A related chair appears as figure 657.)

The decoration on the chair in figures **287–289** is more fluid than on previous examples, and, as in figure 654, the back panel design was laid out with large compass strokes. Serrated inlay of alternating colors enriches the base of the Yorkshire-type crest, the rail between the back panels, and the back posts above the seat. (A similar zigzag line was carved on the molding seen in figure 245.) The motifs on the crest rail and top panel are finished with stamped and chiseled decoration. The ground of the large panel is matted with carved cross-hatching, which looks like quilting. Figure 289 shows the through chamfering of the crest rail, and the corresponding projecting bevel of the ear bracket.

The form and decoration of the crest, the use of vines and diagonal inlay, place the chair in figure **290** once again in Yorkshire. The vines of the back rails include roses and terminate with tulips. The top panel is unusual in having the recessed area form the decorative motif (perhaps this once held inlay). The tops of the arms have chip-carved decoration. The front posts are ring-turned, and the front seat rail has brackets and a central drop. The panels have applied molding, rather than through chamfering, and the chair is placed here to demonstrate once again that the type of edge decoration was within this region a matter of choice.

The tulip-decorated chair, figure **291**, was made in Yorkshire. The back posts have wavy lines flanked by large chip carving, and the resulting pattern echoes the use of alternating colored inlay and vines, as on figures 288 and 290. A single back panel is made to appear as two partially scalloped edge panels. All the tulips, except that in the center of the crest rail, are asymmetrically shaped, with surfaces decorated by punch work. There are rounded stems and midribs. At the top of the center of the crest rail is a pointed oval, or teardrop shape, frequently seen on Yorkshire chairs (for example, figure 667). The front seat rail has lightly carved arches and stamped decoration.

A chair with similar turning and carving, figure **292**, is dated 1690. The scrolling on the crest rail echoes rudimentary snails (more clearly discernible on the chairs in figures 297 and 298). The tulips on the crest rail recall those on the

292

293

294

upper panels of figure 272, and the tulips on the panel those of the preceding chair. The edges of the panel are decorated with punch work in zigzag lines, and the front seat rail with light arches and punch work. The tops of the arms have chip carving and the posts above them larger gauge carving. (The feet are not original.) The related Yorkshire child's chair in figure **293** has wavy lines on the back posts and asymmetrical tulips. These tulips appear also on figures 224 and 225, and as part of the decorative vocabulary of Connecticut carvers (figures 227 and 294).

The panel, figure **294**, carved in the Wethersfield area of Connecticut, was probably used in a chest similar in style to the cupboard seen in figure 227. The tulip with gauged details is like the tulips on the legs and rails of the oak table in figures **295–296**. It has a history of having come from a farmhouse near Whitefield, which is close to Manchester, Lancashire.

295

296

297

298

The through-chamfered 1706 chair, figure **297**, has the crest rail that was popular in Westmorland: decorated with snails, and using a flatter top line. (The lower corners of the crest rail seem to have been cut to allow the fitting of new side brackets.) A more complex Westmorland chair seen in figures **298** and 6 is dated 1742. The stepped through chamfering allows for the difference in the widths of the back panels. (The side brackets may not be original.) Figure **299** is dated "85"—the bowed shape and ears of the crest rail associated with the "Chippendale" style suggest that these numerals signify 1785. Perhaps the

299

300

301

simple tapering of the front parts under the arms is a late feature. The chair is in Townend, Troutbeck, in the Lake District of Westmorland. There is no assurance that this chair did not recently come to the house, but it does have a locally practiced constructional feature: the arms, side seat rails, and side stretchers through-tenon the back posts (figure **300**). Such construction was found on a number of Lake District chairs (see figures 334 through 337).

The English cupboard, figure **301,** is a late nineteenth-century interpretation of earlier pieces. Not typical of early work is the pediment-shaped top or the carved figures above the drops; and the use of pitchers in profile is particularly anachronistic, for on early pieces urns are balanced with two handles. Hundreds of early pieces have later had decoration added, for aesthetic or financial reasons, but probably this one is totally of the late nineteenth century.

After reviewing this related, closely knit group of vernacular furniture, it should be clear that it was not an isolated English craft tradition that gave Connecticut the distinctive groups of Hadley chests. Rather, although the English Hadley-like motifs were rather restricted geographically, the particular construction feature was more widely popular, and, on occasion, appeared in disparate areas. These features did become narrowly concentrated in the colonies, although in a few instances they appeared elsewhere; and, in the Connecticut Valley, alternative decorative schemes and forms of construction were available. The geographical unity of the Hadley pattern was probably the result of a small set of makers trained in this approach settling in a restricted area and influencing others to use similar techniques. Similarly, the Devon area of England, using universal motifs in a personal way, influenced eastern Massachusetts designs (as seen by comparing figures 8 through 10).

The first group of Connecticut chests, represented by figure 230, is in some ways the closest to work executed in north Lancashire, using applied moldings, concentric circles, and inlaid strips of alternating, diagonally oriented light and dark woods. One of the five pieces in the first Connecticut group has undulating vines and these are standard on the second group. The second group has in common with the English pieces undulating vines, through chamfering, and full concentric circles with serrated edges forming roses. The third American group, with two-plane, large painted motifs repeated over the entire front surface, is less closely related to English work. (The American aspect of this expression is discussed further under figure 399 in Chapter 9.) This group easily subdivides: a few lack through chamfering and have applied moldings; others restrict carving to the panels, and a few have turned feet; some have interlaced devices as found in Westmorland; still others employ compass stars, stylized roses with serrated edges, pinwheels, and heart shapes, among other decorative devices.

7

Significant Visual & Constructional Details

Particular motifs or decorative features and construction techniques in furniture design have until recently been accepted as signaling a particular American region. Now, with more understanding of craft practices, it is realized that special features may on occasion occur in a variety of places.[1] In part this is because techniques and motifs migrated between colonies. Also, since all the characteristics once thought to be the exclusive products of American centers were practiced in Europe, and often in more than one country, the dispersal of features along the coast of the New World may be the result of practices from one or more areas of Europe reaching several parts of America. A good case in point is the through-tenon chair construction. As we will see, it is associated with Philadelphia chairs, but did occasionally appear in other areas of America. In part, this resulted from the movements of men who once worked in Philadelphia and later practiced elsewhere. But since this constructional feature was also common in the north of England and on the continent, this craft practice in America may have a variety of origins.

Claw and Ball Feet

In England, claw and ball feet grew in popularity from about 1720. Although they appear only in a very minor way in Chippendale's *Director*, they have become firmly linked with his style. Their origins seem to stem from China, where the form symbolizes a dragon's foot grasping a pearl. They appear in figures **302** and **303**, details of two chairs that support seventeenth-century enameled porcelain figures made during the K'ang-hsi period (1622–1722). The first is from the God of Wealth in His Civil Aspect; the second, from the God of Wealth in His Military Aspect. In other crafts, representations of a dragon's foot grasping a pearl, on textiles for example, often show elongated claws and talons and suggest the form of the foot found in Newport (as seen in figure 311). The all-over form of the chairs in figures 302 and 303 would inspire Queen Anne designs, and animal heads terminating arm rails were made in England through much of the eighteenth century.

Among the most famous details held to demonstrate an American regional source are two forms of the claw and ball foot made between 1745 and 1790: the retracted claw foot, suggesting Massachusetts; and the open or pierced-talon foot, signifying Rhode Island. Although it is true that feet with the side claws raking to the rear are far more frequent on furniture made in eastern Massachusetts (figure **304**; the full chair is figure 850), they were on occasion used on furniture made in other American regions: for example, the Newport chair, figure 892. The chair with retracted claws, figure **305** (1750–85), is English. The other "Massachusetts" features on this example are narrow seat rails without horizontal shaping; a flat, un-

302

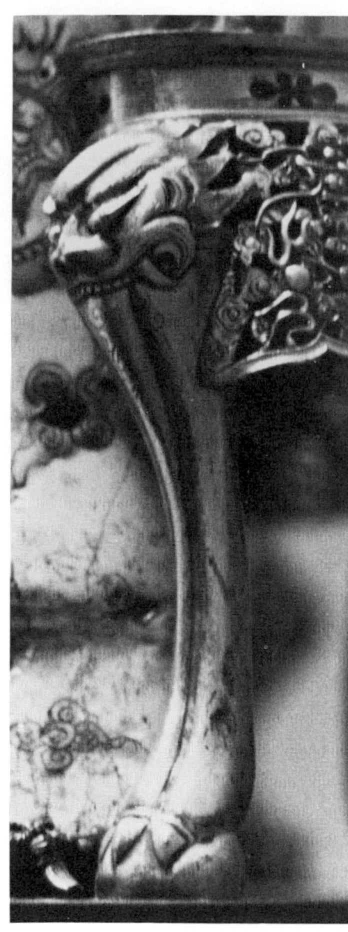

303

304

305

306

308

307

309

310

bowed back; and rear legs ending in square feet. (Most Massachusetts chairs of this period have stretchers and lack articulated rear feet, but when stretchers are absent square feet are standard.) The particular Gothic pattern of the back is not known on American chairs, but it was sufficiently popular in England to appear on chairs with straight legs and cabriole legs ending in turned feet.[2]

The mahogany and oak chair in figure **306** (1750–85) was made in England and brought to Long Island in the eighteenth century. It has a history of belonging to the loyalist Josiah Martin, who imported furniture for Rock Hall in Lawrence. The crest rail is similar to those on figures 1001 and 1002; the shape and decoration of the splat are found on figures 938 through 943. The carving of the English chair with retracted claws (1750–80) in figures **307** and **308** is more richly detailed than on most American chairs. The outline and leafage of the splat of the English chair (1750–85) in figure **309** were used in various American centers (see figures 890 through 892, for example) and the crest rail decoration in Massa-

311

313

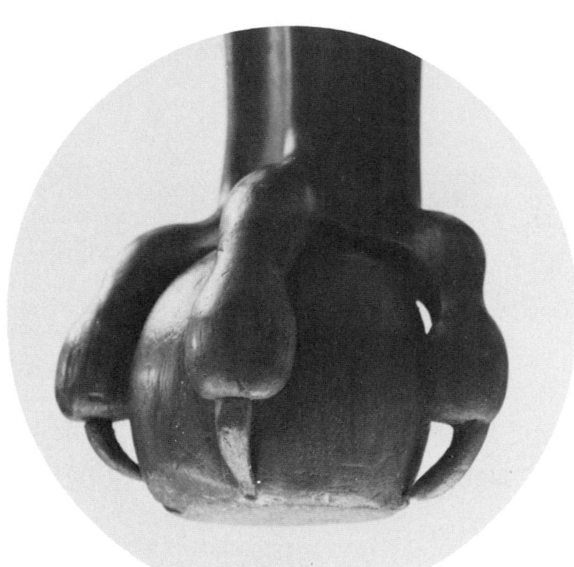

312

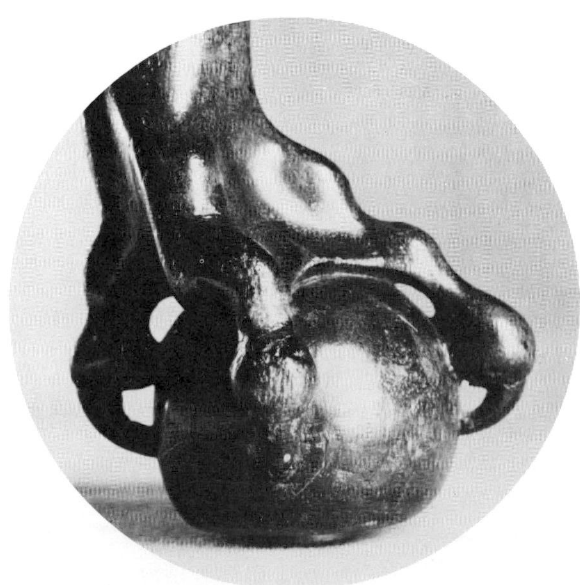

314

315

chusetts (figure 894) and New York (figure 933). The English easy chair (1750–85) in figure **310** is similar to upholstered chairs made in various American centers.

Open talons appear on many developed Newport, Rhode Island, pieces (figure **311**, detail of a highboy, 1750–90), on which, too, the ankle usually has prominent tendons rising from each claw (figure 352). The English chair (1750–85) in figures **312** and **313** has open claws and open talons, and prominent tendons. The profile of the claws is more knobbly than on most Newport feet, although similarly profiled, unpierced feet do appear on a few Newport pieces. Another English foot, figure **314**, is distinctly wavy in profile, recalling Massachusetts feet with similar silhouette. (Open talons appear on the Irish card table in figure 1371.) The use of ivory claws on the English case piece (1725–40) in figure **315** demonstrates the attention that might be paid to these parts of the feet.

Turnings

The similarity of many English and American turnings is evident in the illustrations of the Visual Survey that follows; a detailed study is not necessary here. However, a review of a few turned forms serves to illuminate the issue. The eighteenth-century English stair bannisters, figure **316**, include many of the baluster shapes found on American furniture and as part of American architecture. The form of the applied split-spindle on the English table, figure **317**, was widely used there (see figures 113, 159, 446, and 465) and on some American furniture: for example, the Connecticut chest with drawers (1760–90), figure **318**. The form of the leg turnings on the Connecticut piece also appears in England on figure 694.

Just as many American shapes had precedents in England, so too the continent was the source for English turned forms. Similar turnings appear on the Italian mid-seventeenth-century chair, figure **319**, and the English table (1650–1725) in figure **320** (other English versions appear throughout, for example, on figures 664, 667, 683, 684, 690,

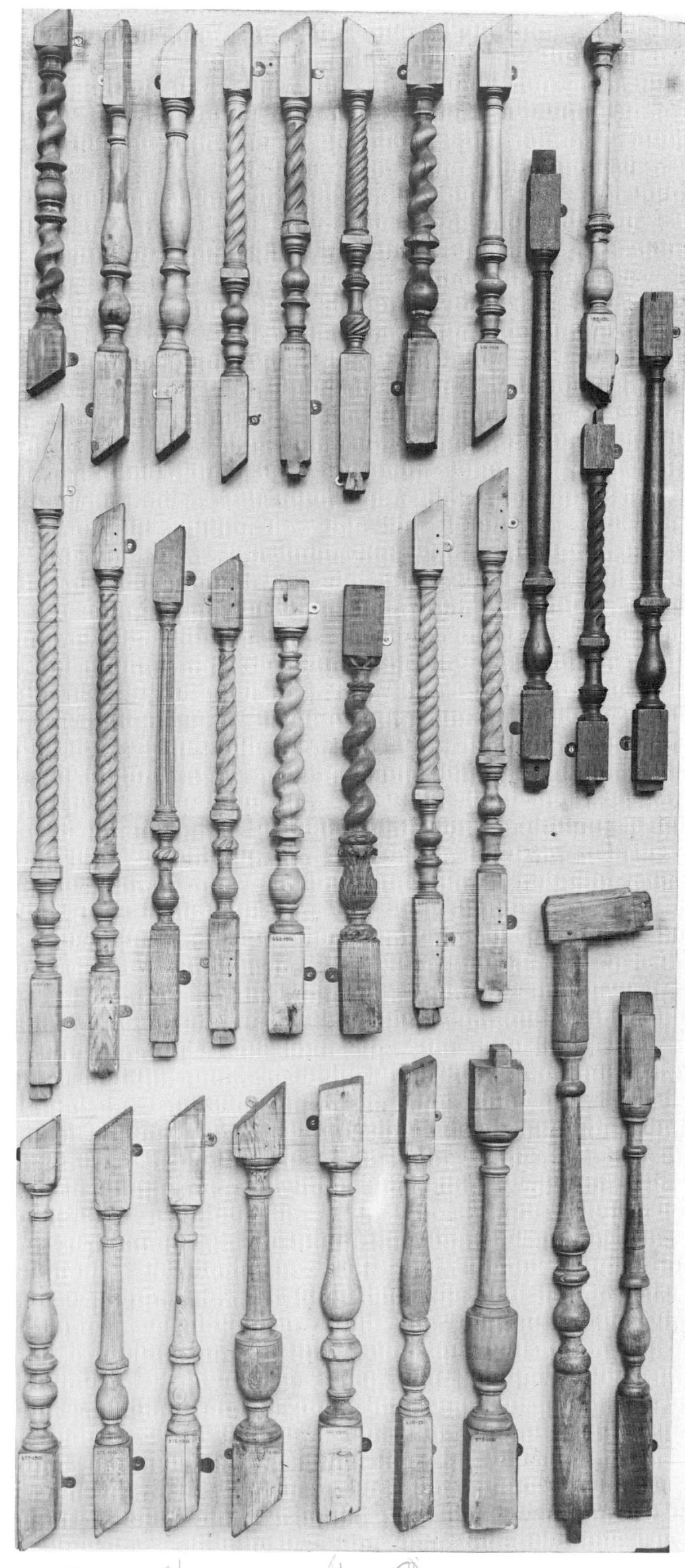

316

317

318

319

320

692, 695). In turn, similar shapes appeared in the colonies, as seen on the lower stage of the New Haven area, late seventeenth-century cupboard, figure **321**. (The turnings flanking the upper cupboard differ slightly in shape from those below and are not original. They were probably similar to those on figure 163.)

The Blockfront Form

The Boston desk and bookcase, figure **322**, is the earliest known dated blockfront piece made in America. It is inscribed "1738," "Job Coit Jr" (1717–1745), and "J. Coit"—perhaps the father, who was also a cabinetmaker (1692–1741). This piece is not particularly distinguished, but it is an important document, for it dates the form fairly early in the eighteenth century; the form was probably made even earlier in Massachusetts, Rhode Island, or New York. (The plate-glass mirrors, desk interior, brasses, and two finials are not original.) The chest of drawers, figure 382, shows the exquisite balance of blocked forms Massachusetts could achieve in the second half of the eighteenth century. Searching for the American form of blocked furniture in an original English example proved fruitless. Related shaping does appear in two designs for library tables in Chippendale's 1762 edition of the *Director* (plates 80 and 82), but the pedestal ends are ovoid in movement and not the source of American work. It seems that the American blocked form came directly from the continent.

322

321

The late seventeenth-century Parisian dressing table, figure **323**, and the early eighteenth-century Parisian chest of drawers, figure **324**, use the sur-

323

324

325

326

face technique made famous by André Charles Boulle (1642–1732) and decorative motifs associated with Jean Bérain. The fronts move very much as in the chest of drawers, figure 382: here the ends of the front project in curves and the center has a flatter line. (The form of the legs in figure 323 appears on English furniture and on a few American pieces.) The desk and bookcase, figure **325**, uses very low-relief movement on the lower case. This example, probably of rosewood or padouk, may be of Dutch colonial origin, although similar minimal shaping was used throughout the continent and England. Deep blocking was made in Scandinavia, Germany, France, and Italy.[3] The early eighteenth-century japanned chest-on-chest, figure **326**, is probably of Dutch or north German origin. German pieces were often dramatically blocked, as evidenced by figure 4, designed by J. G. König about 1740–50.

The form of the long-leg dressing table, with goat feet and hocked ankles, figure **327**, suggests it may have been made in northern Italy between 1720 and 1740, although the use of what is probably walnut veneer, with triple-line stringing, suggests Holland. This piece has flat blocking while that on the previous chest-on-chest was rounded. Although both the rounded and the flat form appeared in the colonies, that on the dressing table was more common.

The Chinese export trade, borrowing a foreign shape, provided blocked pieces to both Europe and America; a typical piece from the late eighteenth century is seen in figure **328**.

The blockfront form gave way in America to the reverse-serpentine, or oxbow, form when the

327

328

329

classical serpentine line dominated. The bulging movement of projection and recess became a sensuous, slow-moving line. Since blocking was not an English shape, the reverse serpentine is rarely found there. The shape did appear in Chippendale's *Director* and on a few pieces such as the japanned dressing commode in figure **329**. It was made *en suite*, 1752–54, by the firm of William & John Linnell for the Chinese bedroom of the fourth Duke of Beaufort (the bed is shown as figure 367).

Through Tenons

In this construction, the tenons of the side rails pass completely through the rear stiles and are visible from behind (figure **330**). This technique was used on about 95 per cent of Philadelphia Queen Anne and Chippendale chairs, and occasionally appeared in Connecticut, New York, and the South. After the Revolution it appeared in other areas such as Rhode Island.

In his *Blue Book, Philadelphia Furniture* (1935), William Macpherson Hornor, Jr., reported that this construction "has been pointed out as a method also used in Lancashire, England." Horner went on: "it was stated in 1795 that on each chair a supplementary charge of six pence was to be made [in Philadelphia] for 'Mortising the back feet through.' "[4] Undoubtedly the extra charge was to compensate for having to make a neat opening at the back of the legs. Some Philadelphia chairs did not use this joint, for example, figures 953 and 965, the latter perhaps because it had stretchers to ensure a firm construction.

The set of walnut chairs represented by figure **331** has through tenons; according to one tradition, these chairs were found in York, England.[5] Another English walnut chair, figure **332**, has through tenons but no provenance. On an English rural elm or yew chair, also without provenance, figure **333**, the side seat rails and the stretchers through-tenon the back posts, as on the wainscot chair, figure 300. (On all the vernacular chairs included here, the through tenons are double-wedged.) The two vernacular chairs, figures 334 through 337, are in the Lake District and are considered local products. The oak chair, figures **334–**

330

333

331

332

334

335

336

337

335, is in Wordsworth's House, Cockermouth. There is no shoe; rather, the straight rail below the Gothic splat is on top of the wooden seat. The front legs have edge molding. (The medial stretcher is missing and the seat may be replaced.) Figures **336–337** show one of a set of three chairs in the Wordsworth Museum also at Cockermouth. The splat is housed in a rail above the seat. The square-tapered legs suggest a date after 1780. The primary wood is oak; the "Philadelphia-type" corner blocks are pine (for a Philadelphia example, see figure 348). A bracing rail runs from the front to the rear of the seat. The two elm chairs, figures **338** through **340**, are at Bolling Hall, Bradford, West Yorkshire, and the staff considers the through tenons to have "come from east of Skipton [northwest of Leeds] in the Whitby, Bridlington, area." Whitby and Bridlington are both on the east coast of Yorkshire. The splats of the chairs are housed in a shoe. The seat of the first is framed in the seat rails; on the second, it rests on top of the rails. The neo-classical splat and crest rail of figure 340 suggest a date after 1780.

Round through tenons were fairly common on turned chairs. Often slender tenons on two rails passed through larger ones on adjacent rails (figure 697).

Through tenons are an ancient practice that possibly began as a logical feature in knockdown furniture. The mid-sixteenth-century chair in figure **341**, like the 1785 wainscot chair in figures 299 and 300, is rife with through tenons. As on early trestle tables, the tenons protrude and are transversely wedged (see figure 1224). This medieval practice appears also on a three-legged plank-seat chair (bottom of seat shown in figure **342**) that probably dates from the seventeenth century. The boards forming the back penetrate the seat near the rounded legs and are wedged below. The meal chest (figures **343–344**) is typical of a form that used through-tenon construction into the eighteenth century. Undoubtedly the form of chest persisted because it was serviceable. The top could be removed, inverted, and the cross bars become feet. Also, the notches in these cross bars fit over carrying poles.

338

339

340

341

342

Through tenons appear in paintings and prints of local scenes in The Netherlands, Germany, and Italy.[6] Sometimes the member is round and part of a stick construction, at other times rectangular. Published examples of Swedish and German chairs and early furniture from China and ancient Palestine all show such tenons. Probably under the influence of Philadelphia work, they also appear in eighteenth-century Bermuda chairs.[7]

Splat and Shoe

It is standard on English and American chairs to use a removable shoe when the upholstery wraps over the front and side seat rails. During upholstering the rear edge of the fabric was tacked onto the top of the rear seat rail; the shoe was then nailed over the raw edge of the textile. It could be removed for re-upholstery. To keep the splat fixed in position, when the shoe was absent, it was housed into the rear seat rail (figure **345**). If there was a loose slip seat that could be removed

343

344

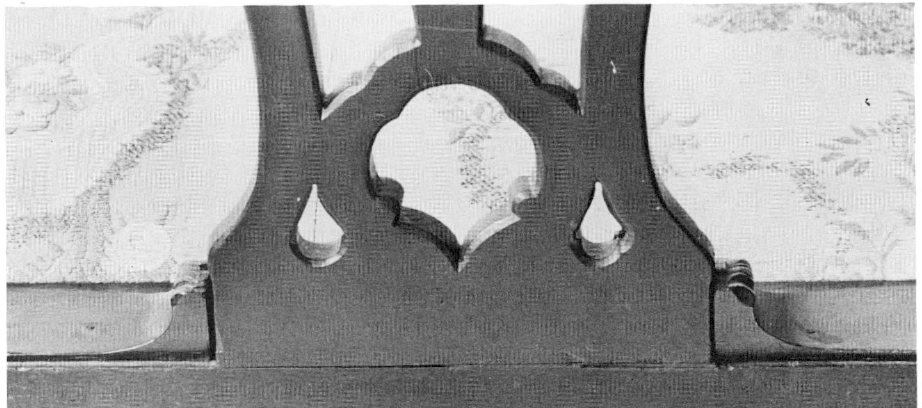

345

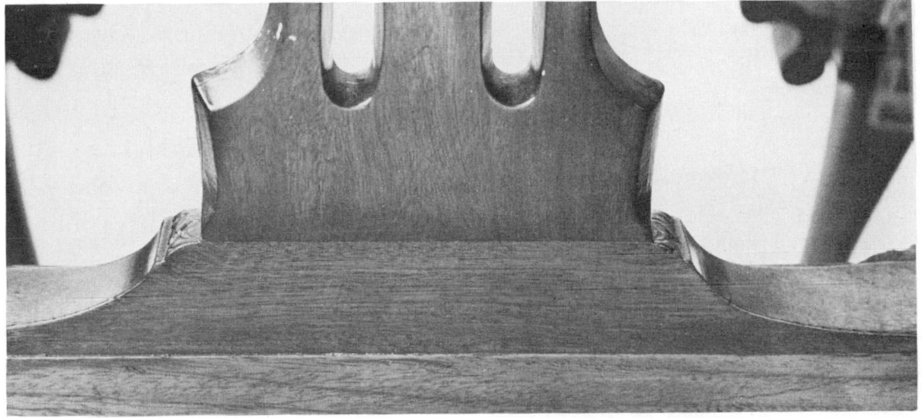

346

for re-upholstery, the splat *may* still have been housed in the rear seat rail, with the shoe fitting around it. Or, the shoe was permanently fixed to the rear seat rail with the splat housed into its top (figure **346**). In England it was fairly common to have the splat housed into the rear rail and the shoe fitting around it even when using a slip seat. This practice was rarer in America but more common in New England than elsewhere—perhaps because upholstery over the rails was more usual there and it became a general shop practice for chairs with either approach to upholstery.

Knee Brackets

On most American chairs the knee brackets are deep and glued between the bottom of the seat rail and the knee of the leg. It is fairly common on English chairs to have the piece of wood forming the seat rail drop down behind the bracket (figure **347**). This allows the seat rails a deep

347

348

349

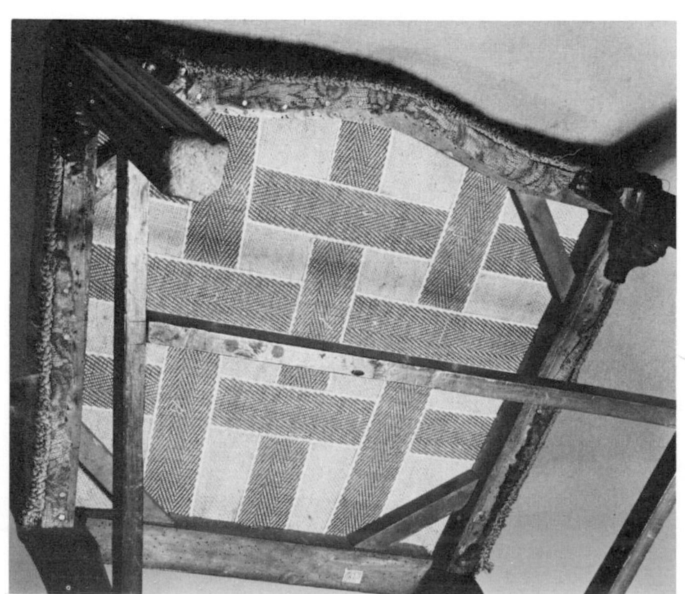

350

tenoned joint in the legs. When this construction is used, a shallow bracket is glued to the downward curve of the rail. Such sturdy construction appears on a few Philadelphia chairs (see figure 953, which was also made without through tenons) and Southern chairs. It was common to glue knee brackets to the face of the rails on both English and American tables.

Seat Bracing

There are two basic forms of corner blocks in American chairs. One is associated with Philadelphia (figure **348**) and related work in Connecticut and the South, although it was also used on a few New York chairs. At the front, two pieces of vertical-grain softwood fit around the leg and are shaped to a quarter round; at the rear, a piece fills the area between the seat rail and the front of the leg, and then a vertical-grain softwood quarter-round block is glued into the corner. (English examples are seen in figure 1017.) The second form of block is associated with New England (figure **349**) and is again also found in some New York chairs. It is triangular in shape, with a horizontal grain (usually of hardwood), and is attached with glue and nails. The nails often have rounded heads.

Both forms appear in England. On many examples front corners have the "Philadelphia" form, and rear corners the "New England" shape—these, too, may use round-headed nails (figure 804). Cross ties, often dovetailed in from above, were a popular means of strengthening English chairs (figure **350**) but rarely appear in American chairs before the neo-classical style, about 1785.

Dovetails

It is a common assumption that American dovetails are distinctive, particularly those made in Newport, Rhode Island, which are noted for coming to a point as they near the face of a drawer. Similar dovetails can be seen on the English drawer, figure **351**—the front is mahogany, the sides are oak. Dovetails have a long tradition and can be found in ancient Egyptian work.[8]

Detachable Legs

Removable legs are associated with Newport (figure 352) and related Connecticut work.[9] The boards forming the ends, front, and back of the lower case are fitted together like a box, and the cabriole legs, where they reach the case, cut back the depth of the case boards and continue up inside the corner. They are kept in place only with glue and glue blocks. On most Newport highboys with this construction, the front of the lower case has a heavy piece of veneer with vertical grain directly above the leg. This veneer *appears* to be an extension of the leg, which therefore seems to form the corner. (On the Newport highboy, figure 352, the left side board of the lower case has a shrinkage crack: if the leg did continue as the corner post, the crack in the side board would not extend to the front face.) It has become accepted that this construction was popular because it allowed shipment with legs detached, and Newport engaged heavily in the venture cargo of the maritime trade. It was not, however, a Newport invention, appearing on the English oak highboy detailed in figure 353 and shown in full as figure 559. Since it also appears on inland Connecticut examples, it seems that this was more a constructional habit than a delivery feature. Indeed, it is difficult to imagine the assemblage of glossy sophisticated pieces once they arrived at some distant home.

352

351

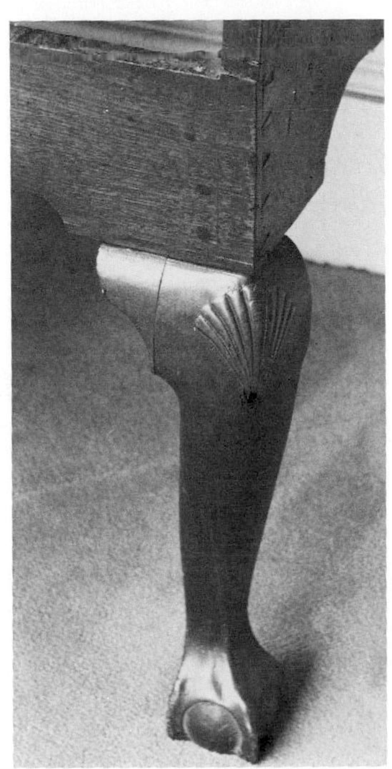

353

8

What America Did Not Do

While constructional features, basic forms, and motifs used in American furniture migrated from Europe, certain expressions were not transferred: court-level magnificence, Palladian styling, and some vernacular details. The furniture shown in figures 354 through 368 presents significant elite work for which there is no parallel American statement.

The bed, figures **354–355** (detail of headboard, figure 203), was made for the first Earl of Melville about 1695: its imposing scale, costly textiles, and aristocratic bearing would have been unimaginable accessories to colonial life. Such an expression was not sustained in America until the "Gilded Age" of the late nineteenth century. The exquisitely complex patterning of rushing textile-covered wooden C scrolls and S shapes, and the voluptuous draping, render it a superlatively sensuous creation. Indeed, the quality is so high that it may be by a maker of French extraction.[1] (The original height of the mattress would have raised the pillows to join their design to that of the headboard; and the cords holding the curtains around the posts are not appropriate.)

The cane chair, figure **356** (detail in figure 41), was made about 1685 under Dutch or French influence, and the movement, balance, and execution of the carving render it the finest known English example. The rhythm of the leaf scrolling on either side of the cane panel is particularly fine. A great continental chair would show a slightly better proportional adjustment between parts: in the relationship of the back posts to the wooden panel composed of crest, side, and base rails, for example.

The cabinet on stand (1690–1710), figure **357**, places an English japanned veneered cabinet of oak and pine between a crest and stand of gilt oak and pine. The square-baluster legs are carved to drapery overlays and are joined by a confection of richly patterned leafage. The crest, with scrolling, leafage, and birds, terminates in a floral basket. (The tops of the side finials are missing. The stand and cresting are re-gilt with some slight evidence that the original finish was a silver-coating, with a gold-tinted varnish.) When compared to the most developed American highboys, such as that in figure 546, the disparity between the expectations of the societies in which these pieces functioned is readily apparent.

The Palladian tables (1730–40), figures **358** and **359**, are in the style of William Kent. The first, with a base painted white to echo the white and gray marble top, uses Roman motifs: foxes support the front corners, and a female mask over a shell centers richly carved scrolls, leafage, and garlands. Designs like the gilt eagle console table in figure 359 would, nearly one hundred years later, influence the early nineteenth-century Regency style and thereby New York card tables such as figure **360**.

The table in figure **361** (1730–45) is one of the

354

356

355

357

finest English forms standing between baroque classicism and rococo disarray. Where figure 359 placed a tense, compact eagle on a firm base, this table orchestrates extraordinary drama: broken reverse-curve legs with hoof feet support mannerist masks; opulent garlands of flowers draped around the legs and across the front are held in the beak of the surging eagle. The rock that the bird grips with its talons is many-faceted, pulsing with light and shadow, above a shell. (An overmantel with a similar eagle and related motifs was probably made by the Linnell firm in 1751.)[2]

The gilded pine marble-top table, figures **362–363**, is similar to a 1739 design by Batty and Thomas Langly, published in *The City and Country Builder's and Workman's Treasury of Designs* (1740), which in turn had been copied from a design in Nicolas Pineau's *Nouveaux Desseins de Pieds de Tables.* Broken-reverse-curve legs (related in form to those on figures 1453 through 1455) are entwined with winged serpents, and merge with finely sculpted hermae. As the detail makes clear, the subtlety of the shaping of the forms, the tension, and balance of parts are of the highest quality, and were unlike anything available in America at this date. (The top and the gilding are new.) The table with related reverse-curve legs and fuller female figures was made for Ham House in Surrey fifty years earlier (figure 1453).

The writing desk (1740–50) in figure **364** was

358

359

360

361

362

363

364

originally one of a pair that stood back to back to form a large library table. The extensive use of brass ornaments and the compact rhythmic flow suggest a German influence. When the top tier (which is really one long fitted drawer) is pulled out, the front corners of the case with dolphin feet pull with it to serve as legs.[3] The nearest American expression is the German-inspired block-and-shell case furniture made in Newport, Rhode Island (figures 3 and 381).

Figure **365** is a reconstructed fragment. It was probably one wing of "His Majesty's Grand Medal Case," made about 1750, and altered for George III by William Vile in 1761. (The original cupboard seems to have been cut into three sections and the two ends are still known: figure 365, and a similar piece, in the Victoria and Albert Museum.[4] In reworking the large cabinet, Vile put carved sides on the fragment in figure 365 and fitted the Victoria and Albert end with plain sides. There are other changes to this piece: the carving and construction of the bottom section—between the corner posts—differ from what is found above; the applied moldings on the front and sides of the bottom section are simpler, less frenzied, and the body of the door has vertical grain. The panels of the upper front doors have

365

366

wood cut to quadrants that continue to the center line; the grain runs around the central leafage. The base was originally open between squared legs.) A garter-star decorates the upper panel; rococo leafage forms panels on a ground of concentric grain; lion heads curve out above stop-fluted Corinthian columns at the front corners of the middle stage; and leafage flows down the original legs. The reason for including a reworked, partial piece is, first, to show the high quality of the early part and, second, to demonstrate the changes that might occur even to major pieces almost from the time of their manufacture. The original detailing is finer than most contemporary English work and more exquisite than mid-century American carving.

The sketch for "Lord Scarsdale's Sofa at Keddleston in Derbyshire" (figure **366**) is by John Linnell and the sofa was furnished by the Linnell firm by 1765. One of the finest English expressions, it combines baroque-rococo play with classical motifs: dolphins, water gods, and a medallion and swag. Rolled cushions, with tassels, added comfort and a horizontal line. The finished piece is in Kedleston.

Although generally less exuberant than the work of a variety of continental centers, the English craftsmen were able to enjoy a degree of rococo fantasy, which remained beyond the American experience until the late nineteenth century. The black, red, and gold japanned dragon bed (1752–54) in figure **367** was designed by John Linnell and made for the fourth Duke of Beaufort, *en suite* with figure 329, for the Chinese bedroom at Badminton House.

The designs for rusticated chairs, figure **368**, appear as plate 26 of Robert Manwaring's *The Cabinet and Chair-Maker's Real Friend and Companion*, published in London (1765). Such objects were suitable for consciously fanciful situations where the gentry played at the rural life.

Presenting with reverence the preceding group of English pieces suggests once again that involved designs are the only successful British statement, leaving plain elegance—the subtlety of the graceful line—as the American achievement. To correct this impression, it seemed appropriate to venture through the full sequence of English styles and select for inclusion certain pieces that demonstrated quality without complex ornamentation. After placing side by side three great pieces (figures 369 through 371) which depend on line,

367

it comes as a surprise to discover that they are all of the same style, Chinese-based, and covered with nervous, small-unit surface decoration. Elegance in other English modes does seem to require a barrage of richness. There are, of course, simple pieces made by major cabinetmakers for lesser situations, such as the plain, Marlborough leg tables executed for Paxton House, Berwickshire, in Scotland, by Chippendale.[5] Indeed, his useful furniture often exhibits a better balance of line and mass than do many of his more involved high-fashion creations.

The early eighteenth-century cupboard on stand, figure **369**, drew inspiration from the Orient for the form and brass enrichment of its cupboard, and for the elements of the stand: the shaping and edge molding, and the square-section cabriole legs, as found on the Chinese table in figure 1267. The tight balance of straights and curves in figure 369 relates it to the Chinese-inspired chair in figure 779—an object that might also be included in this essay. The lower edge of the stand rises from the knee blocks to carry the edge molding of the legs across a slender rail, whose dimension and surface play elegantly against the flats of the legs and the rectilinear forms above.

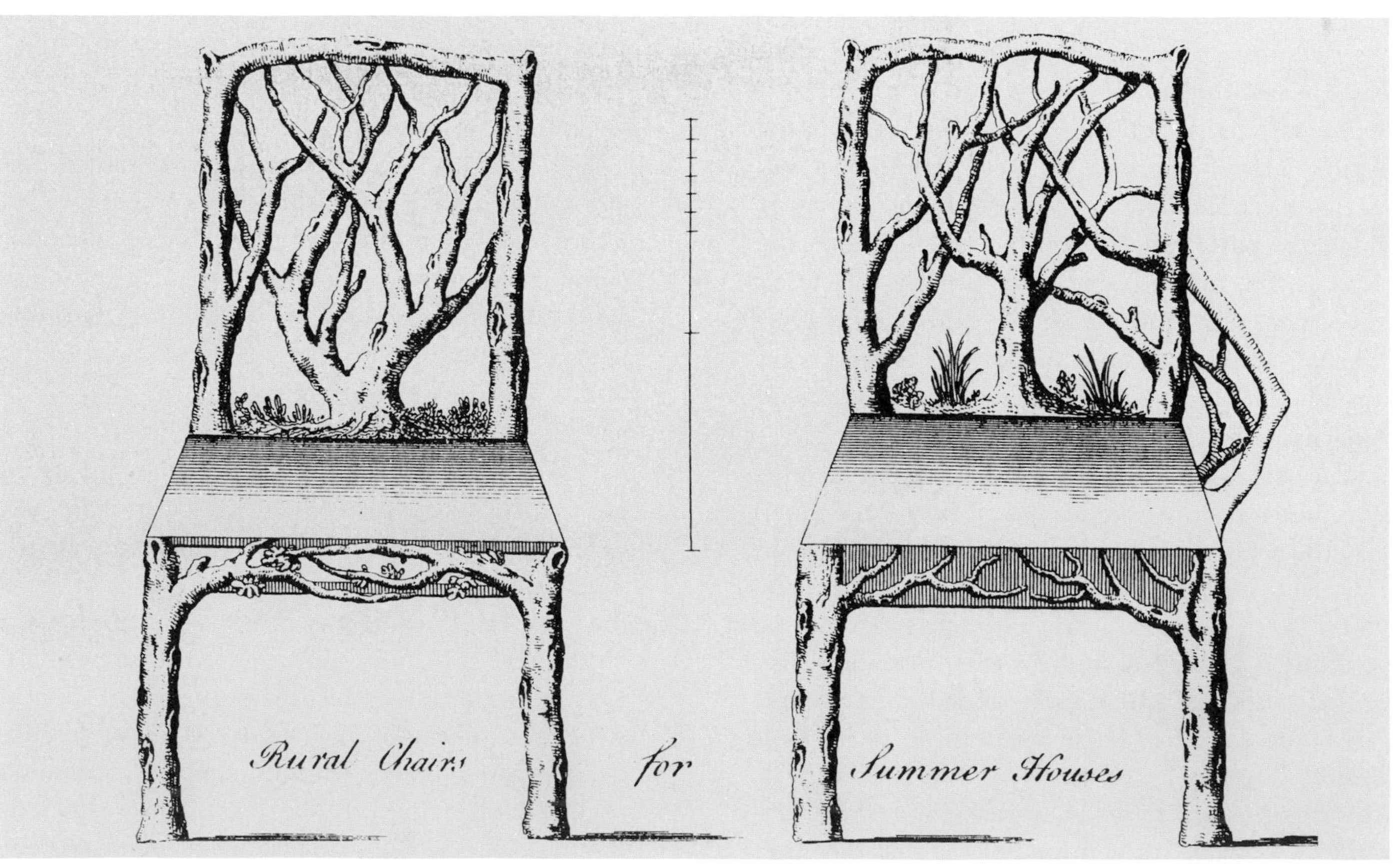

368

The similarly dated chair in figure **370** (the front view appears as figure 780) borrowed Chinese concepts for both its form and surface. The tension between the lines of the forward-curving back posts, the spooned splat, and the reverse-curve legs produce a lean, taut statement unlike the more restful American designs of this period. The cabinet on stand (1710–30), figure **371**, may not have the confident poise of figure 369, but the interplay of flat surfaces and rectangles creates an intriguing counterpoint of related shapes. The line of the sharp-edge cabriole legs shifts to chamfered corners, which decrease on the upper case to broaden again in the cornice.

369

370

371

9

Original American Statements

After reviewing both examples of America's dependence on British furniture and the pieces that had little impact on American work, it is possible to discern the attitude toward form that emerged in the new settings. Although this change in approach rarely placed American furniture outside the English context, its character was clearly new.

The southeastern Massachusetts table, figure **372**, was made about 1640–60. With its tightly unified base and projecting top, it creates a new, un-British statement. By this date wide boards were not readily available in England, where seventeenth-century table tops are usually of several pieces and hug the dimensions of the supporting frame. In this piece the traditional use of oak is continued for the frame, which retains a thin coat of red-brown paint. The turnings, similar to those on the eastern Massachusetts stool in figure 1205, invert the standard English sequence (figure 1206) and rise in ring, reel, rather "straight" baluster with ring, to terminate with another ring. The lower edge of the front rail is shaped to central and end brackets. The tops of the square-section stretchers are edge-molded. The top takes advantage of expansive planks of pine, which cantilever out to produce an early instance in the opening up of designs that would soon become essential to America's new aesthetic.

The drop-leaf table (1690–1720) in figure **373** has a history of use in the Lydia Poore House, West Newbury, Massachusetts. It is made of maple and retains an original or early coat of brown paint. Maple lacks open grain and can be turned to beautiful crisp shapes. Its strength allows a contrasting range of dimensions, and the movement from thick to thin areas is often part of the best American turning—for example, in the leg shaping of the Windsor chair that follows. The only maple furniture so far discovered in England was made after the introduction of the neoclassical taste for light woods, about 1770. The wood is listed in some earlier accounts dated 1586, 1588, and 1624;[1] it appears in the Gillows firm records early in the nineteenth century (see figure 191 and the discussion in the Visual Survey under figure 1201). The table in figure 373 plays the inward angle of the legs against the action of the "butterfly" bracket supports and the thrusting, broad top.

The Windsor arm chair, figure **374**, has the stamp of Walter MacBride (working in New York about 1785–1810), and is one of the better examples of a form that in America encompassed new engineering and aesthetic developments. The chair employs the wood appropriate for each part: maple for the turnings, soft tulip for the sculpted seat, and oak for the springy back. The varying grains and colors of the woods were hidden by unifying paint—a dark color that intensifies the intriguing silhouette. The wide stance of the beautifully formed ring, reel, and baluster-turned

372

373

374

375

376

377

legs provided stability. The arm posts, repeating the turned forms of the legs, thrust out to the arms to provide both a sense of generosity and space for the sitter. The arm rail sweeps in, up, and around, gathering the rayed back and bracing spokes. The forms of Windsor parts are found in England, but the interpretation of the turning and the raking action is new (see the English chairs, figures 1091 through 1130). The larger Windsor arm chair (1770–95), figure **375**, is of painted maple, birch, beech, oak, hickory, and white pine, and was possibly made in New England. Although the parts are less beautiful than in the previous chair, there is majesty, and the raking bracing spokes play against those that form the back.

The turnings of the all-maple table (1740–90), figure **376**, exhibit that sensibility of line which distinguishes the best high-style and vernacular American furniture from its European antecedents. The base retains most of its original red paint. The same sensibility of line is seen on the New England mahogany table (1790–1810) in figure **377**. It is rather unconventional in using long, smooth areas either side of the leg cuffs and smooth reels above reed shafts. The way these and the upper section are leanly drawn makes a great, if idiosyncratic, object. (The piece was photographed with the leaf propped up, diminishing the proper visual weight of two boards across the top. The presence of inlay on the top surface of the top leaf of many card tables made during this period suggests they were originally kept closed except when in use.)

Although the profile of the front legs is slightly awkward, the way line rather than ornamentation is used makes the Philadelphia walnut (walnut, pine) chair (1730–60), figure **378**, one of the greatest pieces of American eighteenth-century sculpture. The play of the shaped parts and the spaces they delineate are contrived to provide rhythm, force, and subtlety: reverse-curve front legs sweep to a similarly shaped seat frame, from which arm supports and back rise in contrapuntal curves. The seat rail and splat are veneered (in England, the back posts and crest rail would have been similarly decorated). The form of the parts can be found on English chairs, but here they are heightened to a lean tautness.

The mahogany Boston tea table (1730–60) in

378

379

figure **379** and the Philadelphia arm chair in figure 378 provide an opportunity to contrast great objects from two American style centers. The New England table is more conservative in approach, creating a design from similarly shaped reverse curves: long reverse-curve legs play against briefer versions on the skirt rails. (A related line is found on the probably Irish table, figure 1279.) The Philadelphia piece engages in a greater contrast of forms.

Newport created the most original American high-style furniture. The active block-and-shell desk and bookcase, figure 3, has been shown as a major new expression. It and the knee-hole chest of drawers (1750–90) in figure 381 are the best of one extreme in Newport's design attitude. At the other end of the spectrum are clean, rectilinear forms of which the dressing table (1740–70) of mahogany (pine, tulip) in figure **380** is a superior example. Both statements depend on a careful control of bold parts.

The dressing table has extraordinary edges, as though the parts were drawn with a sharp pencil. Rising from slipper feet, sinuous square-section legs reverse-curve up to similarly shaped knee brackets; the line is repeated in larger form on the skirt, which rises to encompass a shell with paired reverse curves on its lower edge. The front of the case is articulated only by lipped drawers and their brasses. The quick, projecting top caps the tight, lean form.

The mahogany (tulip, chestnut) knee-hole chest of drawers (1750–90), figure **381**, takes its basic forms from England (figures 533 through 537); but with blocking and shells from the continent (figures 4 and 323 through 327), projection and recess, light and shadow, it intensifies pattern to become original. The raised blocking begins at the floor, with the scrolling inner edge of the feet, and moves through the base molding up the drawers to arch rhythmically over the shells. The recessed shell is echoed within the mass on the cupboard door. The polished brasses are large, charging the front with shining surfaces that join the light reflected from the curving mahogany.

The blocked form, as seen in the Massachusetts mahogany chest of drawers (1750–90), figure **382**, is particularly suited to an American line drawn with assured grace. The drawers divide the case into four horizontals, which in turn are broken by the three verticals of the positive and negative

380

shaping. The resulting curved rectangles are punctuated by shining brasses. The tension of these shapes is enhanced by the cock beading applied to the case around the drawers. Reverse-curve feet, with curving brackets, echo the curves above, and support the base molding, which follows the line of the case. The similarly shaped projecting top stops the vertical thrust and returns it to the design.

Like the Newport dressing table, figure 380, the slightly more provincial designer of the Salem area maple highboy (1740–70) in figures **383–384** worked with sharp edges. The arris of the knees carries the distinctive line one-third of the distance down the legs; the inner edge of the scrolling on the knee brackets is distinctly sharp; the drawer lips form a pattern of rectangles; and the brasses are strict verticals. Tiger maple drawer fronts give additional life to the original painted grain that imitates walnut or mahogany. In deference to the rainbow-painted fans, their drawers have less active graining. Massachusetts highboys with claw and ball feet are rare, whereas turned feet (more in keeping with that area's sense of line) continued until the end of the century.

Until the second quarter of the nineteenth century, carving on better American pieces usually enhances line rather than forms it. The legs on the mahogany drop-leaf table (1750–90) in figure

381

382

383

384

385

386

387

388

385 are strong in line and terminate in handsome claw and ball feet typical of one of four forms of that foot made in New York.[2] The movement of the knees is not disturbed but only made more generous by the leafage. The line formed by the feet, legs, knee bracket, and the arched rail plays against the line of the top.

The carved applied leafage in the pediment of the Philadelphia walnut highboy (1750–90) in figure **386** may perhaps derive its forms from Irish plasterwork,[3] but the interpretation and placement are a Philadelphia expression. Moving to fill the pediment, the leafage overlaps, turns, and twists. Although composed of slender tendrils, it firmly dominates the surface it enriches, maintaining equal power with the adjacent large carved images.

The Philadelphia mahogany (poplar, cedar) desk and bookcase, figure **387**, was made about 1770 for Caspar Wistar, Jr. (1740–1811). Together with the chest-on-chest that follows, it typifies the best furniture made in Philadelphia between 1750 and 1790. The arched-panel style of an earlier period combines with a broken-arch pediment, and a shell and leafage of the rococo style. On an elaborate English piece, the leafage at the corners of the pediment would trail down the corners of the upper case. On a simpler British desk and bookcase, carving might be restricted to rosettes and finials (figures 639 and 640).

The mahogany (poplar, pine) chest-on-chest (1770–90) in figure **388** has the stance and formality of a beautiful pedimented mahogany doorway. More unified than the previous desk and bookcase, the form builds from the lower through the upper case to the fretted frieze, dentilated cornice, and supreme pediment. The horizontal action of the lipped drawers and their swirling grain are contained on both cases by engaged, fluted quarter columns. The vertical thrust is intensified by the brasses, which do not step in as the case narrows but continue a straight line, shifting only on the top tier to pull the eye toward the finial.

Ability to draw an elegant line makes possible the fine American high-style work and supervises the greatness of the vernacular Philadelphia arm chair (1730–60) in figure **389** (made of maple but stained to walnut color). Every part is well conceived as a unit and as a responding part of the total concept. Together, the reverse curves of the square-section legs, front stretcher, seat rail, and

389

390

391

392

baluster arm supports establish an interacting rectilinear frame for the beautifully composed back. Straight lines create a counterpoint to the curves: the top edge of the seat, the lower rail of the back, the long verticals at the base of the splat, and the edges of the back posts. The design has borrowed features from New England chairs, yet it is Philadelphian in attitude; although related to work by William Savery (1721–1788), it surpasses Savery's ability, and the chair may be by his master, Solomon Fussell (c. 1700–1765).[4]

The maple, stained walnut color, arm chair in figure **390** is probably from the same shop as the preceding example, for it exhibits similar details and use of line. Here the massive double-baluster, reel, and ring front stretcher echo the line of the front seat and crest rails. This example is perhaps of a later date (1745–90) than the previous chair, for there are trifid feet and ears on the crest rail and splat. A simple date division of styles is not, however, instructive, particularly with vernacular objects. (See the discussion on "plain chairs" for figures 838 through 842 in the Visual Survey.) Similar arms, arm supports, front stretchers, legs, and clarity of parts appear on some slat-back chairs which may have come from the same shop.[5] All three styles could be contemporary.

The four New England vernacular tables, figures 391 through 394, achieve greatness in different ways. The black-painted, oval-top maple (oak) table (figure **391**) actively opposes form against form: Spanish feet (originally called claw feet),[6] richly molded stretchers, raking turned legs, deeply shaped shirt, and circular projecting top. (It is a form often associated with the Gaines family, who worked in Ipswich, Massachusetts, and Portsmouth, New Hampshire, during the second quarter of the eighteenth century.) A chair of similar expression and quality is seen in figure 22.

A half century later, the maple and pine table (figure **392**) employed the shapes and smooth surfaces required by the neo-classical style, yet maintained a powerful stance. The legs, made without feet, swell and recede to a ring and reel shape. They slope to an unshaped skirt, visually held by the oval top. The original red paint is under a later coat of gray. The serene maple table (1730–70) in figure **393** seems to have a bottom coat of thin red paint, which may be the original color or an undercoat for the next layer, which is green. Over this is a later green, and the top layer is varnish or shellac. The dramatic curve of the ankle was carefully contrived: about 2 inches above the floor a wedge shape was cut from the

393

394

outer face of the ankle and the lower part of the leg bent out to the present angle. This closed the wedge shape so that only the saw line remains. Such attention to achieving the desired line demonstrates how consciously the final appearance of the best vernacular forms was pursued. (A similar cutting of a wedge shape to allow bending was used on figure 405.)

The maple-base and pine-top table (1700–35) in figure **394** may have had the same turner as figure 373. With the oval-top table, there is no dramatic raking or counterthrusting of forms. Rather, like the seventeenth-century table in figure 372, a rectilinear base holds a projecting top. Here the circular action above unites with the rounded form of the legs.

The discord or disquiet produced by deviating from the norm may produce failure, and lesser makers were usually content to stay within established practices. Taking the risk to differ may also produce new and desirable qualities both in high-style and vernacular work. Figures **395** and **396** are examples of fine new expressions. The first highboy was made in Concord, Massachusetts, during the second half of the eighteenth century. (It is often considered the work of Joseph Hosmer, 1736–1821.) It uses cherry, maple, and white pine. Rather vertical feet join almost straight cabriole legs; the skirt is horizontal in orientation, with a central triangle pointing up; the blocking mounts without change in width from lower to upper case, and the brasses are similarly aligned; a carved fan above an upward-pointing ogival brass caps the central recess of the blocking; and the arched line of the fan is echoed in the arch of the cornice. The workmanship, particularly the dovetails, is not very accomplished, but the piece is a new and exciting variation on elite forms. (The skirt drop and center finial are not original.)

The second highboy, figure 396, made of maple (pine), in the area of Windsor, Connecticut, in 1736 (dated upper rear corner of left side), is another successful personal statement. The surface imitates japanning in gold paint on a black ground. The active base moves the deeply shaped skirt out to wildly curving knees, straight legs, and enormous turned feet. Exaggerated knees are found in England (figure 554), but this almost animalistic shaping may result from a personal whim of the maker.

A similar energy of the line raises the Greek-revival, maple and pine fancy chair (1810–40) in figure **397** above most of its contemporaries. The line of the small back spokes moves into the seat

395

396

397

398

shape and that of the larger back spokes into the rear legs. Like the great English Queen Anne chair seen in figure 370, this chair sets thrusting lines against active curves; what had become a general, mass-produced form is here turned into visual excitement.

The maple and pine table (1825–40) in figure **398** uses exaggeration in juxtaposing a freewheeling top and a tightly organized base, uniting them with slashing red on yellow paint. That this was a carefully controlled device is demonstrated by the care taken to enclose the drawer in ebony-color cock beading applied to the case; the knob is also painted black. This piece, in a vernacular form, has the directness and precision of the card table in figure 377. Tables with a similar bold presence are depicted in paintings by Joseph H. Davis (active c. 1832–c. 1838).

The interpretations of Hadley chests were discussed in Chapter 6, where it was evident that of the many variants of the group represented, figures 232 and **399** embody a more original expression. Like the painted graining on figure 398, their decoration was abstracted, pushing further than precedents suggested. Unlike related English work, the entire front of the chests was covered with template-drawn designs. When there was not room for the total design, no subtle adjustment of size, shape, or placement was made; rather, the segment of the template that did not fit was simply eliminated. On the rails of the oak and pine chest made about 1700, the end leaves are not complete; on the top rail, the end leaves do almost coincide with the leaves on the corner post, but this does not occur below. The all-over repetition produced a textilelike pattern, and the paint established broad units of design: red on the rails and panels; black on the stiles, muntins, and drawer. No English piece so fully covers its surface in repeated pattern, and possibly none used paint to relieve an otherwise overly similar carved surface.

The four New England pieces of furniture in figures 400 through 405 are again unlike English work, in part because of the availability of pine boards. The chest over drawers (1700–25) in figures **400–401** is made of hard pine with oak feet and was painted black. Rural chests of drawers were rare in England during this period; when known, they tend to be of framed construction. As the availability of wide boards in America encouraged a new popularity for the six-board chest over the framed expression, it also encouraged simple, board, vernacular chests of drawers, or, as here, a chest over drawers made to look like the fashionable form. The slender proportions of the piece in figure 400 produce an elegant stance. Its turned

399

400

401

402

feet (one seen as figure 401) show the best of American line: there is a sharp, angled break between the massive ball form and the reel shape; above the reel, a straight fillet moves to a flattened ring. This foot joins basic units in the turner's vocabulary to produce a basic baluster form. The New England maple foot of about the same date, figure **402**, employs the same vocabulary but makes a different statement by flattening the ball, accenting its horizontality with an incised groove.

The New England pine chest over drawers (1700–35) in figure **403** raises the form on high, strongly shaped bracket feet, which are partly formed by the extension of the sides. The front is made to look as though there are four drawers, although brasses were not added to the chest section as on figure 400. The exterior, painted blue-gray, meets local fashion, while the interior spaces answer local needs.

The eighteenth-century pine chest over drawer, figure **404**, was constructed with wooden pegs augmented by a few large-headed, handmade

403

404

nails. The surface has an original red-brown paint. While not an extraordinary American piece, it is a form not found in England, where framed chests, once introduced, remained common. Its untouched surface and varying horizontal front members play against the shaped sides to produce a quiet, nicely composed practical object.

The early eighteenth-century cupboard, figure 405, was found in the area of Rehoboth, Massachusetts. It is a useful piece, of local pine painted red (later a coat of green covered the outside and the front edges of the upper shelves). The form was made exciting by incorporating fielded panels and by returning the slant of the upper section with a strongly raking cornice. The front boards on either side of the doors are one piece of wood, even though they angle back for the upper section. The angle change was accomplished by cutting a wedge across the rear of the board and then bending it to the present shape (much like the bending of the ankles of the table in figure 393).

405

Conclusion

American furniture paralleled European, especially British, models until the late nineteenth century, when styles became less dependent on a particular center and more international in scope. Seventeenth-century American furniture was usually similar in construction, form, enrichment, and date to *rural* English furniture (figures 8, 9, 230, and 237). On occasion, London styling did directly affect American urban designs (figures 467 through 475), but normally London's influence flowed first to rural Britain and from there to the colonies. An exception to Britain's dominance during the seventeenth century was the prevalence of Dutch designs in New York. In the eighteenth century there was an increasing correspondence between the furniture made in American urban centers and that made for British clients in similar economic, social, and cultural situations.

Rarely did American designer-craftsmen *consciously* step outside European precedents, although their sources may have been second, third, or fourth hand. There were a few notable exceptions, such as the Newport school, when craftsmen with forethought created successful original designs (figures 380 and 381). But usually the discernible differences between American and European examples stemmed *not* from choice but from the natural changes that resulted from the interjection of time, distance, new materials, and the imposition of a personal taste on a generally available design. What emerged was an American aesthetic that depends primarily on the movement of a dominant line. And this line was surprisingly consistent across diverse regions and style periods within each type of furniture: urban high style, rural high style, urban vernacular, and rural vernacular.

Urban High Style

During the third quarter of this century there was a drive to establish the variations between American regional groups. While it was shown that each center produced significantly different expressions, it is now evident that these had more commonality than dissimilarity. That is, the furniture of all American high-style centers *and* English high-style furniture has more in common than any one group has with continental high-style or English court work. For instance, the English, New England, New York, and Pennsylvania highboys seen in figures 540 through 553 are more alike than any is to the court expression seen in figure 357 or related continental forms.

When aesthetically important urban high-style furniture was made in America, the basic line always controlled the design. These pieces often lacked applied ornamentation, and when complex American forms achieved world significance—for example, in the best block-and-shell furniture (figures 3 and 381)—bold, balanced, well-drawn lines underlay their greatness.

Britain's furniture that relates closely to American work was rarely by her better craftsmen and it lacks a free line, as though conscious of being inferior to England's elaborate, more aristocratic court work. Those often superb objects usually relied on rich details and embellishments, which frequently dissolved the basic forms beneath to become the principal shapes (figures 361 and 362). Successful American furniture, even when ornamented, allowed basic line to dominate. When, as on a few urban high-style pieces, richness became assertive, the results were rarely successful. A set of Philadelphia Chippendale-style chairs made for the Lambert family[1] uses a conventional form similar to that in figure 878, and lathers it with rococo leafage and shells. The unfortunate result is confusion rather than elegance.

Rural High Style

While Europe remained the primary source for urban high-style work, rural high-style pieces looked both to American centers and to European furniture for inspiration. The parallel between the English and Connecticut tables in figures 19 and 20 readily demonstrates the influence of English provincial furniture. The Connecticut chairs in figures 853 and 907 exemplify the influences American urban centers could engender in rural forms. The chairs were probably made by Eliphalet Chapin (1741–1807), who returned to East Windsor in 1771 after working about four years in Philadelphia. Although a survey of the body of his work makes clear that Chapin understood the components of Philadelphia styling, in figure 853 he used them only where they were least visible: ovoid-section rear legs, side rails through-tenoning the back posts, and the Philadelphia form of corner blocks (although he also added nails in the New England manner). For the more visible parts he employed a New England–New York four-C-shape splat; New England blunt and grooved ears; and a crest rail shell with all positive lobes (the Philadelphia form has flutes between the lobes). A shell related to the Chapin design is found on the famous New York Livingston family "cipher" chair.[2] The diverse sources of the elements of the chair are discernible, but their combination and the final visual stance were at the same time Chapin's and compatible with the aesthetic of its region. In the design, the back posts angle out to prominent ears; from these, the action moves in through the crest rail to whip down and around the C shapes. Such an active line on a developed form is not found in urban centers.

This Chapin chair has great quality of design, but a comparison with the less successful Chapin arm chair in figure 907 raises questions that are difficult to answer: to what degree is the success of the piece in figure 853 an accident, and how fragile is greatness, particularly when an artist works outside a supporting context? The splat of the arm chair lacks unity of form. The base is similar to New England, New York, and Philadelphia Gothic splats (figures 898, 900, and 980); the upper looped straps may be based on the movement of the upper straps on Massachusetts chairs, as seen in figure 850; the central X was probably inspired by Philadelphia's use of this device, which is borrowed from designs in Chippendale's *Director* (see figures 846 and 847; Chapin also introduced an X onto the plinths under the central finials of some case pieces). The central shell derives from Philadelphia forms; the blunt, creased ears and "fills" on the crest rail between the straps are from New England; and the forms of the rear legs, arm supports, front legs, and use of through tenons were inspired by Philadelphia practices. Again, the final statement is Chapin's, and although the result is not particularly successful, it suits Connecticut's artistic temperament.

In both Chapin chairs, the American and ultimate English sources are discernible. For many years American and English parallels for the serenely beautiful chair seen as figure 781 evaded me, and I had come to accept it as a rare instance of a great American innovation. Made in the Wethersfield area of Connecticut for Ezekiel Porter (1707–1775), it uses a Philadelphia form of seat (the front legs tenon through the seat frame, which has an applied rim, and the side rails through-tenon the back posts), and the slender parts of the back are unlike anything found in Philadelphia or Boston. Eventually I realized that its slender splat and surrounding parts were based on Queen Anne forms made about 1710 (see figures 782 through 786), whereas nearly all other

American solid splat forms are influenced by later George I and George II work (see figures 789 through 843). Now, grouped with English Queen Anne forms, this great chair takes its proper place in the general sequence of design. Recognizing the influence of the slender Queen Anne style also explained other chairs that seemed to stand without English precedents. There are a few Rhode Island chairs with similarly slender splats[3] and their visual relationship to the Ezekiel Porter chair is obvious. But associating the Connecticut and Rhode Island chairs remained uneasy, for although Newport did condition a group of Connecticut makers, any connection between these chairs was certainly tenuous. The recognition that these chair backs depend on early eighteenth-century English prototypes allowed the proper link between the American chairs to be found in England.

In establishing the full connection between American furniture and related British work, it is inevitable to ask whether there were instances when a maker-designer was free to create totally original pieces. In fact, no maker—whether American or British—was free of his training, the available vocabulary of shapes and forms, and the steadily evolving styling that surrounded him. New ideas in any country develop when a worker imposes his personal insights and abilities on the aesthetics and practices available to all those with similar experience. Greatness can result if a craftsman has a superior eye. Although the Ezekiel Porter chair is ultimately English in inspiration, and reflects both the sources available and the approach of the area in which it was made, the manner of its stance results from the maker's personal handling of forms.

A finely tuned understanding of Connecticut's work allows Chapin's furniture and the Ezekiel Porter chair to fit both within the Anglo-American design sequence and within their region's particular artistic sensibility. While Connecticut's design expression is unique, it has much in common with other high-style rural work—American and English.

In America, there is a clear difference between urban and rural high-style designs; but in England, the distinctions between these categories are less obvious. The objects made in the north by the Gillows firm (figures 566 and 567), and such pieces as the chair made in Norwich by Samuel Sharp (figure 5), are not significantly different from London forms made for equivalent economic and artistic settings. Undoubtedly this is because London dominated England. In America, a similar dominance existed before 1790 between the culturally more powerful Philadelphia and nearby Maryland. Although differences between the furniture of these two American regions are discernible, the similarities are more apparent. Within Britain, only the Dublin makers contributed radical, personal high-style statements, particularly when executing rich designs.

It remains a question whether in America the distance a rural high-style worker was from a major cultural center conditioned the degree of individual expression. The Chapin chairs were made in the center of Connecticut and have an obviously exuberant line that would not have been accepted in urban work. On the other hand, the highboy made near Boston, in Concord, Massachusetts (figure 395), shows equal originality, while being more contained and tightly composed, seemingly echoing an attitude found in blocked chest-on-chests made in the Boston area. Does this reflect conditioning of the maker by nearby urban forces, or simply the maker's personal design sense? Indeed, can the two be separated?

Urban Vernacular and Rural Vernacular

Vernacular forms also simultaneously reveal the attitudes of their sources and the region in which they were made. The chairs seen in figures 389 and 390 have behind them New England, English, and perhaps German sources,[4] but they are unmistakably Philadelphia expressions of the highest quality. It is tempting to ask whether their maker could also achieve greatness in high-style forms, but it should be realized that such questions carry the danger of elitism if they imply that greatness in the high-style mode must outrank all vernacular expressions. It is, however, interesting to speculate whether a maker who has an "eye" for vernacular greatness is able to succeed with high-style forms. Cabinetmakers like William

Savery of Philadelphia produced both vernacular and high-style furniture. His vernacular expressions fall short of the quality found in figures 389 and 390, and his high-style chairs, mostly of the "plain chair" variety, show a similar mundane adeptness, below the best Philadelphia standard. (The two labeled Savery arm chairs in the Winterthur Museum are cases in point. One is seen as figure 1009.)[5]

On the other hand, the painter William Matthew Prior (1806–1873), who advertised a variety of expressions, created his finest works in the vernacular mode. Undoubtedly he thought his academic paintings to be more important achievements than his "flat" paintings: the former, costing $25 to $35 with a gilt frame, were his most expensive works, and the purchasers must have agreed with his ranking. As an alternative, Prior announced that "Persons wishing for a flat picture can have a likeness without shade or shadow at one quarter price." One of the finest pictures was priced under $3. It is inscribed on the back board of the frame: "PORTRAITS PAINTED IN THIS STYLE! Done in about an hour's sitting. Price $2,92, including Frame, Glass, &c. . . ."[6] Although they run contrary to most accepted art historical tenets, which imply that it is preferable to aspire to the more developed expressions, some of the "flat" Prior paintings, rather than his academic work, are now seen as major American statements.

The impetus for this study was to find in Europe everything thought to be personal to American furniture, so that I might distill and clarify what was new in American designs. Over the years, as the list of "unique" American practices diminished, it seemed likely that the result would sweep away any American originality. Only by forcing the emergence of the text—and particularly the last chapter and this Conclusion—have I been able clearly to perceive both the dependence and the independence of American furniture. While the features of an American-made piece are not unique to America or perhaps a particular region, the final combination, the visual taste of a piece, is in fact particular to both the maker and, usually, the region in which it was made, and thus to America.

Perhaps the hardest factor in the process of understanding these pieces has been to achieve sufficient detachment from the layers of past attitudes about American art and American originality in general; to set the objects in relief from previous personally and generally accepted opinions. This was necessary not because of any irreverence for the labor and concern lavished upon American-made objects by generations of scholars, for that is always the foundation of further study. Rather, it seemed vital to accomplish a de-mythologizing, which could then allow fresh insights to wash over the central issue—the nature of originality. But, to do this, it is first necessary to know everything that is ordinary about a piece: sources, local artistic attitudes, training and skill of the maker, shop practices, and the purchaser's requirements. Only then can a true perception of any object's unique quality be attained.

Visual Survey of British & American Furniture

NOTE THAT PIECES CITED AS "BRITAIN" ARE PROBABLY ENGLISH BUT MAY BE FROM IRELAND, WALES, OR SCOTLAND. WOODS ARE INCLUDED WHEN THEY ARE KNOWN; SECONDARY WOODS FOLLOW PRIMARY WOODS, IN PARENTHESES. SALIENT FEATURES ARE MENTIONED ONLY WHEN THEY ARE DFFICULT TO DISCERN IN THE PHOTOGRAPH.

406

407

408

Boxes

406 / 1650–1700; England; oak; old but not original brown paint outside and green inside. (Lock not original.)

407 / 1670–1710; Massachusetts, probably Essex County; oak, pine. Possibly by Thomas Dennis or William Searle.

408 / 1650–1700; England; oak.

409 / 1650–1700; Essex County, Massachusetts, possibly Ipswich; white pine. Sides with channel molding like linen-fold. Similar lunettes and leafage appear on the Massachusetts chair in figure 658.

409

410

411

412

413

414

415

Chests

410 / Medieval?; Britain; oak. Log furniture paralleled in date more sophisticated forms (see discussion under figures 31 and 32), and heavy iron-bound, well-locked chests maintained a role into the eighteenth century as secure storage units.

411 / Late fourteenth-century; England; oak; remains of polychrome decoration.[1] The front, of three horizontal and two vertical boards carved to panels; Gothic tracery on a diapered ground. Photograph inscribed: "Dresingham Church, Norfolk." (Part of the lid, and lock area, replaced.)

412, 413 / Sixteenth- or early seventeenth-century; England; oak: boards 1½" thick; remains of layers of paint including red, white, and blue. In addition to this piece, there are two similar chests at Castle Acre Priory; the three are of slightly different lengths.

414 / 1640–90; eastern Massachusetts; pine: boards 1½" and 1⅛" thick; old but not original red paint.

415 / Dated 1673; New England; front made of two boards. The top one formed to panels by stamped decoration. (The stamp decoration has in modern times been filled with chalk to make it more visible.)

416

417

418

419

420

421

416 / Sixteenth-century; Britain; oak. Linen-fold was made by decorating a long board with creasing planes, perhaps pulled by horses, and cutting it to panel length. The pattern was then smoothed off at the ends to make it appear as though each panel was decorated separately.[2]

417 / 1640–80; Connecticut, probably Guilford; white oak, painted red.

418 / Seventeenth-century; Britain; oak. The panel-construction front is pinned to board-construction sides. (Figures 419 and 440 use the same construction.)

419 / Dated 1685; New England, probably Portsmouth, New Hampshire; oak, pine; painted: vermilion, verdigris, and yellow ochre. As on the previous chest and figure 440, a panel-construction front was attached (here with nails) to board-construction sides. (The original depth of this piece is uncertain because the bottom has been reworked, the end boards have been pieced out, and at least the rear edge of the top is new.)

420 / Late sixteenth- or early seventeenth-century; London area; oak. (Top replaced.)

421 / Late sixteenth-century; England; oak, with painted religious scenes. Panels from an overmantel which, according to tradition, came from a cottage in Uckfield, Sussex.

422

423

424

425

426

427

422 / Early seventeenth-century; England, probably Hampshire; oak. Photograph inscribed: "Panel in God-begot House, Winchester [Hampshire]."

423 / 1640–80; Connecticut, possibly New Haven; white oak, white pine.

424 / Early seventeenth-century; England, probably Gloucester or Somerset; oak. Outer face of the foot of a bed. (This is from the foot rather than the head since the lower rail is channeled for the rope supports, which carry across from hole to hole only on the outer surface of the rails.) Long leaves appear on many pieces.

425 / 1600–50; southwest England. (The drawer level is not original.)

426 / Dated 1664; England. Top rail with dragons. Other areas with tulips, pomegranates, and leaves. (The lettering and the decoration inside the center arch are probably not original: the use of an asymmetrical pattern and the forms suggest a modern hand for the latter.)

427 / Mid-seventeenth-century; Yorkshire. Marquetry and lines of diagonally oriented light and dark inlay. Paneled top.

428

429

430

431

432

433

428 / Dated 1697; England; elm. A six-board chest carved and stamp-decorated to appear as paneled.

429 / Mid-seventeenth-century; Dorset or Somerset; oak. Shallow chest with lift-top over doors.

430 / Mid-seventeenth-century; England, probably Lancashire; oak.

431 / 1640–80; Connecticut, probably Guilford; oak, pine.

432 / Dated 1683; England, probably Cheshire or Lancashire; oak.

433 / About 1674—see similarly carved, dated wainscot chair, figure 273; England, probably Yorkshire or Lancashire. The drawer carving is enclosed in punch-work decoration. (At the extreme right this is on an applied strip, and strips mitred at the corners edge the drawers. All these strips are probably later.)

434

435

436

437

438

439

434 / Early seventeenth-century, with late seventeenth-century additions: foot and hood crestings, and ribbon and flower molding around the sides; England. (The bases of the rockers are later.)

435 / 1670–1710; probably New Haven, Connecticut, possibly Long Island;[3] oak, pine. Cleats serve as hinges.

436, 437 / 1650–1700; England, probably Lancashire; oak and pine. Initialed "SB." (Top replaced.)

438 / 1690–1720; Connecticut; pine and oak. Compass decoration. Similar serrated-edge roses are discussed in Chapter 6. (See figure 231.)

439 / Sixteenth-century; Italian. A wooden mold displaying compass designs that appeared at varying levels of sophistication in many European centers.

440

441

442

443

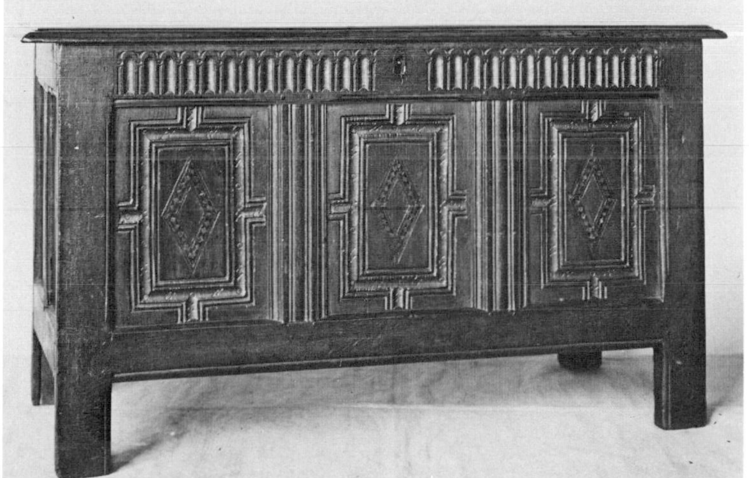

444

445

440 / Mid-seventeenth-century; England; oak. Frame-construction front, pinned to board sides. (Figures 418 and 419 are similarly made.)

441 / Dated 1714; Connecticut, possibly Wethersfield area; pine; red-brown paint. Initialed "SD." Stamped decoration simulating a framed and carved chest.

442, 443 / 1650–1700; Yorkshire; oak and inlay. Similar decoration appears on figures 277 through 281. The detail shows the laying-out lines. Similar lines are seen on figure 279.

444 / First half of the seventeenth century; England, possibly southwest; oak and inlay. Panels carved to appear as though they had inner-frame panels, as found on the Sizergh Castle paneling in figure 109.

445 / Mid-seventeenth-century; England; oak, possibly fruitwood inlay. Simulated inner-frame panels flank an inlaid panel. (The outer panels probably once have had applied edge moldings like those on the center panel.)

446

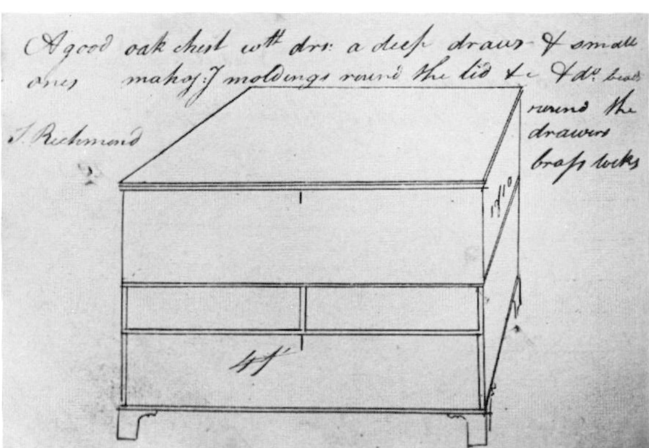

448

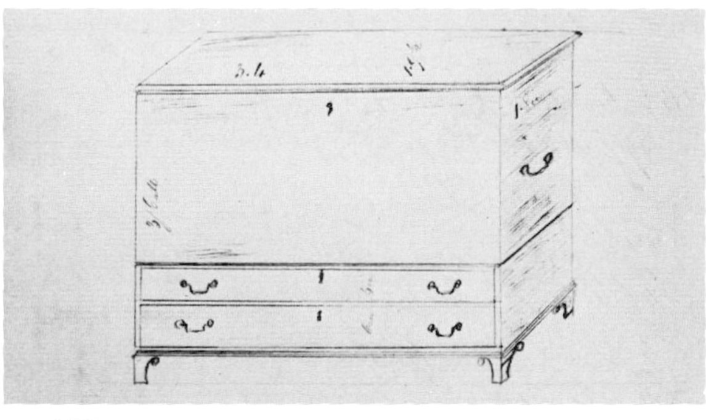

449

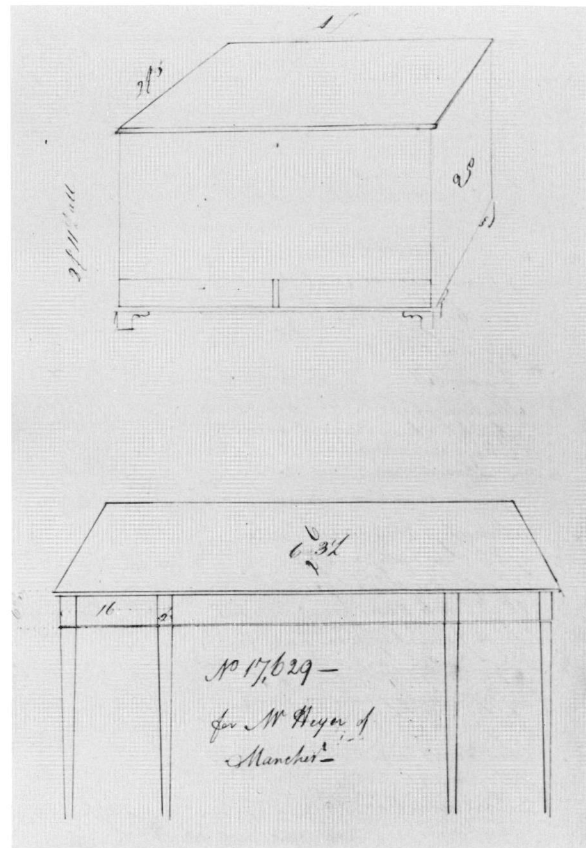

447

450

446 / 1650–90; England; similar turnings are discussed under figure 317. It has been customary to see the evolution of the chest of drawers, which appeared about 1640, as deriving from the gradual addition of more drawers under a chest until the case was entirely filled with drawers. Benno Forman has convincingly argued that such pieces as the chest of drawers with doors in figure 469 predate chests over drawers.[4] Such pieces as figure 446 are, therefore, vernacular responses to the full chest of drawers.

447 / Dated April, 1792. Ink drawing of "A Ceadar Cloathes Chest," page 845 of the Estimate Book of the Gillows firm, demonstrating the continuation of the chest as a popular form. It has post-Chippendale–style proportions. The accounting sheet lists cedar, deal, a chest lock and latch, two drawer locks, two strong lifting handles, and two common [drawer] handles. The maker was paid 14 shillings for executing it in fourteen days. The second drawing is of a square-tapered leg "mahogany Sideboard."

448 / Dated April, 1793. Ink drawing of "A good oak chest," page 962 of the Estimate Book of the Gillows firm. The oak chest was trimmed with mahogany moldings and had four brass lock escutcheons. The maker was paid 14 shillings for one week's work.

449 / Dated May, 1810. Ink drawing of a "Linnen Chest," page 1875 of the Estimate Book of the Gillows firm. Among the materials listed is "½ in[ch] American Oak." (See figure 1434, also listed as American oak.)

450 / 1740–70; Britain; oak. The lipped drawers suggest a date after 1720, the form of the brass pulls a mid-century date, the oval keyhole escutcheon a date after 1765. Late eighteenth-century oak chests were common; in 1770, when Thomas Chippendale was moving from rococo styling to neo-classical forms, his second cousin, William Chippendale, was making a simple six board oak chest with dovetailed corners on a simple bracket base for £1 11s. 6d. in Thomas's home county of Yorkshire. The only applied decorations were three oval lock escutcheons.[5]

451

452

453

454

456

455

451 / 1730–60; Britain; oak. The lock escutcheons are original. The pulls were once of a similar size and form.

452 / 1740–60; Britain, possibly Ireland.

453 / 1740–90; Ireland. The chest section with drawers sits within the top molding of the stand.

454 / 1740–80; Ireland. The chest section sits within a molding on the frame.

455 / 1750–90; Britain, probably Ireland. That the cupboard section does not sit within a retaining molding suggests this is a "married" piece. The base has features found on furniture made in the Philadelphia area: C-scroll legs, and a shaped and scrolled skirt with an applied central shell of scallop form.

456 / 1750–90; detail of a Philadelphia, Pennsylvania, dressing table; mahogany.

457

458

459

460

461

Chests of Drawers; Knee-Hole Chests of Drawers; High Chests; Clothes-Presses

457 / Dated 1678; Ipswich, Massachusetts; red oak (poplar); old but not original paint (see note 69, Chapter 4); possibly by Thomas Dennis. Made for John and Margaret Staniford.

458 / 1660–1700; Britain; oak. Most early chests of drawers originally had feet formed by the extension of the stiles.

459, 460 / 1660–1700; Britain; back dated 1693 (date may not be original); oak. Made in two sections. (The molding under the top and the knobs are not original.)

462

463

464

465

461 / 1660–1700; England. (Later lock escutcheons and feet.)
462, 463 / 1660–1700; Britain. The view with the open drawers shows the sunk fillet for the rail that supports the drawers. The lining paper, in the drawers, is seen as figure 229. (The base molding has been lost.)
464 / 1660–1700; Britain. (The feet are new: they are of a later bracket form, and are of pine dovetailed at the corners.)
465 / 1660–1700; England. Made in two sections. Similar turnings are discussed under figure 317. (The top of the reels of the feet seem too wide for the feet to be original.)
466 / 1680–1710; New England; pine; cleaned of later red paint; traces of black paint on the moldings. The front is paneled in the same manner as the drawer fronts above: strips and moldings are applied to a board. Similar boxes were made in England.[6]

466

467

468

469

470

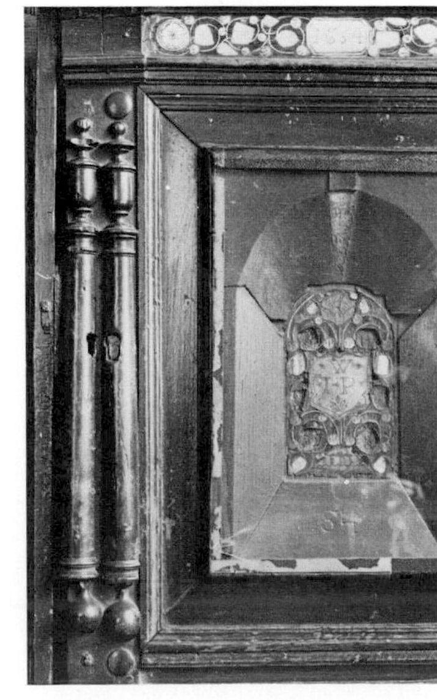

471

472

467 / 1650–70; Boston, Massachusetts; red and white oak, American black walnut, cedar, chestnut, lignum vitae. Made in two sections. The place of this eloquent piece within New England's stylistic development is discussed in the essay on paint, Chapter 4.

468 / 1650–70; England, probably London. Made in two sections. (The small, flat board between the base moldings and the feet suggests that the feet may not be original.)

469 / 1650–70; London, England. Made in two sections. The circular decoration on the center panel of the drawer was lathe-turned, like a treen plate, and separated into quadrants. (The feet are not original.)

470, 471, 472 / Dated 1654; London, England. Hanging cupboard, initialed "I W P" and stamped "S H."

473

474

475

476

477

473 / 1650–70; London, England. The base molding is missing.

474 / 1650–70; Boston, Massachusetts; American red cedar, black walnut, American red oak. (Lower section, probably containing at least one drawer, is missing.)

475 / 1650–70; London, England. Initialed "T E E."

476 / 1700–20; England. Single half-round molding on the case around the drawers, inspired by Chinese usage,[8] stylistically predates double half-round molding, as on figure 478. Lipped drawers, as on figure 477, stylistically follow the double half-round molding.

477 / 1715–35; Boston, Massachusetts; burl maple veneer, walnut, maple (pine). The use of lipped drawers and bail rather than teardrop brasses suggests a date after 1720. This is a rare form for America at this date. Many pieces that now have this form are highboy tops with later feet.

478

479

480

481

482

478 / 1715–35; New England, probably Massachusetts. Chest over two drawers. Patterned veneer is simulated by paint. The feet are an unusual form.

479 / 1700–25; New England, probably eastern Massachusetts; painted pine. Chest over three drawers. The rear feet are extensions of the sides, which are painted with wavy lines to simulate veneer grain. The front, with an early use of a stencil, gives the pattern of inlay as found on figure 480. (Hadley chests such as that in figure 232 had used a template in a similar manner.) The English inlaid pieces echoed the patterns on French furniture veneered with brass and tortoiseshell, as found on figures 481 and 324; the motif of foliated S shapes, however, was not new (see figure 583).

480 / 1700–20; London, England. The top is finished with veneer, suggesting this is a chest of drawers which has lost its feet rather than the upper case of a highboy.

481 / About 1700; Paris. Detail (turned sideways) of an armoire possibly by André-Charles Boulle (1642–1732); brass, tortoiseshell, black and brown ebony veneers on oak; gilt bronze mounts.

482 / 1715–30; England. Other bombé forms appear in figures 571, 572, and 630.

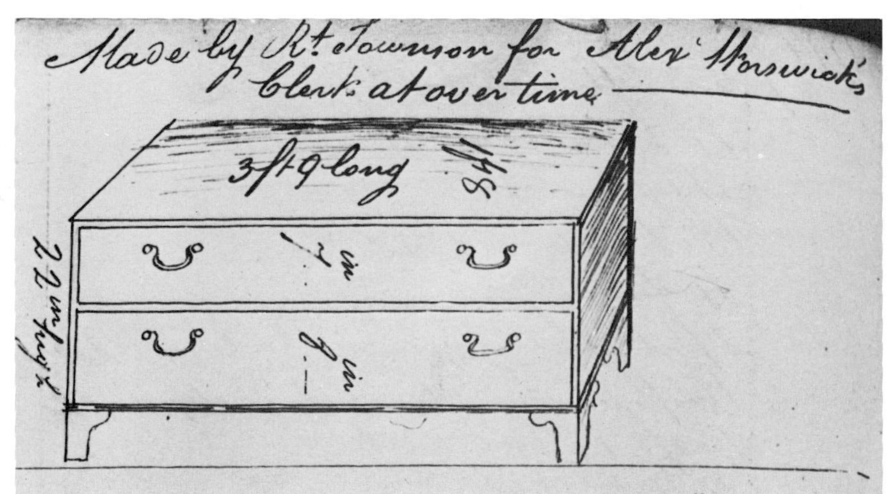

483

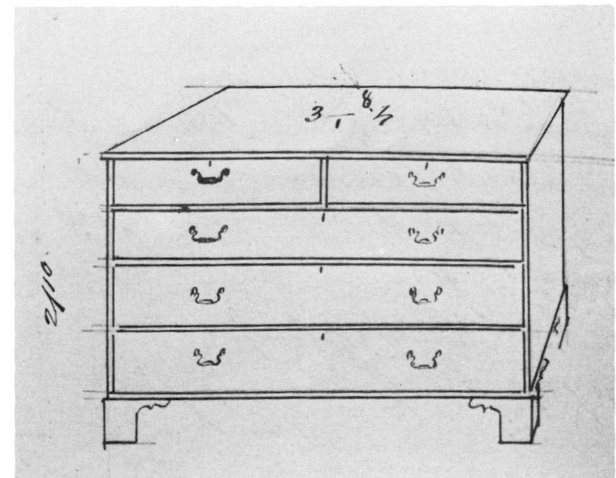

484

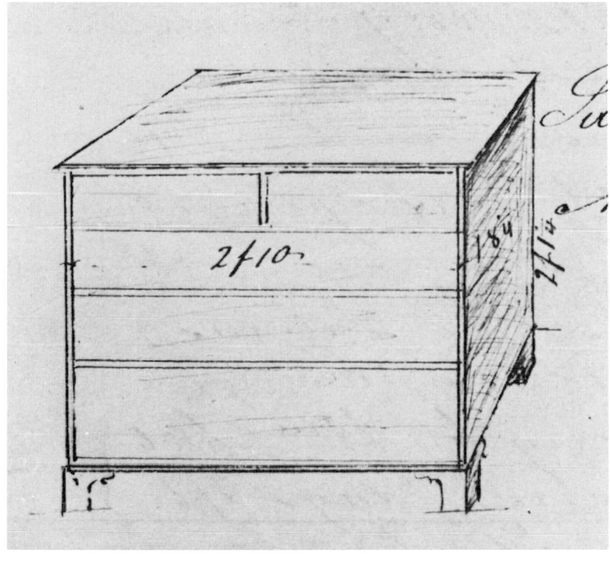

485

486

487

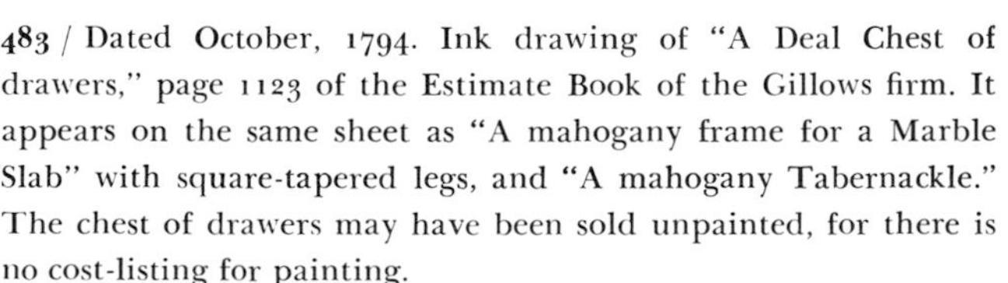
483 / Dated October, 1794. Ink drawing of "A Deal Chest of drawers," page 1123 of the Estimate Book of the Gillows firm. It appears on the same sheet as "A mahogany frame for a Marble Slab" with square-tapered legs, and "A mahogany Tabernackle." The chest of drawers may have been sold unpainted, for there is no cost-listing for painting.

484 / Dated May, 1793. Ink drawing of "A Solid oak chest of draws," page 973 of the Estimate Book of the Gillows firm. The secondary wood was deal. On the same sheet is a half-circle mahogany sideboard with square-tapered legs.

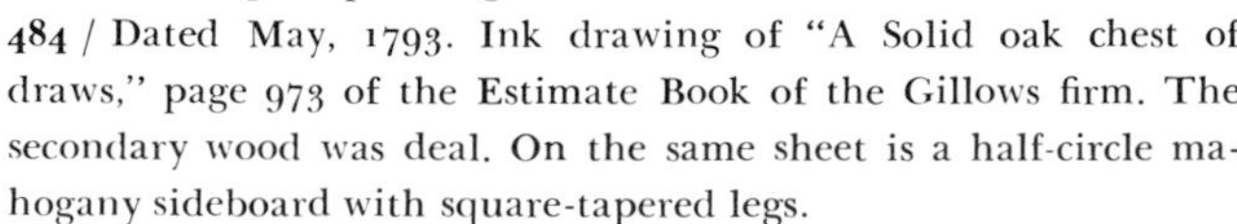
485 / Dated April, 1796. Ink drawing of "A Deal Dressing Chest," on page 1236 of the Estimate Book of the Gillows firm. It may have been sold unpainted. On the same sheet is "A mahogany moving Library," and "A mahogany Table Clock case."

486 / 1750–90; New England, probably Connecticut; cherry.

487 / 1750–80; Britain; mahogany.

488

489

490

491

492

488 / 1760–80; Britain; mahogany.
489 / 1760–90; Britain; mahogany.
490, 491 / 1770–1800; Britain; mahogany.
492 / 1770–1800; Britain; mahogany (cedar).

493

494

495

496

497

493 / 1760–95; Britain; oak (pine, oak). Full pine dust dividers between drawers. Brasses original.

494 / 1760–95; New England, possibly Rhode Island; maple (chestnut). Top tier is one long drawer formed to appear as three.

495, 496, 497 / 1785–1810; Britain.

498

500

502

499

501

498 / 1780–1800; Connecticut; cherry. The reverse-serpentine or oxbow form was not part of the standard British vocabulary of forms (see discussion under figure 329).

499 / 1789; Philadelphia, Pennsylvania; mahogany, gilded gesso (spruce, pine, cedar, tulip). Chest of drawers and stand made by Jonathan Gostelowe for his wife, Elizabeth (Powers) Gostelowe, in 1789.

500 / 1770–90; Britain; mahogany.

501 / 1770–1800; Britain.

502 / 1780–1800; Britain; mahogany.

503

504

505

506

507

503 / 1760–80; considered probably Irish by the National Museum of Ireland.

504, 505 / 1780–1810; Britain.

506 / 1785–1810; Britain.

507 / 1785–1810; Charleston, South Carolina; mahogany (pine, cedar).

508

509

510

511

512

508, 509, 510, 511, 512 / 1785–1810; Britain; mahogany.

513

514

515

516

517

513, 514, 515, 516 / 1785–1810; Britain; mahogany.
517 / 1790–1810; New England, possibly New Hampshire; mahogany and a lightwood veneer, possibly birch.

518

519

520

521

522

518, 519, 520 / 1790–1810; Britain; mahogany.
521 / 1790–1810; Southern, probably Norfolk, Virginia; mahogany, mahogany veneer, lightwood stringing (poplar, yellow pine).
522 / 1790–1810; Britain, mahogany.

523

524

525

526

527

523 / 1790–1810; Britain; mahogany.

524 / 1790–1815; Britain; mahogany.

525 / 1800–15; Salem, Massachusetts; mahogany (white pine). The corner posts and legs are similar to those on the sideboard William Hook made for his sister, Hannah, in 1808/9.[9]

526, 527 / 1785–1810; Britain. A related chest, but with a straight front and four drawers, was made by the Gillows firm in December, 1789 (Estimate Book, p. 554).

528

529

530

531

532

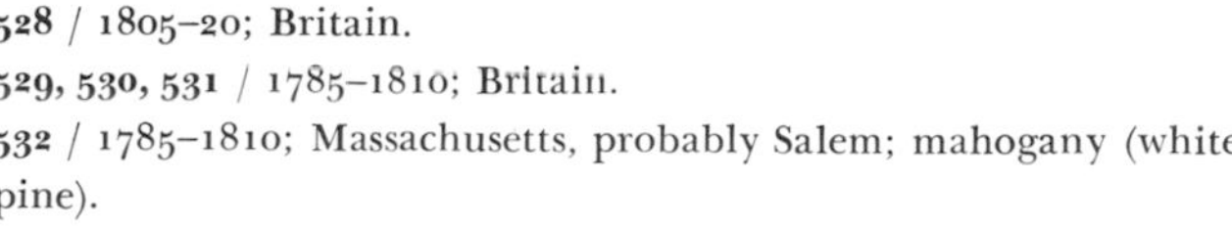

528 / 1805–20; Britain.
529, 530, 531 / 1785–1810; Britain.
532 / 1785–1810; Massachusetts, probably Salem; mahogany (white pine).

533

534

535

536

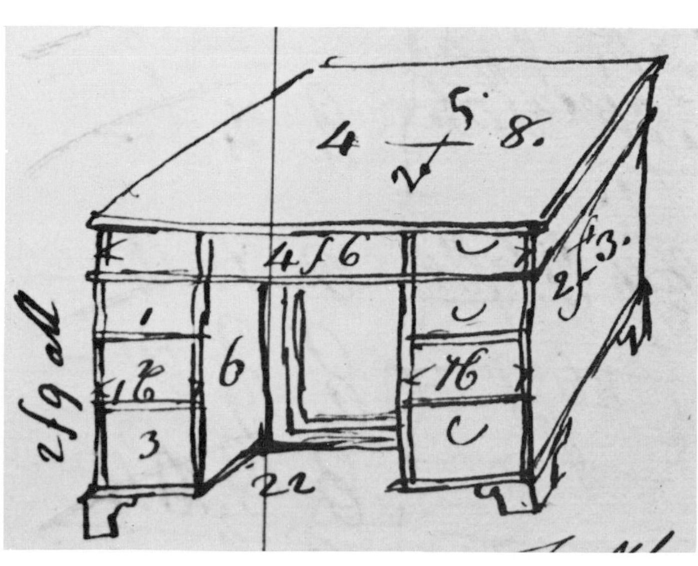

537

533 / Dated May, 1794. Ink drawing of "A mahogany Knee hole Chest of drawers," page 1087 of the Estimate Book of the Gillows firm.

534 / 1750–90; Philadelphia, Pennsylvania; mahogany (pine, tulip). (The inner front feet are restored: evidence that they were once present appeared on the bottom board.) Chippendale's 1754 and 1755 *Director* shows designs for "Buroe Tables," also referring to the form as "A Bureau Dressing-Table."[10] Two of the designs, plate XLI, were in a simple rectilinear style with straight bracket feet (four across the front).

535 / 1760–85; Britain. The top "drawer" opens to form a writing surface, as in figure 536.

536 / 1760–90; Newport, Rhode Island; mahogany.

537 / Dated May, 1789. Ink drawing of "A Buroe Writ[in]g Table," page 344 of the Estimate Book of the Gillows firm.

538

539

540

541

538 / 1680–1700; England; walnut, marquetry of walnut and various woods (pine carcass, oak). A Connecticut piece simulating marquetry appears as figure 168. During this style period developed English pieces have cross-banded half-round moldings. (The condition report states: "The legs restored, the stretchers original.")

539 / 1690–1720; Britain. The deep drawer, serving like a chest, may have precluded higher legs, or, as in figure 548, they may be lost.

540 / 1700–25; New York, New York; walnut, veneers of walnut and burl: probably ash (American yellow pine of the taeda group, North American white pine).

541 / 1690–1715; England; walnut.

542

543

544

545

542 / 1690–1715; England.
543 / 1700–20; New England; walnut (pine, oak).
544 / 1695–1720; England; walnut, walnut veneer. Inverted shallow cups forming leg turnings were not an American practice.
545 / 1700–20; New England; painted pine and maple. Slender cup turning is rare in British and American work.

546

547

548

549

546 / 1710–35; Boston, Massachusetts, or New York, New York;[11] burl and walnut veneer, walnut, maple, tiger maple (chestnut). Legs painted or stained dark. Tiger maple stretchers. The pulvinated frieze faces a thin drawer.

547 / 1690–1715; England. The central part of the front stretcher does not repeat the shape of the skirt above, although all the other stretchers do. The drawers in the stand have a space between them as found on Philadelphia area pieces (see figure 553). In other American regions these drawers normally touch (see figure 546).

548 / 1695–1720; England. The label on the photograph says: "Veneered with walnut and inlaid with narrow strips of sycamore and rosewood on the faces of the drawers." (The drops, legs, and stretchers, and probably the cock beading of the skirt, are missing.)

549 / 1695–1720; Britain; oak. (Rear stretcher missing.)

550

551

552

553

550 / 1690–1720; Britain; oak. (The fill between the upper cupboard and the retaining molding on the top of the stand suggests that the glazed case is not original to the stand.) A similar form of cup turning on the legs appears on the Connecticut piece in figure 168. Cross stretchers are common in America on dressing tables, as on figure 545, with a related finial.

551 / 1695–1720; Britain. The use of a shaped rear stretcher is rare in Britain and America. It appears on an eastern Massachusetts highboy.[12] (The lower case seems reworked: there is no skirt below the side drawers; the cross-banded edges on the sides of the upper case do not appear on the sides of the lower case.)

552 / 1695–1720; Britain.

553 / 1700–25; Pennsylvania; butternut (white cedar). In Pennsylvania, the drawers of the stand are spaced as though the center legs continued up between them, and each drawer has two brass pulls. In more northern regions, there is no space between the drawers and usually each side drawer has only one pull (figure 546). The line of the half-round molding below the side drawers of the stand runs to the corners and turns to continue along the sides. Similar detailing appears on some Pennsylvania desks and English case pieces (see figure 603), as though the top part still lifted off as a desk box.

554

555

556

557

554 / 1720–50; Britain; oak. The cupboard is of a finer quality oak than the stand, and may have been added later. The exaggerated swing of the top of the square-section cabriole legs is found on some American pieces (figure 396).

555 / 1720–50; Britain. Turned bosses were used instead of knee brackets.

556, 557 /1725–50; Britain.

558

559

560

561

558 / 1750–1800; Britain; oak. Skirt with a central pendant shell. Legs with shell-carved knees and trifid feet.

559 / 1750–1800; Britain; oak. Detachable legs (see detail in figure 353). (Skirt carving probably not original.)

560 / 1750–90; Ireland.

561 / 1750–90; Ireland. This form, which relates to Philadelphia highboys, was also made with engaged fluted quarter columns.[13] An English highboy with claw and ball feet appears as figure 315.

562

563

564

565

562 / 1750–85; Britain; mahogany. Lipped drawers suggest a date before 1780.
563 / 1750–85; Britain; mahogany. Chamfered and fluted upper case with "lamb's tongue" terminals at base.
564 / 1765–80; England.

565 / 1770–1810; Britain. The late date is suggested by the form of the brasses and the similarity to the pieces shown in the Gillows drawings that follow. They are dated 1786, 1792, and 1792. A similar chest-on-chest appears as figure 27.

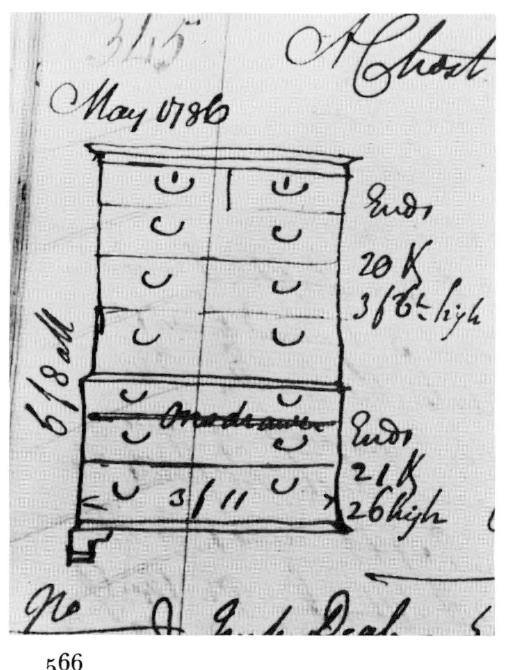

566

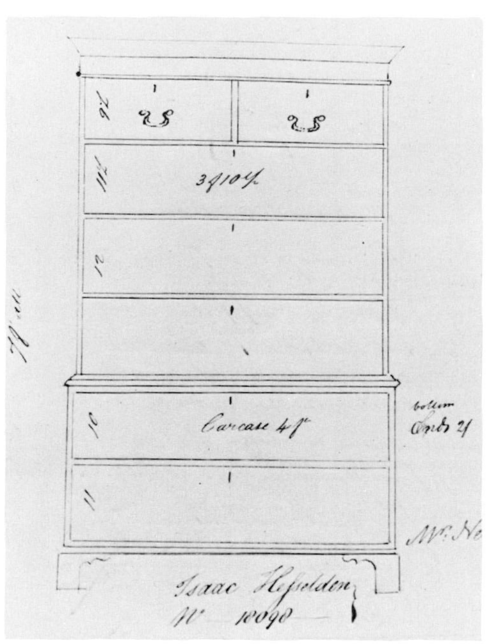

567

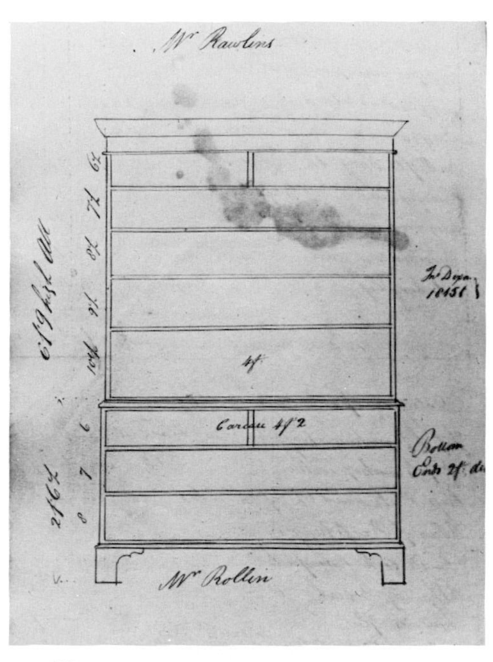

568

569

570

566 / Dated May, 1786. Ink drawing of "A Chest on D° [ditto]," page 345 of the Estimate Book of the Gillows firm. The front was veneered on mahogany; the ends were solid mahogany; the secondary woods were oak and deal. The sketch indicates that the top and second tier in the lower case opened as one deep drawer.

567 / Dated August, 1792. Ink drawing of "A Chest upon Chest," page 884 of the Estimate Book of the Gillows firm. The front was mahogany; the ends bay wood; secondary woods were deal and oak. There was a "plain frieze & Tuscan Cornice, a Desk drawer wth prospect door." The desk area was fitted with various-sized drawers.

568 / Dated August, 1792. Ink drawing of "A mahogany Chest upon d° [ditto]," page 894 of the Estimate Book of the Gillows firm. The front was mahogany veneer on bay wood; the ends bay wood; the frieze was veneered deal; and the cornice inch-thick mahogany and deal.

569 / 1780–1810; Britain; mahogany.

570 / 1790–1810; Britain; mahogany.

571[1]

572[2]

573

574

571 / 1740–50; Netherlands. The ends of the drawers follow the shape of the case. Other bombé pieces are listed under figure 482.

572 / 1745–60; England; mahogany (oak, deal). According to tradition, this clothes-press was once owned by Charles Apthorp (1698–1758) in Boston, Massachusetts. In his 1759 estate inventory, the "Great Parlour" contained "a Mohogony Beauro with Glass doors . . . £32: 0: 0," and in the "Dining Room up Stairs" there was a "a Mohogony Cabinet with glass doors . . . £30: 0: 0."[14] Either may be referring to this piece, although the "Cabinet" seems more likely. Other bombé pieces are listed under figure 482.

573 / 1750–80; England; mahogany (pine). This illustration is included despite its poor quality because it is close to Philadelphia work in using a pendent shell and Marlborough legs and feet.

574 / 1760–85; Britain.

575

576

577

578

579

580

Cupboards

575, 576 / Dated 1679; Massachusetts, probably Ipswich; white oak, red oak, white pine. Initialed "T H," which may stand for a member of the Hart family of Lynnfield, Massachusetts. Interior shows drawer pulls made of iron curtain rings.

577, 578, 579 / 1660–1700; Britain; oak. Back with "rose-headed" nails, top and drawers with sprig (wirelike) nails (shown in figure 579). Drawers with pulls made of iron curtain rings.

580 / Dated 1639; Britain; oak. Initialed "D M C."

581

582

583

581 / Late sixteenth- or early seventeenth-century; England; oak.

582 / Early seventeenth-century; England; oak.

583 / Mid-seventeenth-century; England, possibly Yorkshire; oak and inlaid woods.

584, 585 / 1650–1700; Britain; oak; circular and strip inlay of alternating colors. (Some rebuilding, particularly to the ends.)

584

585

586

587

588

589

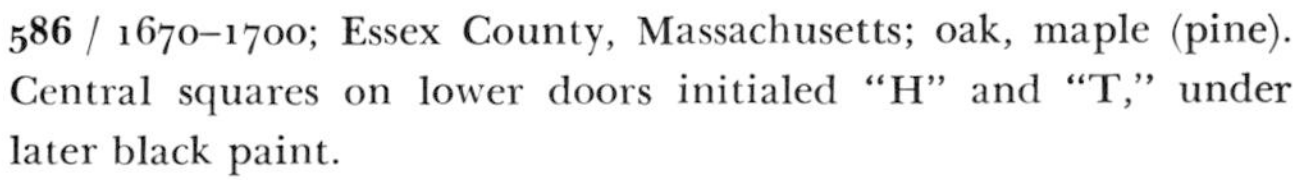

586 / 1670–1700; Essex County, Massachusetts; oak, maple (pine). Central squares on lower doors initialed "H" and "T," under later black paint.

587 / 1660–90; England; oak.

588 / 1700–20; northern England; oak. Fielded panels and pulvinated frieze suggest an early eighteenth-century date.

589 / 1700–35; Hampton area of New Hampshire; tiger maple and pine. Top inscribed: "Sarah Rowell," drawer inscribed: "S.R." The combination of the "tiger" stripe and black squiggly lines effects the motion of contemporary patterned veneers on this board-construction cupboard. The seventeenth-century form has narrowed and scales to William and Mary proportions.

590 / 1690–1720; England; oak.

590

591

592

593

594

591 / 1690–1720; England. Stop fluting divides and flanks the upper doors. The overall design is vertical in emphasis, reflecting early eighteenth-century taste. (Base molding and feet not original.)

592 / Dated 1721; probably England, possibly Ireland. Initialed "R I" and "R J." Sides made with through chamfering. (The cornice is late nineteenth-century, and the feet are Elizabethan fragments that have been attached, perhaps when the cornice was added. Bottom front rail missing; bottom of sides reworked.)

593 / Dated 1733; Britain. The back of the photograph is inscribed "Height 5ft. Sunk inscription on frieze filled with red composition: E.D. 1733. NOVA PULCHRA. R. R. F. FECIT. (E D = E. Davis.)"

594 / 1740–90; Britain; oak. Small in size.

595

596

597

598

595 / Mid-eighteenth-century; Britain; oak and pine. (The projecting base is not original.)

596 / Eighteenth-century; Britain; oak. The pulls, if original, would place it after 1765.

597, 598 / 1785–1810; Britain; mahogany.

599

600

601

602

Desks

599 / 1690–1715; England.
600 / 1700–25; Britain; oak.
601 / 1700–20; Boston, Massachusetts; maple burl and walnut veneer, walnut (pine).
602 / 1700–20; England. Beautiful early brasses.
603 / 1705–25; England; walnut. Well-shaped bracket base.
604 / 1710–25; Britain.
605 / 1720–35; Britain; walnut, yew, and amboyna veneer (oak, pine).
606 / Early eighteenth-century; Britain. (Pulls replaced in a later style. Bracket feet seem too long to be original.)

603

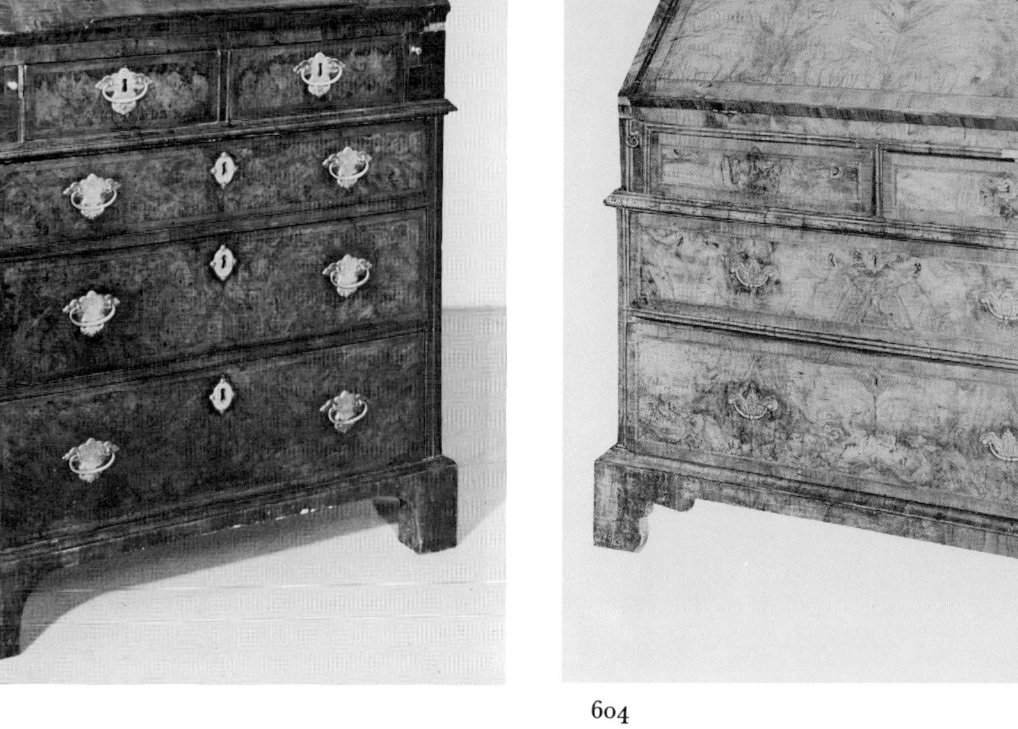

604

605

606

607

608

609

610

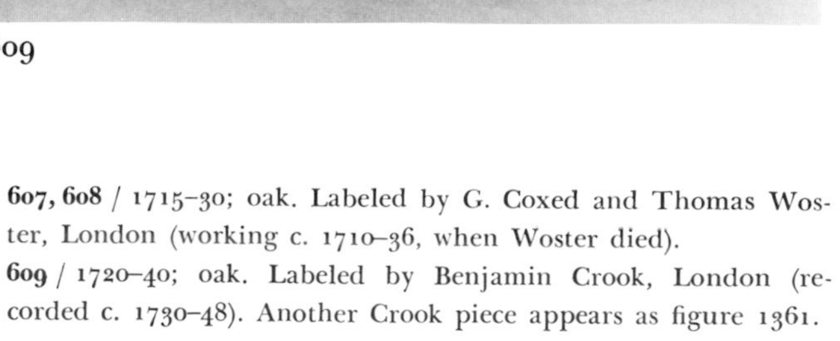

607, 608 / 1715–30; oak. Labeled by G. Coxed and Thomas Woster, London (working c. 1710–36, when Woster died).

609 / 1720–40; oak. Labeled by Benjamin Crook, London (recorded c. 1730–48). Another Crook piece appears as figure 1361.

610 / 1750–80; Britain; mahogany. The interior door is inlaid with a military figure. Back of photograph inscribed: "McIlhenny."

611

612

613

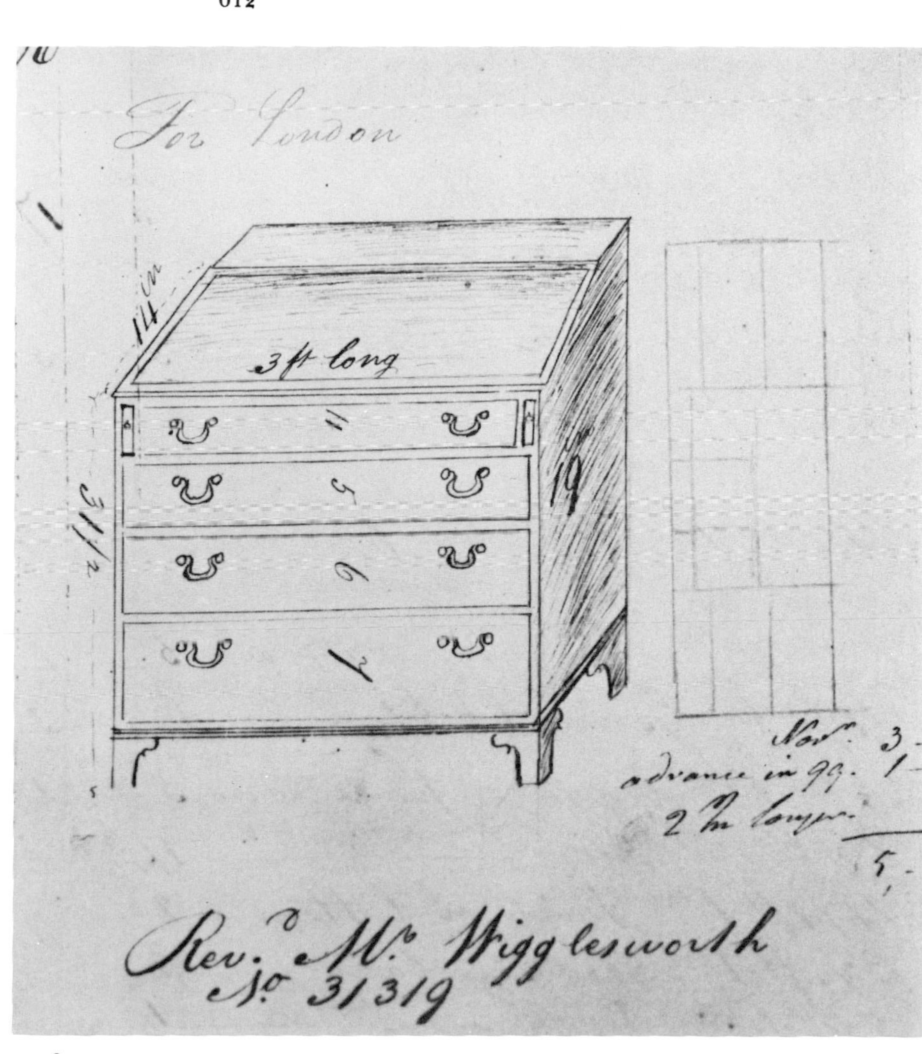

614

611 / 1750–80; Britain; mahogany.
612, 613 / 1760–85; Britain; mahogany.
614 / Dated July, 1794. Ink drawing of "A mahogany Desk," page 1106 of the Estimate Book of the Gillows firm. Oak and deal were secondary woods. The pigeon-hole divisions are shown at the right. "For London" above the drawing indicates it was made for the firm's London outlet. On the same sheet appears "A Satin wood work Table" made of satinwood veneer on oak, satinwood, and mahogany; oak was the secondary wood.

615

616

617

618

615 / 1750–1800; New England; maple (pine). According to tradition, it was owned by the Codman family of Camden, Maine.
616, 617 / 1750–1800; Britain; mahogany (oak, deal).
618 / 1750–1800; Britain; oak. The straight rear legs suggest a date after 1750. Although mixed in style, the brasses seem original, and the later-style pulls would place the date after 1765. Round turned feet are dated in the Gillows papers as late as 1793 (figure 1255).

619

620

621

622

619 / 1710–35; England; walnut, walnut veneer.
620 / 1720–40; probably Britain, possibly the continent; japanned.

621 / 1750–90; American, probably Pennsylvania; cherry (hard pine). Turned rear feet.
622 / 1740–80; Britain.

623

624

625

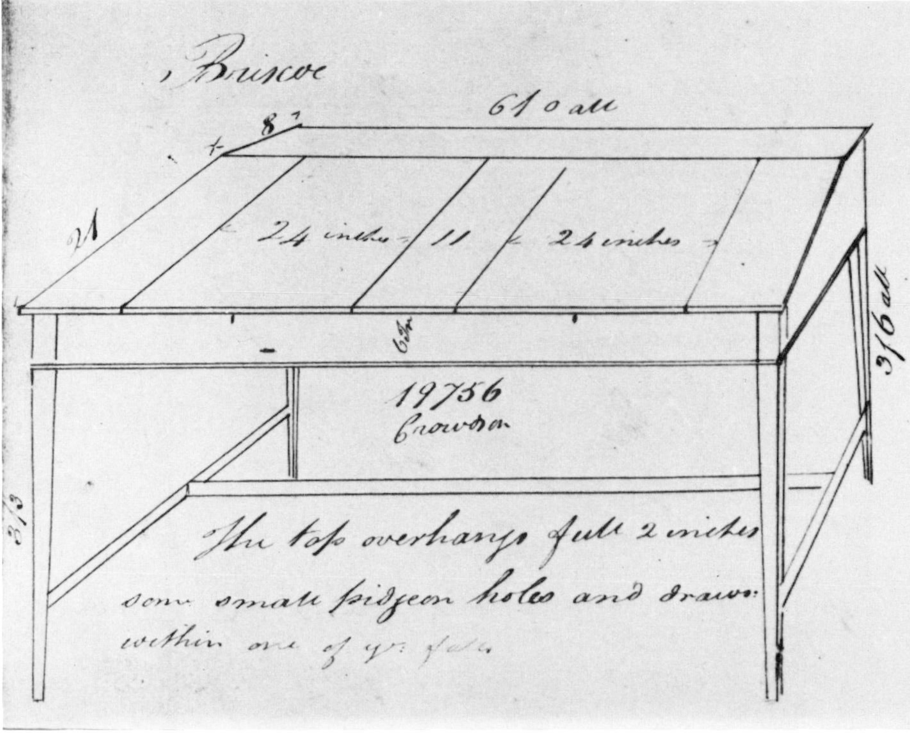

626

623, 624 / 1785–1810; Britain. A related American piece was probably made by John Shaw in Annapolis, Maryland, about 1797 for the Maryland Statehouse.[15]

625 / 1785–1810; Britain.

626 / 1793. (Although the page is undated, it appears between sheets dated June, 1793). Ink drawing of "An Accounting house desk," page 984 of the Estimate Book of the Gillows firm. It was made of mahogany and bay wood, with oak as the secondary wood.

627 / 1690–1710; England. (Veneer and cross banding enrich the entire front except the bracket feet, suggesting they are not original.)

628 / Dated 1707; Philadelphia, Pennsylvania; walnut (white cedar, white pine): Signed and dated by Edward Evans (1679–1754).

629 / Early eighteenth-century; Britain; oak.

630 / 1760–80; Britain. The ends of the drawers follow the curve of the case. Other bombé pieces are listed under figure 482.

627

628

629

630

631

632

633

634

631 / 1710–25; oak veneered with burl walnut and marquetry panels (oak). Signed "Samuel Bennett London fecit" (recorded working 1723, died 1741). Door inset with looking glass. (The leafage of the pediment rosettes should flow down and in.)

632 / 1720–30; England. Doors and pediment inset with looking glass.

633 / 1735–50; Massachusetts, probably Boston; walnut veneer and various inlays, walnut (pine, maple). The "star" inlay design in the pediment is found etched in the looking glass set in the pediment of figure 632. (Finials probably not original.)

634 / 1730–45; England.

635

636

637

638

635 / 1725–45; England; burl walnut veneer on oak (oak). Mirrored doors. (Gilt eagle restored.)

636 / 1750–1800; Connecticut; cherry, black birch (red gum, butternut, white pine, tulip). A Connecticut cherry bookcase on desk has a carved shell in a niche in the bottom drawer and base molding.[16]

637 / 1770–1800; Britain.

638 / 1760–95; Britain.

639

640

641

642

639 / 1750–80; Britain, possibly Ireland; mahogany. (Finial partly missing.)

640 / 1740–80; Ireland, possibly County Cork.[17] Vertical-grain veneer placed only on the pediment appears on various pieces associated with Ireland (see also figures 643 and 644). (Finial probably not original.)

641, 642 / 1740–80; Britain, possibly Ireland; walnut. (Finial missing.)

643

644

645

646

643 / 1740–70; Britain, probably Ireland; mahogany. (Finial and one cornice rosette missing.)

644 / 1740–70; Britain, probably Ireland; mahogany. (Finial surprisingly large.)

645 / 1740–70; Britain; mahogany. Bead on inner edge of feet and base molding.

646 / 1780–1810; Britain; mahogany.

647

648

649

650

Seating Furniture

CHAIRS

647 / Late sixteenth- or early seventeenth-century; southwest England; oak.

648 / 1640–1670; Connecticut; white oak. Long associated with Yale University,[18] the form of the columnar turned front posts and arms relates it to the preceding and following chairs. The seat rail shaping is found on such examples as figures 652, 655, 1206, and 1208. Fielded panels facing forward appear on a few British chairs and a possibly Connecticut chair, figure 228.

649 / Christchurch Mansion describes this oak chair as the "Ipswich Ducking Chair," and dates it 1579.

650 / Dated 1595; England; oak and various inlays. Vines and flowers inlaid in top rail, back posts, and top of arms. (Top of crest rail altered.)

651

652

653

654

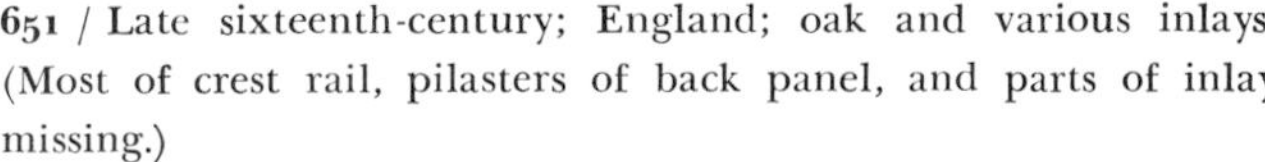

651 / Late sixteenth-century; England; oak and various inlays. (Most of crest rail, pilasters of back panel, and parts of inlay missing.)

652 / 1640–90; Yorkshire or East Anglia; oak and various inlays.

653 / 1640–90; East Anglia, probably Suffolk; oak and various inlays.

654 / 1650–1700; northern England; oak. Carved panel laid out with large compass strokes.

655

656

657

658

659

655, 656 / 1650–1700; England; oak. The interlaced lunettes, spandrel design, use of an arch, and shaping of the seat rail all suggest the southwest, particularly Somerset and Gloucestershire. (Walnut finials and seat not original.)

657 / 1650–1700; probably Somerset or Gloucestershire; oak. Similar features are found on figure 286.

658 / 1670–1700; Essex County, probably Ipswich, Massachusetts; red and white oak. Square balusters do not result from lack of a lathe to turn them, but were part of the vocabulary of mannerist decoration, as found on the pilasters in figure 195 and the posts in figure 213. Related lunettes and leafage appear on the Massachusetts box in figure 409. (Front two boards of seat replaced; rear legs built up.)

659 / Seventeenth-century; England; oak. The flat crest, arch, cable carving, and leafage-filled lunettes suggest the West Country, particularly Gloucestershire.

660

661

662

663

664

665

660, 661, 662, 663, 664 / 1650–1720; England; oak. The proportions and turnings of some chairs of this type, such as those in figures 662 and 664, suggest the early eighteenth century. The pyramidal form of finial is found on chairs made in Lancashire and North Cheshire. Figure 661 was formerly at Cakwen Hall, Batley, West Yorkshire. The cresting of figure 664 is related to that on the North Netherlands chair, figure 669.

665 / 1700–35; Pennsylvania; walnut. The shape of the crest rail is like that on the preceding chair and the one from the North Netherlands in figure 669.

666

667

668

669

670

671

666 / 1680–1720; Lancashire; oak. (Top of back posts missing.)
667 / 1680–1720; Yorkshire; oak. The scroll terminals move like the outline of the lions on the North Netherlands chair, figure 669. The centers of the back rails have pointed oval faces, which are associated with the likeness of Charles I, although similar portraits appear in varying manners on the capitals of a Norman nave in the Midlands (figure 668). The small drops are related to turnings found on the following chairs.

668 / About 1088; capital, Blyth Church, Nottinghamshire.
669 / Mid-seventeenth-century; North Netherlands; rosewood and ebony. Based on Italian chairs.
670, 671 / 1680–1720; Yorkshire or Derbyshire; oak; original cushion on figure 670. The scrolling of the ears, turnings and arcading of the backs, and turning of the front posts all derive from North Netherlands chairs (figure 669).

672

673

674

675

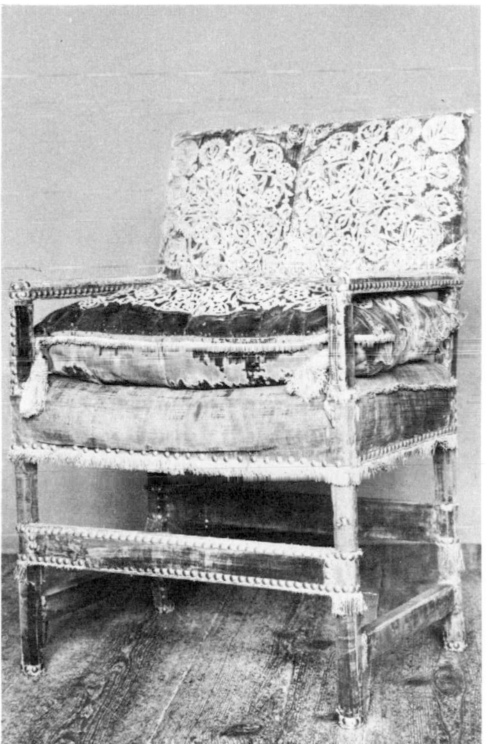

676

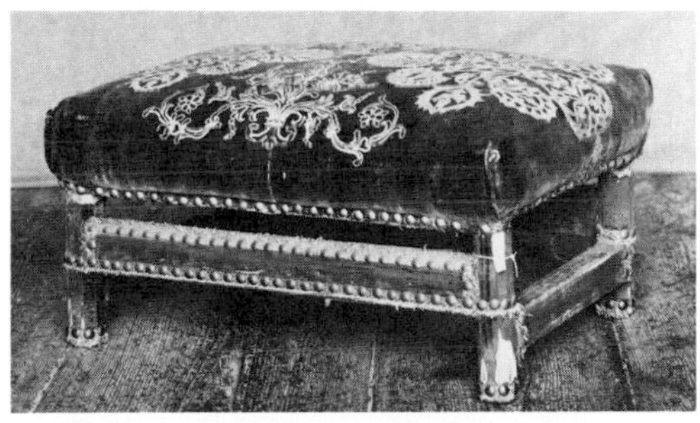

677

678

672 / 1680–1720; England, probably Yorkshire, possibly Derbyshire; oak.

673 / Dated 1724; Yorkshire; oak. (Front feet not original.)

674 / Dated 1633; England; probably chestnut. Stamped, scratched, inlaid, chip-carved, and turned decoration. (Seat replaced, arms shortened.)

675 / 1640–70; Boston, Massachusetts; soft maple, oak; original Russia leather. According to tradition, the chair descended in the Endicott family of Salem, Massachusetts. (The cushion is too densely filled and thus appears disproportionately large.)

676, 677, 678 / 1625–40; England. The arm chair, its foot stool, and one of the X-frame stools that flanked the chair are entirely covered with fabric (as figures 144 and 197). The textile is velvet (probably originally purple but now black) with an exotic material cut up and applied. Peter Thornton reports that it was probably Turkish embroidery executed in silver strip over what looks like leather or vellum.

679

680

681

682

683

684

679 / 1620–40; England; oak; original covering. Much of the applied strapwork on the blue wool ground is missing. There are the remains of blue and red fringe on the lower edge of the seat rails. The square padding of the seat has been pressed outwards.
680 / Mid-seventeenth-century; Italian; original upholstery. Similar chairs were made as far north as Norway.[19]
681 / 1640–80; Britain; oak; original leather. (Lower row of brass nails and much of the separate strip of leather that covered the sides of the seat rails missing.)
682 / 1650–90; Boston, Massachusetts; maple (oak); traces of red paint stain. Maple was used where it showed, and oak behind the upholstery. The present leather is new. It is certain that the chair was originally upholstered in leather, for pieces were found under the original tacks. The present leather was cut to knife marks made when the original leather was cut in place. Seventeenth-century brass-head nails (with square shafts) were placed in the square holes left by the original nails. The pattern of five nails at each front corner appears also on the pieces in figures 675, 683, 684, and 1175.
683 / Made in 1692 for Christ Church College, Oxford, by John Williams;[20] oak; original leather. The centers of the seats were pulled down nearly to the webbing to create a comfortable shape.
684 / 1690–1710; Britain; oak. The tall proportions reflect the late seventeenth-century sensibility. (Feet not original.)

685

686

687

688

689

685 / 1670–1700; Boston, Massachusetts; maple (oak); traces of paint; original turkeywork covering. Turkeywork—a woven fabric knotted on a loom in imitation of Turkish rugs—was produced in appropriate-size panels for chair backs and seats in England, probably Norwich. The panels were used in England, and exported to America and the continent, where frames were made to meet their dimensions.[21] Ball turning echoed more expensive spiral turning. (See figure 690, where the latter appears only on the back.)

686 / Mid-seventeenth-century; Italy; original upholstery: applied floral work on velvet.

687 / Dated 1649; England. From Leyburn, Wensleydale, Yorkshire. Initialed "S G C." (Original seat covering partly lost and re-backed.)

688 / Embroidery 1641–55; England; frame walnut. The arms in the tent stitch embroidery are of Hill of Spaxton Yarde and Pounsford, Somerset, impaling Gurdon of Assington Hall, Suffolk, and Letton, Norfolk; they relate to the marriage, in 1641, of Roger Hill of Pounsford (d. June 29, 1655) to his second wife Abigail, born Gurdon. The chair has a history of coming from Dedham Place, Buckinghamshire.

689 / 1660–80; England; walnut.

690

691

692

693

694

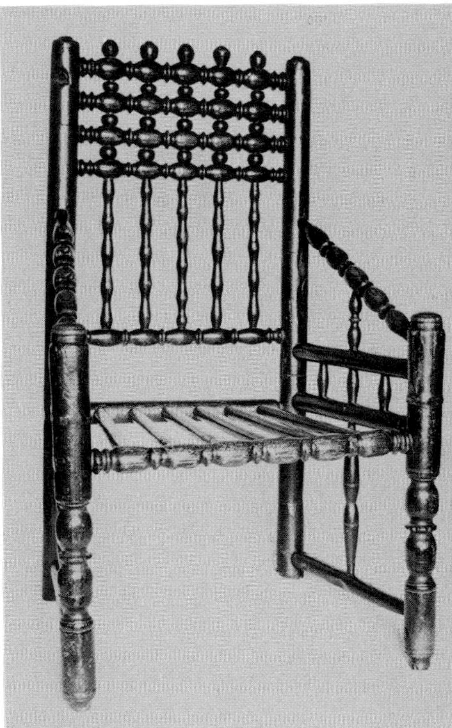

695

690 / 1660–90; England. Spiral turning appears only on the back. The chair is at Nostell Priory, Yorkshire.

691 / 1699?; Philadelphia, Pennsylvania, or New York, New York; American walnut, white oak. The chair has an old label that reads: "This chair belonged originally to the first Robert Pearson. He emigrated to America A.D. 1680. Settled on Crosswicks Creek [New Jersey]. The chair was manufactured A.D. 1699. . . ."[22]

692 / 1660–1700; England; the wood appears to be maple, but is probably beech.

693 / 1670–1700; England; walnut. According to tradition, the chair came from Shropshire.

694 / 1670–1710; England.

695 / 1680–1710; England; ash; painted brown on white over black, and the chair had some wear before the black coat was applied. The tradition of turned chairs with button terminals, rather than finials, on the top of the back stiles may not have transferred to America until early in the nineteenth century, when they appear on fancy chairs. (This chair may, in fact, have lost finials, but figures 764 through 766 certainly never had them. Front stretcher missing.)

696

697

698

699

700

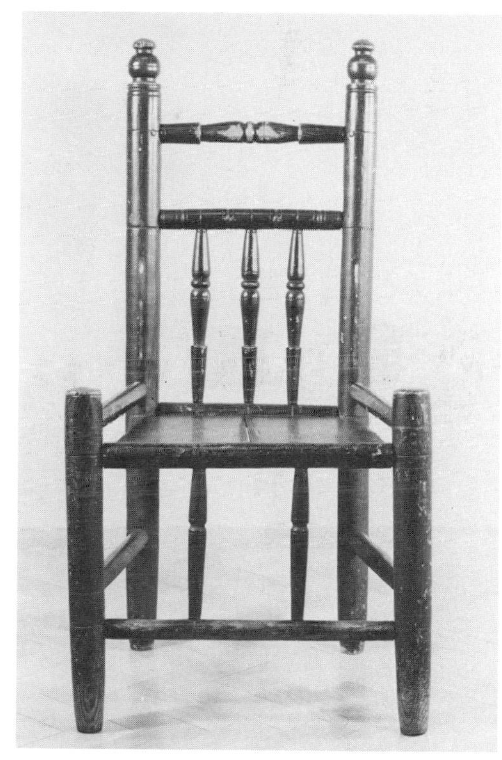

701

696 / 1610–60; England; possibly a fruitwood.

697 / 1630–70; England; ash; perhaps original, red paint. The round tenons of the seat rails pass through the posts—the thinner tenons of the side rails transect the heavier ones of the front and rear rails. A hole in the top center of the top rail may have held a third finial. (The side spokes of the back are replacements.)

698 / 1640–70; America, possibly New York; American ash. According to tradition, this chair belonged to the New York Stryker family; a similar chair has a Connecticut history.[23] (Tops of finials, hand holds, and board seat missing.)

699 / 1610–60; Britain.

700 / 1660–90; Plymouth, Massachusetts; American ash; possibly by Ephraim Tinkham II. According to tradition, this chair belonged to John Carver (c. 1576–1621), a prominent member of the original group which founded Plymouth Colony, and signator of the Mayflower Compact. This ownership caused early scholars of American furniture to call chairs with turned spindles only in the back "Carver chairs." Similar turnings, including front posts of a narrower dimension above the seat, were made in the Plymouth area, possibly by Ephraim Tinkham II.[24] (Hand holds mostly lost. Later seat covering.)

701 / Mid-nineteenth-century; England; elm and oak; original dark green paint. The tapered feet, plainness of posts, and side rails above seat (to keep cushion in place) suggest this date.

702

703

704

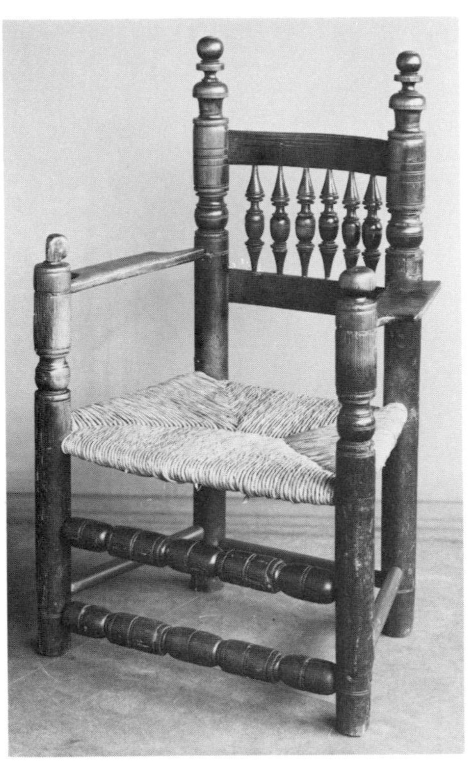

705

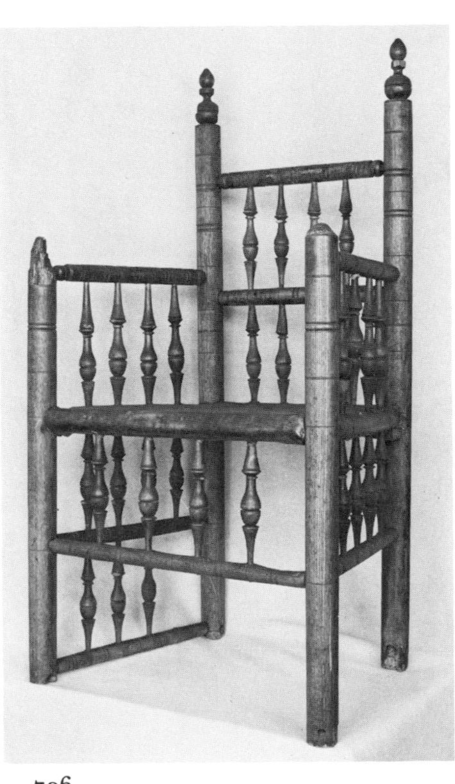

706

707

702 / Eighteenth-century; probably continental, possibly Britain. Many turned and Windsor chairs of expansive form were made to be draped, or covered with a fitted cloth, to protect the sitter from drafts, as in wing chairs and settles.

703 / 1680–1710; Guilford area, Connecticut; American ash; traces of black over green paint. According to tradition, it descended in the Gardiner family of Saybrook,

704 / 1680–1710; England; ash.

705 / Mid-seventeenth-century; England; ash.

706 / Mid-seventeenth-century; eastern Massachusetts, probably Boston area; American red ash or "green" ash.[25] According to tradition, this chair belonged to William Brewster (1567–1644), prominent member of the group that founded the Plymouth Colony, and signator of the Mayflower Compact. This ownership caused early scholars to term all turned chairs with spindles above and below the seat "Brewster chairs." (Hand holds and some stretchers and spindles missing. Later seat covering.)

707 / 1645 Danish engraving from Søren Terkelsen's *Dend hyrdinde Astrea,* showing a turned chair with spindles.

708

709

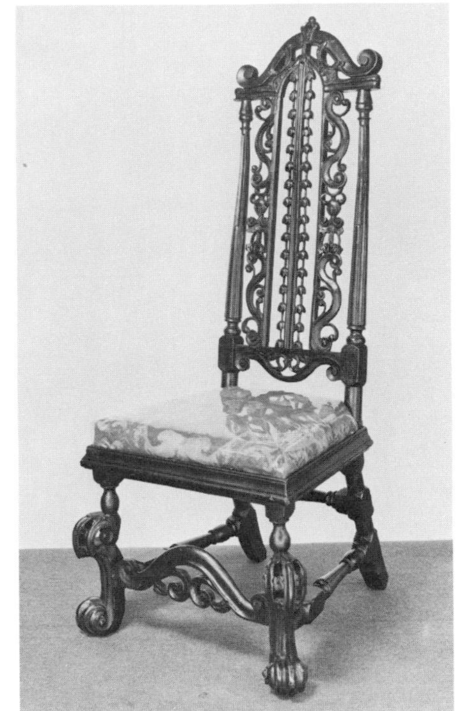

710

711

712

713

708 / 1675–90; England; walnut. The form of the back stiles appears on the American chair, figure 719. Stylistically early cane chairs had the crest rail between the stiles, which terminated in finials. The next styling placed the crest rail on top of the back posts (figure 710), and then the back posts became one continuous line with stiles (figure 711). Simpler chairs, such as figure 712, and American bannister-back chairs (figure 750) continued the first styling. (It was standard to have the front stretcher echo the crest rail's shape and high accent. Therefore, the center on this crest rail has probably lost a floral design.)

709 / 1690–1720; Ireland. (Board seat not original.)

710 / 1685–1700; London, England; beech; painted black. Upholstered seat. The use of a baluster turning above a reverse-curve leg continued into the following periods (see figures 721 and 776).

711 / 1685–1700; London, England; walnut. The complex form of the cup turning on the front legs is German in origin, and related to turnings on some early eighteenth-century Pennsylvania pieces (see figure 170).

712, 713 / 1690–1710; England. Both chairs originally had cane seats. The mount of the photograph of figure 713 is inscribed: "Lacock Abbey [Lacock, near Chippenham, Wiltshire]."

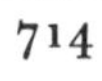

714

715

716

717

718

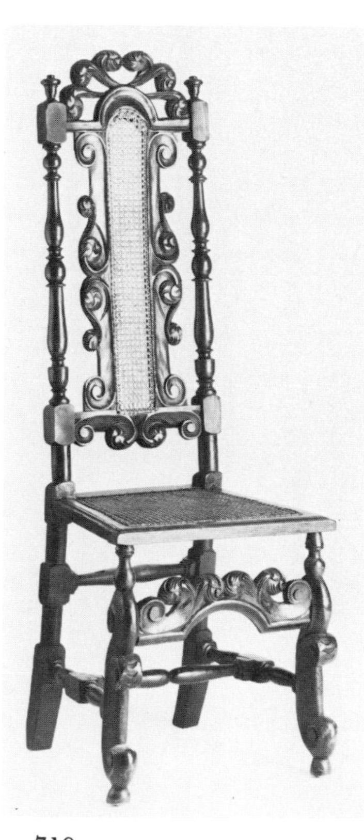

719

714 / 1690–1710; Ireland; oak. According to tradition, this chair came from Alderford, County Roscommon. (Wooden seat not original.)

715 / 1690–1710; English; walnut. The form of the stiles and their finials on this unusual chair relate it to Pennsylvania slat-back chairs (see figure 761); the crest rail to such Pennsylvania chairs as figure 745; and the shape of the cane panel to the English chairs in figures 717 and 731.

716 / 1690–1710; England; walnut. Initials "S. S." incised on back of upper part of leg.

717 / 1690–1710; England.

718 / 1690–1710; England; walnut. (The front stretcher replaced.)

719 / 1695–1735; South Shore, Massachusetts; American beech. The form of the back posts appears on figure 708 and is similar to those of figure 744.

720

721

722

723

724

725

720 / 1680–1700; North Netherlands.
721 / 1700–20; England; walnut. The use of a cabriole leg on a simple chair suggests a date after 1700. Square-section cabriole legs continued on vernacular furniture throughout the eighteenth century. Baluster turnings above cabriole legs are discussed under figure 710.
722, 723, 724 / 1700–25; England. The early twentieth-century mount of the photograph of figure 723 is inscribed: "Brigstock (Northants) [Northamptonshire]: Church."
725 / 1700–35; Boston or Charlestown, Massachusetts; maple.

726

727

728

729

730

731

726 / 1700–25; England. Baluster turnings above cabriole legs are discussed under figure 710. (Cane panels covered with later upholstery.)

727 / 1700–35; Boston area, Massachusetts; maple, oak.

728 / 1700–25; England; beech.

729 / 1700–35; America, probably Massachusetts; American beech.

730 / 1700–35; Pennsylvania; American black walnut. To achieve the great dimension of the baluster forms on the front legs, additional pieces were glued to the basic stock.

731 / 1700–25; England; walnut. The early twentieth-century mount of the photograph says: "Lent by C. H. Talbot, Esq., Lacock Abbey [Lacock, near Chippenham, Wiltshire]."

732

733

734

735

732 / 1700–35; Boston, Massachusetts; American red oak, soft maple. The turnings of the back stiles appear on many English chairs of varying quality (see figure 356). Leather panels, which had been used horizontally during the seventeenth century, were an alternative to cane.

733 / 1700–35; New York; maple (cherry, oak). Original Russia leather and brass nails. (The iron arm braces are not original.)

734 / 1700–35; New York; maple.

735 / 1690–1730; England; beech, painted black.

736

737

738

739

740

736 / 1700–30; England; oak. The early twentieth-century mount of the photograph is inscribed: "Didmarton (Gloucs.) [Gloucestershire] New Church."

737 / 1680–1705; England; oak?

738 / 1670–1700; England; walnut; iron reading board supports and back ratchets. Attenuated cup-baluster turnings are rare in America, but do appear, for example, on the stretchers of Pennsylvania chairs in figure 745.

739 / 1700–20; England. Photograph inscribed: "Parish Clerks Hall, London."

740 / 1725–45; Boston area, Massachusetts; maple (red oak).

741

742

743

744

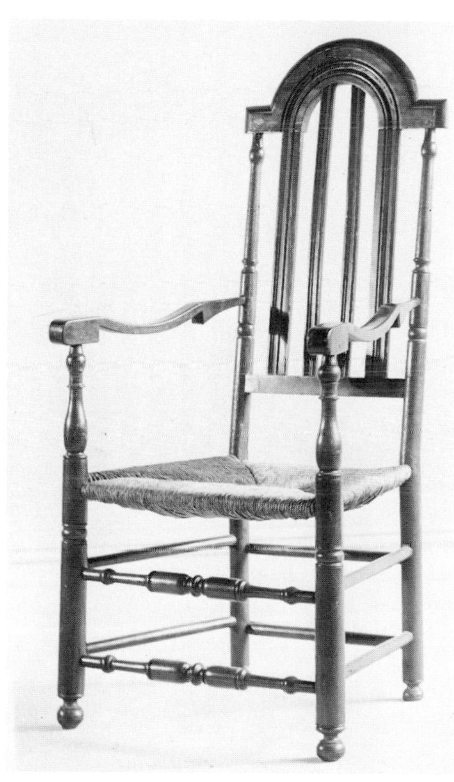

745

746

741 / 1710–30; England; vertical slats and a panel seat often appeared in place of cane on vernacular British chairs. The former also appeared in high-style chairs, figure 743.

742 / Dated 1726; Ireland; oak. (Front feet probably once had attached toes.)

743 / 1690–1710; England; walnut. According to tradition, formerly at Hampden House, Buckinghamshire. Molded slats were sometimes part of the high-style taste.

744 / 1690–1710; England.

745 / Late eighteenth- or early nineteenth-century; Pennsylvania. The attenuated cup-baluster form of stretcher is rare in America, but common in Europe (see figure 738).

746 / 1710–60; America, probably Connecticut, Avon area; soft maple, white pine. The double ball turning, tightly formed sausage turnings, and the form of the front feet associate this chair with figures 754 through 756. (Top front stretcher replaced.)

747

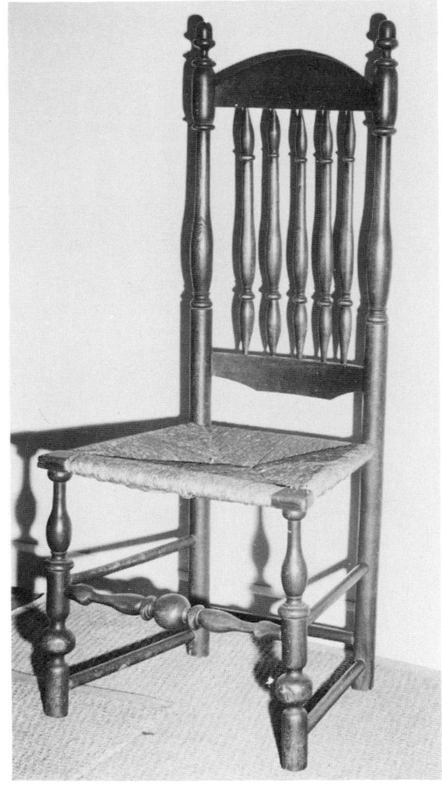

748

749

750

751

747 / 1700–25. The early twentieth-century mount of the photograph inscribed: "Bristol (Gloucs.) [Gloucestershire] Quaker Friars."

748 / 1700–1735; England; ash; red-brown finish.

749 / 1690–1710; England. According to tradition, this chair has always been at Hatfield House, Hertfordshire.

750 / 1700–35; Boston area, Massachusetts; maple; painted black. A fine interpretation of the bannister-back form which, in America, took the role of the cane chair in England. (Board seat and paint old but not original; the seat was originally rushed.)

751 / 1690–1700; England; walnut. Recorded as formerly at Bramshill Park, Hampshire. Matching chairs accompanied this piece.

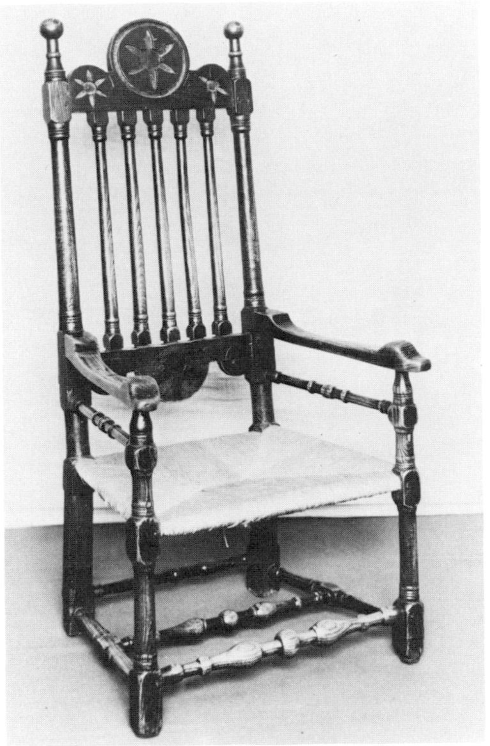

752

753

754

755

756

752 / 1700–1750; continental; possibly ash. The shape of the turnings and arms, and the use of star inlay, suggest Germany as the place of origin.

753 / 1745–60; England, possibly London area. A rural use of a colonnade appears on the chair in figure 988.

754 / 1680–1710; America? According to tradition, similar chairs were found in New Jersey and the Hudson River Valley, and they may have originated in New York City. They were based on Netherlands forms, such as figures 755 and 756. Wood analysis of this chair raises the question whether or not it is American, revealing: right front leg, European or American cherry; left rear leg, European walnut; rear seat rail, European or American ash; and lower right stretcher, hickory. (As noted earlier, scientific wood analysis is helpful but not totally dependable.) Double ball turning and tightly formed sausage-turned stretchers appear on the probably Connecticut chair in figure 746.

755 / 1660–90; North Netherlands; nut wood.

756 / 1660–90; Netherlands.

757

758

759

760

761

762

757 / Late seventeenth-century; ash. Probably English, although the shape of the slats and finials recall some Netherlands chairs. (Restorations include: turned rail below right arm; lower straight part of left front leg; base of the other three legs; front, back left, and lower right stretchers. The seat was originally rushed.)

758 / Late seventeenth-century; America, probably New York, New York; soft maple, American hickory.

759 / Eighteenth-century; England. English use of button terminals rather than finials is discussed under figure 695.

760 / 1720–1800; probably England, possibly Netherlands. (Feet and lower front stretcher are not original. Top of upper slat missing.)

761 / 1725–1800; Pennsylvania; maple, ash (stenciled paint removed and chair stained red to match original finish).

762 / 1720–1800; possibly England, probably continental, perhaps Netherlands, cherry. The dealer who sold the chair to the Yale University Art Gallery considered it to be "From East Anglia." Similar feet are discussed under figure 1255.

763

764

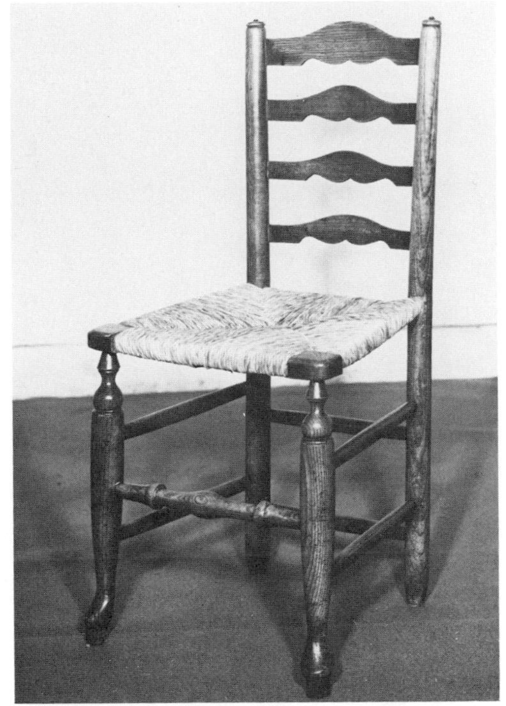
765

766

767

763 / 1730–1800; England.

764 / Probably 1790–1850; England. Similar chairs appeared in the catalogue *Old World Lancashire Chairs* (c. 1920), published by H. J. Berry & Sons, Chipping, near Preston, Lancashire. Those in the catalogue lack the bulging cabriole form found on this chair and have a reel turning above the cabriole part of the legs.[26] (This catalogue is also discussed under figure 1089.)

765, 766, 767 / Nineteenth-century; England.

768 / Nineteenth-century; North Netherlands dolls' chairs; poplar, beech, cherry.

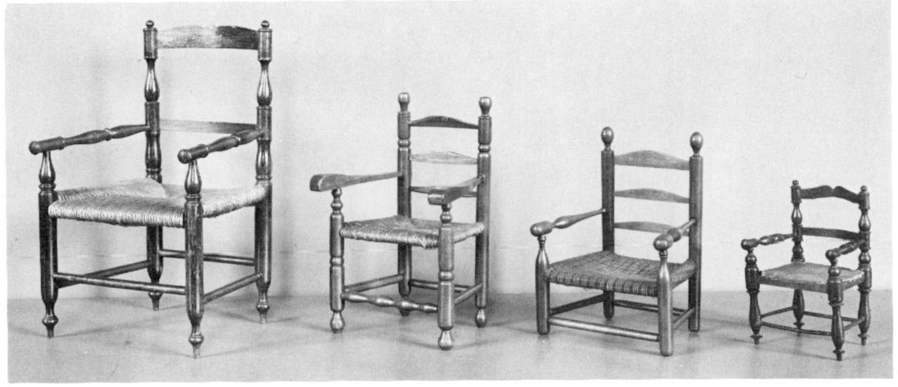
768

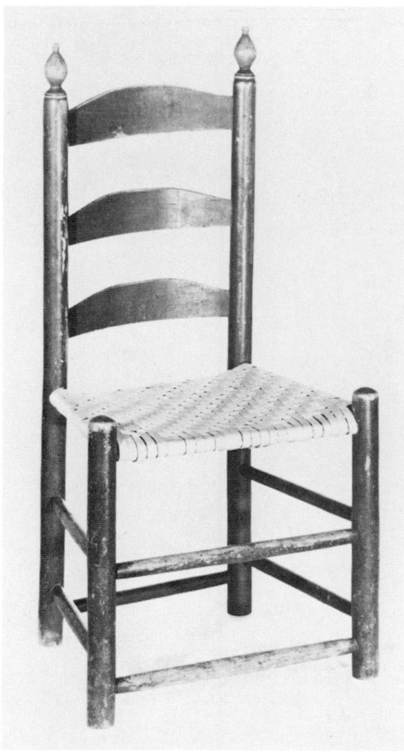
769

770

771

772

769 / Nineteenth-century, probably after 1850; New England, found in New Hampshire; maple, ash; remains of red paint. (Seat new.)

770 / Late eighteenth-century; England; probably ash.

771 / Late eighteenth- and early nineteenth-century; Netherlands.

772 / 1624; Dutch engraving from Johannes de Brunc's *Emblemata of Zinnewerck*, showing slat-back chairs with shaped slats. The slats through-tenon the back posts.

773

774

775

776

777

778

773 / 1720–1800; Britain.

774 / 1740–90; probably England. The early twentieth-century mount inscribed: "Maiden Bradley (Wilts.) [Wiltshire] Church." Similar chairs with naive floral carving were made in Scandinavia. A related American chair appears as figure 22, and related splats are found on the pieces in figures 775 and 813.

775 / 1740–90; England?; oak. (Medial stretcher not original.)

776 / 1720–50; England; ash or yew.

777 / 1700–20; England; walnut.

778 / About 1680; England. Bearing the cipher and coronet of Elizabeth Dysart, Duchess of Lauderdale. This may be one of the set of "12 back Stools with cane bottoms, japaned" mentioned in the 1683 inventory of Ham House, Petersham, Surrey. Chinese forms and decoration influenced English designs from the late seventeenth century and dominated early eighteenth-century styling.

779

780

781

782

783

784

779 / 1710–20; England; beech, japanned green and gold on a red ground. An exquisitely shaped and balanced chair based on Chinese designs.

780 / 1710–20; England. The side view appears as figure 370. Closely based on Chinese designs, this is one of the most exciting of the early eighteenth-century English forms.

781 / 1725–60; Wethersfield area, Connecticut; cherry (soft maple, pine). Side seat rails through-tenon the back posts. This and a few other American chairs echo the slender Queen Anne forms rather than, as in figure 792, the broader George I and early George II chairs seen in figures 793 and 805. This chair is discussed in the Conclusion.

782 / 1710–20; England? Turned knee bosses, rather than brackets, which are repeated on the crest rail.

783 / 1731–33. English mezzotint by John Faber after Thomas Hudson's portrait of Samuel Scott. The print was used as the basic design by John Singleton Copley for his Boston, Massachusetts, portrait of John Amory. The chair in the print has a splat silhouette like those found on figures 784 and 785. Although borrowing much from the print, Copley replaced this chair with a New England rush-seated example.

784 / 1710–25; England. Inlaid splat.

785

786

787

788

789

790

785 / 1710–25; England; walnut. (Medial and left side stretcher missing.)

786 / 1720–35; England. Inlaid splat.

787 / 1725–60; Newport, Rhode Island; mahogany, splat veneered on maple. The use of only three stretchers is unusual, but does appear on figure 801.

788 / 1730–50; England.

789 / 1725–45; England. Shapes developed under Queen Anne became broader during George I and George II styling.

790 / 1745–1800; England; cherry. The straight front legs place it in the second half of the century.

791

792

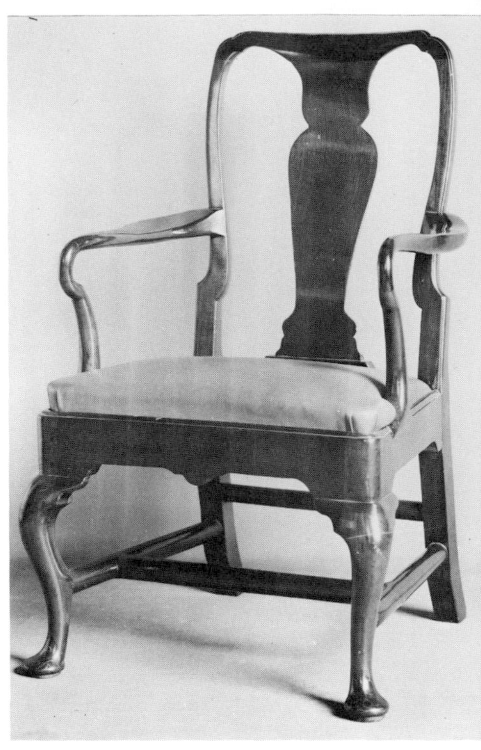
793

794

795

796

791 / 1720–45; England; walnut. Straight-turned stretchers were common in England but not in America. They echo the straight line of the edges of the seat rails.

792 / 1730–60; Boston area, Massachusetts; walnut. Based on George I styling.

793 / 1720–45; England. Back legs retaining their square section, even when stretchers are present, were used in Rhode Island.

794 / 1720–40; England.

795 / 1720–40; England; walnut. Square front feet. No evidence of corner blocks. (The shoe is damaged, the slip seat replaced.)

796 / 1730–60; Newport, Rhode Island; walnut (maple).

797

798

799

800

801

802

797 / 1725–60; England. Photograph inscribed "Trinity House, Hull [southeast Yorkshire]." Square front feet.

798 / 1715–25; England. Probably the chair was lacquered in the Orient; certainly the original crests appear to have been applied there, although there is later overpainting. In the colonies the role of wooden hall chairs, resistant to damp and uncouth clothing, was often taken by Windsor chairs.

799 / 1720–40; England.

800 / 1735–60; Britain, possibly Ireland; fruitwood.

801 / 1730–60; England; walnut. Seat braced with nailed cross ties.

802 / 1730–60; New York, New York; cherry (pine, maple). Related feet appear on figures 795, 836, and 1281.

803

804

805

806

807

808

803, 804 / 1725–35; London, England; gilt gesso. The quality of line and decoration places this chair among the best examples of early eighteenth-century furniture. Its dolphins, paterae, shells, and leafage link it with the classical statements of the Renaissance and antique Rome. The corner blocks are like those used in Massachusetts; see figure 349.

805 / 1725–40; England; walnut. Veneered splat, back posts above the seat, and seat rails.

806 / 1740–70; New York, New York; walnut (pine, red gum). In America, this form of shoe seems to have been restricted to New York City. A shoe on a Philadelphia chair has the same form, but it is not original.[27] Similar knee brackets appear on figures 828 and 832. Other related chairs appear in figures 23 and 24.

807 / 1740–70; probably Newport, Rhode Island; walnut.

808 / 1740–70; Britain, probably Ireland; mahogany. Pointed feet.

809

810

811

812

813

814

809, 810 / 1730–70; Britain, probably Ireland.

811 / 1730–70; New York, New York; mahogany (tulip, maple). The splat is veneered on maple. The form of the front feet appears on the preceding chair and figure 918; a crest rail shell flanked by leafage on figure 934.

812 / 1730–40; England; walnut (beech). (Japanning old but not original.) Detail of leg appears as figure 33. (Top edge of shoe missing.)

813 / 1725–50; England; mahogany.

814 / 1740–60; Newport, Rhode Island; walnut (maple). Detail of a similar front leg is seen as figure 34.

815

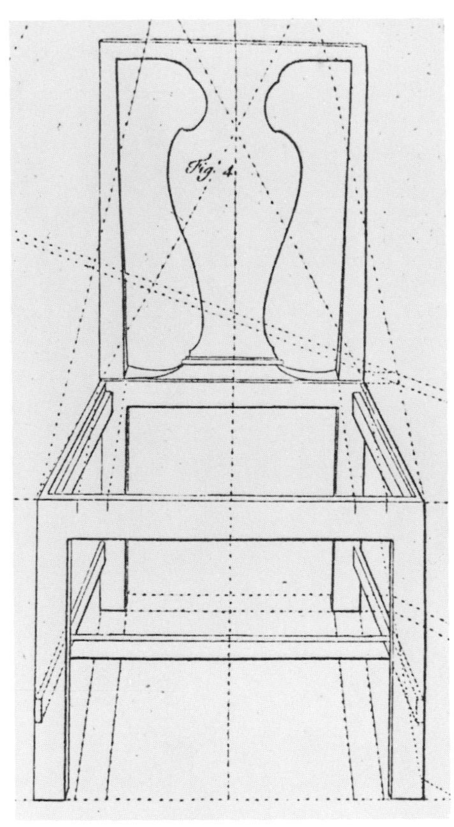

816

817

818

819

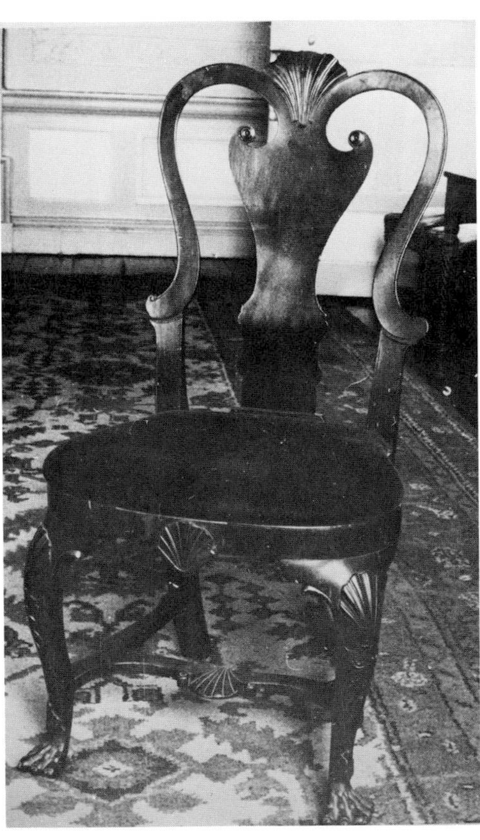

820

815 / 1720–40; England. Veneered back and seat rail. Figure 331 has a similar back.

816 / Thomas Chippendale's *Director*, 1754 edition, plate 9.

817 / 1740–60; Pennsylvania, near Philadelphia; American black walnut (cherry). Through tenons. Front feet with distinctive turned pads are a typical Philadelphia form.

818 / 1730–60; Britain; mahogany.

819 / 1730–60; Ireland; walnut (white oak). Front legs tenon through the seat frame.

820 / 1730–60; Ireland.

821

822

823

824

825

821 / 1730–60; Ireland; mahogany.

822, 823, 824 / 1730–60; Ireland; mahogany. Seat construction as found in Philadelphia,[28] except that the tenons of the front legs passing through the seat frame are square rather than round in section. The side rails of the seat do not through-tenon the back posts.

825 / 1735–45; London, England; rosewood, rosewood and brass veneer.

826

827

828

829

830

831

826 / 1745–60; Philadelphia, Pennsylvania; walnut (pine).
827 / 1740–60; Britain, probably Ireland.
828 / 1725–35; London, England. Beautifully organized and finely detailed, for example, in the movement of the knee shells and the integration of the shapes of the veneered back and seat rails.

829 / 1740–70; New York, New York; mahogany (white pine, maple, red oak).
830 / 1725–45; England.
831 / 1740–60; probably Scandinavian; japanned walnut, cane seat.

832

833

834

835

836

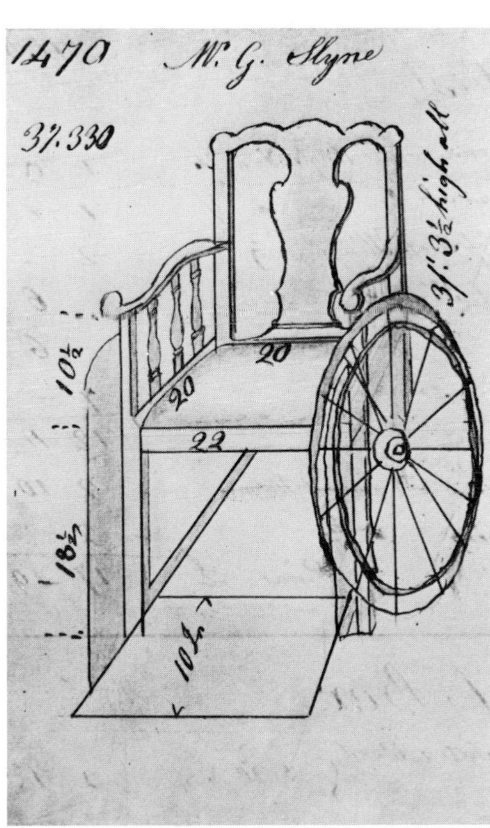

837

832 / 1730–60; England; walnut, walnut veneer.

833 / 1740–60; Philadelphia, Pennsylvania; walnut (pine). According to tradition, this chair descended in the Wistar family.

834 / 1740–70; Britain; mahogany.

835 / 1750–1800; Britain.

836 / 1740–70; Britain. Pointed front foot.

837 / "A Gouty Chair," dated September, 1798, page 1470 of the Estimate Book of the Gillows firm. It was made of beech, ash, and deal, and had a "Canvas Bottom." The grains and colors of the various woods were united by stain, for which 8d. was charged.

838

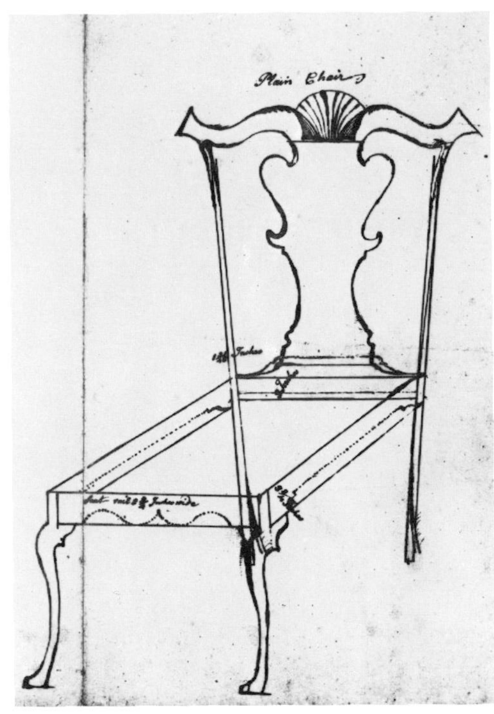

839

840

841

842

843

838 / 1745–90; Philadelphia, Pennsylvania; American black walnut (pine, tulip).

839 / Detail from a group of ink drawings by Samuel Mickle of Philadelphia, one of which is dated 1766. The chair is headed "Plain Chair." Plain chairs appear in the Philadelphia cabinetmakers' price list of 1772,[29] where objects are priced in both walnut and mahogany. Each furniture form begins with the basic, undecorated version. This is followed by increasingly elaborate versions at higher costs. The simplest chair with cabriole legs has "plain feet & bannester [splat] with leather Bottoms [seats]." Features that might be added were arms, claw feet, shells, leaves, fluted or ogee (molded) back stiles, piercing the slat; "for Releiving the Bannesters [carving the splat] ad acording to the Work on them." The profile of the front feet in the drawing suggests the trifid forms, as seen in the preceding illustration. Lathe-turned feet, as on figure 840, were probably the cheapest form, the trifid foot the next in cost—its three-prong thrust suggesting the most expensive form, the claw and ball foot.

840 / 1745–90; Pennsylvania, probably Philadelphia; walnut (pine, walnut).

841 / 1745–65; England; walnut.

842 / 1745–70; England; oak. (Board seat replaced.)

843 / 1745–80; England; walnut. According to tradition, the chair was one of three Masonic chairs made for Royal Alpha Lodge, South Middlesex.

844

845

846

847

Interpretations of published designs

It has been customary to see the design of American Chippendale chairs as deriving wholly or in combination of parts from the published designs of Thomas Chippendale. Indeed, a few American chairs were taken from the *Director* or other source books, but most pre-Revolutionary chairs were based on actual British examples. When American Chippendale chairs are closer to English chairs than to published English designs, it must be assumed that *they*, not books, are the sources. (See figures 935–7.) The balance shifted after the Revolution when the design books of George Hepplewhite and Thomas Sheraton had a stronger and more direct influence on American furniture in the neoclassical style.

844 / 1765. Plate 9 in Robert Manwaring's *The Cabinet and Chair-Maker's Real Friend and Companion*.

845 / 1765–90; Salem or Boston, Massachusetts; mahogany (pine, maple).

846 / Dated 1753; on plate 12, 1754 edition, and plate 13, 1762 edition, of Chippendale's *Director*.

847 / 1754–90; Philadelphia, Pennsylvania; mahogany (white cedar).

848

849

850

851

Similar to Massachusetts and related chairs

(Chairs with "figure 8" splats are under figures 999 through 1006.)

848 / This room view was published in *Old English Furniture for the Small Collector* (London, 1930) by J. P. Blake and A. E. Reveirs-Hopkins, and includes three pierced-splat English chairs that might pass as Massachusetts in origin. At the left, the Gothic splats are like that in figure 898; the splat and crest of the center chair are similar to those in figure 890; the chair at the right has a splat with four interlaced C shapes and a rising central strap, as found in figure 852.

849 / 1750–85; England; mahogany. Made for the Løvenborg Manor House, Denmark.[30] Molding back posts to two distinct lines seems not to have been an American practice. This form of foot, with rather pudgy claws, appears on an arm chair with a similar splat and crest rail, which is considered to be from Massachusetts.[31] Massachusetts chairs without stretchers have similar back legs and feet.

850 / 1750–90; Boston or Salem, Massachusetts; mahogany (pine, soft maple). Similar to the previous chair in the use of an unbowed back, shape of the splat and crest rail, narrowness of the seat rail, and knee leafage coming from under the seat. A detail of one front leg appears as figure 304.

851 / 1750–90; Newport, Rhode Island; mahogany (maple). The shaping of the front legs and feet, and the large scale of the back posts and crest rail shell, secure this example to Newport. This form of splat is rare on high-style Newport chairs, but common on Rhode Island vernacular chairs, and standard in eastern Massachusetts.

852

853

854

855

856

857

852 / 1750–90; New England, probably Massachusetts; American black walnut (soft maple, white pine). Splats with four interlaced C shapes were common in the American colonies except Philadelphia, where the active straps do not all come from the crest rail (figure 878). The late use of lathe-turned feet was discussed under figure 58.

853 / 1771–95; East Windsor, Connecticut; cherry (white pine, white oak); probably by Eliphalet Chapin (1741–1807). This chair is discussed in the Conclusion.

854, 855, 856 / 1750–85; Britain. The first has leafage edging the larger C shapes; the second chip carving on the "fill" between the straps where they join the crest rail, as on the Massachusetts example, figure 850; the third leaf carving on the crest rail. A similar splat appears on the chair made by Samuel Sharp of Norwich, England (figure 5).

857 / 1745–80; Britain, possibly Ireland. The photograph is inscribed: "Irish says D[esmond Fitz-Gerald, The Knight of Glin]."

858

859

860

861

862

863

858 / 1750–90; Massachusetts, possibly the Hingham area (it descended from Peter Oliver of Hingham); American walnut (cherry, maple, walnut). This is the only known scroll-foot New England chair.

859 / 1750–85; Britain; English walnut (pine, beech). Creased ears appeared in New York (figure 941).

860 / 1750–85; Britain; walnut. (The side stretchers are probably not original.)

861 / 1750–85; Britain.

862 / 1750–90; Denmark. Formerly at the Løvenborg Manor House, Denmark.

863 / 1750–85; England. Carved straight legs and pierced stretchers appeared infrequently in American work.

864

865

866

867

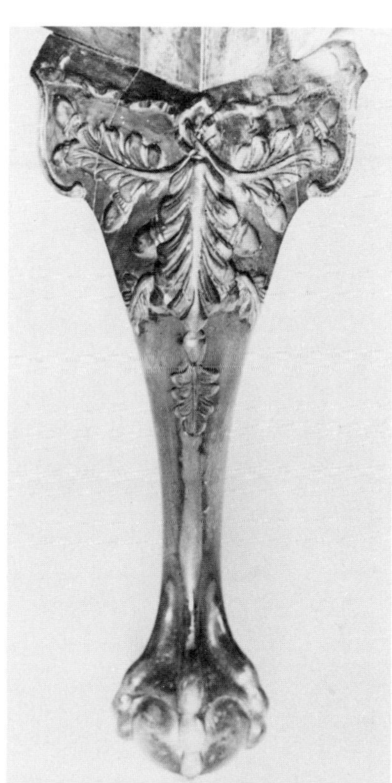

868

869

864 / 1750–85; Britain. Back stiles continuing as scrolls on the crest rail appeared in the Pennsylvania area.

865 / 1750–85; English. This version of the four C-scroll splat terminates the inner two scrolls at a lower point than on those preceding. The outer and inner scrolls are more parallel.

866 / 1750–90; New England, possibly Portsmouth, New Hampshire; mahogany (soft maple). Rear seat rail stamped "D. AUSTIN." During the claw and ball period, a deeply turned front foot gave a similar mass. In Philadelphia, the trifid foot was an inexpensive substitute for the claw and ball foot. The rear legs are similar to those on figure 870.

867, 868 / 1750–85; Britain, possibly Ireland. The use of only a rear stretcher or stretcher of rectangular section on cabriole leg chairs was not an American practice. Knees carved to oak leaves and acorns.

869 / 1750–90; Boston or Salem, Massachusetts; mahogany.

870

871

872

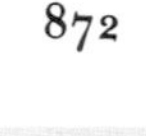

873

874

875

870 / 1750–85; England; mahogany. (Corner blocks and slip-seat frame new.)

871 / 1750–85; England.

872 / 1750–85; Britain; mahogany (elm). Leafage on the outer C scrolls. (Slip-seat frame new.)

873 / 1750–90; New York, New York; mahogany (tulip). The central crest rail ornament appears on figures 859 and 897.

874 / 1750–85; Britain. A similarly decorated crest rail appears on the New York chair in figure 933. The cable form of the gadrooning attached under the front seat rail appears on New York examples.

875 / 1750–85; Britain; mahogany. Despite the darkness, this photograph shows some important features: the rear stiles continuing into scroll ears; leafage on the outer C scrolls and scroll ears; front feet with retracted side claws; and square rear feet.

876

877

878

879

880

881

876 / 1770–1800; Britain; mahogany. The squareness of the back suggests a date after the introduction of the neo-classical style.

877 / 1750–90; Britain; mahogany. It was more customary to lace the diamond through the strapwork. A similarly unintegrated diamond appears on a few Connecticut chairs, which were probably made by Eliphalet Chapin in East Windsor, as with the X in figure 907.

878 / 1750–90; Philadelphia, Pennsylvania; mahogany (tulip). Philadelphia scroll strapwork uses two scrolls from the crest rail and three from the shoe which become two outer straps; these four straps are linked in the center by two central straps. Although this form is common in Philadelphia, it seems rare in England.

879 / 1750–85; Britain. A rare occurrence in Britain of the form of scroll strapwork used in Philadelphia.

880 / 1750–90; Britain, probably Ireland; mahogany.

881 / 1750–1800; Sweden.

882

883

884

885

886

887

882 / 1750–90; Boston, Massachusetts; mahogany (pine, maple). According to tradition, this chair belonged to the family of James Swan (1754–1830) of Boston and Dorchester. Radically retracted claws. The squareness of the back legs, without chamfering, was standard on a group of Rhode Island chairs.

883, 884, 885, 886, 887 / 1750–85; Britain. Diamond cross-section stretchers, as found on figure 884, did not become an American practice.

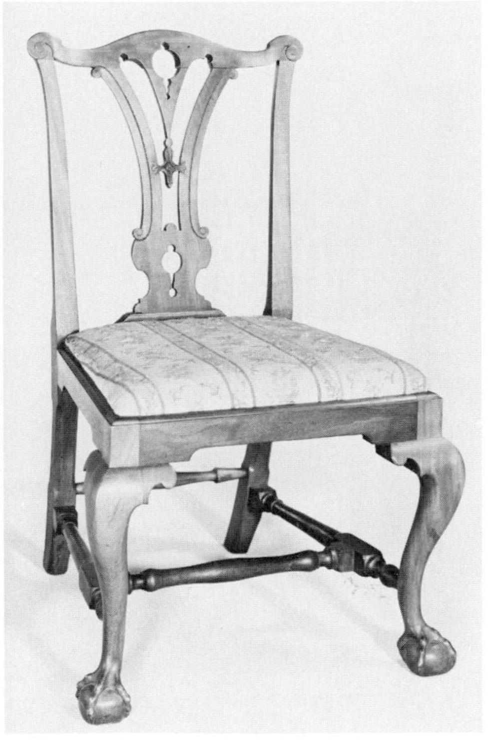
888

889

890

891

892

893

888 / 1750–90; Massachusetts, possibly Boston; mahogany (soft maple). A chair with a similar splat appears in paintings by John Singleton Copley: Daniel Rogers, 1767, Gloucester; Joseph Sherburne, 1767–70, Boston; and Joseph Hooper, 1770–71, Marblehead. The chair may have been a prop in the artist's Boston studio. The scroll knee brackets appear on various English chairs, often with a carved scroll, as in figure 891.

889 / 1750–85; Britain; mahogany.[32]

890 / 1750–90; Massachusetts, probably Boston; mahogany (soft maple, white pine). A similar chair appears in the room view, figure 848. A related Massachusetts chair has leaf carving on the splat, as in figures 891 and 892.[33]

891 / 1750–85; Britain; mahogany. A similar splat silhouette appeared in Rhode Island, New York, and Philadelphia (see figures 939 through 946).

892 / 1750–90; Newport, Rhode Island; mahogany (maple). The proportions, movement of parts, and form of the shells denote Newport. The front feet have retracted side claws.

893 / 1750–85; Britain; mahogany.

894

895

896

897

898

899

894 / 1750–90; Boston, Massachusetts; mahogany (soft maple, birch). A side chair from the set uses soft maple, American black ash, and white pine.[34] The carving is just perceptibly shallower than on the following chair.

895 / 1750–85; England; mahogany (English beech). Similar paw feet appear on a small number of American pieces.

896 / 1750–85; Britain; mahogany (beech).

897 / 1750–85; Britain. A related central crest rail ornament appears on various chairs, such as figures 859 and 873. (A part may be missing between the top scrolls of the splat.)

898 / 1750–90; Massachusetts, probably Boston; mahogany (pine, maple).

899/ 1750–85; England; mahogany. The molding of the front legs steps out from the plane of the seat rail; this also occurs on various chairs and tables, figure 906, for example.

900

901

902

903

904

905

900 / 1750–90; New York, New York; mahogany (pine, maple).
901, 902, 903, 904, 905 / 1750–85; Britain; mahogany. The overlapping of the straps of the splats varies.

906

907

908

909

910

906 / 1750–85; Britain. The molding of the front legs steps out from the plane of the seat rail.

907 / 1771–95; East Windsor, Connecticut; cherry (pine); probably by Eliphalet Chapin. This chair is discussed in the Conclusion.

908 / 1750–85; England. The wooden seat may be a replacement.

909 / 1750–80; England; mahogany (beech). A rear view of a similar chair appears in the following illustration.

910 / 1765; London; *The American School* (oil on canvas), by Matthew Pratt, born in Philadelphia. American-born artist Benjamin West is seen standing at the left; Pratt may be the figure seated beside him.

911

912

913

914

915

916

911 / 1750–85; England; mahogany (pine).
912 / 1750–80; England; mahogany (beech).
913 / 1750–90; eastern Massachusetts; mahogany.
914 / 1760–95; Massachusetts, possibly Newburyport; mahogany. Chairs with related features are associated with the work of Joseph Short.
915 / 1750–85; England; mahogany. (Right front knee bracket missing.)
916 / 1770–90; Britain; mahogany. The square-tapered legs suggest a date late in the century.

917

918

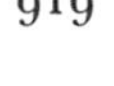

919

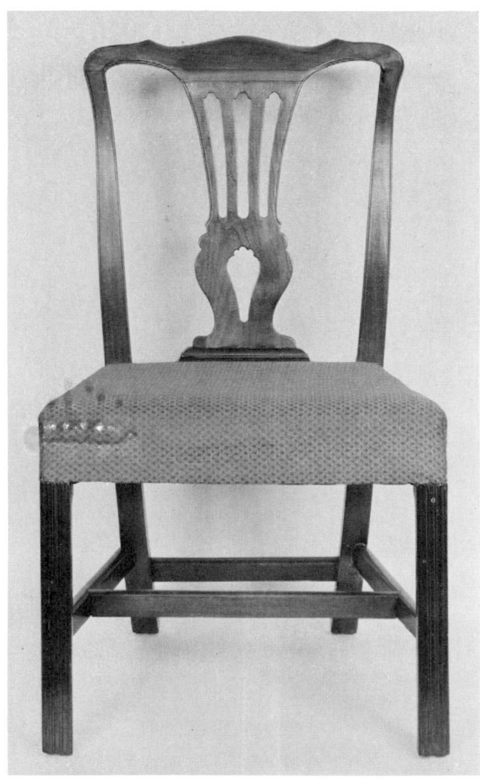

920

921

922

Similar to New York and related chairs

917 / 1750–90; New York, New York; mahogany (tulip). Scroll ears also appear on figure 934. Many pieces of New York furniture made during these years continued the mass of George II forms, perhaps a legacy of the early ownership by the Dutch.

918 / 1740–65; England; mahogany. Veneered back and seat rail. The form of the front foot appears in figures 810 and 811.

919 / 1750–80; England; mahogany. An elegant interpretation of the design.

920, 921 / 1755–90; Britain; mahogany.

922 / 1755–90; Ireland. The two features—a straight top rail and long reverse-curve knee brackets—appear together or singly on other possibly Irish chairs (figures 927, 994, 1020, 1025, 1047, and 1134).

923

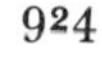

924

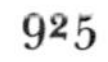

925

926

927

928

923 / 1760–90; rural England; elm or ash. Photograph inscribed: "Trinity House, Hull [southeast Yorkshire]."

924 / 1794?; American, possibly Southern; walnut (yellow pine). Leather seat probably original. Side rails tenon through the back posts. Signed "Saml. Winters 1794" on inside of the rear seat rail. A stretcher joins the front legs.

925 / 1750–75?; Williamsburg, Virginia; mahogany (beech); possibly by Peter Scott (1694–1775). Knee carving as on figure 828.

926 / 1760–1800; New England; maple or birch.

927 / 1750–90; Ireland. Photograph inscribed: "G. Russell, Dunhathel, Glanmire, [County] Cork." Prototype "Philadelphia" trifid feet and flat stretchers. (The straight, rectangular-section rear stretcher was not an American practice in cabriole-leg chairs. Crest rails shaped on their lower edges to reverse curves either side of the splat appeared in various regions of the Southern colonies. There, too, splats with vertical ribs were favored. (Other possibly Irish chairs with similarly shaped crest rails appear as figures 994, 1020, 1025.)

928 / 1750–85; England. The photograph mount is inscribed: "Syon [House, Brentford, Middlesex]."

929

930

931

932

933

934

929 / 1750–90; New York, New York; mahogany (soft maple, birch).

930, 931, 932 / 1750–85, England. The first has Gothic fret-carved front legs, and square stretchers in a "diamond" cross section; the second stop-fluted front legs; the third plain legs. This back also appeared on English chairs with slip seats.

933 / 1750–90; New York, New York; mahogany. Similar crest rail, legs, and a gadrooned skirt appear on figure 874.

934 / 1745–85; Britain; mahogany. New York used similarly scrolled ears (figure 917) and crest rail shells flanked by leafage (figure 811).

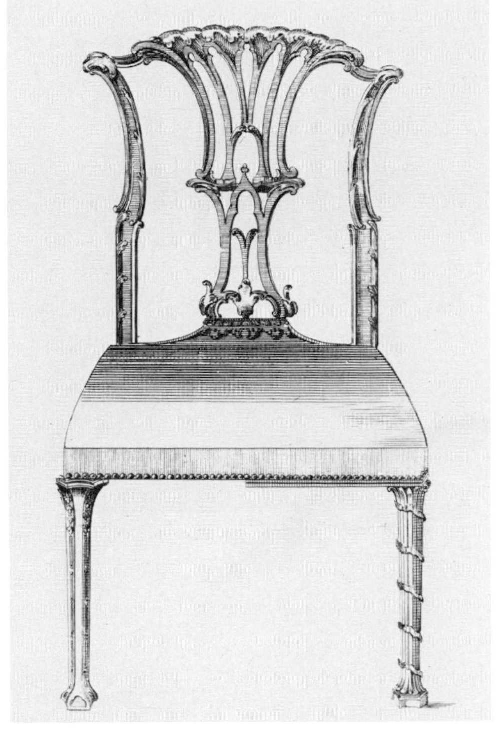

935

936

937

938

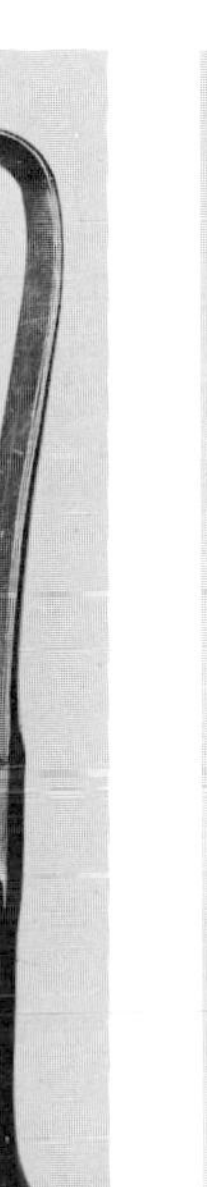

939

940

935 / Engraving from Chippendale's *Director*, 1762 edition only, plate 12.

936 / 1762–85; England. A simplified version of the preceding design.

937 / 1762–90; New York, New York; walnut (pine, tulip). It follows more closely the chair in figure 936 than the engraved design in figure 935.

938 / 1740–60; England; mahogany. The silhouette of the splat is similar to those in figures 890 through 897.

939 / 1750–90; Newport, Rhode Island; mahogany (maple). Chip-carved lines enriching the splat. They appear on the preceding and following chairs, and also on figures 888, 919, and 929 through 932. Stop-fluted legs appear on various English pieces (for example, figure 931). In 1765, Robert Manwaring published a somewhat related, simpler splat on plate 9 of *The Cabinet and Chair-Maker's Real Friend and Companion*, but English chairs are the *direct* precedent.

940 / 1760–1800; Britain; walnut.

941

942

943

944

945

946

941 / 1750–90; New York, New York; mahogany (red gum, mahogany). A similar crest rail ear appears on figures 860 and 861.

942 / 1750–90; New York; mahogany (pine, maple). The silhouette of the splat is similar to those that precede and follow. There are very few known New York chairs with turned front feet.

943 / 1750–90; England; mahogany (ash?).

944 / 1750–90; New York, New York; mahogany (pine, tulip).

945 / 1750–90; Philadelphia, Pennsylvania; walnut (pine).

946 / 1750–90; New York, New York; mahogany (pine, oak, cherry). According to tradition, this chair descended in the Verplanck family.

947

948

949

950

951

952

Similar to Philadelphia and related chairs

(Scroll-splat Philadelphia chairs are discussed under figures 878 and 879.)

947 / 1750–90; Philadelphia, Pennsylvania; mahogany (pine, white cedar). Philadelphia chairs of this pattern were once assigned to the workshop of Benjamin Randolph, but this attribution has been questioned.[35] The lower edges of the seat rails are not horizontally lightened between the legs. There are through tenons. American chairs, particularly those made in Philadelphia, have been described as more vertical than English ones, but this does not hold true, particularly in this group with vase-baluster splats.

948 / 1750–85; Britain; mahogany.

949 / 1750–90; Southern, possibly Baltimore, Maryland; mahogany (yellow pine). This chair does not have through tenons.

950, 951, 952 / 1750–85; Britain; mahogany.

953

954

955

956

957

958

953 / 1750–90; Philadelphia, Pennsylvania; mahogany (pine of the taeda group). Unlike most related Philadelphia side chairs, the seat rail is not shaped to lighten its lower edge between the knee brackets. The knee brackets are applied to the face of the seat rail, which drops behind them (as in figure 347). The bracket responds, at the rear of the side seat rails, are cut from the solid. There are no through tenons.

954 / 1760–1800; Southern, possibly South Carolina; mahogany (yellow pine). The chair does not have through tenons.

955, 956 / 1750–85; Britain; mahogany.

957 / 1750–85; Britain; mahogany (mahogany nailed cross ties).

958 / 1750–90; Portugal. Peculiar to this country is the recessed, serpentined front seat rail and projecting hock of the ankles.

1055

1056

1057

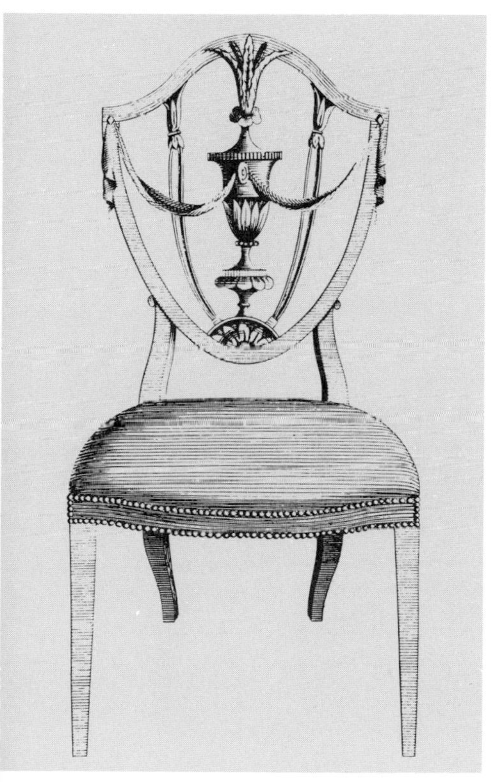

1058

1059

1060

1055 / 1785–1810; Britain. Recessed rectangles in the front legs at seat-rail level probably held applied plaques.
1056 / 1790–1810; eastern Massachusetts; mahogany (soft maple, ash, birch).
1057 / 1790–1810; New England; maple.
1058 / Dated 1787; the design first appeared in George Hepplewhite's *Guide* (1788), plate 2.
1059 / 1788–1810; Britain; mahogany. The chair differs from the engraving, figure 1058, in having a rounder base to the back shield shape and a more slender splat below the urn form.
1060 / 1790–1810; Salem, Massachusetts; mahogany. Carving possibly by Samuel McIntire, who did carving for Elias Hasket Derby and his family, the original owners of this chair.

1061

1062

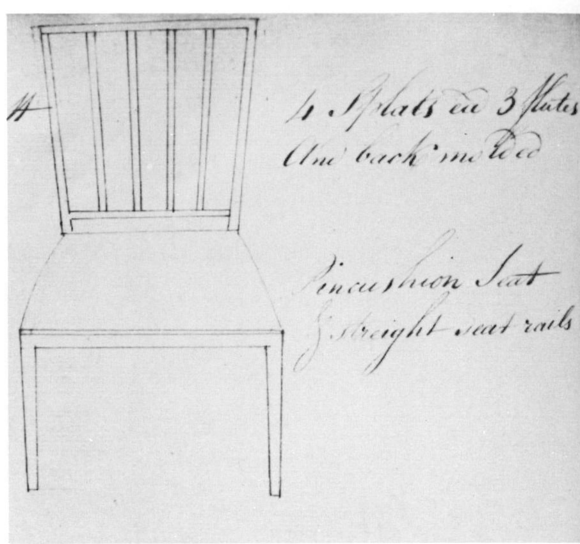

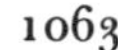

1063

1064

1065

1066

1061 / 1790–1810; Salem, Massachusetts; mahogany, ebony (birch, ash, white pine). The original carving may be by Samuel McIntire, for this chair matches examples in the possession of the Derby family of Salem for whom McIntire worked ("the three feathers and ribbons of the back have recently been exactly executed to match faithfully the original surviving chair [in the Derby family]").[37]

1062 / 1785–1810; Britain.

1063 / Dated July, 1790; mahogany with "4 Splats ea[ch with] 3 flutes And back molded." Ink drawing in the Estimate Book of the Gillows firm, page 613.

1064 / Late nineteenth-century; England. The photograph mount is inscribed: "Syon [House, Brentford, Middlesex]." The use of a drop-in rushed seat, paired medial stretchers, and hard-edge rectilinear shapes suggest this date.

1065 / 1790–1810; Britain.

1066 / 1790–1815; Britain.

1067

1068

1069

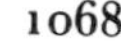

1070

1071

1072

1067, 1068, 1069 / 1790–1815; Britain.
1070 / Dated 1792. Plate 33 in Thomas Sheraton's *Drawing-Book*.
1071 / 1792–1810; Salem, Massachusetts; mahogany (birch, white pine, mahogany). According to tradition, this chair was part of a set of twelve made for the parlor of the Peirce-Nichols House in Salem, and may date from the completion of the room in 1802. The room, and probably the chairs, were carved by Samuel McIntire.
1072 / 1792–1815; Britain or the continent; mahogany.

1073

1074

1075

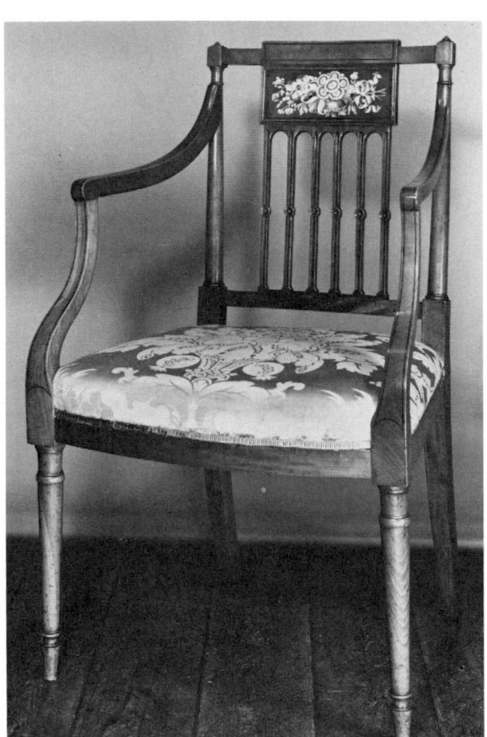

1076

1077

1078

1073 / 1805–15; Boston, Massachusetts; mahogany, figured birch veneer (birch). Work with this styling has been attributed to the workshop of John Seymour (c. 1738–c. 1818) and/or his son, Thomas Seymour (1771–1848), both of whom emigrated from Axminster, Devon, in 1785. *The London Chair-Makers' and Carvers' Book of Prices for Workmanship* (1802) listed prices for chairs with "scroll upper end back legs," veneer "on a straight back rail," and veneered "tablets in tops."[38]

1074, 1075 / 1800–15; Britain.

1076 / 1790–1810; Britain. A chair of similar splat design but with square-tapered legs appears on page 1396 of the Gillows firm Estimate Book, and is dated November, 1797. It was made of painted beech and deal.

1077 / 1790–1810; America, possibly Maryland; mahogany (black ash, pine of the taeda group, tulip). Based on plate 9 of Hepplewhite's *Guide* (1788). The plate is dated 1787.

1078 / 1788–1810; Britain; mahogany. Based on plate 1 of Hepplewhite's *Guide* (1788). The plate is dated 1787.

1079

1080

1081

1082

1083

1084

1079 / 1790–1810; England or Ireland.

1080 / 1795–1810; England. Photograph inscribed: "Cutlers."

1081 / 1800–1820; Britain. A chair with a similar base, dated April, 1809, appears on page 1860 of the Estimate Book of the Gillows firm.

1082 / 1805–20; New York, New York; mahogany (oak). A sketch that has been attributed to Duncan Phyfe shows a similar back, and possibly dates from 1815 or 1816.[39]

1083 / 1800–15; Britain; mahogany.

1084 / 1800–15; England. Photograph inscribed: "Painted, brass mounts."

1085

1086

1087

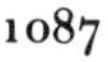

1088

1089

1090

1085 / 1820–50; England; beech with elm seat. The form of the back posts, top rail, and mid-rail of the back continues the Grecian style at the vernacular level. (The left front leg is probably a replacement.)

1086 / 1820–50; England; beech with elm seat. The back continues Grecian styling.

1087 / 1810–40; England; ash with elm seat. The back continues neo-classical-style Gothic forms.

1088 / 1840–60; England. Photograph inscribed: "Typical Beech Wycombe [Buckinghamshire] chair."

Windsor chairs and bench

1089 / About 1800; England. The form of the rear stiles, scrolling of the ears, and deep scooping of the crest rail suggest mid-eighteenth-century styling; the urn form of the front posts under the arms and the lightness of the spindles, the neo-classical taste. H. J. Berry & Sons, Chipping, near Preston, Lancashire, made copies of similar chairs about 1920. They did not continue the cabriole line of the leg to the arm support, but stopped it in a reel shape below the seat. (The entry for figure 764 also discusses this publication.)

1090 / 1810–40; England; fruitwood.

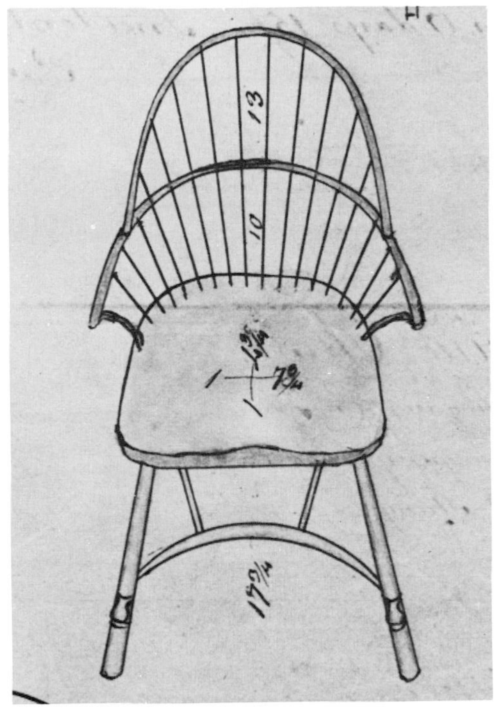

1091

1092

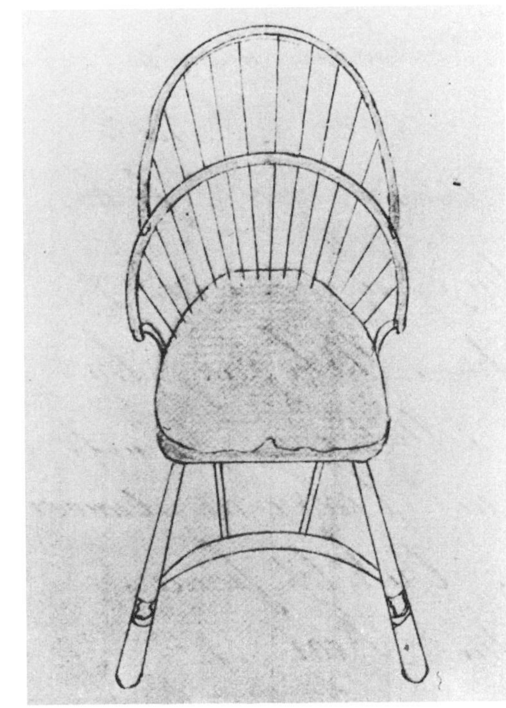

1093

1094

1095

1096

1091 / Dated September 11, 1798. Ink drawing of a mahogany chair with "Cherry Tree" arm and top rails in the Estimate Book of the Gillows firm. This mostly mahogany chair cost 22s. 0d. (Another Gillows Windsor appears as figure 187.)
1092 / Dated December, 1798. Ink drawing of "A Windsor Chair" made of cherry with an elm seat on page 1490 of the Estimate Book of the Gillows firm. It was sold at 9s. 6d., half the price of a mahogany one made the same year (figure 1091).
1093 / Dated 1806. Ink drawing of "A High Back Ash Windsor Chair" with some use of deal, and painted green, on page 1804 of the Estimate Book of the Gillows firm. It was priced at 9s. 9½d.
1094 / 1740–60; England; ash. The legs tenon completely through the seat. Features associated with the earliest Windsors are found here and on figure 1095: worked (draw knife) or plain-turned legs, often without stretchers; D-shaped seats with the front straight or double-scooped; front arm supports of a bent, curved member, or formed to a bladelike shape; bent, single-piece arm rails; and crest rails with multiple scoopings.[40]
1095 / 1740–60; England; ash, elm, oak. The crest rail is shaped like a classical pediment and is edge-molded. The molding is repeated on the top of the seat at the side and rear. (One or both rear legs are restored.)
1096 / 1760–80; Britain; ash with elm seat. The form of the crest rail suggests the mid-eighteenth-century style. H-stretchers appeared about 1750. (The central back lath is not original.)

1097

1098

1099

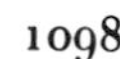

1100

1101

1102

1097 / 1750–60; England; ash, painted green. According to tradition, this chair was made for Oliver Goldsmith, who bequeathed it in 1774 to Dr. William Howes. Oval seats were popular during the middle of the eighteenth century. C-shape arm supports (not bent but cut from the solid), attached to the side of the seat, appeared about 1750. The baluster-form legs end in a ball flanked by rings, over the beginnings of another baluster facing downwards, and were called "Colt" feet. The arm rail is made of three pieces with straight grain and looks like one thin, bent piece.

1098 / 1760–80; England; beech with an elm seat. Splats—solid or pierced—were introduced about 1750. The seat is narrower at the back and echoes high-style "round" seats (see figure 824).

1099 / 1755–60; England. The metal plaque on the crest rail reads: "This being one of the Cabin Chairs which was on board His Majesty's Ship 'Resolution,' Capt. James Cook, on his last Voyage round the World . . . about 1760." From this date chairs usually had a bracing over the joints of the three pieces that formed the arm rail.

1100 / 1770–90; England; ash; the arm rail is possibly oak. (Stretchers missing: the legs have holes for them.)

1101 / 1770–90; England; beech, with an elm seat.

1102 / 1770–1800; America, possibly Pennsylvania; oak, ash, maple, and pine. Not common to English work of this period: this form of leg and foot, and the downward scrolling crest rail ears.

1103

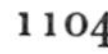

1104

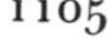

1105

1106

1107

1108

1103 / 1750–70; England. The flat and scooped front arm supports and the D-shaped seat are early features. Lath end spokes forming the edges of the crest appeared about 1750.

1104 / 1750–90; America, possibly Philadelphia, Pennsylvania; maple, hickory, oak, tulip. Splats rarely appeared in American examples. (The feet are missing.)

1105 / 1750–70; England. An early date is suggested by the shape of the arm supports, seat, hocked ankles, and arm rail without a raised support.

1106 / 1760–90; England; beech, with an elm seat. The front arm supports of this fine chair are shaped to paired reverse curves; the inner arm supports are baluster-turned; the knees have raised C shaping; the front feet are of the trifid form; and the rear legs have Colt feet. The slender strapwork of the splat suggests a late date.

1107 / 1750–1800; England.

1108 / 1760–90; Philadelphia, Pennsylvania; walnut. The pad form of the turned front feet and the form of the back legs and medial stretcher are typical of Philadelphia.

1109

1110

1111

1112

1113

1114

1109, 1110 / 1760–1810; England. Ends of the crest rail shaped to reverse curves leaving a raised central scoop. Baluster forms turned into the legs began about 1760 and are seen in figures 1091 through 1093. Crescent front stretchers began about 1750, but usually appear on chairs with a similarly bowed crest rail (as in figure 1117) where the line of the stretcher, rear edge of the seat, arm rail, and top rail oppose curve against curve.

1111 / 1790–1810; England. Turned front arm supports began about 1760 and gradually became heavier and more complicated through the eighteenth and nineteenth centuries. The mass and complexity of the front arm supports and stretchers, and the heavy crest rail, suggest a late date.

1112 / 1770–90; Pennsylvania; soft maple, American hickory, maple. The lower row of spindles is baluster-turned. Baluster-form legs with Colt feet and X-stretchers. The latter is as rare in England as America (an English example appears as figure 1124).

1113 / 1760–1800; America, probably Connecticut; lower spindles, maple; upper spindles, oak; seat, soft maple. The form of the spindles resembles English turnings as found on the stretchers of the following chair.

1114 / 1790–1820; England. The form of the seat and front arm supports, and the degenerate form of the Colt feet, suggest a late date.

1115

1116

1117

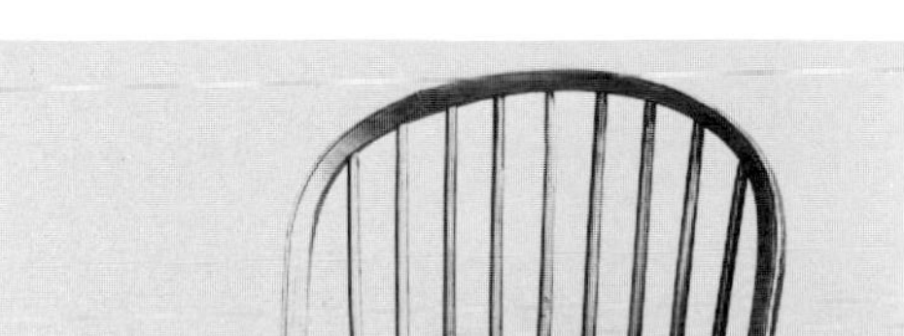

1118

1119

1120

1115 / 1760–80; England; beech with ash bows. Made without the use of a lathe.

1116 / 1750–80; England; yew with walnut legs. Early form of front arm support.

1117 / 1750–70; England.

1118 / 1760–1800; England.

1119 / 1760–80; England. The shape of the front of the seat, turnings of the arm supports, and form of the legs all suggest an early date.

1120 / 1780–1810; England; ash, seat possibly oak. Scroll hand holds. (One spoke damaged; stretchers missing: the legs have holes for them.)

1121

1122

1123

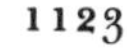

1124

1125

1126

1121 / 1770–1800; America; white oak arm rails and spindles, white pine seat, birch legs, stretchers, and arm supports. A beautiful balance of parts and use of space.
1122 / 1795–1815; Massachusetts; yellow birch, ash, white oak, white pine. The neo-classical style is seen in the bamboo-shape turning, ovals in the stretchers, plain front edge of the seat, and squeezing of the base of the top rail to form a circular shape.
1123 / 1790–1820; Britain; ash back; beech seat, arms, and arm supports; oak legs. The form of the arms and arm supports suggest an early nineteenth-century date. (Third spoke from left replaced.)
1124 / 1780–1810; England; mahogany. The carving and piercing of the splat includes neo-classical motifs: urns, rosettes, husks, and wheat-heads. A rare use of an X-stretcher in England.
1125 / 1780–1800; England. The urn form in the back leg suggests early neo-classical styling. Photograph inscribed: "Curriers."
1126 / Probably late eighteenth-century; Britain. (Legs shortened; medial stretcher missing; top of cabriole legs notched—probably to receive a board; damage to the splat.)

1127

1128

1129

1130

1131

1127 / 1820–40. Stamp of Thomas Simpson (1797–1878) of Boston, Lincolnshire, on chair in figure 1128.

1128 / 1820–40; England. The heaviness and complexity of the front arm supports (which do not match) and the legs suggest this date. (The left rear leg, and its turned stretcher, do not match those at the right.)

1129 / 1840–60; England; beech. The heavy legs suggest this date.

1130 / 1860–1900; England. During the second half of the nineteenth century the form of the splats, arm supports, and legs became ever more complex and heavy.

1131 / 1755–80; England. The form of the crest rail, arm supports, and front legs with Colt feet suggest a mid-century date. (The rear legs appear to be late replacements.)

1132

1133

1134

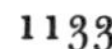

1135

1136

1137

Upholstered chairs

(Further examples appear in the essay section and in this section, under categories such as seventeenth-century and early eighteenth-century chairs.)

1132 / 1715–25; England; walnut, covered with original embroidery (the fringe may be of a later date).[41] C-scrolled knees.

1133 / 1720–35; England; walnut.

1134 / 1750–70; Britain, possibly Ireland. Photograph inscribed: "D[esmond Fitz-Gerald] says Irish?" For chairs of possible Irish origin with this form of knee bracket, see the entry to figure 922.

1135 / 1750–80; England. Twenty similar chairs, but with lower, straight top rails, were supplied by Chippendale in 1766 to Sir Rowland Winn, probably for the dining room in his house in St. James's Square.[42]

1136, 1137 / 1750–90; New England, possibly Massachusetts; mahogany (birch). As in similar British work, the primary wood of the rear legs is attached to the secondary wood, which makes the back; the tops of the front legs angle up to secure the corners of the upholstery; and there are cross ties.

1138

1139

1140

1141

1142

1143

1138 / 1725–40; England; walnut. Fragments of original red damask. The form of the arm supports appears on Philadelphia chairs made early in this style.

1139, 1140 / 1750–80; England; mahogany (beech). Mahogany rear leg spliced to beech back post.

1141 / 1750–80; Britain; mahogany. Bird heads carved on knee brackets of all four legs. Similar knee decoration appears on figure 1356. Bird heads were used in America as arm terminals and knee brackets (figure 1154).

1142, 1143 / 1750–85; Britain; mahogany. Similar chairs were designed by John Linnell about 1760 and others were made by Chippendale's shop in 1766.[43]

1144

1145

1146

1147

1148

1149

1144, 1145 / 1750–85; Britain; mahogany. Back legs spliced to back posts.

1146 / 1750–85; Britain; mahogany. Arm supports continue in scrolls above the arms.

1147 / 1720–30; England, probably London. A beautiful gilt-finished Palladian-style chair with flat and turned stretchers. The square-section front legs terminate in hoof feet below a line of carved hair.

1148 / 1715–25; England; walnut. Original tent and cross-stitch embroidery in wools. Similar chairs appear in figures 15 and 16. (Front of the turned front feet lost.)

1149 / 1720–35; England. Knees with raised edge and lambrequins with pendent husks.

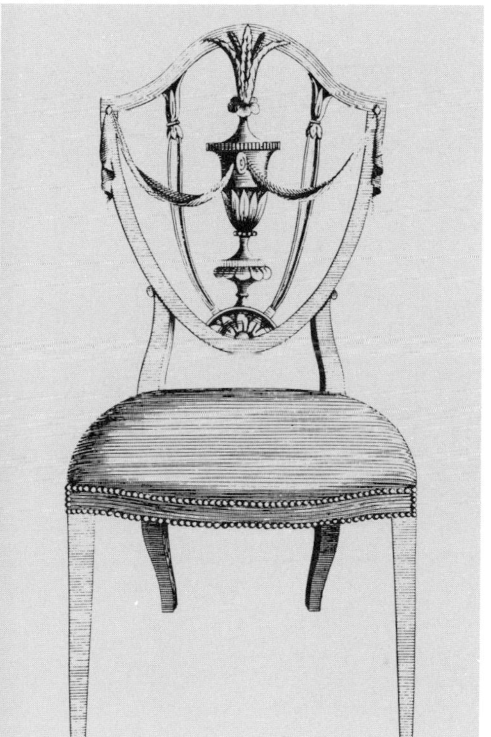

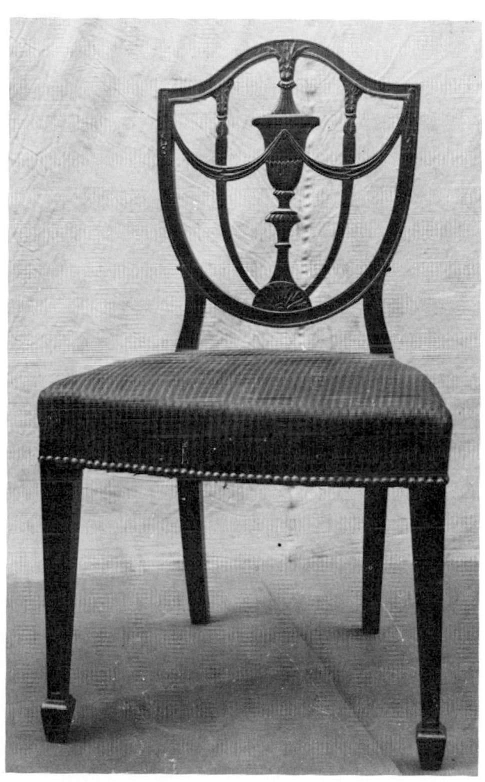

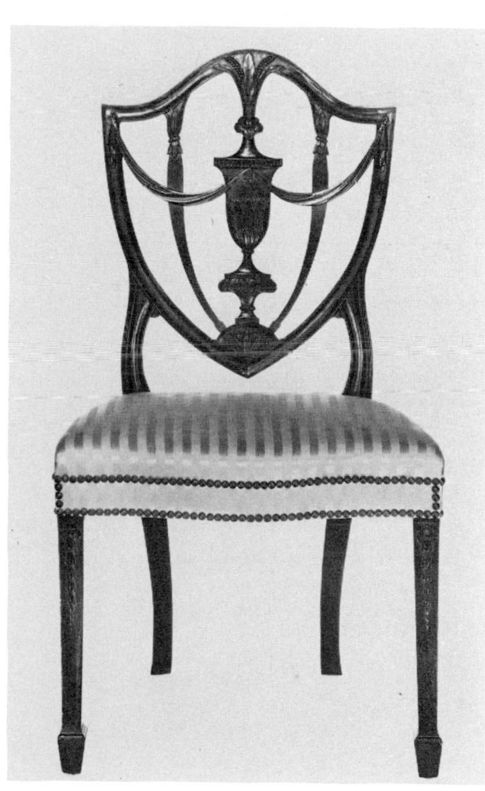

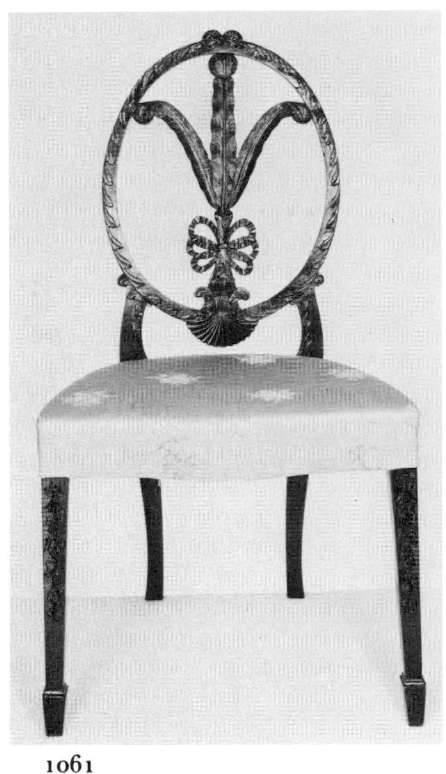

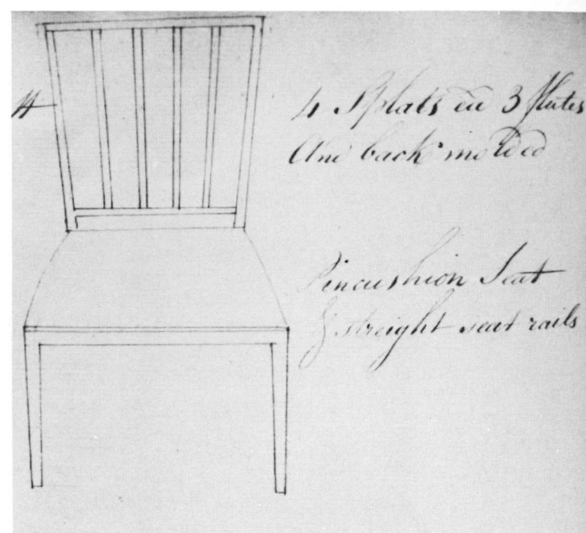

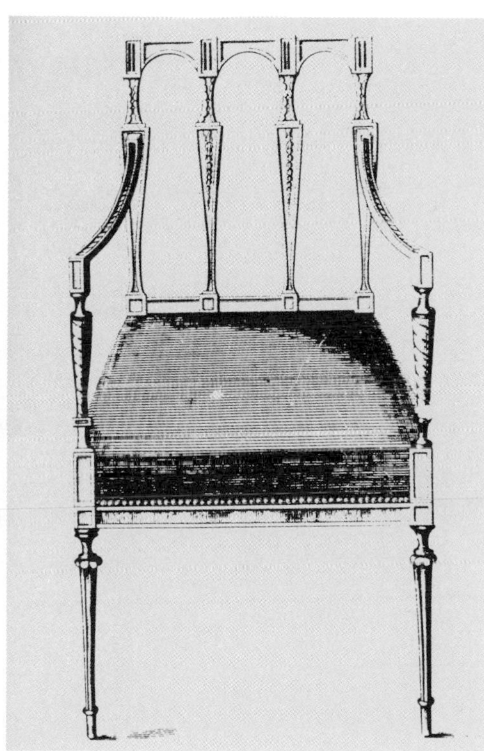

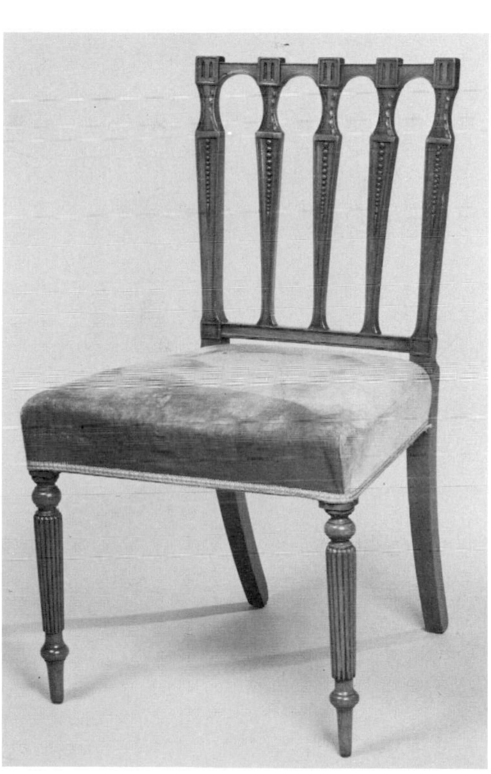

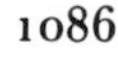

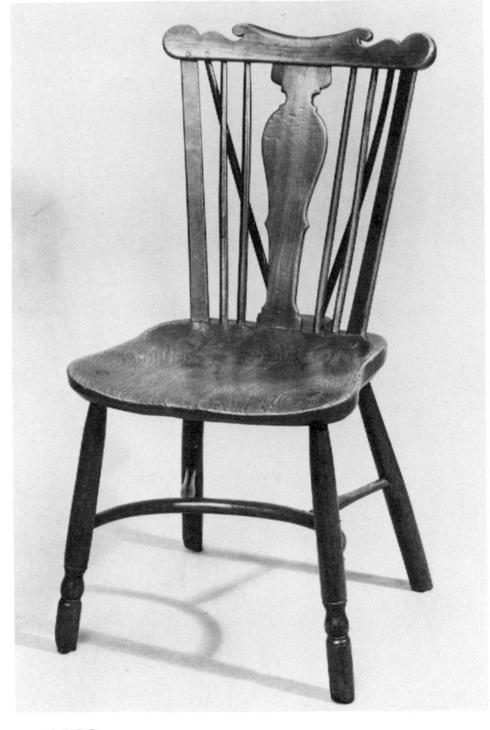

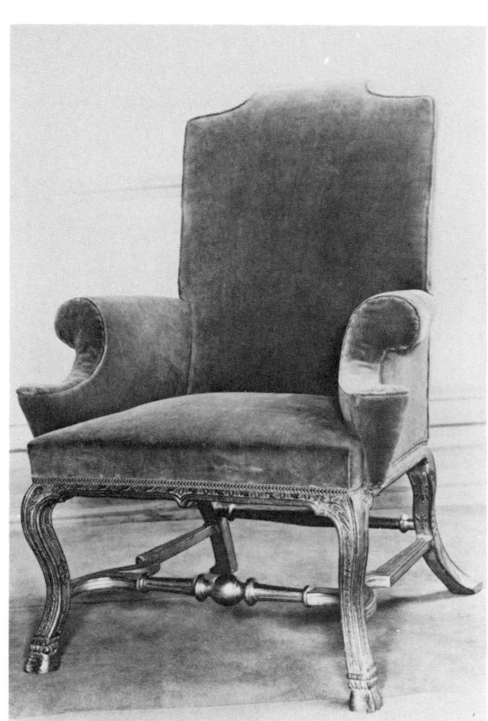

1150

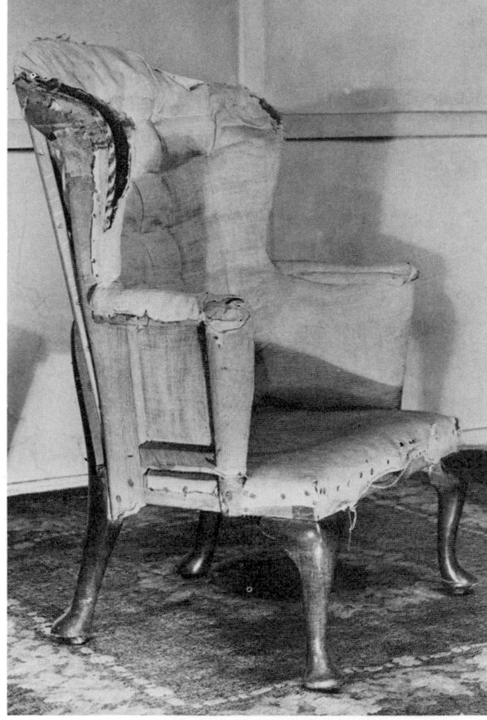
1151

1152

1153

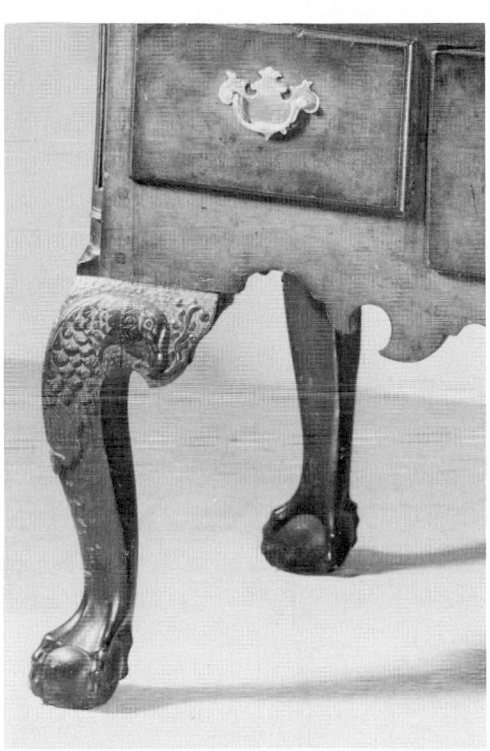
1154

1155

1150 / 1730–60; Britain. Vertically rolled arms stylistically predate horizontally rolling arms (figure 1155). The use of turned feet continued to the end of the century (see figure 1255). The disk or pad form of the turned front feet became standard in Philadelphia.

1151 / 1730–60; Britain. Back legs spliced to the back post (which has been replaced).

1152 / 1730–65; Britain. Straight-turned stretchers.

1153 / 1730–50; Britain. A rounded front shaping to the seat was popular in Philadelphia.

1154 / 1750–90; Pennsylvania; cherry (hard pine). Detail from a highboy.

1155 / 1735–50; Britain.

1156

1157

1158

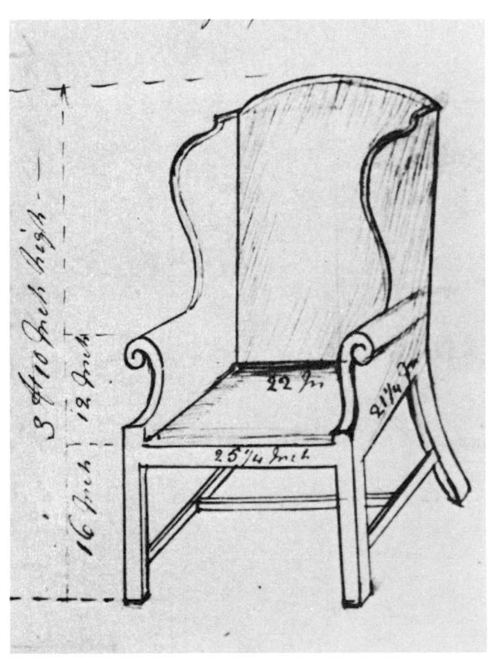

1159

1160

1161

1156 / 1750–90; Charleston, South Carolina; mahogany (mahogany, red bay, poplar, yellow pine).
1157 / 1745–85; Britain. Back leg spliced to back posts.
1158 / 1745–85; Britain.
1159 / Dated February 14, 1788. Ink drawing of "a Easy Chair Made of Beech" in the Estimate Book of the Gillows firm. The use of the square-section leg continued on some examples long after the beginning of the neo-classical style. (See the drawing of a sofa with straight legs dated 1798, figure 1185.)

1160 / 1750–90; Britain.
1161 / 1775–1810; Britain. The active serpentine line of the crest rail and wings suggests the classical revival style. The arm supports and front legs lack age and are replaced. Some chairs and sofas are "earlied-up" by replacing tapered legs with "Chippendale"-style straight legs; some are enriched with molding or stop fluting; and some are made "American" by changing certain secondary woods.

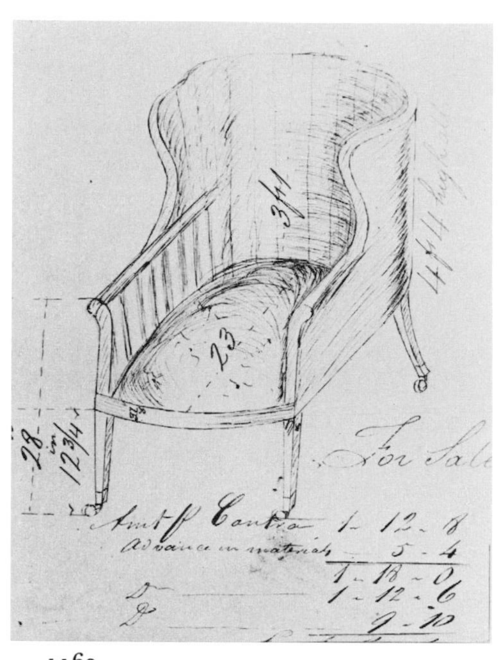

1162

1163

1164

1165

1166

1167

1162 / Dated March 6, 1795. Ink drawing in the Estimate Book of the Gillows firm.
1163 / 1780–1810; Britain. Back legs spliced to back posts.
1164 / 1790–1810; America, possibly Baltimore; mahogany (pine of the taeda group, tulip, white pine). The wings are removable for upholstery. Plate 15 of Hepplewhite's *Guide,* dated 1787, shows a similar chair that probably had removable wings. (Medial stretcher restored since this photograph.)
1165 / 1780–1810; Britain; mahogany.
1166 / 1790–1810; Massachusetts; mahogany (soft maple). Top of each arm carved to a rosette and triple bead edging.
1167 / 1780–1810; Britain.

1168

1169

1170

1171

1172

1168 / 1805–20; Britain. Various designs in Sheraton's 1812 edition of *Designs for Household Furniture* are similar in form.

WOODEN EASY CHAIRS; SETTLES; SOFAS

1169 / 1750–1800; England; pine painted red. A front view of this chair appears as figure 182. The shaping of the crest rail suggests a date after the middle of the century. A variety of forms was devised to protect the sitter from drafts intensified by open fires. The wing chair and settle are the most familiar, but others, such as this wooden wing chair and draped or cloth-fitted Windsors, could also serve.

1170 / Probably early nineteenth-century; America, probably New England; pine painted blue-green. A similar English pine piece is seen as figure 183.

1171 / Probably early nineteenth-century; Britain. Probably a removable seat board to allow access to a potty. Holes in the hand holds may once have held a restraining rail.

1172 / Late seventeenth century; Britain; oak. The central part of the seat lifts to allow access to a storage area. Many British settles were made of pine.

1173

1174

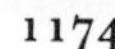

1175

1176

1177

1178

1173 / 1750–1800; America, possibly Connecticut; Atlantic white cedar. A related settle has a history of having belonged to the Trumbull family of Lebanon, Connecticut.[44] The hand holds are not dissimilar to those on the preceding English settle. The central board of the back has beaded edges. Tapered boards, preserving the full dimension of the sawn board, occur also in contemporary architectural board sheathing.

1174 / Possibly late seventeenth-century; Britain; oak. Known as the "Shakespeare courting settle."

1175 / 1640–80; England. Original leather and nails.

1176 / 1660–1700; Boston, Massachusetts; maple (oak). Possibly made for John Leverett (1662–1724).[45] (Adjustable wings similar to those on the couch in figure 1175 are missing.)

1177 / Late seventeenth-century; England. The pyramidal finial suggests Lancashire and North Cheshire (see figure 660).

1178 / Early eighteenth-century; England. Fielded panels.

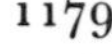

1179

1180

1181

1182

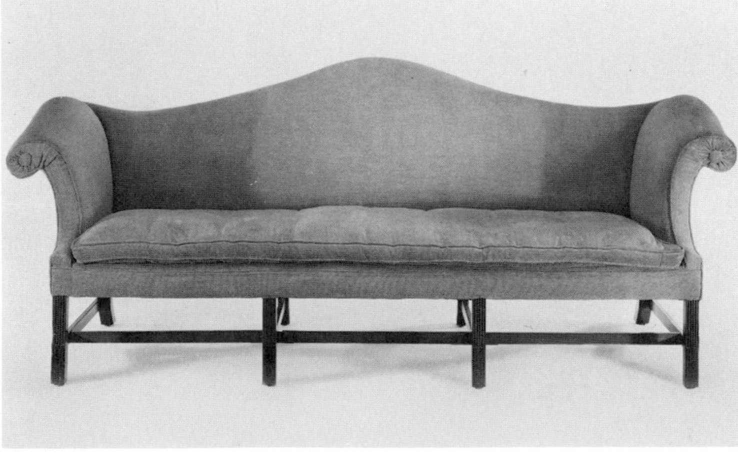

1183

1184

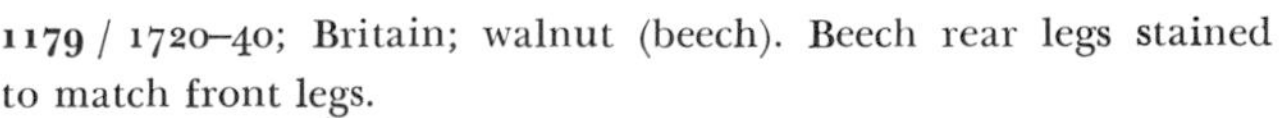

1179 / 1720–40; Britain; walnut (beech). Beech rear legs stained to match front legs.

1180 / 1730–60; Ireland. Veneered back and seat rails.

1181 / 1730–60; Ireland; walnut (oak, pine). Seat rails veneered.

1182 / 1745–90; Philadelphia, Pennsylvania; mahogany (white oak). (Probably the stretchers are new: the area of the legs around the stretchers shows reworking and there is no evidence on the present stretchers for medial stretchers, which should be present.)

1183 / 1760–90; Newport, Rhode Island; mahogany (pine, cherry, ash, chestnut). According to tradition, made for John Brown's house in Providence, Rhode Island.

1184 / 1750–85; Britain. Sofas with straight legs, square in cross section, were made at least as late as 1798 (see figure 1185).

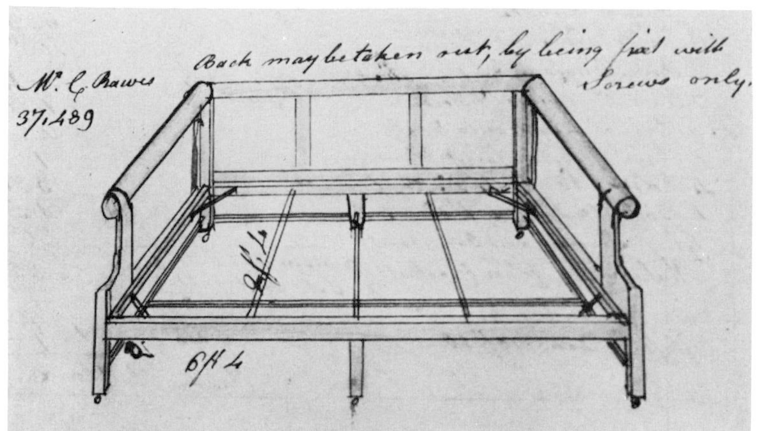

1185

1186

1187

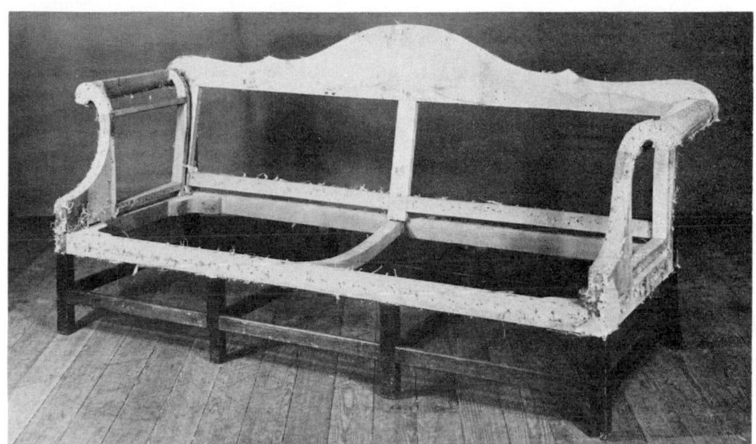

1188

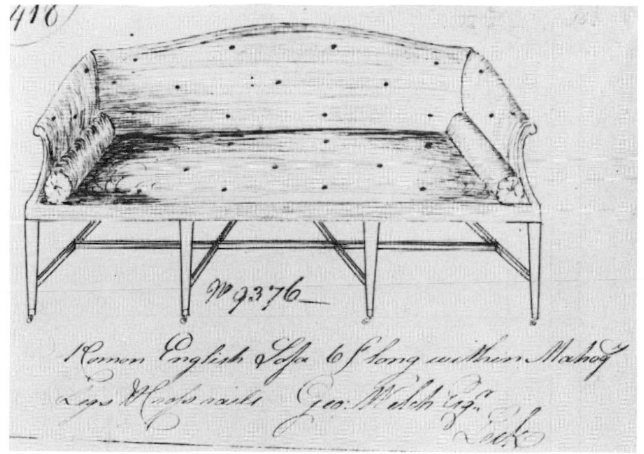

1189

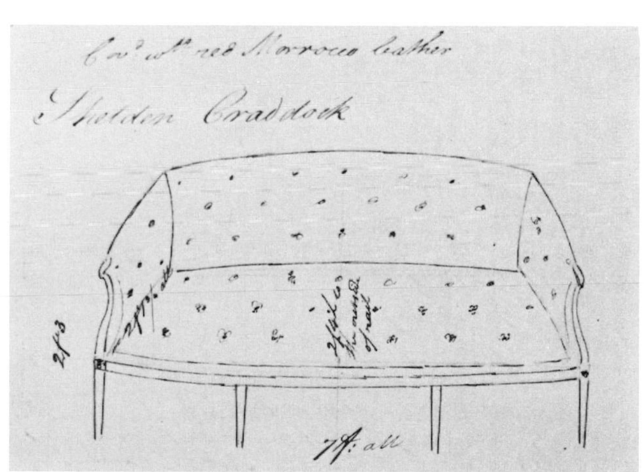

1190

1185 / Dated October, 1798. Ink drawing of "A Sofa," on page 1479 of the Estimate Book of the Gillows firm. There were mahogany "Feet & Stritching rails [stretchers]," a deal back, and the other secondary wood was beech; it had "6 three Wheel Iron Casters." This drawing and figure 1159 document the use of straight, untapered legs of square section until the end of the eighteenth century. The straightness of the top line of the crest rail and arms is like those on figures 1195 through 1200. Another 1798 Gillows drawing (page 1463) of "A Cabriole Sofa" has straight legs "moulded on the front and Side only." Its crest rail is wavy, like that on figure 1193.

1186 / 1750–85; Britain.

1187, 1188 / 1750–90; Britain. The use of stretchers between the front legs suggests a provincial origin. The front legs of the first are joined to the scrolled front of the arms in a scarf joint.

1189 / Dated October, 1788. Ink drawing of "A Comon English Sofa," page 418 of the Estimate Book of the Gillows firm. Mahogany legs and stretching rails.

1190 / Dated June, 1793. Ink drawing of "A mahogany sofa," page 982 of the Estimate Book of the Gillows firm. Mahogany "end feet & elbows [front of the arms]," "legs and X [cross] rails." Other woods were beech with "X band ven[ee]r" and white wood. The sofa was covered with "red Marrocco leather." On the lower half of the page was written: "One exactly simular only a foot shorter & the back curved a little at one end to suit the room," which demonstrates how precisely items could be made to the customer's needs.

1191

1192

1193

1194

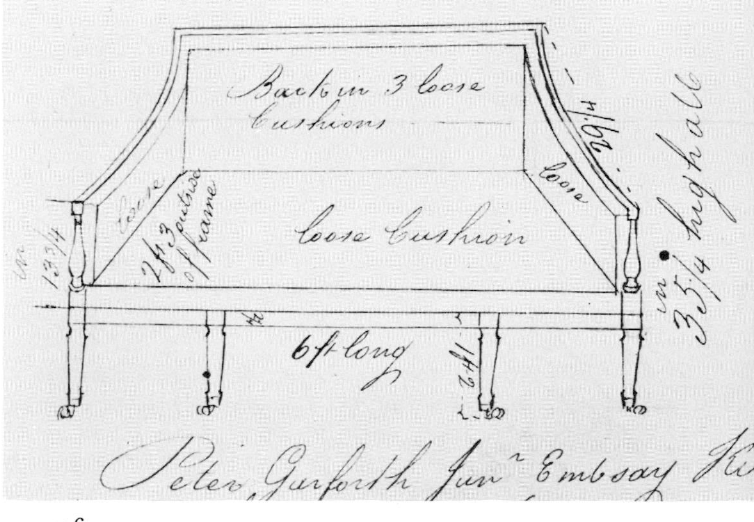

1195

1196

1191, 1192 / 1785–1805; Britain.
1193 / 1785–1805; Britain. A 1798 drawing of "A Cabriole Sofa" in the Estimate Book of the Gillows firm (page 1463) has a similarly shaped arm and top rail, but the legs are straight, not tapered.
1194, 1195 / 1785–1805; Britain.

1196 / Dated November, 1794. Ink drawing of "A painted Beech Sofa," page 1134 of the Estimate Book of the Gillows firm. "Painted to match his [Peter Garforth's] Drawing Room Chairs." The inside of the seating space was covered with loose cushions, one on the seat, one at each end, and three across the back.

1197

1198

1199

1200

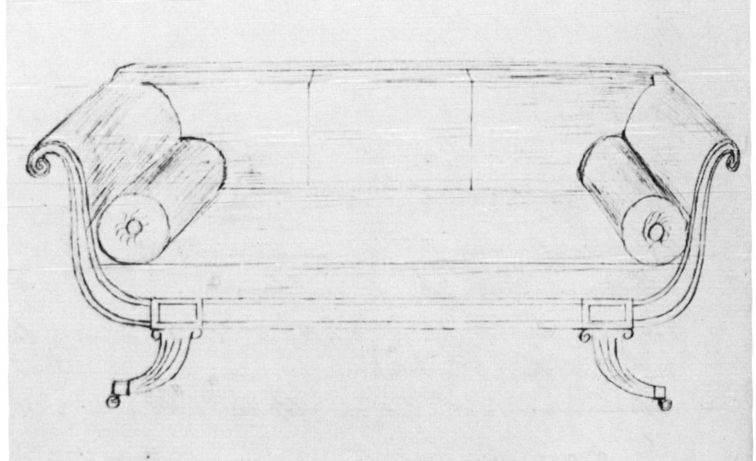

1201

1202

1197 / 1790–1810; America, probably New York, New York.
1198 / 1785–1810; Britain; mahogany.
1199 / Dated May, 1795. Ink drawing of "A Beech Sofa with mahogany Legs," page 1167 of the Estimate Book of the Gillows firm. The legs were turned round.
1200 / 1790–1810; Britain. A sofa with a similar line for the back and end rails appears on plate 21, dated 1787, of Hepplewhite's 1788 *Guide*, although the back, ends, and seat are upholstered, and the legs are of the square-section tapered form.
1201 / Dated April, 1809. Ink drawing of "A Grecian Sofa," page 1860 of the Estimate Book of the Gillows firm. Made of ash, it was japanned black and had 44 feet of brass bead and "claw Casters." The next entry on this page was a similarly styled and decorated cane-seat chair. A related "Mahogany Grecian Couch" (the right end higher than the left) of "Mapple" and "Mahogany" appears on page 1765, dated 1805. Another item of similar form, but without a back, was "A Mahogany Grecian Window Stool," dated April, 1811, page 1896. The right end rose as high as that of figure 1201, the left end curved down.
1202 / 1800–15; Britain.

1203

1204

1205

1206

FORMS: STOOLS

1203 / 1650–1700; Plymouth County, Massachusetts; white pine, black ash, soft maple. Similar turnings appear on a number of pieces made in Plymouth County. The overhang of the top is greater than on related English pieces.

1204 / 1630–80; England; oak. Related turnings appear on the chair in figure 655.

1205 / 1650–1700; eastern Massachusetts; American red oak. As in figure 372, the turnings are an inverted version of a standard English pattern.

1206 / 1650–1700; England; oak. Related turnings and rail shaping appear on figure 655.

1207

1208

1209

1210

1211

1212

1213

1207 / 1650–1700; England; oak.
1208 / 1650–1700; England; oak. (The lower parts of the legs have been restored incorrectly; they place the stretchers too far from the floor.)
1209 / 1670–1710; England; walnut.

1210 / 1720–45; England.
1211 / 1730–70; New England, probably Connecticut; cherry (hard pine). Corners of slip-seat frame made with lap-joints.
1212, 1213 / 1720–60; Britain; walnut.

1214

1215

1216

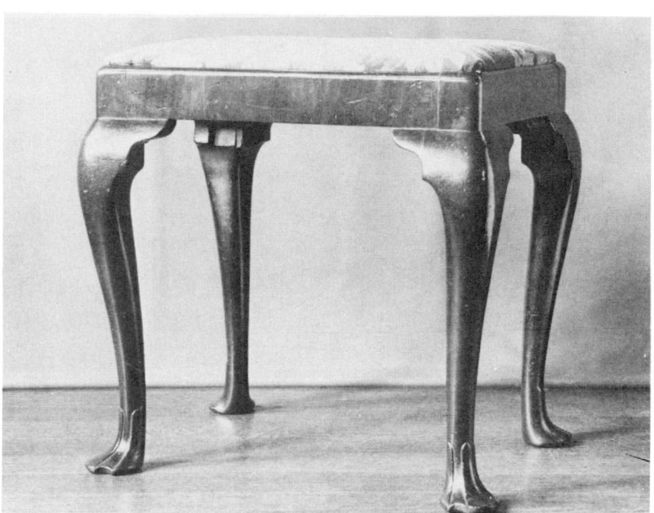
1217

1218

1219

1214 / 1720–60; Britain; walnut. Photograph inscribed: "Hampton Court."

1215 / 1720–60; Britain; walnut.

1216 / 1740–70; Ireland or England; walnut.

1217 / 1740–70; Britain, possibly Ireland. A detail of one foot appears as figure 35.

1218 / 1750–85; Britain.

1219 / 1755–90; Britain.

1220

1221

1222

1223

1224

1225

Tables

EARLY

1220 / Table probably eighteenth-century; stool nineteenth-century; Britain.

1221 / 1590–1640; England; oak. The rear central leg has a simple octagonal shape: when used as a head table that leg would not be seen.

1222 / 1630–50; England; oak.

1223 / 1670–1700; America, probably Little Compton area of Rhode Island; white oak (white pine, soft maple).

1224 / Early seventeenth-century; probably Britain. Similar tables were made from Scandinavia to Italy.[46] (The corners of the top were probably rounded at a later date.)

1225 / Seventeenth-century; probably Britain; oak.

1226

1227

1228

1229

1230

1226 / 1675–1700; Britain; oak.
1227 / 1670–1705; Britain.
1228 / 1670–1700; Connecticut, probably New London; maple and pine. According to tradition, it descended in the Allyn family of New London.
1229 / 1690–1720; Britain. (Pulls of a later date.)
1230 / 1670–1700; Britain; walnut, end rails with inlaid walnut and fruitwood in a diaper pattern (oak). (Feet not original.)

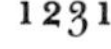

1231

1232

1233

1234

1235

1231 / 1690–1720; Britain; walnut.
1232 / 1700–35; New England, found in Rhode Island; maple with remains of red paint.
1233 / 1680–1710; Britain.
1234 / 1665–90; England; oak. An end rail with shadow molding is unusual. (Feet restored.)
1235 / 1670–1700; England; oak. Column turning reemerged as a popular form late in the seventeenth century. (Drop leaves missing.)

1236

1237

1238

1239

1240

1241

1242

1243

1244

1236 / 1700–40; Britain; oak. (The drawer and the rail below its front edge are not original. They have been fitted into a stand that may not have had a drawer originally.)
1237 / 1700–40; Britain.
1238 / 1680–1700; England; walnut. One drop leaf. Six legs with urn forms below baluster shapes.
1239 / 1710–80; Southern, possibly North Carolina or coastal Virginia; walnut. Urn turnings below baluster shapes.
1240 / 1685–1715; England; oak.
1241 / 1690–1720; Britain; walnut. (The feet have lost their attached toes.)
1242 / 1690–1720; Britain. The top barely overhangs the open gate leg, which suggests that the top itself is not original.
1243 / 1710–50; Southern, southeast Tidewater Virginia; yellow pine and cypress.
1244 / 1700–40; Britain.

1245

1246

1247

1248

1245 / 1680–1700; England; oak.
1246 / 1690–1730; Britain.
1247 / 1680–1720; England.
1248 / 1680–1710; England; oak. Drawer front carved to central flower flanked by scrolls, above carved spandrels. (The top is new, and the feet have lost their attached toes.)

1249

1250

1251

1252

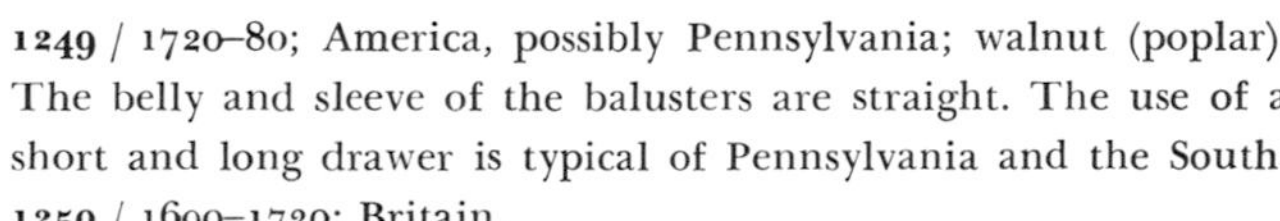

1249 / 1720–80; America, possibly Pennsylvania; walnut (poplar). The belly and sleeve of the balusters are straight. The use of a short and long drawer is typical of Pennsylvania and the South.
1250 / 1690–1730; Britain.
1251 / 1690–1730; Britain; oak.
1252 / 1690–1720; Britain. The height of the restored feet is too great. The use of swing brackets to support raised leaves is not common in England; the piece may be a joined stool converted to this form. (Another published example of this form is also questionable.)[47]
1253 / Probably nineteenth-century; Britain. Splayed-leg "cricket" tables were made in great numbers as a serviceable form that would not rock on uneven surfaces. Similar tables were made on the continent (see figure 771).

1253

1254

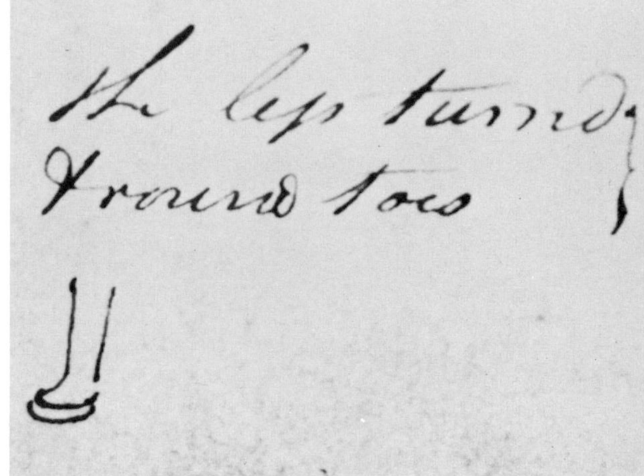

1255

1256

1257

TURNED LEGS WITH ROUND TOES

1254 / 1740–1800; America, probably Rhode Island; mahogany. It is not possible to narrow the dating of straight-turned legs with offset turned feet unless other distinguishing features are present. They appear on high-style items by about 1720 (figure 1358) and remain as an optional form throughout the century. (The following 1793 drawing of this form of leg and foot from the Gillows firm records is headed: "The legs turned & round toes.") The straight-turned form, with claw and ball feet or rounded toes, often appears as rear legs on developed pieces, confining elaborate decoration and shaping to the front (figures 1361 and 1377).

1255 / Dated May, 1793. Detail from an ink drawing showing a table and a detail of the lower part of one of its legs, page 977 of the Estimate Book of the Gillows firm. The table is shown as figure 92. The detail is headed: "The legs turned & round toes."

1256, 1257 / 1740–1800; England; walnut (beech stained brown-red). Molded corners on the blocks at the top of the legs appeared also on Philadelphia and Southern tables.

1258

1259

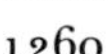

1260

1261

1258 / 1740–1800; Britain; walnut.
1259 / 1740–1800; America, possibly Newport, Rhode Island; mahogany (maple, chestnut).
1260 / 1760–90; Britain, possibly Ireland; mahogany. The photograph is inscribed: "Irish, mahog[any]." Similar tables were made in England.
1261 / 1740–1800; Britain, possibly Ireland; mahogany. The photograph is inscribed: "Irish"

1262

1263

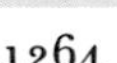

1264

1265

1266

1262 / 1740–1800; Britain; mahogany, veneered rails.
1263 / 1740–1800; New England; maple with red-brown paint.
1264 / 1740–1800; Surrey-Sussex County area, Virginia; walnut (yellow pine).
1265 / 1740–1800; Tidewater Virginia; walnut (walnut).
1266 / 1740–1800; Britain; mahogany.

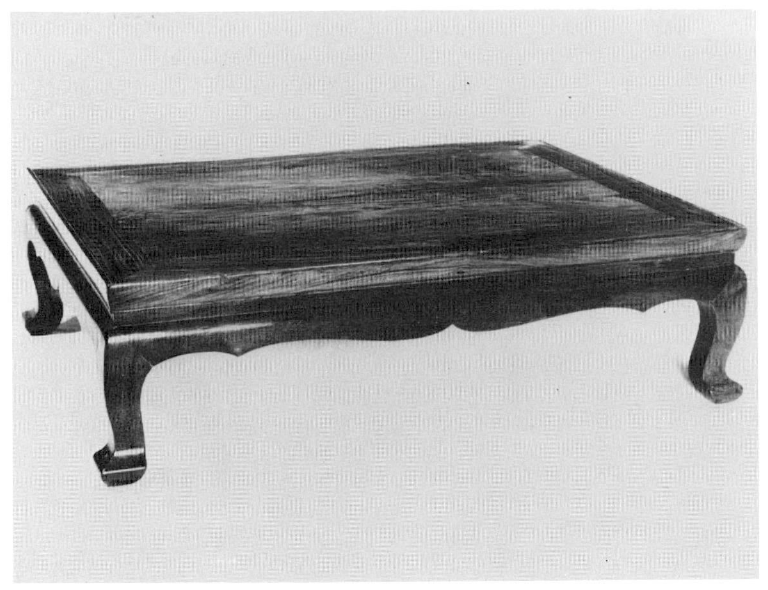

1267

1268

1269

1270

1271

CHINESE-BASED; SIMPLE CABRIOLE FORMS, INCLUDING IRISH; PHILADELPHIA-RELATED: IRISH AND ENGLISH

(Some examples are under other categories, such as card tables.)

1267 / Fifteenth-century; China; rosewood. The Chinese cabriole leg and foot (which are square in section) and the paired reverse-curve shaping of the rails influenced English design from the late seventeenth century through the first third of the eighteenth century. Many Chinese tables were low, like this example, but others were as high as Western examples.[48]

1268, 1269 / 1710–20; England; walnut. Many tables such as these have veneered rails, usually with vertical grain, and cross-banded veneer skirts.

1270 / 1715–30; England.

1271 / 1710–20; England.

1272

1273

1274

1275

1276

In 1713–14, London exported one hundred tea tables to New England at the cost of £31 10s.[49] Contemporary inventories often list tea board and stand as separate items. Possibly the tops on many rectangular tea tables, although now fixed in place, originally lifted off. (Inspection of a number of examples shows the glue blocks holding the tops to the frames to be new.) On other examples, fixed tops held removable trays of wood or another material, as on the table seen in figure 1297, with a silver tray. On a few tables, the molded edge of the fixed top stepped down rather than up; this recessed edge held the tray in place.[50]

1272 / 1740–70; Britain, probably Ireland; mahogany (pine). Photograph inscribed: "Irish Solid Mahogany pine blocks—Found in Dublin." A related form was made in China in the sixteenth century and the Chinese design was used in Japan in the seventeenth century, figure 1273.

1273 / Seventeenth-century; Japan; lacquered and inlaid with

1277

1278

1279

1280

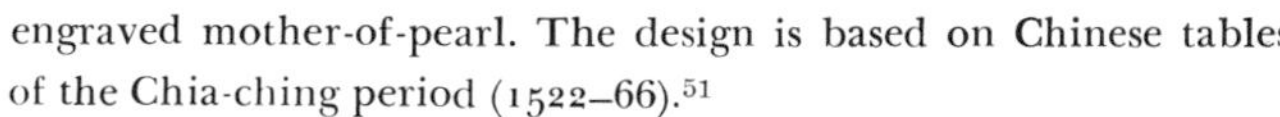

engraved mother-of-pearl. The design is based on Chinese tables of the Chia-ching period (1522–66).[51]

1274 / 1740–90; America, probably Long Island, New York; cherry. Similar pointed feet appear on various English pieces, for example, figure 1281. The top was made to look like a separate tray.

1275 / 1750–90; America, probably Rhode Island, probably Newport; cherry.

1276 / 1715–40; England. Japanned stand for a cabinet.

1277 / 1740–80; Newport, Rhode Island; walnut (hard sugar maple).

1278 / 1740–80; Britain, probably Ireland. The photograph is inscribed: "Irish."

1279 / 1740–70; Ireland or England; mahogany, mahogany veneer on skirt and rails (pine).

1280 / 1740–80; Britain, probably Ireland; mahogany.

1281 / 1730–70; Britain. Pointed feet.

1281

1282

1283

1284

1285

1286

1287

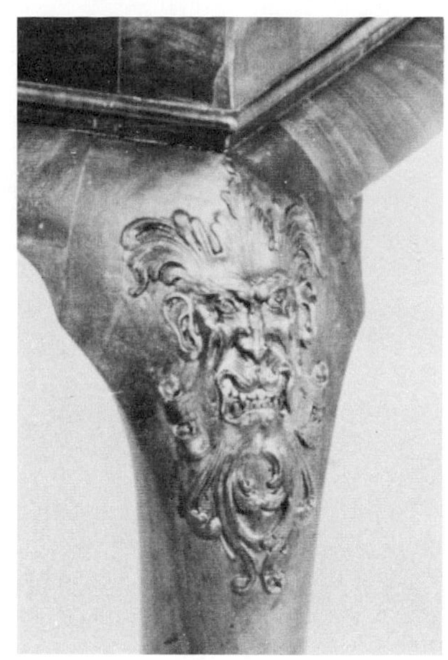

1288

1289

1290

1282 / 1720–35; London, England; gilded wood. Similar leaf-carved feet appear on the tea table in figure 1297 and the complex side table, figure 1322.

1283 / 1725–40; London, England; gilded wood. Leaf-carved knees and feet.

1284 / 1730–45; London, England; walnut?, brass inlay. Photograph inscribed: "Cartouche with crest of the Marsh family of Longden and of Denton in Kent." Brass shell forms inlaid into the feet.

1285 / 1730–45; London, England; mahogany? with brass inlay. Writing slide and drawer in front rail.

1286 / 1725–50; England.

1287, 1288 / 1730–60; Ireland; mahogany (pine, oak). Finished on all four sides. The knee masks are similar to those on a three-leg pier table and a desk on stand associated with Boston, Massachusetts. Research suggests, however, that the pier table is "made up" from three old, probably British, legs, and that only the desk section of the desk on stand is original. (Its base seems of recent manufacture, employing four old, probably Irish, legs.)[52]

1289 / 1730–60; Britain, possibly Ireland; mahogany.

1290 / 1740–70; Britain; mahogany.

1291

1292

1293

1294

1295

1291 / 1740–70; Britain; mahogany.
1292 / 1730–55; history of being in Berwick, Maine, but probably made in Boston, Massachusetts; walnut (maple, white pine). Feet turned with a projecting pad are more common in the Philadelphia area, but appear on a few New England pieces.
1293 / 1730–60; Britain, possibly Ireland; mahogany.
1294 / 1735–60; New England, probably Rhode Island, possibly Massachusetts; mahogany. Finished on all four sides.
1295 / 1730–70; Britain.

1296

1297

1298

1299

1296 / 1720–40; England; japanned. Very close to Chinese forms. Probably worked rather than turned feet.
1297 / 1725–45; England; gilded wood. A silver tray rests on a wooden top shaped to hold it in place. Feet carved to scrolling leafage.
1298 / 1730–80; Britain, possibly Ireland; mahogany.
1299 / 1730–80; Ireland or England. A related table that is equally like New England work was sold as English in 1964.[53]
1300 / 1730–60; Ireland or provincial England.

1300

1301

1302

1303

1304

1305

1306

1307

1308

1309

1301 / 1725–60; Britain, possibly Ireland.

1302 / 1730–50; London, England; mahogany, mahogany veneer. Similar knee carving appears on the London card tables in figures 1361 and 1362, and on New York and Newport pieces. (Top replaced.)

1303 / 1745–80; Britain, probably Ireland.

1304 / 1745–85; Britain, probably Ireland; mahogany (pine).

1305 / 1745–85; Britain, possibly Ireland.

1306 / 1745–85; Ireland; oak. (Knee bracket missing.)

1307 / 1745–85; Britain, probably Ireland; mahogany.

1308 / 1745–85; Ireland; mahogany.

1309 / 1745–85; Britain, possibly Ireland. (Edge of top and parts of skirt rebuilt.)

1310 / 1745–85; Ireland; mahogany.

1310

1311

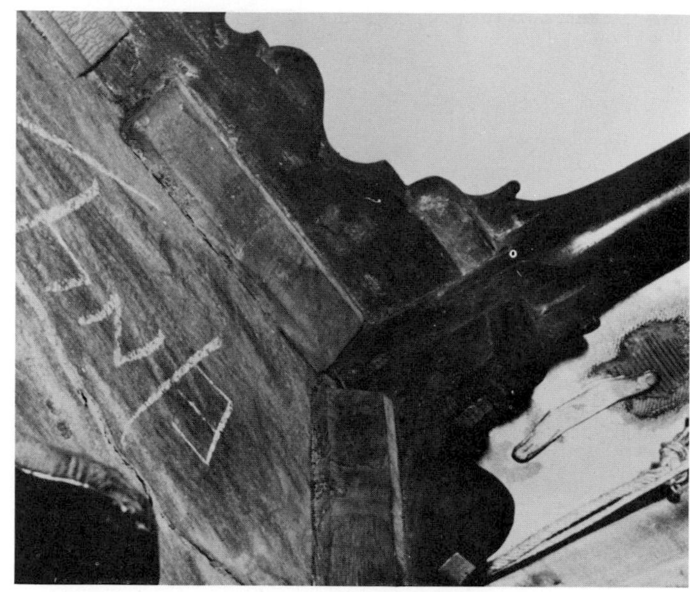

1312

1313

1314

1315

1316

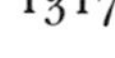

1317

1318

1319

1320

1311, 1312 / 1745–85; Ireland; mahogany. Detail shows skirt pieced out behind knee brackets, and glue blocks securing top to frame.

1313 / 1745–90; probably Philadelphia, Pennsylvania, possibly Ireland; mahogany. The legs do not have pins securing the rail tenons; the knee brackets may be replacements; the molding edging the top is applied. This example was published as one of five known Philadelphia eighteenth-century tea tables and as having descended from George Gray of Whitby Hall, at the foot of Gray's Ferry Road.[54] Its visual relationship to Irish examples is strong, and it is made entirely of mahogany. To assign a place of origin, it is necessary to depend on family history and stylistic analysis. The first is treacherous as a basis for attribution, for even if the history is correct, the original owner may have imported the piece. The second involves personal judgments, which may shift with new understanding. The line of the legs is possibly Philadelphian rather than Irish. Compare the legs with those on figure 1323, which is probably closer to Philadelphia work than any other Irish piece in this book.

1314, 1315 / 1745–85; Britain, probably Ireland; mahogany. The second photograph is inscribed: "Irish."

1316, 1317, 1318, 1319 / 1745–85; Ireland; mahogany.

1320 / 1745–85; Ireland. Applied bosses with concentric rings appear on a variety of eighteenth-century European forms.

1321

1322

1323

1324

1325

1326

1327

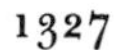

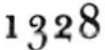

1328

1329

1321 / 1750–85; Ireland; mahogany.
1322 / 1725–40; London, England; gilt gesso on wood.
1323 / 1745–90; Ireland; mahogany (pine, oak). The table has a history of having come from Corenly, County Leitrim.
1324 / 1750–90; Britain, probably Ireland; mahogany. The skirt is shaped on four sides.
1325 / 1750–90; Britain, possibly Ireland.
1326 / 1745–85; Ireland or England; mahogany (pine).
1327 / 1745–85; Ireland; mahogany.
1328 / 1745–85; Britain, probably Ireland; mahogany (pine).
1329 / 1750–85; Britain, possibly Ireland; mahogany.
1330 / 1745–85; probably Netherlands.

1330

1331

1332

1333

1334

1335

1336

1337

1338

1339

1331 / 1750–85; Ireland or England; mahogany.
1332, 1333, 1334, 1335 / 1750–85; Britain; mahogany.
1336 / 1750–90; Philadelphia, Pennsylvania; mahogany (arbor vitae, white pine). (The top is not original. Family tradition states that it once had a marble top that was broken about 1875.)
1337 / 1750–90, possibly 1774; Philadelphia, Pennsylvania; mahogany (cherry, pine). The back of the table has a plain cherry rail that was permanently placed against a wall. It stood in the Lockerman homestead, Dover, Delaware, until the mid-1960s; Vincent Lockerman (d. 1785) purchased pieces from the Philadelphia shop of Benjamin Randolph (1721–1791) and Hercules Courtenay (1744?–1784) in 1774.[55] This may have been among them.
1338 / 1745–85; Ireland; mahogany.
1339 / 1745–85; Ireland. On a group of Irish tables the pulvinated skirt curves to the top without an intervening vertical rail. Similar decoration, including the mask, appears on an easy chair usually assigned to the shop of Benjamin Randolph.[56] The ground of its skirt has a diapered pattern similar to that on figures 1342, 1344, 1345, and 1349–51.

1340

1341

1342

1343

1340 / 1750–90; Philadelphia, Pennsylvania; mahogany (white cedar, white oak).

1341, 1342, 1343 / 1750–85; Ireland; mahogany.

1344 / 1750–85; Ireland.

1345 / 1750–85; Ireland. The ankles have scale carving. (The gadrooned top is probably not original and the lower part of the mask may once have had a circular backing with additional carved hair, as on the preceding table.)

1346 / 1750–85; Ireland. The narrow front and side rails have vertical-grain veneer. The lower part of the mask may once have had a circular backing with more hair, as on figure 1344.

1344

1345

1346

1347

1348

1349

1347 / 1750–85; Ireland. (Top not original.)

1348 / 1750–85; England or Ireland. The cabriole part of the front legs pull out with the front skirt and rail.

1349 / 1745–65; London, England; mahogany. Possibly made by the London cabinetmaker Giles Grendey (1693–1780). Provincial pieces rarely achieve this balance of forms and quality of carving.

1350, 1351 / 1750–85; Ireland; mahogany.

1352 / 1750–85; Britain, probably Ireland, possibly England.

1353, 1354 / 1750–65; Neuwied, Germany; fruitwood. Made by Abraham Roentgen (1711–1793). When the second top is open a case with drawers, pigeon holes, and reading stand can be drawn up from inside the frame. The carving and the veneer continue onto the side and rear rails. All the shapes and motifs found here are known on British examples. The line and sprightly flowing movement of this German decoration are close to known Philadelphia examples.

1350

1351

1352

1353

1354

1355

1356

1357

1355 / 1750–85; England. Photograph inscribed: "Coopers."
1356 / 1750–85; Britain. Similar knee carving appears on figure 1141.
1357 / Dated June, 1821. Ink drawing of "A Mah[ogan]y Carv'd frame (for Marble Slab)" with mahogany cross-band veneered frieze and deal as secondary wood; page 3107 of the Estimate Book of the Gillows firm. The carving alone cost £10 10s.

1358

1359

1360

CARD, MARLBOROUGH LEG, AND PEMBROKE TABLES; STANDS

(Examples from these categories are also found under other headings.)

1358 / 1715–35; London, England; laburnum veneer.

1359 / 1720–40; London, England.

1360 / 1730–50; New England, probably Boston, Massachusetts; walnut.

1361 / 1730–40; London, England; walnut. The drawer in the front rail contains a label of Benjamin Crook of London. (Another Crook piece appears as figure 609.) The rear legs are straight. The use of turned rear legs, often with turned feet, along with more developed front legs and feet, does not denote a transitional piece; rather, it was often a means of providing a more frontal design. Newport, in the second half of the eighteenth century, used turned rear feet and claw and ball front feet to intensify the frontal unity on rectalinear forms (see figure 352).

1362 / 1730–40; London, England. See the caption for the preceding table, which has similar features.

1361

1362

1363

1364

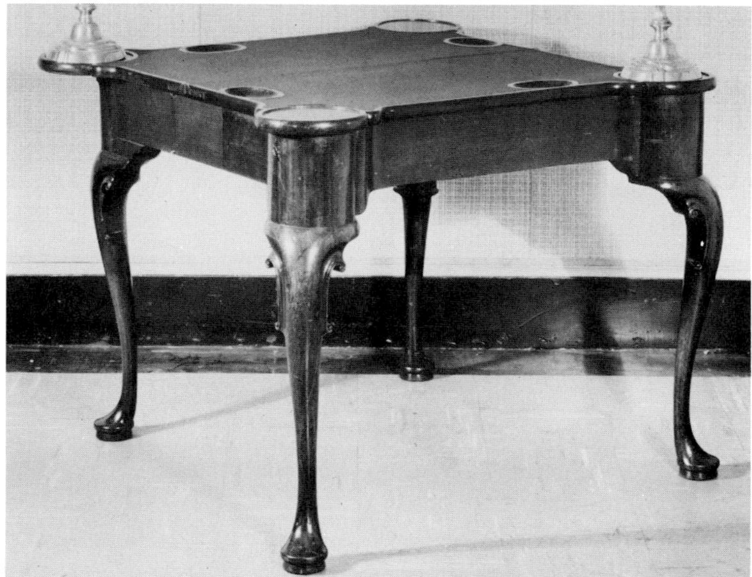

1365

1366

1367

1363 / 1745–70; Ireland?; mahogany (oak, deal).
1364 / 1745–85; Virginia, possibly Norfolk; mahogany (white oak, tulip poplar).
1365 / 1745–80; England or Ireland. "Accordion" form.
1366, 1367 / 1745–85; Ireland.

1368

1369

1370

1371

1372

1368 / 1745–85; Britain, probably Ireland; mahogany.

1369 / 1745–85; Britain, probably Ireland. A similar table but with square corners appears as figure 1376.

1370 / 1745–85; Ireland; mahogany. Three-layer top. As on many examples, the front rail pulls out as the front of a drawer.

1371 / 1750–85; Ireland; mahogany. Claw and ball feet with open claws and talons.

1372 / 1750–85; Britain. Bird heads appear as terminals on some New York and Massachusetts chairs, and as knee brackets on a few Pennsylvania pieces (see figure 1154).

1373

1374

1375

1376

1377a

1377b

1378

1380

1373 / 1740–70; Britain. A simple form that was made into the second half of the century; see figure 1377.
1374 / 1740–70; Boston, Massachusetts; mahogany (pine).
1375 / 1740–70; Ireland or England; mahogany, mahogany veneer (oak). Triple top.
1376 / 1745–85; Ireland; mahogany. A similar table, but with round front corners, appears as figure 1369.
1377 / About 1760. Labeled by "Elizabeth Bell & Son" of London (the label dates from about 1760).
1378 / 1750–85; England. Turned rear legs and feet. (See discussion of straight legs on a developed piece, figure 1361.)
1379, 1380, 1381 / 1750–85; England; mahogany. The feet on the first have retraced side claws.
1382 / 1750–90; Philadelphia, Pennsylvania; mahogany (pine). New York gaming tables of this period are discussed under figure 26.

1379

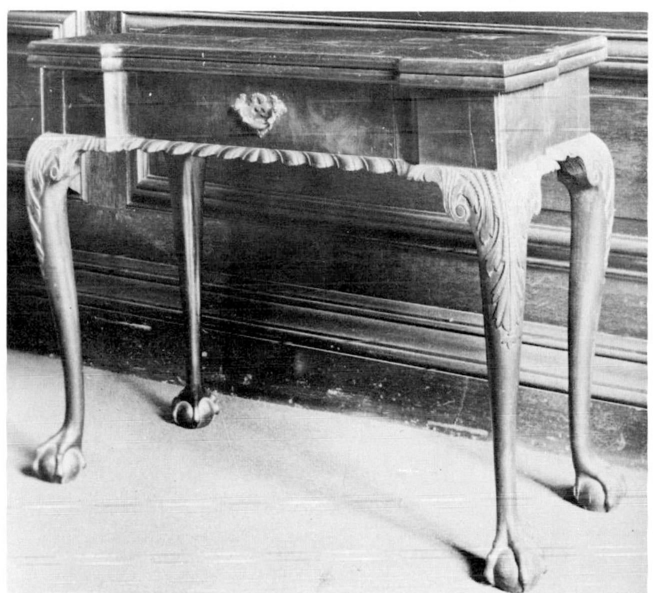

1381

1382

1383

1384

1385

1383 / 1760–90; Britain; mahogany.
1384 / 1750–90; Britain; oak.
1385 / 1760–90; Britain; mahogany.
1386 / 1760–90; Philadelphia, Pennsylvania; mahogany.
1387 / Dated June, 1816. Ink drawing of "An Oak Hall Table 4ft by 1ft 10," page 2020 of the Estimate Book of the Gillows firm.

1386

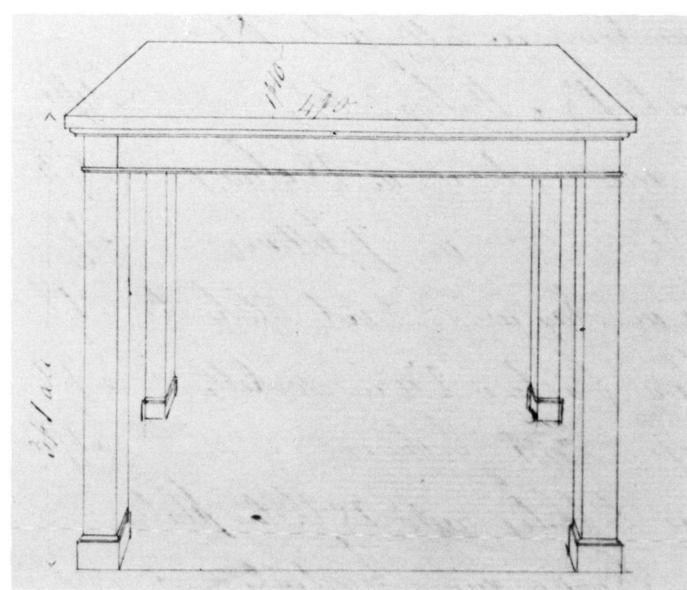

1387

1388

1389

1390

1388 / 1760–90; England; mahogany, mahogany veneer (oak). Interior surface of top recessed for a cloth covering (the top of the swing leg retains traces of green baize).
1389 / 1755–85; England; mahogany.
1390, 1391, 1392 / 1760–90; Britain; mahogany.

1391

1392

1393

1394

1395

1396

1397

1393, 1394, 1395, 1396 / 1785–1810; Britain; mahogany.

1397 / 1790–1810; America, possibly Rhode Island; mahogany, mahogany veneer, and a lightwood inlay. The dark areas were achieved by scorching the wood.

1398

1399

1400

1401

1398, 1399, 1400, 1401, 1402 / 1785–1810; Britain; mahogany.

1402

1403

1404

1405

1406

1407

1403, 1404 / 1790–1815; Britain.

1405 / Dated January, 1826. Ink drawing of "A Mahogany Card table on reeded legs," page 3473 of the Estimate Book of the Gillows firm. It was made of mahogany and various expensive veneers, with deal as secondary wood. The "inside" was lined with "Green cloth." The presence of slender turned legs, even after the introduction of much heavier versions (see the drawing in figure 1489), makes it difficult to put an early date securely on similar examples. The rounding of the corners of the top and frame is probably a late feature.

1406 / 1800–25; Britain; rosewood. Saber legs appear in the Estimate Book of the Gillows firm by 1794, for example, on the table in figure 1437, but become more common after 1800.

1407 / 1800–25; Britain.

1408

1409

1410

1411

1412

1408 / 1760–90; England; mahogany.

1409 / 1785–1810; Britain; mahogany.

1410 / 1760–90; Britain; mahogany.

1411 / 1760–90; Britain; mahogany. Similar legs and stretchers were used in October, 1784, on "A Mahogany Tea Kitchen Stand Lined wth Tin," page 118 of the Estimate Book of the Gillows firm.

1412 / 1765–90; Massachusetts, probably Newburyport; mahogany.

1413

1414

1415

1416

1417

1413, 1414 / 1765–90; Britain; mahogany.

1415 / 1790–1810; Philadelphia, Pennsylvania; mahogany (oak, tulip, cedar). According to family tradition, this piece belonged to John Brown of Providence, Rhode Island. (The faces and bases of the spade feet are replacements.)

1416, 1417 / 1785–1810; England; mahogany. The photograph of the first inscribed: "Syon."

1418

1419

1420

1421

1422

1418, 1419 / 1785–1810; Britain; mahogany.
1420 / 1800–25; Britain; mahogany.
1421 / 1785–1810; Britain; mahogany.
1422 / 1785–1820; Britain; mahogany.

1423

1424

1425

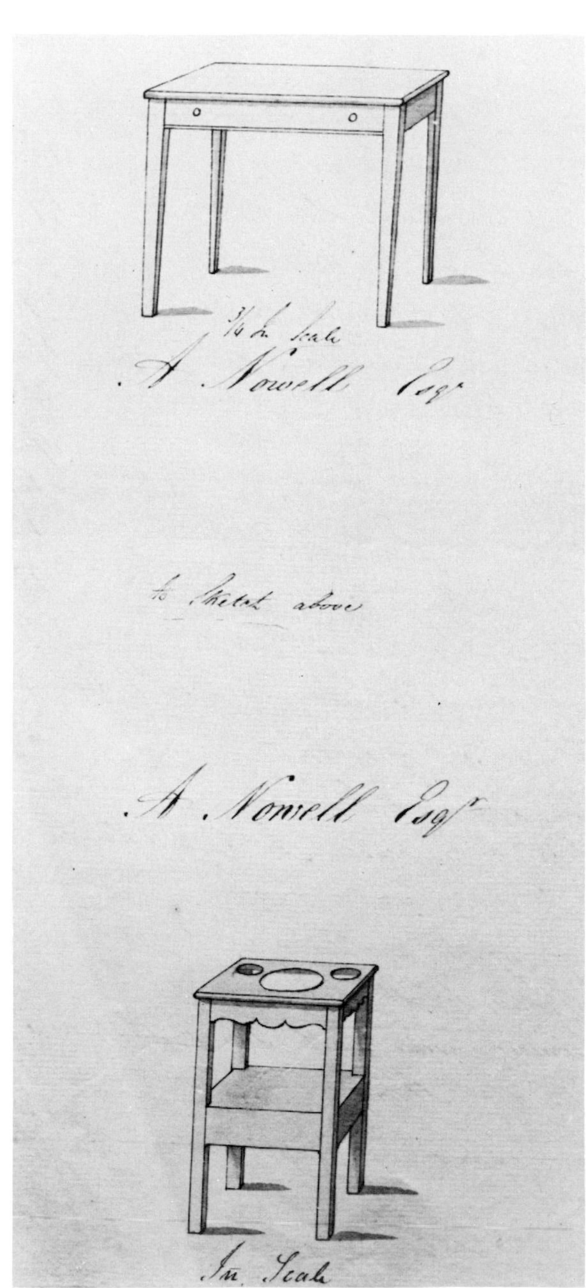

1426

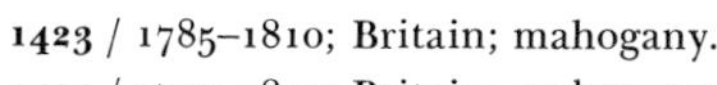

1423 / 1785–1810; Britain; mahogany.
1424 / 1790–1815; Britain; mahogany.
1425 / 1790–1820; Britain; mahogany.
1426 / Dated June, 1822. Ink drawings of "A Deal Chamber Table with one drawer" and "A Square Deal Washstand," page 3166 of the Estimate Book of the Gillows firm. Both pieces were painted "cane color," perhaps to match bamboo. The table had metal knobs. The washstand was sold with a "Blue Jug & Bason" and turned "top & cups." A third item, denoted at the center of the page by "to Sketch above," was "A Deal Chamber Table (no drawer)." It was painted white. As with figure 1488, it may have been used with a textile skirt.

1427

1428

1429

1430

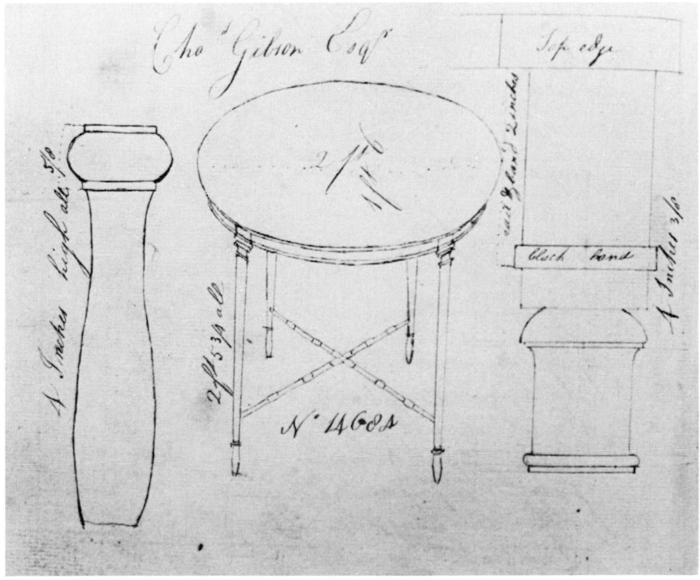

1431

1427 / 1790–1810; America, probably Newport, Rhode Island, or New York, New York; mahogany, mahogany veneer with light inlay (birch, white pine, tulip).

1428 / 1785–1810; Britain; mahogany.

1429 / 1800–20; America, probably New York, New York; mahogany (tulip).

1430 / 1800–20; Britain; mahogany.

1431 / Dated November 15, 1790. Ink drawing in the Estimate Book of the Gillows firm.

1432

1433

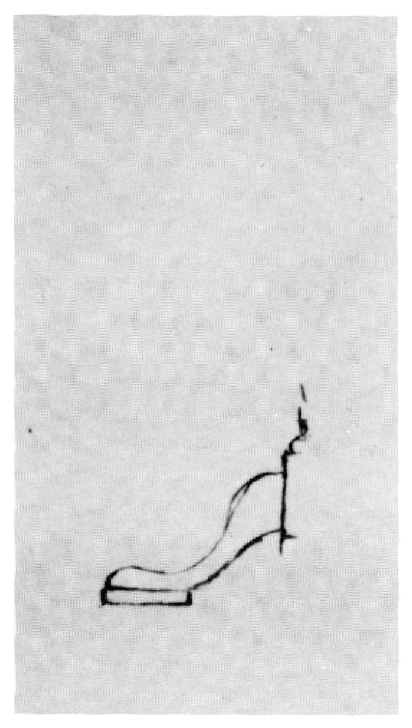
1434

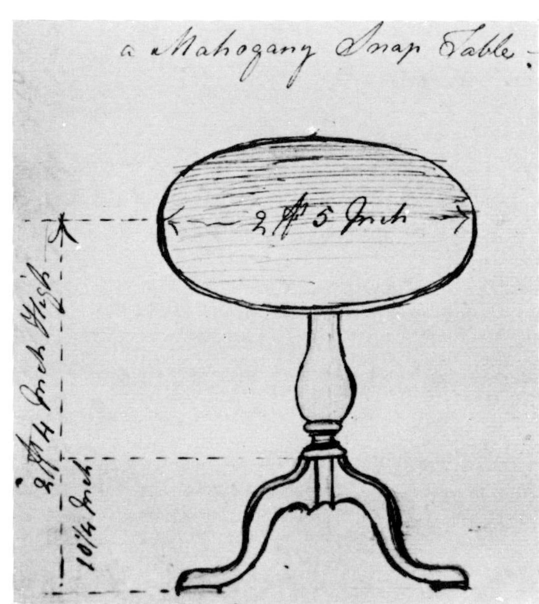

1435

1436

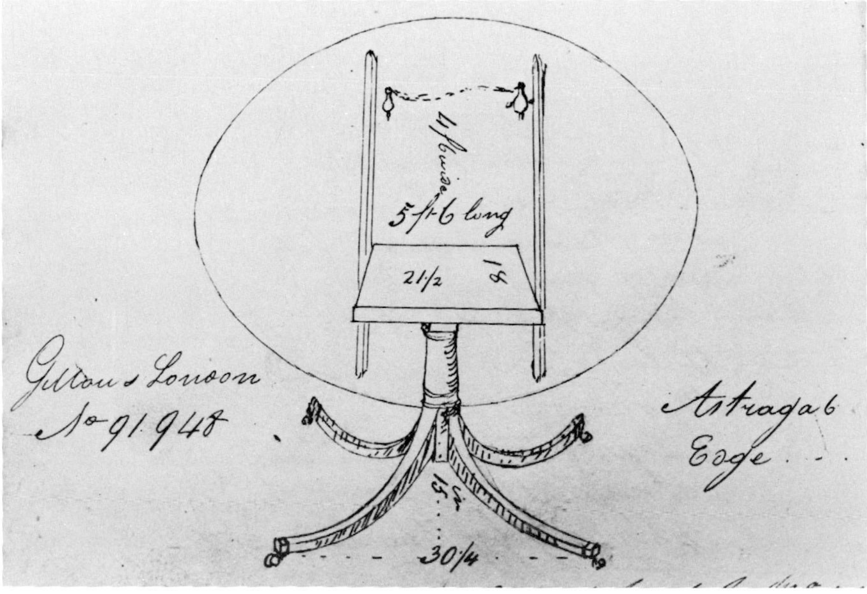

1437

1438

1439

1440

1441

PILLAR TABLES AND STANDS

(Examples from these categories are also found under other headings, in Chapter 3, for example.)

1432 / 1760–85; Britain; mahogany.

1433 / 1765–90; Britain.

1434 / Dated April, 1802. Ink drawing of a "claw" from "An Oak Stand" that was in part of American oak, page 1688, Estimate Book of the Gillows firm.

1435 / Dated February 2, 1788. Ink drawing of "a Mohogany Snap Table," in the Estimate Book of the Gillows firm. The block and bars were oak. A brass snap fastener held the top horizontal.

1436 / 1810–40; Britain; beech painted with red varnish. The legs lack horizontal shaping.

1437 / Dated November, 1794. Ink drawing of "A mahogany Snap table," page 1127 of the Estimate Book of the Gillows firm. The secondary wood was oak. There was an "Astragal Edge" (round) and "4 large brass casters lackered."

1438 / 1750–85; England; mahogany.

1439 / 1750–85; England; mahogany. On most English tables, the four small turned columns of the cage connecting the top to the pillar are columnar in shape. On American tables, a baluster shape—as seen on the preceding English example—is standard.

1440 / Hung-lo period (1403–25); China; dish of carved red lacquer. The form of pie crust tables derives from similarly shaped Chinese dishes, trays, and tables.

1441 / About 1900; England. The scale of the parts, shape of the legs, and profusion of carving suggest this date.

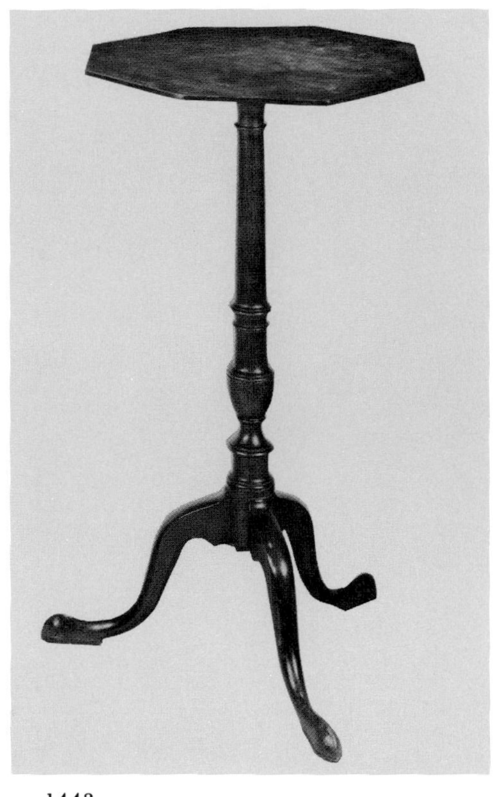
1442

1443

1444

1445

1446

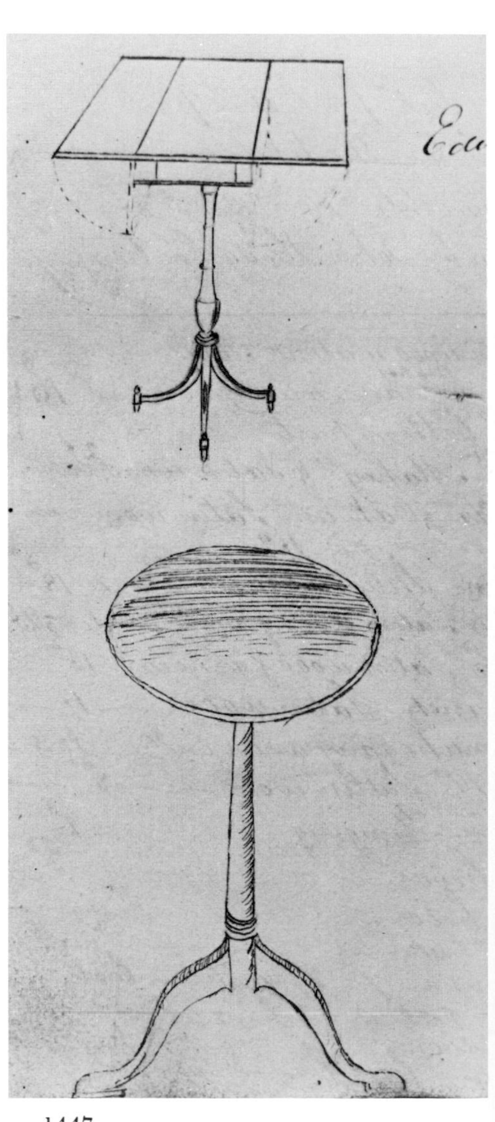
1447

1448

1449

1450

1451

1452

1442 / 1780–1810; Britain; mahogany.

1443 / 1790–1810; Massachusetts, Boston or Salem; mahogany (birch).

1444 / 1785–1810; Britain; mahogany.

1445 / 1770–90; Britain.

1446 / 1785–1810; Britain.

1447 / Dated April, 1794. Ink drawings of "A small mahog[an]y work table" (above) and "A mahogany Stand" (below), page 1074 of the Estimate Book of the Gillows firm.

1448, 1449, 1450 / 1760–90; Britain.

1451 / 1768–74. Labeled in the drawer by Philip Bell, at "The White Swan, against the South Gate in St. Paul's Church Yard, London."

1452 / 1760–90; Newport, Rhode Island; mahogany (maple). According to family tradition, this table originally belonged to John Brown of Providence, Rhode Island.

1453

1454

1455

1456

1457

DRESSING TABLES

1453 / About 1670; London, England. The top (its wood has been renewed) has silver plaques bearing the initials of Elizabeth, Countess of Dysart, who became Duchess of Lauderdale in 1672. It appears in the 1679 Ham House inventory as "one ebony table granished with silver." This superior baroque court piece was probably made in London by a Dutch craftsman. The basic mass of the top and molding, the action of the reverse curve of the legs, and the shape of the stretchers appear in the two simpler tables that follow. A few grand tables were entirely veneered with silver.

1454 / 1670–85; London, England. The top was made from part of a Chinese "Coromandel" lacquer panel, while the base has English japanning simulating Chinese lacquer. The forms of the parts are similar to those on the preceding table—even the

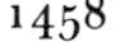

1458

1459

1460

1461

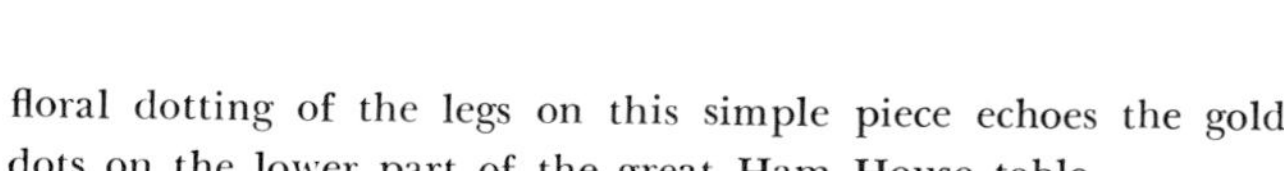

floral dotting of the legs on this simple piece echoes the gold dots on the lower part of the great Ham House table.

1455 / 1675–90; England; oak and pearwood. A similar stretcher form appears on the French table, figure 323.

1456 / 1685–95; Netherlands; veneered with rosewood, ebony, and various other woods and ivory, gilded brass mounts.

1457 / 1690–1710; Britain. As with related high chests of drawers, there is no molding at the end of the drawer. (See figures 538, 541, etc.)

1458 / 1690–1715; England. The cup-turned form of the foot is unusual.

1459 / 1700–20; America, possibly Pennsylvania; cedar (pine).

1460 / 1700–25; Britain. (Brasses replaced; drops, finial, and feet probably not original.)

1461, 1462 / 1690–1710; England; oak. (Pulls replaced.)

1462

1463

1464

1465

1466

1467

1463 / 1700–20; Philadelphia, Pennsylvania; walnut (pine). The open spacing of the drawers and use of paired brasses in Pennsylvania are discussed under figure 553. Another Pennsylvania table of this style but with German influences appears as figures 169 and 170.

1464 / 1700–25; Britain; oak. Additional stock was glued to the legs to accomplish the width of the cup turnings. (The loose line of the feet and rounded edges of the stretchers suggest that these have been replaced.)

1465 / 1690–1715; Britain; walnut.

1466 / 1710–35; Massachusetts, probably Boston; walnut, probably maple burl veneer, maple (pine). The top was imported from Switzerland. This piece is one of the great American statements.

1467 / 1690–1710; European, possibly Britain; apple (poplar, European elm).

1468

1469

1470

1471

1472

1468 / 1710–25; England; gilt and japanning.
1469 / 1730–60; Britain; oak. Cock beading on drawer.
1470 / 1695–1720; England or the continent.
1471 / 1690–1715. The exaggerated movement of the skirt, legs, and feet imply a continental—possibly Dutch or north German—maker.
1472 / 1730–50; England; oak. Cock beading on drawers. The knee scrolling and leafage are gilded. (The gilding may not be original.)

1473

1474

1475

1476

1477

1473 / 1745–70; Britain. Lipped drawers. Feet with raised edges. Front corners of case chamfered.

1474 / 1745–70; Britain. Cock-beaded drawers. Pad-turned feet. Cove molding between case and top.

1475 / 1750–85; Britain. Lipped drawers. Ridged and pointed feet.

1476 / 1745–85; Britain. Drawer with simulated cock beading. The use of differing front and rear legs does not denote a transitional date. (See discussion under figure 1361.)

1477 / 1745–60; Britain.

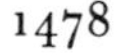

1478

1479

1480

1481

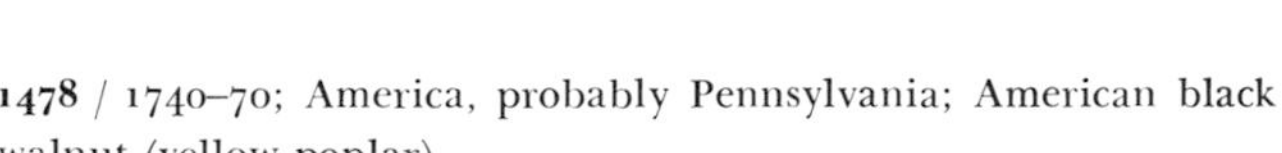

1478 / 1740–70; America, probably Pennsylvania; American black walnut (yellow poplar).

1479 / 1750–90; Britain; oak (oak). Cock-beaded drawers. (Only the central brass is original.)

1480 / 1755–90; Pennsylvania; American black walnut (yellow poplar, white cedar, white oak).

1481 / 1785–1810; Britain; mahogany. Lipped drawers. Square-tapered legs.

1482 / Late nineteenth- or early twentieth-century; Britain; oak (pine). Cock-beaded drawers. The form was used as part of the late Victorian revival of country oak furniture, influenced by such designers as Charles Robert Ashbee (1863–1942).

1482

1483

1484

1485

1486

1487

1483 / 1785–1810; Winchester, England; mahogany, mahogany veneer. This dressing table bears the label of a Winchester, Hampshire, cabinetmaker and upholsterer named [?] Mant.

1484 / 1790–1810; New England, Salem, North Shore of Massachusetts, or Portsmouth, New Hampshire; mahogany, mahogany and lightwood veneers (white pine).

1485, 1486, 1487 / 1785–1810; Britain; mahogany.

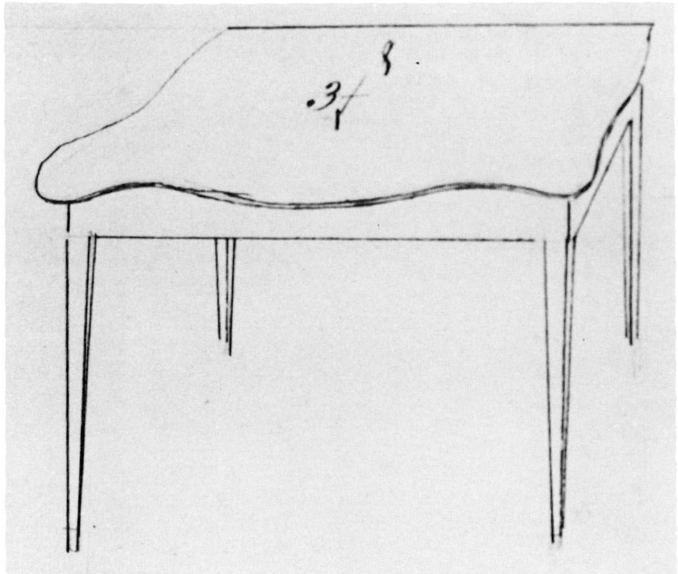

1488

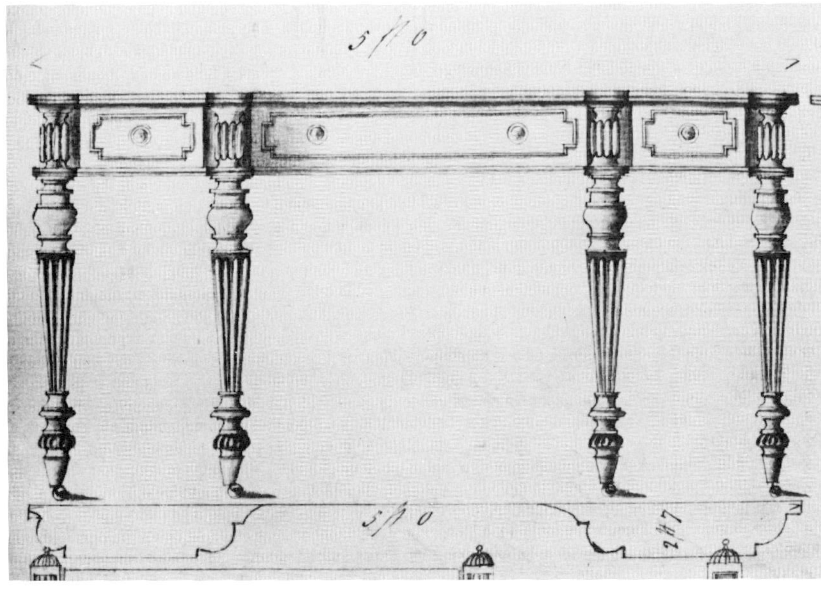

1489

1490

1491

1488 / Dated May, 1793. Ink drawing of "2 deal chamber tables," page 975 of the Estimate Book of the Gillows firm. Such tables were often painted and supported a textile covering that reached to the floor. A similar table with the front of the top cut to a partial circle (rather than a serpentine) descended in the family of the Providence, Rhode Island, merchant John Brown.[57] It is pine painted blue-gray.

1489 / Dated September, 1814. Ink drawing of "A Mahogany Washing Table," page 1961 of the Estimate Book of the Gillows firm.

1490, 1491 / 1785–1810; Britain; mahogany.

1492 / 1790–1810; America, probably Portsmouth, New Hampshire; mahogany, mahogany veneer, various inlays (pine). An elegant New England statement. The poise is accentuated by the increased tapering of the foot below the inlaid cuff. The edges of the drawers are made to flicker by including the sapwood with the cross-banded veneer.

1492

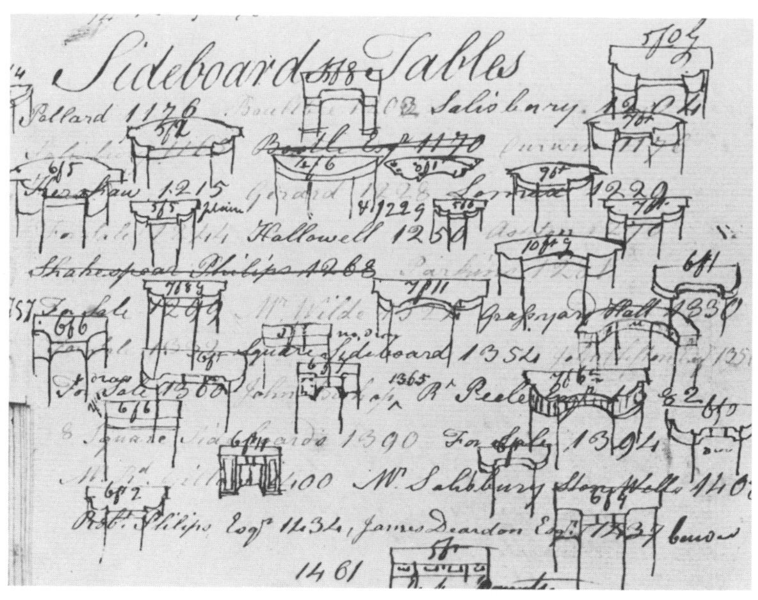

1493

1494

1495

1496

1497

SIDEBOARDS

1493 / From page cxii of the 1795–8 Index of the Estimate Book of the Gillows firm. Ink drawing of "Sideboard Tables."

1494, 1495, 1496, 1497 / 1785–1810; Britain.

1498 / 1785–1810; Britain.

1499 / 1790–1810; America, probably Newport, Rhode Island; mahogany, mahogany and lightwood veneer (tulip). According to family tradition, it descended in the Joseph Allen family of Newport.

1500 / 1785–1810; Britain.

1501 / 1790–1810; New England, possibly Boston, Massachusetts. Lunette inlay like that in the preceding English piece. Similar stringing has been associated with the workshop of John and Thomas Seymour, but it also appears on pieces documented to other American makers. It appears also on the cornice of "A Cylinder Desk and Book Case" in Sheraton's 1791–4 pattern book, plate 47, dated August 6, 1792. Stringing and other inlays could be purchased from American specialists and imported from Europe.

1502 / Detail of figure 1500.

1503 / Detail of figure 1501.

1504 / 1825–35; Britain. (The feet are possibly not original.)

1498

1499

1500

1501

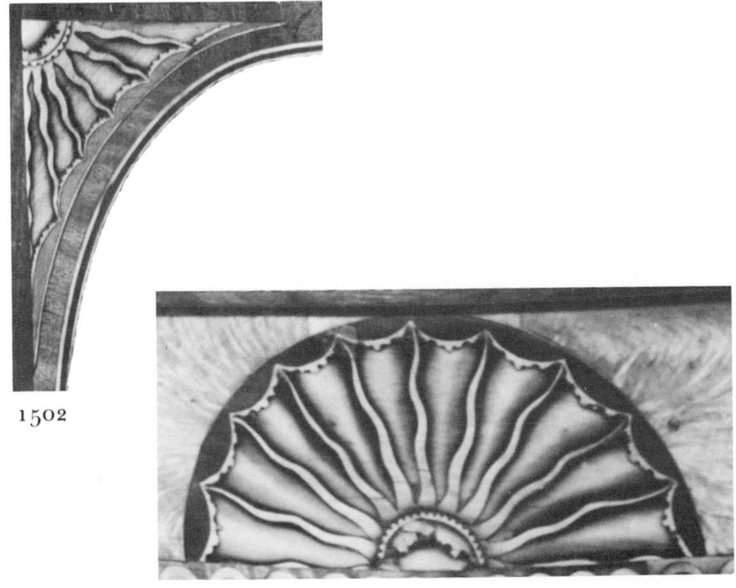

1502

1503

1504

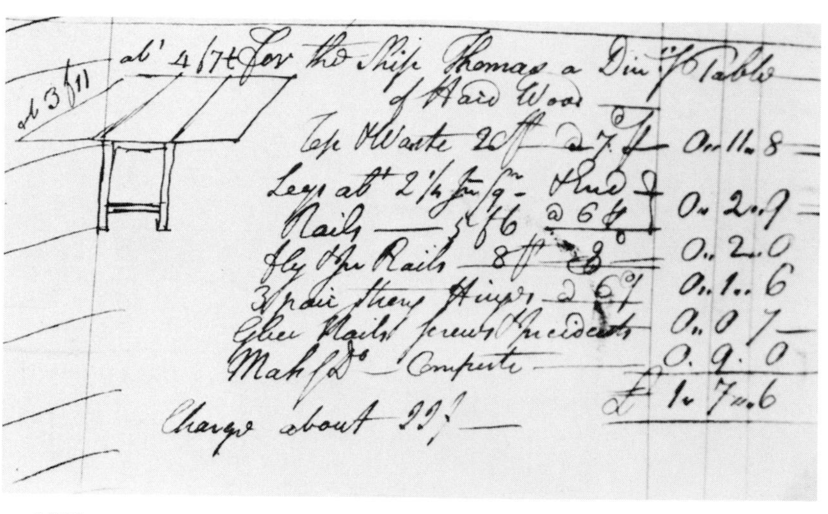

1505

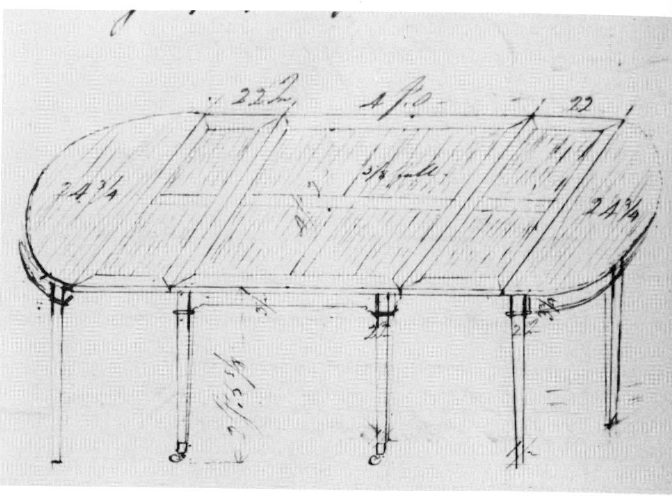

1506

1507

1508

DINING TABLES

(See also Chapter 3.)

1505 / 1789. Ink drawing titled "for the Ship Thomas a Din[in]g Table," page 538 of the Estimate Book of the Gillows firm. It was made of "Hard Wood."

1506 / Dated October, 1790. Ink drawing of "An Universal Table with sliding leaves," page 660 of the Estimate Book of the Gillows firm.

1507 / 1760–90; Britain. Photograph inscribed: "Found in Ireland." The great variety of possible dining table forms is discussed in Chapter 3.

1508 / 1785–1810; Britain.

NOTES

PICTURE CREDITS

INDEXES

Notes

Preface

1. Margaret Burke Clunie, Anne Farnam, and Robert F. Trent, *Furniture at the Essex Institute* (Salem, Mass., 1980), p. 21.

2. Minor Myers, Jr., and Edgar deN. Mayhew, *New London County Furniture 1640–1840* (New London: Lyman Allyn Museum, 1974). Donna-Belle Garvin, James L. Garvin, and John F. Page, *Plain & Elegant, Rich & Common: Documented New Hampshire Furniture, 1750–1850* (Concord: New Hampshire Historical Society, 1979).

3. Trevor J. Fairbrother, "John Singleton Copley's Use of British Mezzotints for His American Portraits: A Reappraisal Prompted by New Discoveries," *Arts Magazine* 55 (March, 1981), pp. 122–30.

4. Anna Wells Rutledge, "Fact and Fancy: Portraits from the Provinces," *Antiques* 72 (November, 1957), pp. 446–8.

5. Daniel Robbins, "Folk Sculpture Without Folk," in *Folk Sculpture USA*, ed. Herbert W. Hemphill, Jr. (catalogue for an exhibition, The Brooklyn Museum and Los Angeles County Museum of Art, 1976), pp. 11–30. For an injudicious response to Mr. Robbins, see Amy Goldin, "Problems in Folk Art," *Artforum* 14 (June, 1976), pp. 48–52. For Vlach on Hicks, John Michael Vlach, "Quaker Tradition and the Paintings of Edward Hicks: A Strategy for the Study of Folk Art," *Journal of American Folklore* 94 (April–June, 1981), pp. 145–65; quote: p. 151. Contrary to Vlach's opinion, Hicks was as original in nineteenth-century Pennsylvania as Eliphalet Chapin in eighteenth-century Connecticut (see discussion of Chapin in the Conclusion). For both artists, their creative artistic independence is as discernible as their sources.

6. Fairbrother, "Copley," p. 127.

Issues Relating British to American Furniture

Chapter 1

1. I am indebted to Morrison H. Heckscher, who reminded me of this copy of the *Director* given to the museum by Maxim Karolik, and to Robert F. Trent who went through the volume with me. The inside of the back cover has been mostly relined, and the remaining small area of original paper has an ink inscription "Thomas Goddard." The original surface is so disturbed it is difficult to be certain whether the signature is early writing. This has called into question the authenticity of the tradition that the volume belonged to Stephen Goddard's father, John. However, close scrutiny of all the pages revealed that plate 77, titled "Library Tables," has the penciled inscriptions "Thomas Goddard" and "Library Tables." (Although these are now mostly erased, the impressions in the paper are clear.) It appears that Thomas Goddard was practicing script by copying the engraved heading of the plate. On the untitled plate 99, a pencil drawing follows the outline of the plinth of the right-hand design for a column. On plate 159, titled "Six Designs of Tea Chests," the lower right design, which is most like a Newport form, has ink splatters, and the lower center chest a few ink drops. The history of the volume is reviewed in a letter from Duncan A. Hazard to Maxim Karolik dated October 9, 1929 (a copy accompanies the book). The *Director* had been purchased from a Miss Goffe. Her grandfather, who had been a cabinetmaker in Newport seventy-five years earlier, had bought it at an auction of a descendant of John Goddard. Albert W. Goddard, John Goddard's great-grandson (age about eighty-two), identified the book as one owned and used by his great-grandfather.

2. Christopher Gilbert, *The Life and Work of Thomas Chippendale*, 2 vols. (New York, 1978), vol. 1, pp. 65 and 83.

3. *Ibid.*, vol. 2, figs. 245–7, 409, 133, and 204. Gilbert dates the illustration of the clothes-press 1766, although the accounts, p. 185, date it 1767.

4. The history of the Gillows firm of furniture makers in Lancaster began under Robert Gillow, who became a Freeman of the town in 1728. In 1769, the firm opened an outlet at 176 Oxford Road, London. Nearly two hundred volumes of their records survive, covering the years from 1784 to 1905. Their so-called Estimate Books record over twenty thousand pieces of furniture and the entry for each item is specified as to costs for materials and labor, usually accompanied by a sketch of the object. The firm sold simple painted pieces and elaborate mahogany forms to customers throughout the land. I have referred to this firm as Gillows rather than Gillow, for they often did so in their papers and when they marked their pieces. For a detailed study of one house they furnished, see Nicholas Goodison and John Hardy, "Gillows at Tatton Park," *Furniture History* 6 (1970), pp. 1–39, pls. 1A–24C. Page 1 dates the opening of the London shop 1760. In a letter to the author dated March 11, 1982, Sarah Nichols states that "Gillow and William Taylor were first rated at 176, Oxford St., in 1769. The first entry in the 'Gillows and Taylor, London' partnership account is May 1770. . . ."

5. Trevor J. Fairbrother, "John Singleton Copley's Use of British Mezzotints for His American Portraits: A Reappraisal Prompted by New Discoveries," *Arts Magazine* 55 (March, 1981), pp. 122–30.

6. For example, both Kenneth L. Ames and John Michael Vlach would exclude from the designation "folk art" the work of makers such as Wilhelm Schimmel who carved dramatic eagles and other forms, because he was rejected by his community for deviant behavior. Ames: *Beyond Necessity, Art in the Folk Tradition* (catalogue for an exhibition at the Brandywine River Museum, Winterthur, Delaware, 1977). Vlach: "American Folk Art: Questions and Quandaries," *Winterthur Portfolio* 15 (Winter, 1981), pp. 345–55.

Chapter 2

1. I am indebted to Benno M. Forman for researching and photographing the chest. He learned of it from Abbott Lowell Cummings, who recorded the date and inscription on the left end. Cummings had been told about the chest by Katharine Simonds Thompson.

2. Joseph Downs, *American Furniture, Queen Anne and Chippendale Periods* (New York, 1952), figs. 11 and 12.

3. The notorious beech rear seat rail of one of the New York chairs was reported after three separate microanalyses by the same person as: cherry, red gum, and finally American beech. See John T. Kirk, *American Chairs: Queen Anne and Chippendale* (New York, 1972), fig. 127.

4. R. W. Symonds's Papers, ms. 75 x 69.45, p. 57. Joseph Downs Memorial Manuscript Library, Winterthur Museum. Robert Wemyss Symonds, a scholar of English furniture, amassed a large collection of references to early English art, particularly furniture, from various early manuscripts and books. The Symonds Papers are indexed no. 6598, shelf nos. 75 x 69.1-58.

5. It appears on a chair of possible Philadelphia origin, but the shoe is not original to the chair: Helen Comstock, *American Furniture* (New York, 1962), fig. 156, first chair at the left.

6. I am indebted to Vincent Luti for providing these photographs, and the information about them. Peter Benes directed me to Mr. Luti.

7. I am grateful to Abbott Lowell Cummings for suggesting these two images.

8. Jonathan L. Fairbanks told me of the recent discovery that is discussed in *New England Begins: The Seventeenth Century, 1620–1700* (catalogue for an exhibition, Museum of Fine Arts, Boston, 1982), cat. no. 436, x-ray fig. 60.

9. I am indebted to Jane Nylander for suggesting these examples and providing much of the information that accompanies them.

10. I am grateful to Linda Wesselman, who contacted the American dealer who purchased the hangings in England.

11. John L. Nevinson, *Catalogue of English Domestic Embroidery* (1938; reprinted London: Victoria and Albert Museum, 1950), pp. 64 and 65, pls. 47 and 48.

Chapter 4

1. Florence M. Montgomery, "A Set of English Crewelwork Bed Hangings," *Antiques* 115 (February, 1979), p. 334, fig. 4.

2. Florence M. Montgomery, *Printed Textiles, English and American Cottons and Linens, 1700–1850* (New York, 1970), p. 333, fig. 385.

3. The accession number of the tapestry is 1370–1864.

4. Celia Jenning, *Early Chests in Wood and Iron* (London, 1974), pp. 2, 8, and figs. 1, 2.

5. *Ibid.*, pp. 3, 8, and fig. 3.

6. Robert Wemyss Symonds Papers, ms. 75 x 69.7, section entitled "Chests," p. 7. Joseph Downs Memorial Manuscript Library, Winterthur Museum.

7. *Ibid.*, p. 3.

8. Helena Hayward, "English Interiors in the Seventeenth Century," in *Arts of the Anglo-American Community in the Seventeenth Century*, ed. Ian M. G. Quimby (Charlottesville, Va., 1975), p. 172.

9. Henry Shaw, *Specimens of Ancient Furniture Drawn from Existing Authorities by Henry Shaw* (London, 1836), p. 38, pl. 32.

10. Symonds Papers, ms. 75 x 69.12, section entitled "Painter," p. 2.

11. *Ibid.*

12. *Ibid.*, p. 1.

13. *Ibid.*

14. Symonds Papers, ms. 75 x 69.7, first page written on and entitled "Chests."

15. Symonds Papers, ms. 75 x 69.12, section entitled "Painter," p. 2. The date given is *Mary I.*

16. *Ibid.*, p. 1.

17. Symonds Papers, ms. 75 x 69.7, first page written on and entitled "Chests."

18. Symonds Papers, ms. 75 x 69.12, section entitled "Painter," p. 2.

19. Symonds Papers, ms. 75 x 69.16, p. 32.

20. James Orehard Halliwell, *Ancient Inventories of Furniture, Pictures, Tapestry, Plate* (London, 1854), p. 121.

21. Douglas Ash, "Gothic," in *World Furniture*, ed. Helena Hayward (Secaucus, N.J., 1965), p. 31, fig. 74.

22. Dorothy Erskine Muir, *An Historical Guide to Southwold Parish Church* (5th ed., Southwold, Suffolk, 1972), p. 3. All documentation about the church is taken from this publication.

23. Randle Holme, *The Academy of Armory: or a Display of Heraldry* (London and Westminster, 1701 ed.), vol. 1, p. 147. Holme compiled a massive manuscript covering an enormous range of topics. Books 1 and 2 and the first thirteen chapters of Book 3 were first published in 1688 as volume 1. What could be found of the remaining manuscript was edited by I. H. Jeayes and published by the Roxburghe Club of London in 1905.

24. W. and G. Audsley wrote *Polychromatic Decoration As Applied to Buildings in the Medieval Style* in 1882. It is a plea for the reintroduction of paint on architecture, and provides thirty-six colorplates based on early designs. The colors, as printed, all have milky, unclear tones not found in original early paint. This effect is part of the color sensibility of the later nineteenth century.

25. Quoted in Muir, *Historical Guide to Southwold Parish Church*, p. 23.

26. Symonds Papers, ms. 75 x 69.16, p. 8.

27. Christopher Gilbert, *The Life and Work of Thomas Chippendale*, 2 vols. (New York, 1978), vol. 1, p. 52.

28. *Fonts and Font Covers* (London, 1908), p. 253.

29. John Summerson, *Architecture in Britain, 1530 to 1830* (3rd ed., Harmondsworth, Baltimore, Mitcham, 1958), pp. 2–10.

30. Edward Croft-Murray, *Decorative Painting in England 1537–1837*, 2 vols. (London, 1962), vol. 1, p. 155.

31. See *The Inlaid Room from Sizergh Castle* (Victoria and Albert Museum, 1928 ed.).

32. John Hunt, "Byzantine and Early Medieval," in *World Furniture*, p. 21, fig. 41.

33. John L. Nevinson, *Catalogue of English Domestic Embroidery* (1938; reprinted London: Victoria and Albert Museum, 1950), p. 62, pl. 45.

34. Symonds Papers, ms. 75 x 69.18, p. 199.

35. Salmon, *Polygraphice; or The Arts of Drawing, Engraving, Etching, Limning, Painting, Varnishing, Japaning, Gilding, Ec* (8th ed., London 1701), p. 889, gives a detailed description of how best to treat different types of wood.

36. Symonds Papers, ms. 75 x 69.16, p. 80.

37. *Ibid.*, p. 94.

38. Croft-Murray, *Decorative Painting in England*, vol. 1, pp. 87–8, pls. 17–20.

39. *The Academy of Armory*, vol. 1, p. 145.

40. *Polygraphice*, pp. 897–8.

41. George Smith, *The Laboratory or School of Arts* (London, 1755), pp. 148 and 224.

42. Symonds Papers, ms. 75 x 69.18, p. 28.

43. *Polygraphice*, pp. 862 and 903.

44. Symonds Papers, ms. 75 x 69.18, pp. 154–6.

45. Symonds Papers, ms. 75 x 69.12, section entitled "Stainer," p. 3.

46. *Ibid.*, p. 2, under subheading "Household stuff at Holecroft."

47. *Ibid.*, p. 3.

48. *Ibid.*, pp. 1, 2.

49. Roy Strong and Julia Trevelyan Oman, *Elizabeth R* (London, 1971), pp. 46–7.

50. Roy Strong, *National Portrait Gallery Tudor & Jacobean Portraits*, 2 vols. (London, 1969), vol. 2, pls. 421–4.

51. James Ayres, *British Folk Art* (London, 1977), p. 106, lower left plate.

52. *The Academy of Armory*, vol. 1, p. 149.

53. Salmon, *Polygraphice*, p. 188, xcii.

54. Strong and Oman, *Elizabeth R*, p. 11.

55. *Ancient Coffers & Cupboards* (London, 1902), pp. 115–16.

56. I am grateful to Peter Thornton, who brought this piece to the attention of Benno M. Forman in a letter dated November 6, 1971. Mr. Forman shared the letter and additional information on the maker with me. See also Benno M. Forman, "Continental Furniture Craftsmen in London: 1511–1625," *Furniture History* 7 (London, 1971), p. 113, no. 233, where the maker is listed as Lodeuyke Tyves, virginal maker.

57. The stones include, among others, garnets, turquoises, and lapis lazuli. The "clavichord" was made by Annibale del Rossi and is illustrated in *Musical Instruments as Works of Art* (London: Victoria and Albert Museum, 1968), figs. 8a–8c.

58. I am indebted to Derek Shrub for directing me to this piece.

59. I am grateful to Benno M. Forman, who supplied this information from the Symonds Papers Misc. Notes, vol. 2, p. 71.

60. Peter Thornton, *Seventeenth-Century Interior Decoration in England, France and Holland* (New Haven and London, 1978), p. 195, fig. 169.

61. *The Academy of Armory*, vol. 1, p. 146. This is a slightly expanded version of the 1672 description in Salmon's *Polygraphice*, p. 41.

62. Thornton, *Seventeenth-Century Interior Decoration*, pp. 171–4.

63. In conversation, November, 1974.

64. Inventory of the estate of John Freake, July 24, 1675, Suffolk County Probate Records, vol. 5, pp. 294–6. Suffolk County Court House, Boston, Massachusetts.

65. Abbott Lowell Cummings, "Decorative Painters and House Painting at Massachusetts Bay, 1630–1725," in *American Painting to 1776: A Reappraisal*, ed. Ian M. G. Quimby (Charlottesville, Va., 1971), pp. 71–125. In July, 1979, Mr. Cummings informed me that the dentils over the fireplace in the Hart House room are from another Ipswich house of the same date.

66. John T. Kirk, "The Tradition of English Painted Furniture; Part I: The Experience in Colonial New England," *Antiques* 117 (May, 1980), p. 1079, pl. 2. The cupboard made about 1680–1710, was reported to have square-cut nails, raising the question of its date. In fact the cupboard was originally assembled with wooden pegs assisted by a few wrought "rose-headed" nails. The square-cut, nineteenth-century nails were added later to tighten the piece.

67. Abbott Lowell Cummings, *Rural Household Inventories* (Boston, 1964), p. xxxiv.

68. The Society for the Preservation of New England Antiquities owns a small fragment. Their files contain a photograph of a much larger piece (in a private collection) and a copy of a label that reads: "This is a piece of the tapestry or wall covering on the old Levett house [formerly the Thaxter house] that stood where the Catholic Church now does in Hingham, Mass. The right hand room was covered with it, representing a fishing scene on a brook or river."

69. Perhaps the most famous piece of painted seventeenth-century New England furniture is the John and Margaret Staniford chest of drawers dated 1678 and possibly made by Thomas Dennis (figure 457). Unfortunately, its paint is not original. Benno M. Forman revealed in conversation that new research found that the formula for the light blue paint on the dentils was invented in Berlin, Germany, between 1704 and 1707, and kept secret until 1742, after which the color was also made in England. Originally, it would have appeared similar to figure 586, with black details playing against oak.

A recently published English chest of drawers with vivid coloring has newly painted decoration: Victor Chinnery, *Oak Furniture, The British Tradition* (Woodbridge, Suffolk, 1979), pp. 90, 91, and 209, pls. 5 and 6, and figs. 2:235, 2:235a and b. The paint enters areas damaged before the application of this layer, and the style of the decoration (both in the color and the handling of the forms) is modern.

70. Inventory of Jacob Smith, March 25, 1700, Suffolk County Probate Records, vol. 14, p. 165; inventory of Mary Nash, December 6, 1700, Suffolk County Probate Records, vol. 14, pp. 315–16. I am indebted for these references to Frederica Richards's [Struse's] term paper, "Evolution of 17th Century [Suffolk County] Inventories (1692–1702)," and to Ellen Smith for sharing her further work on the subject.

71. I am grateful to Frank H. Sommer for providing this information and illustration.

72. I am indebted to Fred Licht and Judith Oliver, who informed me of the Tree of Jesse and references for other vine and mask images.

73. Benno M. Forman provided this reference and took the photograph.

74. Kathleen Basford, *The Green Man* (Ipswich, England, 1978), pl. 92. This book traces the vine and mask motif from ancient times to the eighteenth century.

75. I am indebted to Elizabeth Reilly for discussing with me American, English, and German printers' ornaments.

76. This group of pieces is often assigned to Peter Blin (c. 1639/40–1725) of Wethersfield (Houghton Bulkeley, "A Discovery on the Connecticut Chest," *Bulletin* of the Connecticut Historical Society, vol. 23, no. 1 [January, 1958], pp. 17–19; reprinted in Houghton Bulkeley, *Contributions to Connecticut Cabinet Making* [Connecticut Historical Society, 1967], pp. 24–7). However, the documentation linking the chests to Blin is slight. Moreover, the manner of carving and the turning of the chest shown in figure 172 suggest that it may be by a different hand altogether.

77. On a pew end and door made in 1659 by John Norman, for the first meeting house in Marblehead, Massachusetts, there are applied moldings on the more visible upper panels. On the bottom panels, the moldings are simply run directly into the stiles and rails (see Peter Benes and Philip D. Zimmerman, *New England Meeting House and Church: 1630–1850* [catalogue for an exhibition, Boston University and the Currier Gallery of Art, 1979], pp. 47–9 and figs. 85a and b).

78. A chest over drawers dated April 15, 1704, combines turnings and carvings with painted motifs: the side panels have carved tulips, but the dated center panel and the drawers have painted floral designs (see John T. Kirk, *Connecticut Furniture, Seventeenth and Eighteenth Centuries* [catalogue for an exhibition, Wadsworth Atheneum, 1967], p. 14, fig. 18). Benno M. Forman has raised the question of the age of the painted decoration; and indeed the motifs of the design, particularly on the drawers, suggest a later style.

79. Linda R. Baumgarten, "The Textile Trade in Boston, 1650–1700," in *Arts of the Anglo-American Community in the Seventeenth Century*, pp. 249, 253, 262, 263, and 261.

80. *Estimate Book*, p. 163.

81. *Ibid.*, p. 840.

82. *Ibid.*, p. 1032.

83. There is a Gunthorpe in Norfolk and one in Nottinghamshire. The latter is probably intended, as the cradle is now in a museum a few miles from that county. *Lilla* is Swedish for "little"; its use may signal the influence of a Swedish-trained worker in central England in the mid-nineteenth century, or it may reflect the lingering influence of the earlier emigration from Scandinavia to England.

84. *Estimate Book*, p. 1661.

Chapter 5

1. See Peter Ward-Jackson, "Some Main Streams and Tributaries in European Ornament from 1500 to 1750," in *Victoria and Albert Museum Bulletin* 3 (April, July, and October, 1967), pp. 58–71, 90–103, and 121–34.

2. Elizabeth Reilly in conversation, February, 1981.

Chapter 6

1. Patricia E. Kane, "The Seventeenth-Century Furniture of the Connecticut Valley: The Hadley Chest Reappraised," in *Arts of the Anglo-American Community in the Seventeenth Century*, ed. Ian M. G. Quimby (Charlottesville, Va., 1974), pp. 79–122.

2. For a discussion of the subdivision of this group, see Kane, *ibid.*

3. For the other four, see Clair Franklin Luther, *The Hadley Chest* (Hartford, Conn., 1935), nos. 10, 28, 55, and 60.

4. The turnings on no. 28 of Luther's *The Hadley Chest* are modern: they are more curvilinearly bulbous than seventeenth-century forms.

5. Luther, *The Hadley Chest*, no. 15.

6. Kane, "The Hadley Chest Reappraised," p. 86.

7. The lower bevel extensions of the muntins between the panels of the chest initialed "P W" at Winterthur Museum cover black paint on the bevel of the rail below them—Luther, *The Hadley Chest*, no. 95.

8. John T. Kirk, *Connecticut Furniture, Seventeenth and Eighteenth Centuries* (catalogue for an exhibition, Wadsworth Atheneum, Hartford, 1967), fig. 271.

9. Anthony Wells-Cole, *Oak Furniture from Lancashire & the Lake District* (catalogue for an exhibition, Temple Newsam, Leeds, 1973), fig. 12.

10. Luther, *The Hadley Chest*, no. 10.

11. See note to Chapter 4, no. 77.

12. Robert Blair St. George, "Style and Structure in the Joinery of Dedham and Medfield, Massachusetts, 1635–1685," *Winterthur Portfolio* 13 (1979), p. 8, fig. 8, and p. 30, fig. 30a.

13. *Ibid.*, p. 4. I am grateful to Benno M. Forman for sharing his photograph of this piece, and to Robert Blair St. George for making the negative available.

14. *Ibid.*, p. 34, fig. 30r.

15. Christopher Gilbert, Anthony Wells-Cole, and Richard Fawcett, *Oak Furniture from Yorkshire Churches* (catalogue for an exhibition, Temple Newsam House, Leeds, 1971), p. 11.

Chapter 7

1. John T. Kirk, *American Chairs, Queen Anne and Chippendale* (New York, 1972), pp. 63–4.

2. F. Lewis Hinckley, *A Directory of Queen Anne, Early Georgian and Chippendale Furniture* (New York, 1971), p. 172, figs. 275 and 276.

3. Scandinavia: Sigurd Erixon, *Möbler Och Heminredning I Svenska Bygder* (Stockholm, 1926), vol. 2, p. 220, fig. 1018. Germany: fig. 4, and Hermann Schmitz, *Deutsche Möbel des Barock und Rokoko* (Stuttgart, 1925), pp. 162, 222, 225, 232, etc. Italy: Raffaella Del Puglia and Carlo Steiner, *Mobili e Ambienti Italiani dal Gotico al Floreale*, 2 vols. (Milan, 1963), vol. 1, p. 67.

4. William Macpherson Hornor, Jr., *Blue Book, Philadelphia Furniture* (Philadelphia, 1935), p. 207.

5. Colonial Williamsburg's archives record the chairs as being purchased in Bath, England. David Stockwell reported in conversation in September, 1980, that John Graham purchased them for Williamsburg in York, England, and that they were considered local chairs.

6. The Netherlands, fig. 772. Flanders and Italy: Irving Phillips Lyon, "Square-Post Slat-Back Chairs," *Antiques* 20 (October, 1931), pp. 210–16, figs. 10, 11, 13, 15, 17, and 19 among others. Germany: Robert Rosenblum, *Transformations in Late Eighteenth Century Art* (Princeton, 1967), fig. 208.

7. Swedish: Erixon, *Möbler*, title page and figs. 611, 612, etc. German: Otto Von Falke, *Deutsche Möbel Des Mittelalters Und Der Renaissance* (Stuttgart, 1924), pp. 2, 3, 4, and 73. China: Michel Beurdeley, *Chinese Furniture*, trans. Katherine Watson (Tokyo, New York, and San Francisco, 1979), p. 72, fig. 90. Ancient Palestine: Hollis S. Baker, *Furniture in the Ancient World* (New York, 1966), p. 219, fig. 354: excavated at Jericho, made about 1600 B.C. And Bermuda: Colin Cooke and Sylvia Shorto, "Some Notes on Early Bermudian Furniture," *Antiques* 116 (August, 1979), p. 333, figs. 10 and 10a.

8. Various forms of dovetails are found in many of the outer coffins for sarcophagi displayed in the British Museum. See also drawings of Eighteenth Dynasty (c. 1567–1320 B.C.) joints in Baker, *Furniture in the Ancient World*, pp. 304–6, figs. 465–6.

9. John T. Kirk, *Connecticut Furniture, Seventeenth and Eighteenth Centuries* (catalogue for an exhibition, Wadsworth Atheneum, Hartford, 1967), fig. 87.

Chapter 8

1. Peter Thornton, *Seventeenth-Century Interior Decoration in England, France and Holland* (New Haven and London, 1978), p. 101, fig. 97.

2. Helena Hayward and Pat Kirkham, *William and John Linnell, Eighteenth-Century London Furniture Makers*, 2 vols. (New York, 1980), vol. 1, facing p. 42, pl. 1. For a classical Roman sarcophagus with similar eagle and swags, see Erwin Panofsky, *Tomb Sculpture*, ed. H. W. Janson (New York, 1964), fig. 121d.

3. This and other examples of eighteenth-century brass-ornamented English furniture are discussed in John Hayward, "English Brass-inlay Furniture," *Victoria and Albert Museum Bulletin* 1 (January, 1965), pp. 10–23.

4. For an extended analysis of the two ends, see Derek Shrub, "The Vile Problem," *Victoria and Albert Museum Bulletin* 1 (October, 1965), pp. 26–35.

5. Christopher Gilbert, *The Life and Work of Thomas Chippendale*, 2 vols. (New York, 1978), vol. 2, figs. 398 and 426.

Chapter 9

1. Victor Chinnery, *Oak Furniture, The British Tradition* (Woodbridge, Suffolk, 1979), p. 162.

2. John T. Kirk, *American Chairs, Queen Anne and Chippendale* (New York, 1972), pp. 44–5.

3. Meyric R. Rogers, "Philadelphia via Dublin: Influence in Rococo Furniture," *Antiques* 79 (March, 1961), pp. 272–5.

4. Benno M. Forman, "Delaware Valley 'Crookt Foot' and Slat-Back Chairs," *Winterthur Portfolio* 15 (Spring, 1980), pp. 41–64. Forman establishes that this and related chairs are aesthetically better than those made by Savery. That his master Fussell made them is only a hypothesis.

5. John T. Kirk, *Early American Furniture* (New York, 1970), p. 37, fig. 24.

6. Benno M. Forman has found early references using this term for this form of foot.

Conclusion

1. John T. Kirk, *American Chairs, Queen Anne and Chippendale* (New York, 1972), p. 81, fig. 71.

2. *Ibid.*, p. 112, fig. 127.

3. For example, see *ibid.*, p. 129, figs. 160 and 161.

4. Benno M. Forman, "Delaware Valley 'Crookt Foot' and Slat-Back Chairs," *Winterthur Portfolio* 15 (Spring, 1980), pp. 41–64.

5. For the other, see Kirk, *American Chairs*, p. 90, figs. 88 and 88a.

6. Nina Fletcher Little, "William M. Prior, Traveling Artist," *Antiques* 53 (January, 1948), p. 45, man's portrait in fig. 3. I am also grateful for additional information supplied by Mrs. Little.

Visual Survey of British & American Furniture

1. Ralph Edwards, *The Shorter Dictionary of English Furniture* (London, 1964), pp. 186–7, fig. 6.

2. Clive Wainwright, in conversation, January, 1975.

3. I am grateful to Benno M. Forman for providing this information.

4. Benno M. Forman, "The Origins of the Joined Chest of Drawers," *Nederlands Kunsthistorisch Jaarboek* (Leyden, 1981), pp. 169–83.

5. Christopher Gilbert, *The Life and Work of Thomas Chippendale*, 2 vols. (New York, 1978), vol. 2, p. 15, fig. 27.

6. Edwards, *Dictionary*, pp. 63–4, fig. 7.

7. I am indebted to Benno M. Forman, who shared his photograph of the piece with me.

8. Michel Beurdeley, *Chinese Furniture*, trans. Katherine Watson (Tokyo, New York, and San Francisco, 1979), figs. 122, 127, etc.

9. Richard H. Randall, Jr., *American Furniture in the Museum of Fine Arts Boston* (Boston, 1965), pp. 102–3, fig. 70.

10. Nancy A. Goyne [Evans], "The Bureau Table in America," *Winterthur Portfolio* 3 (1967), pp. 24-5, fig. 1.

11. I am indebted to Benno M. Forman for his suggestion that this may not be a Massachusetts piece because: the brasses are a type used in New York; the drawer arrangement at the top of the upper case is not a Massachusetts pattern; the low-hanging ogee curves of the skirt are found in New York; flat bottom turnings on the legs above the ankle baluster combined with a flare under the cup are New York features; and finally, the veneer panel down the center of the cases again indicates New York.

12. Dean A. Fales, Jr., *American Painted Furniture 1660–1880* (New York, 1972), p. 38, fig. 43. Unfortunately, the rear edge of the back stretcher, which is shaped to follow the front edge, was airbrushed out on the photograph and appears as a straight line.

13. Desmond Fitz-Gerald, "Irish Mahogany Furniture: A Source for American Design?" *Antiques* 99 (April, 1971), p. 568, fig. 1.

14. Jonathan L. Fairbanks, Wendy A. Cooper, Anne Farnam, Brock W. Jobe, and Martha B. Katz-Hyman, Intro. by Walter Muir Whitehill, *Paul Revere's Boston: 1735–1818* (catalogue for an exhibition, Museum of Fine Arts, Boston, 1975), p. 44, fig. 49.

15. Randall, *American Furniture*, pp. 77–80, figs. 59–59c.

16. Joseph Downs, *American Furniture, Queen Anne and Chippendale Periods* (New York, 1952), fig. 231.

17. Fitz-Gerald, "Irish Mahogany Furniture," fig. 4.

18. Patricia E. Kane, *300 Years of American Seating Furniture* (Boston, 1976), p. 29, fig. 1.

19. *Nordsjøkulturen British Kunsthåndverk 1650–1850* (catalogue for an exhibition, Kunstindustrimuseet, Oslo, 1955), p. 107, fig. 38, which has English turkeywork upholstery.

20. Side chair from the set: Pauline Agius, *101 Chairs* (catalogue for an exhibition, Divinity School, Oxford, 1968), fig. 13.

21. Peter Thornton, *Seventeenth-Century Interior Decoration in England, France and Holland* (New Haven and London, 1978), pp. 110–11.

22. *Philadelphia: Three Centuries of American Art* (catalogue for an exhibition, Philadelphia Museum of Art, 1976), p. 9, fig. 6.

23. John T. Kirk, *Connecticut Furniture, Seventeenth and Eighteenth Centuries* (catalogue for an exhibition, Wadsworth Atheneum, Hartford, 1967), p. 113, fig. 198.

24. See Robert Blair St. George, *The Wrought Covenant* (catalogue for an exhibition, Brockton Art Center, Mass., 1979), figs. 46–9.

25. Benno M. Forman informed me of the woods used in this chair. Robert Blair St. George suggested Boston as the source of this and similar chairs.

26. Christopher Gilbert, *An Exhibition of Town and Country Furniture* (catalogue for an exhibition, Temple Newsam House, Leeds, 1972), fig. 51.

27. Helen Comstock, *American Furniture* (New York, 1962), first chair at the left of fig. 156.

28. John T. Kirk, *American Chairs, Queen Anne and Chippendale* (New York, 1972), pp. 27–8, figs. 16 and 17.

29. Martin Eli Weil, "A Cabinetmaker's Price Book," *Winterthur Portfolio* 13 (Chicago and London, 1979), pp. 175–92.

30. Kirk, *American Chairs*, p. 100, fig. 105.

31. Downs, *American Furniture*, fig. 56.

32. For a similar chair with identical upholstery and probably from the same set, see F. Lewis Hinckley, *A Directory of Antique Furniture* (New York, 1953), p. 251, fig. 785.

33. Downs, *American Furniture*, fig. 154.

34. Kane, *300 Years of American Seating Furniture*, p. 117, fig. 98.

35. Kirk, *American Chairs*, pp. 87 and 172–4, figs. 83, 83a, and 233.

36. Helena Hayward and Pat Kirkham, *William and John Linnell, Eighteenth-Century London Furniture Makers*, 2 vols. (New York, 1980), vol. 2, p. 28, fig. 48.

37. Charles F. Montgomery, *American Furniture, The Federal Period* (New York, 1966), p. 77, fig. 16.

38. *Ibid.*, p. 91, fig. 38.

39. *Ibid.*, pp. 126–7, figs. 72a and 72b.

40. For a detailed discussion of English Windsors, see Nancy Goyne Evans, "A History and Background of English Windsor Furniture," *Furniture History* 15 (1979), pp. 24–53, pls. 68A–95B.

41. Desmond Fitz-Gerald, Simon Jervis, John Hardy, Intro. by

Ralph Edwards, *English Chairs* (London: Victoria and Albert Museum, 1970), p. 21, fig. 47.

42. Gilbert, *Chippendale*, vol. 2, p. 84, fig. 133.

43. Hayward and Kirkham, *Linnell*, vol. 2, p. 24, fig. 40; Gilbert, *Chippendale*, vol. 2, p. 84, fig. 134.

44. Kirk, *Connecticut Furniture*, p. 144, fig. 260.

45. Margaret Burke Clunie, Anne Farnam, and Robert F. Trent, *Furniture at the Essex Institute* (Salem, Mass., 1980), p. 13, fig. 7.

46. Scandinavia: Sigurd Erixon, *Möbler Och Meminredning I Svenska Bygder* (Stockholm, 1926), vol. 2, figs. 438–9 and 457–8. Italy: Raffaella Del Puglia and Carlo Steiner, *Mobili e Ambienti Italiani dal Gotico al Floreale*, 2 vols. (Milan, 1963), vol. 1, unpaged, fig. 42.

47. Victor Chinnery, *Oak Furniture, The British Tradition* (Woodbridge, Suffolk, 1979), p. 310, fig. 3:231.

48. Beurdeley, *Chinese Furniture*, figs. 118, 120, etc.

49. Robert Wemyss Symonds Papers, ms. 75 x 69.45, p. 49, Joseph Downs Memorial Manuscript Library, Winterthur Museum.

50. Downs, *American Furniture*, fig. 374.

51. See Beurdeley, *Chinese Furniture*, p. 118, fig. 160.

52. Pier table: Edwin J. Hipkiss, *Eighteenth-Century American Arts* (Boston, 1941), pp. 92–3, fig. 50. Desk: Randall, *American Furniture*, pp. 72, 74–5, figs. 57–57B. The research on the pieces was done by Sue Wheeler and Anne Elizabeth Rogers.

53. Parke-Bernet Galleries, New York, Sale no. 2304, October 30–31, 1964, fig. 357.

54. Wood and constructional information supplied by Deborah Ducoff-Barone, in a letter to the author, July 17, 1981. Gray family history: David Stockwell, Inc., advertisement, *East Side House, Winter Antiques Show* (catalogue for a show held January 19–25, 1962), p. 63.

55. *Philadelphia: Three Centuries*, pp. 127–8.

56. *Ibid.*, pp. 112–13, fig. 89 and detail.

57. It descended in the Brown family to Norman Herreshoff, and is on display in the John Brown House, Providence.

Picture Credits

TO SIMPLIFY THE LISTING,
THE FOLLOWING ABBREVIATIONS ARE USED:

Author	Location of the object unknown; photograph in the author's collection.
Author's neg.	Photograph taken by the author.
CID	Council of Industrial Design, London. Some photographs carry this name and "High Wycombe." Those with the additional designation are listed as High Wycombe (see below).
CW	Colonial Williamsburg, Williamsburg, Virginia.
Gillows	Estimate Books, Gillows of Lancaster papers, City of Westminster Public Library, London. Author's negatives.
High Wycombe	High Wycombe Art Gallery and Museum, High Wycombe, Buckinghamshire.
MESDA	Museum of Early Southern Decorative Arts, Winston-Salem, North Carolina.
MFA	Museum of Fine Arts, Boston.
Private Coll.	Private Collection.
RISD	The Museum of Art, Rhode Island School of Design, Providence, Rhode Island.
Sack	Israel Sack, Inc., New York, New York.
Shreve	Shreve, Crump and Low Co., Boston, Massachusetts.
Sotheby	Sotheby & Co., London.
SPNEA	Society for the Preservation of New England Antiquities, Boston, Massachusetts.
Stockwell	David Stockwell, Inc., Wilmington, Delaware.
Symonds, Winterthur	Robert Wemyss Symonds Collection of Photographs, Joseph Downs Memorial Manuscript Library, Winterthur, Museum.
V & A	Furniture owned by the Victoria and Albert Museum, London.
V & A archive	Archive of furniture photographs, Victoria and Albert Museum, London.
Winterthur	Furniture owned by The Henry Francis du Pont Winterthur Museum, Winterthur, Delaware.
Yale	Yale University Art Gallery, New Haven, Connecticut.

1. V & A
2. From Ole Wanscher, *The Art of Furniture*, trans. David Hohnen (London, 1968), p. 149.
3. Yale
4. From Heinrich Kreisel, *Die Kunst des deutschen Möbels, Zweiter Band Spätbarock und Rokoko* (Munich, 1970), fig. 1081.
5. V & A
6. Townend, Troutbeck, Westmorland; author's neg.
7. Private Coll.
8. Lady William Powlett
9. MFA; 29.1015; gift of J. Templeton Coolidge
10. Wadsworth Atheneum, Hartford, Connecticut
11. V & A
12. Yale

13–15. Winterthur

16. Author
17. Winterthur
18. Peel's Antiques, London; author's neg.
19. Author
20. Yale
21. Peel's Antiques; author's neg.
22. Sack
23. V & A archive
24. The Brooklyn Museum, Brooklyn, New York; photo: Sack
25. Temple Newsam House, Leeds, Yorkshire
26. Yale
27. Shreve
28. Yale
29. Author
30. Winterthur
31. Private Coll.; author's neg.
32. Robert W. Withington, Inc., Oliver E. Williams Sale, July 26–28, 1966, no. 38
33. Christchurch Mansion, Ipswich, Suffolk; author's neg.
34. National Society of Colonial Dames of America in the State of Rhode Island and Providence Plantations
35. Symonds, Winterthur
36. RISD
37. Priory Church of St. Mary & St. Martin, Blyth, Nottinghamshire; author's neg.
38. V & A
39. Sudbury Hall, Sudbury, Derbyshire

40. Towneley Hall, Burnley, Lancashire; author's neg.
41. V & A
42. Yale
43. Nichols-Wanton-Hunter House, Newport
44–45. Vincent F. Luti
46. Henry Glassie
47. Yale
48. Museum of Art, Carnegie Institute, Pittsburgh, Pennsylvania; Ailsa Mellon Bruce Collection, 1970
49. Essex Co. Record Office, Chelmsford, Essex
50. SPNEA
51. Worcester Art Museum, Worcester, Massachusetts
52. Massachusetts Historical Society, Boston, Massachusetts
53. Private Coll.
54. Massachusetts Historical Society
55. SPNEA
56–57. V & A archive
58–59. V & A
60. MESDA
61. Author
62–99. Gillows
100. V & A
101. Dean and Chapter of Westminster Abbey, London
102–107. Southwold Parish Church, Southwold, Suffolk; author's negs.
108. Musée du Louvre, Paris
109. V & A
110–111. City Art Museum of Saint Louis, Saint Louis, Missouri
112. V & A
113. Author
114. Symonds, Winterthur
115–117. V & A
118–119. Kederminster Library in Langley Marish Church, Buckinghamshire; author's negs.
120. Wallace Collection, London
121–122. Kederminster Library in Langley Marish Church; author's negs.
123–125. Screen, Langley Marish Church; author's negs.
126. Detail of tapestry, "Feeling," Haddon Hall, Bakewell, Derbyshire; author's neg.
127–134. Christchurch Mansion; author's negs.
135–137. V & A
138–143. V & A; author's negs.
144. V & A
145. V & A Knole, Kent; photo: Symonds, Winterthur
146–149. V & A; author's negs.
150. Symonds, Winterthur
151–152. Hardwick Hall, nr. Chesterfield, Derbyshire
153. V & A
154. The Detroit Institute of Arts, Detroit, Michigan
155–160. V & A; author's negs.
161. Church of St. Botolph, Boston, Lincolnshire; author's neg.
162. Winterthur
163–164. Yale
165. Wadsworth Atheneum
166. Frank H. Sommer
167. Photo: Benno M. Forman
168. Winterthur
169–170. Philadelphia Museum of Art, Philadelphia, Pennsylvania; '40-16-28; bequest of R. Wistar Harvey
171. Yale
172. Historic Deerfield, Inc., Deerfield, Massachusetts
173. MFA; 50.3786; gift of Philip Spaulding Oakes and Ames Spaulding and Hobart Ames Spaulding
174–176. The Connecticut Historical Society, Hartford, Connecticut
177. V & A; author's neg.
178. Temple Newsam House
179. Author
180. V & A
181. Osterley Park House, Middlesex; photo: V & A
182–183. Rufford Old Hall, Rufford, Lancashire; author's negs.
184. The Old Hall, Gainsborough, Lincolnshire; author's neg.
185–187. Gillows
188. Rufford Old Hall; author's neg.
189–190. The Old Hall, Gainsborough; author's negs.
191. Gillows
192–196. V & A
197. Knole; photo: Symonds, Winterthur
198–205. V & A
206. Private Coll.; photo: Richard Cheek
207–209. V & A
210. Osterley Park House; photo: V & A
211–212. Rufford Old Hall; author's negs.
213. Valley Farm, Dedham, Essex; photo: V & A
214–215. Christchurch Mansion; author's negs.
216. Author
217. V & A
218. V & A; author's neg.
219. Yale
220–221. V & A
222–223. Temple Newsam House; author's negs.
224. Haddon Hall; author's neg.
225. Church of St. Wulfrom, Grantham, Lincolnshire; author's neg.
226. V & A
227. Yale
228. The Connecticut Historical Society
229. Author
230. MFA; 32.218; bequest of Charles Hitchcock Tyler
231. Yale
232. Sack
234. Symonds, Winterthur
235–236. Towneley Hall; author's negs.
237–241. Turton Tower, Turton, Lancashire; author's negs.
242–246. Rufford Old Hall; author's negs.
247–250. Temple Newsam House; author's negs.
251. Towneley Hall; author's neg.
252. V & A
253–255. Astley Hall, Chorley, Lancashire; author's negs.
256. Symonds, Winterthur
257. V & A
258–261. The Old Hall, Gainsborough; author's negs.
262–264. Hall i'-th-Wood, Bolton, Lancashire; author's negs.
265. Photo: Benno M. Forman
266. Sotheby
267. V & A
268–270. Hall i'-th-Wood; author's negs.
271–272. V & A
273. Symonds, Winterthur
274. V & A
275. Bolling Hall, Bradford, Yorkshire
276. Symonds, Winterthur
277. Shibden Hall, Halifax, Yorkshire; author's neg.
278–279. Towneley Hall; author's negs.
280. Bolling Hall; author's neg.
281. Towneley Hall; author's neg.
282. Smithills Hall, Bolton, Lancashire; author's neg.
283. Bolling Hall; author's neg.
284. Shibden Hall; author's neg.
285. Temple Newsam House; author's neg.
286. V & A
287–289. Towneley Hall; author's negs.
290. Symonds, Winterthur
291. The Old Hall, Gainsborough; author's neg.
292–293. Symonds, Winterthur
294. Old Sturbridge Village, Sturbridge, Massachusetts
295–296. V & A
297. Symonds, Winterthur
298–300. Townend; author's negs.
301. Rufford Old Hall; author's neg.
302–303. The Metropolitan Museum of Art, New York, New York
304. Yale
305. Author
306. Rock Hall, Lawrence, Long Island, New York; photo: Society for the Preservation of Long Island Antiquities

307–308. Mr. and Mrs. Robert W. Chambers, on loan to the Sterling and Francine Clark Art Institute, Williamstown, Massachusetts
309–310 V & A archive
311. Winterthur
312–313. Author
314. Symonds, Winterthur
315–316. V & A
317. Author
318. Yale
319. V & A
320. Bolling Hall
321. The Metropolitan Museum of Art
322. Winterthur
323. V & A
324. Wallace Collection
325. Sotheby
326. Shreve
327. Symonds, Winterthur
328. Author
329. V & A; photo: Symonds, Winterthur
330. Sack
331. CW
332. Douglas C. Morris & Co., London
333. Author
334–335. Wordsworth House, Cockermouth, Cumberland; author's negs.
336–337. Wordsworth Museum, Cockermouth, Cumberland; author's negs.
338–340. Bolling Hall; author's negs.
341. Symonds, Winterthur
342–344. Towneley Hall; author's negs.
345–346. RISD
347. V & A; author's neg.
348–349. RISD
350–351. V & A
352. Yale
353. Author
354–356. V & A
357. Temple Newsam House
358–359. V & A
360. MFA; 58.19; 1951 Purchase Fund (Francis Bartlett Fund)
361. Symonds, Winterthur
362–364. V & A
365. The Metropolitan Museum of Art; Fletcher Fund, 1964
366–367. V & A
368. From Robert Manwaring, *The Cabinet and Chair-Maker's Real Friend and Companion* (London, 1765; reprinted Tiranti, 1947).
369. Symonds, Winterthur
370. Author
371. V & A
372–373. RISD
374–375. Winterthur
376. Private Coll.
377. Yale
378. Winterthur
379–380. Sack
381. Yale
382. Sack
383–384. Yale
385. The Henry Ford Museum, Dearborn, Michigan
386. Yale
387. Philadelphia Museum of Art; '29-178-1; given by George H. Lorimer
388. Bayou Bend, The Museum of Fine Arts, Houston, Texas
389–390. Winterthur
391. The Metropolitan Museum of Art
392. Roger Bacon, Exeter, New Hampshire
393. Winterthur
394. Private Coll.; photo: Richard Cheek
395–396. Winterthur
397–398. Private Coll.; photos: Richard Cheek
399. Yale
400–401. Private Coll.; photo of full chest: Richard Cheek
402. Private Coll.
403. Private Coll.; photo: Richard Cheek
404. Private Coll.
405. Roger Bacon
406. Bolling Hall; author's neg.
407. Yale
408. Rufford Old Hall; author's neg.
409. Winterthur
410. Symonds, Winterthur
411. Author
412–413. Castle Acre Priory, Castle Acre, Norfolk; author's negs.
414. Roger Bacon
415. Old Sturbridge Village
416. Sotheby
417. Yale
418. V & A
419. MFA; 1978.382; gift of a friend of the Department of American Decorative Arts and Sculpture
420–421. V & A
422. Author
423. Yale
424–425. V & A
426. Christchurch Mansion; author's neg.
427. Author
428–430. V & A
431. The Metropolitan Museum of Art
432. Christchurch Mansion; author's neg.
433. V & A
434. Author
435. Sack
436–437. Towneley Hall; author's negs.
438. The Henry Ford Museum
439–440. V & A
441. Winterthur
442–443. Gawthorpe Hall, nr. Burnley, Lancashire; author's negs.
444–445. V & A
446. Symonds, Winterthur
447–449. Gillows
450. Shreve
451. Peacock Hotel, Rowsley, Derbyshire; author's neg.
452–453. V & A archive
454. V & A
455. V & A archive
456. Sack
457. Winterthur
458–460. Symonds, Winterthur
461. Shreve
462–463. Author
464–465. Sotheby
466–467. Yale
468. Symonds, Winterthur
469. Rufford Old Hall; photo: Benno M. Forman
470–472. Christchurch Mansion; author's negs.
473. Symonds, Winterthur
474. SPNEA
475–476. V & A archive
477. Yale
478. Sack
479. Yale
480. V & A
481. The Metropolitan Museum of Art
482. V & A archive
483–485. Gillows
486. Sack
487. V & A archive
488–489. Author
490. V & A archive
491. Author
492. Yale
493. Black Swan Hotel, Helmsley, Yorkshire; author's neg.
494. Sack
495–496. Author
497. Shreve
498. Sack
499. Yale
500. V & A archive
501–502. Author
503. National Museum of Ireland, Dublin
504. V & A archive
505. Author
506. V & A archive
507. Yale
508–509. Author
510. Shreve
511. Author
512. V & A archive
513–516. Author
517. Shreve
518–520. Author
521. MESDA

522. Author
523. V & A archive
524. Author
525. Shreve
526. Author
527–528. V & A archive
529–531. Author
532. Sack
533. Gillows
534. Yale
535. Shreve
536. Estate of John Nicholas Brown, Providence, Rhode Island
537. Gillows
538. V & A
539. Shreve
540. Oxford-Gail Collection, Long Beach, California
541. From Ralph Fastnedge, *English Furniture Styles* (Harmondsworth, Middlesex, 1955; reprinted 1961), fig. 14.
542. V & A archive
543. The Henry Ford Museum
544. V & A archive
545. Shelburne Museum, Shelburne, Vermont
546. Yale
547. Symonds, Winterthur
548–549. Author
550. Symonds, Winterthur
551. Shreve
552. V & A archive
553. Yale
554. Bolling Hall; author's neg.
555. Author
556. Symonds, Winterthur
557–558. V & A archive
559. Author
560. V & A archive
561. Author
562. V & A archive
563. Author
564. Sotheby
565. V & A archive
566–568. Gillows
569–570. Shreve
571. Symonds, Winterthur
572. MFA; 1971.737; gift of Albert Sack
573. Southwell Cathedral, Southwell, Nottinghamshire; author's neg.
574. Sotheby
575–576. Winterthur
577–579. Shibden Hall; author's negs.
580. Shreve
581. Symonds, Winterthur
582–583. V & A
584–585. Rufford Old Hall; author's negs.
586. MFA; 32.251; bequest of Charles Hitchcock Tyler
587. V & A archive
588. Towneley Hall; author's neg.
589. Yale
590. From Esther Stevens Fraser, "Pioneer Furniture from Hampton, New Hampshire," *Antiques* 17 (April, 1930), p. 314, fig. 3.
591. Christchurch Mansion; author's neg.
592. National Museum of Ireland
593. Author
594. Christchurch Mansion; author's neg.
595. Shreve
596. V & A
597–598. Shreve
599. Sotheby
600. Symonds, Winterthur
601. Mrs. Charles L. Bybee
602–603. Sotheby
604. Shreve
605. V & A
606. Sotheby
607–608. V & A
609. Symonds, Winterthur
610. V & A archive
611–612. Shreve
613. V & A
614. Gillows
615. Historic Deerfield
616–617. V & A archive
618. Bolling Hall; author's neg.
619–620. Author
621. Yale
622–624. Author
625. Shreve
626. Gillows
627. V & A
628. Colonial Williamsburg, Williamsburg, Virginia
629. Symonds, Winterthur
630. From F. Lewis Hinckley, *A Directory of Queen Anne, Early Georgian and Chippendale Furniture* (New York, 1971), fig. 440.
631. V & A
632. Sotheby
633. MFA; 39.176; gift of Mr. and Mrs. Maxim Karolik Collection
634. Sotheby
635. V & A
636. Winterthur
637–638. Shreve
639. Author
640. V & A archive
641–642. Author
643. V & A
644–645. Sotheby
646. Author
647. V & A
648. Yale
649. Christchurch Mansion
650. Symonds, Winterthur
651. V & A
652. Author
653. V & A
654. The Old Hall, Gainsborough; author's neg.
655–656. Hall i'-th-Wood; author's negs.
657. Symonds, Winterthur
658. Winterthur
659–664. V & A
665. Sack
666–667. V & A
668. Priory Church of St. Mary & St. Martin, Blyth; author's neg.
669. Rijksmuseum, Amsterdam
670–673. V & A
674. Christchurch Mansion; author's neg.
675. MFA; 1977.711; William E. Nickerson Fund
676–678. Knole; photos: Symonds, Winterthur
679. V & A
680. From Raffaella Del Puglia and Carlo Steiner, *Mobili e Ambienti Italiani dal Gotico al Floreale*, 2 vols. (Milan, 1963), vol. 1, unpaged, fig. 204.
681. V & A
682. Yale
683. Christ Church College, Oxford; photo: author
684. Author
685. The Metropolitan Museum of Art
686–689. V & A
690. V & A archive
691. Winterthur
692. Shibden Hall; author's neg.
693. V & A
694. Symonds, Winterthur
695. Strangers Hall, Norwich, Norfolk; author's neg.
696. Author
697. Private Coll.
698. The Metropolitan Museum of Art
699. Symonds, Winterthur
700. Plymouth Hall Museum, Plymouth, Massachusetts
701. Rector and P.C.C. of Guiseley; photo: Temple Newsam House
702. Shreve
703. Yale
704. Symonds, Winterthur
705. V & A
706. Plymouth Hall Museum
707. V & A archive
708. V & A
709. National Museum of Ireland
710–712. V & A
713. Author
714. National Museum of Ireland
715. Peacock Hotel; author's neg.
716. V & A
717. Author
718. V & A
719. Winterthur
720. V & A
721–723. Author
724. Symonds, Winterthur

725. Roger Bacon
726. Symonds, Winterthur
727. Milwaukee Art Center, Milwaukee, Wisconsin
728. Author
729–730. Winterthur
731. Author
732. Winterthur
733. MFA; 1971.624; Arthur Tracy Cabot Fund
734. Mrs. Charles L. Bybee
735. Trinity House, Hull, Yorkshire; photo: V & A archive
736. Author
737–739. V & A
740. Yale
741. Author
742. National Museum of Ireland
743. High Wycombe
744. Symonds, Winterthur
745. Formerly Francis P. Garvan Coll.
746. Yale
747. Author
748. Haddon Hall; author's neg.
749. Author
750. Private Coll.; photo: Richard Cheek
751. Author
752. Symonds, Winterthur
753. Sotheby
754. Yale
755–756. Rijksmuseum
757. Strangers Hall; author's neg.
758. Winterthur
759. V & A archive
760. Christchurch Mansion; author's neg.
761. Winterthur
762. Yale
763. High Wycombe
764. V & A
765–767. Author
768. Rijksmuseum
769. Private Coll.
770. Belgrave Hall, Leicester, Leicestershire
771. Openluchtmuseum, Arnhem, The Netherlands
772. V & A archive
773–775. Author
776. Belvoir Castle, nr. Grantham, Leicestershire; author's neg.
777. V & A
778. Ham House, Petersham, Surrey; photo: V & A
779. V & A
780. Author
781. Yale
782. Author
783. Author
784. Shreve
785. V & A
786. Author
787. Preservation Society of Newport County, Newport, Rhode Island
788. Shreve
789. Author
790. Roger Bacon
791. Author
792. Winterthur
793–794. Author
795. Christchurch Mansion; author's neg.
796. George Waterman, Jr.
797. Trinity House, Hull; photo: V & A archive
798. V & A
799. Author
800. V & A archive
801. Astley Hall; author's neg.
802. Winterthur
803–804. Ashmolean Museum, University of Oxford
805. Sotheby
806. Winterthur
807. Sack
808. Shreve
809. National Museum of Ireland
810. Author
811. Museum of the City of New York, New York, New York
812. Christchurch Mansion; author's neg.
813. Shreve
814. Mr. and Mrs. Bayard Ewing
815. High Wycombe
816. V & A archive
817. Yale
818. V & A
819. Stockwell
820–824. V & A archive
825. V & A
826. Milwaukee Art Center
827. V & A archive
828. Author
829. Winterthur
830. Author
831. V & A
832. The Old Hall, Gainsborough; author's neg.
833. Private Coll.
834. Author
835. Strangers Hall
836. Shreve
837. Gillows
838. Yale
839. Philadelphia Museum of Art
840. Robert Y. Swanson
841. Author
842. Southwell Cathedral; author's neg.
843. V & A
844. From Manwaring, *The Cabinet and Chair-Maker's Real Friend and Companion*, pl. 9.
845. The Metropolitan Museum of Art
846. From Thomas Chippendale, *The Gentleman and Cabinet-Maker's Director* (London, 1762; reprinted Dover, 1966), no. 13.
847. Winterthur
848. From J. P. Blake and A. E. Reveirs-Hopkins, *Old English Furniture for the Small Collector* (London, 1930; reprinted 1944); p. 76, fig. 63.
849. Author
850. Yale
851. Sack
852–853. Yale
854. Shreve
855. Author
856. Shreve
857. V & A archive
858. MFA; 41.66; gift of Mrs. Edward Jackson.
859. Yale
860. Shelburne Museum
861. National Museum of Ireland
862. Author
863. The Old Hall, Gainsborough; author's neg.
864. Shreve
865. Bolling Hall
866. Yale
867–868. Ulster Museum; photo: V & A archive
869. Sack
870. Temple Newsam House; author's neg.
871. Author
872. Robert W. Skinner, Inc., Bolton, Massachusetts
873. CW
874–875. Author
876. V & A archive
877. Author
878. Yale
879. Shreve
880. National Museum of Ireland
881. Author
882. Yale
883. Author
884. V & A archive
885–887. Author
888. Yale
889. From Wallace Nutting, *Furniture Treasury* (New York, 1928; reprinted, 1954), fig. 2249.
890. Winterthur
891. Author
892. The Rhode Island Historical Society, Providence, Rhode Island
893. Author
894. Yale
895. Winterthur
896. Yale
897. Author
898. MFA; 60.1176; gift of Mrs. F. Carrington Weems
899. V & A
900. Museum of the City of New York

901–902. Author
903. Yale
904. Author
905. Shreve
906. Author
907. The Connecticut Historical Society
908. Author
909. V & A
910. The Metropolitan Museum of Art
911. The Old Hall, Gainsborough; author's neg.
912. The Metropolitan Museum of Art
913. Shreve
914. Sack
915. Yale
916. Shreve
917. Winterthur
918. Author
919. V & A
920. Shreve
921. Author
922. Stockwell; photo: V & A archive
923. Trinity House, Hull; photo: V & A archive
924. Paul Maynard
925. CW
926. Old Sturbridge Village
927–928. Author
929. Winterthur
930–932. Author
933. Museum of the City of New York
934. From Hinckley's *Directory of Queen Anne, Early Georgian and Chippendale Furniture*, p. 78, fig. 112
935. V & A archive
936. Author
937. Museum of the City of New York
938. National Museum of Ireland
939. Winterthur
940. High Wycombe
941. Yale
942. Ginsburg and Levy, Inc.
943. The Old Hall, Gainsborough; author's neg.
944. Albany Institute of History and Art
945. Author
946. The Metropolitan Museum of Art
947. Yale
948. Author
949. CW
950–952. Author
953. Yale
954. CW
955. CID
956. V & A archive
957. Stockwell
958. Sotheby
959. Symonds, Winterthur
960. V & A
961. Yale
962. Sotheby
963. Shreve
964. Sack
965. Yale
966. Sotheby
967. Author
968. V & A
969. Winterthur
970. Shreve
971. Sotheby
972. Author
973–974. Yale
975–978. Author
979. Ginsburg and Levy, Inc.
980. Yale
981–982. Author
983. Sack
984. Sotheby
985. Shreve
986. National Museum of Ireland
987. Yale
988. Author
989. Sack
990. Author
991. Shreve
992. Winterthur
993. Shreve
994. V & A archive
995. Winterthur
996. CID
997. Author
998. V & A
999. RISD
1000. From Hinckley's *Directory of Queen Anne, Early Georgian and Chippendale Furniture*, p. 80, fig. 122
1001. Yale
1002. RISD
1003. V & A
1004. Author
1005. MESDA
1006. Sotheby
1007. Author
1008. Yale
1009. Winterthur
1010. Author
1011. V & A archive
1012. MESDA
1013–1014. Author
1015. The Henry Ford Museum
1016. Shreve
1017. Peel's Antiques; author's neg.
1018. Author
1019. Shreve
1020. V & A archive
1021. Shreve
1022. Author
1023. CW
1024. V & A archive
1025. National Museum of Ireland
1026. Mr. and Mrs. Graham Hood
1027. CW
1028. Sotheby
1029–1030. Author
1031–1032. Yale
1033–1034. Author
1035. Shreve
1036. V & A archive
1037. Author
1038. Sack
1039. Historic Deerfield
1040. Author
1041. Shreve
1042. Gillows
1043–1044. Shreve
1045. National Museum of Ireland
1046. The Henry Ford Museum
1047–1048. National Museum of Ireland
1049. Sack
1050. Yale
1051. Shreve
1052. National Museum of Ireland
1053. Yale
1954. Winterthur
1055. Sotheby
1056. Yale
1057. Old Sturbridge Village
1058. From George Hepplewhite, *The Cabinet-Maker and Upholsterer's Guide* (London, 1794; reprint Dover, 1969), pl 2.
1059. Author
1060. The Henry Ford Museum
1061. Winterthur
1062. Author
1063. Gillows
1064. Author
1065–1066. High Wycombe
1067. Symonds, Winterthur
1068–1069. High Wycombe
1070. From Ralph Edwards, *Sheraton Furniture Designs* (London, 1949), fig. 39.
1071. The Metropolitan Museum of Art
1072. Sotheby
1073. MFA; 41.610; gift of Mr. and Mrs. Maxim Karolik Collection
1074–1076. Author
1077. Yale
1078. V & A
1079. National Museum of Ireland
1080. Author
1081. Shreve
1082. Yale
1083–1084. V & A archive
1085–1088. High Wycombe
1089. Shreve
1090. Black Swan Hotel; author's neg.
1091–1093. Gillows
1094. Peacock Hotel; author's neg.
1095. V & A
1096. High Wycombe
1097. V & A
1098. High Wycombe
1099. V & A archive
1100. Peacock Hotel; author's neg.
1101. High Wycombe

1102. Sack
1103. CID
1104. Winterthur
1105. CID
1106. High Wycombe
1107. CID
1108. Sack
1109–1110. CID
1111. Southwell Cathedral; author's neg.
1112. Winterthur
1113. Yale
1114. CID
1115. High Wycombe
1116. CID
1117. Author
1118. CID
1119. High Wycombe
1120. Southwell Cathedral; author's neg.
1121. Yale
1122. Winterthur
1123. Black Swan Hotel; author's neg.
1124. High Wycombe
1125. Author
1126. High Wycombe
1127–1128. Sotheby
1129–1130. CID
1131. Symonds, Winterthur
1132. V & A
1133. Sotheby
1134. V & A archive
1135. V & A
1136–1137. Sack
1138. Symonds, Winterthur
1139–1141. Author
1142. V & A archive
1143. Sotheby
1144–1145. Author
1146. Sotheby
1147. Symonds, Winterthur
1148. V & A
1149–1151. Author
1152. Shreve
1153. V & A archive
1154. Yale
1155. Shreve
1156. MESDA
1157. Author
1158. Sotheby
1159. Gillows
1160. V & A
1161. Author
1162. Gillows
1163. V & A archive
1164. Yale
1165. Shreve
1166. Yale
1167. Author
1168. Symonds, Winterthur
1169. Rufford Old Hall; author's neg.
1170. Private Coll.
1171. Author
1172. Symonds, Winterthur
1173. Yale
1174. Anne Hathaway's Cottage, Stratford-upon-Avon, Warwickshire
1175. Rufford Old Hall; author's neg.
1176. Essex Institute, Salem, Massachusetts
1177. The Old Hall, Gainsborough; author's neg.
1178–1179. Author
1180. Sotheby
1181. Stockwell
1182. Winterthur
1183. The Rhode Island Historical Society
1184. V & A archive
1185. Gillows
1186. Author
1187. V & A archive
1188. Author
1189–1190. Gillows
1191–1192. Shreve
1193–1195. Author
1196. Gillows
1197. Shreve
1198. Author
1199. Gillows
1200. Author
1201. Gillows
1202. Author
1203. Winterthur
1204. V & A
1205. Winterthur
1206. Hall i'-th-Wood; author's neg.
1207–1209. V & A
1210. Sotheby
1211. The Metropolitan Museum of Art
1212–1215. Author
1216. V & A
1217. Symonds, Winterthur
1218. Author
1219. Sotheby
1220. Symonds, Winterthur
1221. Author
1222. V & A
1223. Winterthur
1224–1225. Symonds, Winterthur
1226–1227. Author
1228. Yale
1229. Author
1230. Peacock Hotel; author's neg.
1231. Shreve
1232. Roger Bacon
1233. V & A archive
1234. V & A
1235. Rufford Old Hall; author's neg.
1236. Southwell Cathedral; author's neg.
1237. Shreve
1238. V & A
1239. MESDA
1240–1241. V & A
1242. Sotheby
1243. MESDA
1244. Shreve
1245. Temple Newsam House
1246. V & A archive
1247. Symonds, Winterthur
1248. V & A
1249. Yale
1250. Shreve
1251. Peacock Hotel; author's neg.
1252. Symonds, Winterthur
1253. Shreve
1254. Sack
1255. Gillows
1256–1257. The Old Hall, Gainsborough; author's negs.
1258. Peel's Antiques; author's neg.
1259. Sack
1260–1262. V & A archive
1263. Shelburne Museum
1264–1265. MESDA
1266. Author
1267. V & A archive
1268. V & A
1269–1270. Author
1271. Sotheby
1272. Stockwell; photo: V & A archive
1273. From advertisement of Mallet & Son (Antiques) Ltd., London, *Connoisseur* 181 (December, 1972), front section: p. 52
1274. Yale
1275. Gary C. Cole, New York, New York
1276. Christchurch Mansion; author's neg.
1277. The Brooklyn Museum, Brooklyn, New York
1278. V & A archive
1279. Stockwell
1280. V & A archive
1281. Shreve
1282. Sotheby
1283–1284. Author
1285. V & A
1286. Author
1287–1288. Stockwell
1289. V & A archive
1290–1291. Author
1292. Winterthur
1293. Stockwell
1294. Sack
1295. V & A archive
1296. Author
1297. Symonds, Winterthur
1298–1299. V & A archive
1300–1301. Author
1302. V & A
1303. V & A archive
1304. Stockwell
1305. CW; photo: V & A archive
1306. National Museum of Ireland; photo: V & A archive
1307. V & A archive
1308. Stockwell
1309. Sotheby
1310–1312. V & A archive
1313. Philadelphia Museum of Art;

'62-17-1; purchased: John D. McIlhenny Fund
1314–1315. V & A archive
1316. National Museum of Ireland
1317. V & A archive
1318. Author
1319. Stockwell
1320. Author
1321. V & A archive
1322. Sotheby
1323. Stockwell
1324. Symonds, Winterthur
1325–1326. Author
1327. V & A archive
1328–1331. Stockwell
1332. Author
1333. V & A archive
1334. Author
1335. Ginsburg and Levy, Inc.
1336. Winterthur
1337. Philadelphia Museum of Art; '74-223-1; given by H. Richard Dietrich, Jr.
1338. Author
1339. V & A archive
1340. Winterthur
1341. V & A archive
1342. National Museum of Ireland
1343. Author
1344. Philadelphia Museum of Art; photo: V & A archive
1345–1348. V & A archive
1349. V & A
1350–1352. V & A archive
1353–1354. V & A
1355–1356. Author
1357. Gillows
1358. V & A
1359. Author
1360. Sack
1361. Christie's International, Ltd.
1362. Author
1363–1364. CW
1365. Shreve
1366. Stockwell; photo: V & A archive
1367. Shreve
1368. V & A archive
1369. Author
1370. National Museum of Ireland
1371. V & A archive
1372. Author
1373. Shreve
1374. Yale
1375. CW
1376. National Museum of Ireland
1377. Christie's International, Ltd.
1378. V & A
1379. Shreve
1380. Author
1381. V & A archive
1382. Sack
1383. Author
1384. Southwell Cathedral; author's neg.
1385. Author
1386. Sack
1387. Gillows
1388. The Old Hall, Gainsborough; author's neg.
1389. V & A archive
1390–1392. Shreve
1393–1396. Author
1397. Sack
1398. Sotheby
1399. Shreve
1400–1401. V & A archive
1402. Shreve
1403. V & A archive
1404. Author
1405. Gillows
1406–1407. Shreve
1408. Author
1409. Shreve
1410. V & A archive
1411. Author
1412. Sack
1413. V & A archive
1414. Author
1415. Norman Herreshoff; photo: Antiques Library, by Helga Photo Studio
1416. V & A archive
1417. Author
1418–1419. V & A archive
1420. Shreve
1421–1422. Author
1423–1425. Shreve
1426. Gillows
1427. Winterthur
1428. V & A archive
1429. Winterthur
1430. Shreve
1431. Gillows
1432. Author
1433. Shreve
1434–1435. Gillows
1436. Trevor J. Fairbrother
1437. Gillows
1438. Shreve
1439. V & A
1440. From Martin Feddersen, *Chinese Decorative Art,* trans. Arthur Lane (London, 1961), p. 199, fig. 191
1441–1442. Author
1443. Winterthur
1444. Author
1445–1446. Shreve
1447. Gillows
1448. Shreve
1449. RISD
1450. Author
1451. Parke, Bernet, Inc., New York, New York
1452. Sack
1453. Ham House; photo: V & A
1454. Author
1455–1456. V & A
1457–1458. Symonds, Winterthur
1459. Yale
1460. Symonds, Winterthur
1461–1462. Smithills Hall; author's negs.
1463. Philadelphia Museum of Art; '25-69-1; purchased Elizabeth S. Shippen income
1464. Sotheby
1465. Shreve
1466. Dietrich Brothers Americana Corporation
1467. Winterthur
1468. Sotheby
1469. Author
1470. Sotheby
1471. Author
1472. Symonds, Winterthur
1473–1474. Author
1475. Shreve
1476. Author
1477. Shreve
1478. Yale
1479. Peacock Hotel; author's neg.
1480. Yale
1481. Shreve
1482. Photographed in an antique shop (name withheld) in Lincoln, Lincolnshire; author's neg.
1483. Author
1484. Sack
1485–1487. Author
1488–1489. Gillows
1490–1491. Shreve
1492. RISD
1493. Gillows
1494. Shreve
1495. City Art Museum of Saint Louis
1496. Author
1497. Symonds, Winterthur
1498. Author
1499. Sack
1500. Author
1501. The Henry Ford Museum
1502. Detail of 1500
1503. Detail of 1501
1504. National Museum of Ireland
1505–1506. Gillows
1507. Stockwell; photo: V & A archive
1508. Shreve

Indexes

List of English Pieces, Organized by County or Region (*Place of origin or early use*)

(Numbers refer to illustrations.)

List of Irish or Possibly Irish Pieces (*Others cited as British may also be from Ireland.*)

(Numbers refer to illustrations.)

Dated Furniture and Related Pieces

(Numbers refer to illustrations.)

General Index

(Boldface numbers refer to illustrations.)

A Note About the Author

John T. Kirk is a native of Newtown Square, Pennsylvania, and a graduate of George School and Earlham College. In addition to taking an M.A. in art history from Yale University, he studied cabinetmaking at the School for American Craftsmen, Rochester, New York, and furniture design at the Royal Danish Academy of Fine Arts, Copenhagen. He has been Assistant Curator for the Garvan Collection, Yale University Art Gallery; Consultant Curator for the Pendleton House, the Rhode Island School of Design; Director of the Rhode Island Historical Society; Research Associate of the Fogg Art Museum, Harvard University; and Director of Boston University's American and New England Studies Program. He is currently Professor of Art History and Artisanry at Boston University and Research Associate, Museum of Fine Arts, Boston, a member of the New England Advisory Committee of the Archives of American Art, the Advisory Council of the Institute of Early American History and Culture, and the Editorial Board of the *William & Mary Quarterly*. Mr. Kirk is the author of *Connecticut Furniture, Seventeenth and Eighteenth Centuries* (1967), *Early American Furniture* (1970, 1974), *American Chairs: Queen Anne and Chippendale* (1972), and *The Impecunious Collector's Guide to American Antiques* (1975).

A Note About the Type

This book was set on the Linotype in Baskerville. Linotype Baskerville is a facsimile cutting from type cast from the original matrices of a face designed by John Baskerville. The original face was the forerunner of the modern group of type faces. John Baskerville (1706–1775), of Birmingham, England, was a writing master with a special renown for cutting inscriptions in stone. About 1750 he began experimenting with punch cutting and making typographical material, and in 1757 he published his first work, a Virgil in royal quarto, with great-primer letters; the types throughout had been designed by him. This was followed by his famous editions of Milton, the Bible, the Book of Common Prayer, and works by several Latin classical authors. His types, at first criticized as unnecessarily slender, delicate, and feminine, in time were recognized as both distinct and elegant, and his types as well as his printing were greatly admired. Four years after his death, Baskerville's widow sold all his punches and matrices to the Société Philosophique Littéraire et Typographique, which used some of the types for the sumptuous Kehl edition of Voltaire's works in seventy volumes.

Composition by Maryland Linotype Composition Company, Inc., Baltimore, Maryland. Printing by The Murray Printing Company, Westford, Massachusetts. Four-color printing by Coral Color, Amityville, New York. Binding by American Book–Stratford Press, Saddle Brook, New Jersey.

Design by Cynthia Krupat

BOATHOUSES

PHOTOGRAPHS BY John de Visser / TEXT BY Judy Ross

The BOSTON MILLS PRESS

The authors would like to thank all those who allowed us to photograph their boathouses.

A BOSTON MILLS PRESS BOOK

Published by Boston Mills Press, 2006
132 Main Street, Erin, Ontario N0B 1T0
Tel: 519-833-2407 Fax: 519-833-2195
e-mail: books@bostonmillspress.com
www.bostonmillspress.com

In Canada:
Distributed by Firefly Books Ltd.
66 Leek Crescent
Richmond Hill, Ontario, Canada L4B 1H1

In the United States:
Distributed by Firefly Books (U.S.) Inc.
P.O. Box 1338, Ellicott Station
Buffalo, New York 14205

The publisher gratefully acknowledges the financial support for our publishing program by the Canada Council for the Arts, the Ontario Arts Council and the Government of Canada through the Book Publishing Industry Development Program.

Library and Archives Canada Cataloguing in Publication

De Visser, John, 1930-
Boathouses / photographs by John de Visser ; text by Judy Ross.

Includes At the Water's edge, and Shelter at the shore,
both published previously.
ISBN-13: 978-1-55046-484-9
ISBN-10: 1-55046-484-1

1. Boathouses — Ontario–Muskoka (District municipality) — Pictorial works. 2. Boathouses — Pictorial works.
I. Ross, Judy, 1942- II. Title.

NA6920.D473 2006 725'.87'0971316 C2005-907037-4

Publisher Cataloging-in-Publication Data (U.S.)

De Visser, John, 1930-
Boathouses / John de Visser and Judy Ross.
[264] p. : col. photos. ; cm.

Includes two previously published titles: Shelter at the shore : the boathouses of Muskoka / photographs by John de Visser ; text by Judy Ross ; Erin, Ont. : Boston Mills Press, 2001; At the water's edge : Muskoka's boathouses / photographs by John de Visser ; text by Judy Ross ; Toronto : Stoddart, 1993.

ISBN-13: 978-1-55046-484-9
ISBN-10: 1-55046-484-1
1. Boathouses — Ontario — Muskoka — Pictorial works. I. Ross, Judy, 1942- II. Title.
725/.87/0971316 –dc 21 NA6920.D48 2006

Design by Gillian Stead
Printed in Singapore by KWF Printing Pte Ltd.

CONTENTS

The Willardby porch, as close as you can get to living on the water without being in a boat.

LIFE IN A BOATHOUSE

My summer days begin when the sun rises over Crown Island on Lake Muskoka. Shafts of sunlight ripple across the lake and bounce off the water into my boathouse bedroom. Without moving from my bed I can see this miracle of day breaking. I get up and put the coffee on. As the boathouse fills with gauzy light, I pad about in bare feet and enjoy the quiet while others continue to sleep.

With warm coffee mug in hand, I make my way outside to water the flowers in the window boxes that line two sides of the boathouse. I pick off dead blossoms, poke at the soil, and breathe in the fresh air, fragrant with pine. The dock underfoot is damp with dew, and the sun is just beginning to drink up the morning mist as I slide into the lake for my ritual morning swim. All is silent, except for a seagull calling to me from the boathouse roof. Treading the soft water a short distance from shore, I watch my cat, the only other creature stirring, as she rounds the corner of the boathouse, crosses a patch of rock, then curls into the base of the cedar tree next to the bird feeder.

This routine happens every summer morning at our island boathouse-cottage in Muskoka. It is my family's treasured retreat. The boathouse is our emotional anchor, the place that roots us, the place to which we all return. I've been coming to these two small islands belonging to my aunt since I was a child — long enough to know every inch of lichen-covered rock, the shoreline's every nook, and the height of every pine tree. Now my daughters perpetuate this loving attachment to our small patch of earth. "Can't we go up just for an hour or two?" my younger daughter implored recently because she hadn't been to the boathouse for months. In our family "go up" has always meant "go up to the lake." The island's cottage has existed, in various forms, for a long time, but our livable boathouse is new. Its construction was an all-consuming project that took place in the summer of 1988.

That was a summer of much building activity around the Muskoka Lakes. A construction boom took place in this cottage country between 1985 and 1990. Property was selling for unprecedented prices and many extravagant new cottages were built with immense boathouses at the water's edge. The last time the lakes experienced such epic boathouse-building was between 1905 and 1930, during Muskoka's steamboat era, when cottagers depended on boats to get to their summer homes. Few roads had been opened into the area, so the early cottagers arrived by train, then boarded the appropriate lake steamers that would carry them and their belongings to their cottages.

In 1905 the Muskoka Lakes Navigation and Hotel Company ran the largest inland-waterway steamboat line in the country, ferrying cottagers and hotel guests from one end of the lakes to the other. Fifty thousand guests could be accommodated at scores of fashionable summer resorts. Many cottage owners found the navigation company's timetable too erratic, so they bought their own steam-driven launches. These launches were large enough to hold family groups with their attendant trunks, wicker baskets, packing

Many families depended on the commercial steamboats run by the Muskoka Lakes Navigation and Hotel Company to deliver them to and from their cottages. Long delays were inevitable. Here, resplendent in their travelling clothes, a family waits for a steamboat at Browning Island in 1915.

crates and hat boxes. Some of these private steamers were enormous. The *Wanda II*, for example, was a 94-foot steamer built in 1905 for Timothy Eaton, the Toronto department store tycoon. It could hold fifty passengers. Before long, dozens of private steamers plied the lakes, each requiring a boathouse for shelter.

Before the advent of the steamboat, the only shoreline buildings were crude sheds put up by settlers to store their canoes and rowboats, or the somewhat more elaborate dry-slip boathouses belonging to the cottagers. The latter had ramps that sloped into the water so that unmotorized craft could be pulled out of the lake for winter storage. But when the large new private steamers arrived on the lakes, they required buildings that had long slips and tall, pitched roofs. Sheets of tin were used to cover the ceilings, and smokestacks were cut into the rooftops because the boats' wood-fired engines were stoked while the craft were still in their berths. This hazardous arrangement caused frequent boathouse fires. Many early steam yachts were destroyed this way, including the lovely *Wanda II*, which burnt in a boathouse fire at the Eaton's summer estate on Lake Rosseau in 1914.

The Eaton family arrives at the 1921 Muskoka Lakes Association Regatta aboard their private steamer, the Wanda III.

By their nature, boathouses are intrusions on the landscape. Every one built obliterates another patch of scenic shoreline. But many have architectural merit that goes beyond their function. Architect Tony Marsh, who has been involved in twelve Muskoka boathouse projects, maintains that "the design of the boathouse is more important than the cottage because it's more visible. It's a less serious building, really just a garage for boats, so there's room for some whimsy in the design. Details like fish-scale shingles in the gable ends, trellises and window boxes are what make them interesting as buildings." In the architecture of boathouses, it seems, form can follow fancy.

In the early years, architects were rarely involved in the building of boathouses or cottages. Many turn-of-the-century cottage designs came from pattern books, popular building guides published during the Edwardian era. The one architect known to work in Muskoka around the turn of the century was from Pittsburgh. In the early 1900s Brendan Smith was hired to build cottages and boathouses for a few of the Pittsburgh group who summered at Beaumaris. Most notable are the much-photographed Clemson boathouses that look like big and little brother due to their jaunty matching roof lines and porthole windows. Another Brendan Smith structure is found at the Hillmans' property on Gibraltar Island, where two look-alike brown boathouses with fanciful white trim stand side by side. Both these sets of boathouses were built by Peter Curtis, a local builder who left his trademark in the form of wooden cutouts. At the Clemsons' the cutouts are heart-shaped and can be seen on railings, shutters and dock benches. At the Hillmans' the cutouts are diamond-shaped.

∽

Second storeys were often added to boathouses to accommodate staff. In those early days, families often stayed for the entire summer — mothers and children, assorted grandparents and aunts, cousins and others. Servants ensured the smooth running of such large enterprises. On Lake Muskoka at the turn of the century, James Kuhn, a banker from Pittsburgh, built a huge estate on Belle Isle and then brought to the island a staff of twenty-six, a number of whom lived in the family's boathouse. At some cottages the boathouse's upper storey was used as a dance hall and was festooned with streamers and paper lanterns for Saturday-night parties.

As gasoline-powered motorboats took over from steamboats and steam-powered launches, the need for large waterfront buildings lessened, and from 1930 to 1965 few boathouses were built. Some of the older ones that hadn't burnt or fallen down were altered to get rid of their smokestacks and tall, covered slips. In some cases a floor was added to increase upper-level living space, and because family servants were now a thing of the past, the second storey became dormitory space for the children.

∽

For years boathouses — particularly those located along Millionaires' Row at Beaumaris — have been focal points for afternoon cruises around the lakes. But it wasn't until the early 1980s that there emerged a renewed interest in "Old Muskoka" cottages and boathouses. Muskoka once again became a fashionable summer place, much as it had been during the golden years of the 1920s, when Muskoka events and gatherings were reported weekly in the society columns of Toronto's newspapers.

Many of the old boathouses were restored, and new ones were built to imitate the old style. Upper levels that over the years had become storage space, or recreation rooms for children, were also looked at with renewed interest and in many cases renovated for adults, either as guest rooms or granny flats. "What happened at our boathouse," explains a Lake Joseph cottager, "is that we planned the space perfectly for weekend guests, then spent one night in it ourselves, listening to the water, and never moved back to the cottage."

Living in a boathouse wrapped in blue lake is different from living fixed to the ground in a cottage. There is a feeling of buoyancy in the daytime, and at night the lulling sensation of water lapping beneath you as you sleep. It is like being on a large vessel that is permanently anchored in the same snug harbour. "It gives me a psychological lift," claims a boathouse-dweller from Lake Rosseau. "The light is special. It glints off the water even on the dullest days." The full spectrum of light can be seen. Dawn comes in with its pale and shimmery waves of yellow, and at dusk the afterglow of sunset is like a mauve cocoon.

∽

Summer days are ruled by the lake's many moods — by the rhythms of the water, the cycles of the sun and moon, the closeness of the night sky. Like sailors, boathouse-dwellers study the wind. At our island we're exposed to an open stretch of lake, and at times "the north wind doth blow." And blow. And blow. On such days, as the wind rattles the windows and shakes the foundation cribs, we dismiss all loving thoughts about the place. Curled up in the deep cushions of our sofa, with stacks of books and magazines at our side, we turn up the music to drown out the crashes and thuds. We haven't let the real world intrude on our boathouse in the form of television and VCR, but we do have such civilized comforts as hydro, hot water, telephone and stereo. My kitchen typifies the simplicity of our existence, with its two-burner hot plate and absence of gadgets. We try to balance our boathouse life along the fine line between rusticity and comfort.

In her book *Gift from the Sea*, Anne Morrow Lindbergh wrote about "the art of shedding" and how little one needs for beach living. Boathouse living is, or should be, similar. It demands less. Fewer clothes make their way into limited closet space, furniture is kept simple, and outdoor cooking dictates a casual approach to meals. Being surrounded by a vast, cooling body of water tempers our hot summer days.

One of my favourite times at the lake is twilight, when my husband and I inch our way out of the boathouse in our old motorboat and put-put along the shore. We watch as the last sliver of daylight disappears from the horizon and the twinkle of cottage lights begins to appear along the shore. As darkness falls and the rush of cool air rises from the lake, we idle back to the boathouse, pull down the door, and bid goodbye to the day.

In the early 1900s boathouses were built to shelter the cottagers' steam launches. Back then, when few roads reached the Muskoka area, these canopy-topped steamers were the primary means of transportation, carrying the family and their belongings from the train station wharf to the cottage. Moored at this boathouse in 1906 is Arthur Blachford's steamer Fidelia.

On warm and sunny Sundays, the steamer was loaded with food and taken for a cruise up the lake to a favourite picnic spot. Pictured here is a gathering of the O'Brien clan.

The weekly scribbles in our family diary show how insular our boathouse life becomes. Little of the outside world is noted. Instead there are jottings about the weather; the temperature of the lake ("still too cold for a midnight skinny dip"); the day the swallows arrived and started to nest beneath the eaves; the comings and goings of friends and family ("Jane arrived today with the three kids"); the number of saplings gnawed by the beaver; and details about the size of the moon and its silvery path across the lake. And for each of the four summers that we have lived in the boathouse, the final entry in October reads: "All is drained, antifreezed, emptied and shut down. We hate to leave."

∽

Until 1965, Muskoka boathouses were built without restrictions. No by-laws had been imposed by any government to control the building of these waterfront dwellings. Then, as concern for the vanishing shoreline increased, permits were required and various regulations applied. Now the rules change on an almost yearly basis. But since 1989 the maximum allowable size for boathouse living quarters has been 650 square feet, with a maximum height of 25 feet. The neighbours' approval is required before a permit can be granted. In addition, the Ministry of Natural Resources must examine the lake bed to ensure that fish spawning grounds will not be disturbed by the foundation cribs, and Canadian Coast Guard permission stating that the structure will not impede navigation must also be obtained.

In 1990 the Ministry of Natural Resources began to look even more closely at buildings on Crown lands (which include all waterways) and decreed that no more two-storey boathouses may be built in Ontario waters. Permits will only be granted for single-storey structures. And so the boathouses of Muskoka, these quirky, often elegant harbingers of the cottages that lie hidden in the woods, will become historic treasures, never to be duplicated.

A sandblasted cedar sign identifies Loon's Nest on Lake Joseph.

1

LOON'S NEST

LAKE JOSEPH

"Building a house on water is different from building a house on land," says Gordon Brown, the contractor who built this Lake Joseph boathouse for Barry and Louise Needler. For one thing, the foundation work takes place in winter on top of a frozen lake. At that time of year the water level is usually two feet lower, so the underwater foundation and the first layer of stringers can be built more easily.

There are two common methods for building the foundation of a boathouse. In the traditional method, a set of cribs, or square log boxes, is assembled using the ice as a building platform. Then a hole the appropriate size is cut in the ice and the crib is lowered into the water. Rocks are poured into the cribs to anchor them to the lake bottom. The number and size of the cribs depends on the square footage of the decking. If built well and protected from the push of ice in winter, these wooden cribs can last indefinitely. Wood that is permanently underwater never rots.

Recently there has been a trend toward the use of a different method called the steel-piling dock system. In this system, steel beams are driven into the lake bottom to form a foundation, instead of using wooden cribs. When building Loon's Nest, Gordon Brown used thirty-two steel piles, some over 30 feet long, to create a 2,600-square-foot dock platform for the boathouse. The upended steel beams were slotted down through holes in the ice and driven through the silt and into the bedrock with a jackhammer. "This system is preferred by the Ministry of Natural Resources," explains Brown, "because it takes up less square footage on the lake bottom and there's less disturbance of fish spawning areas." The foundation work was completed during the winter of 1992 and the structure was in place by June. In honour of two loon families who "wake us up at 2:30 every morning," the Needlers christened the boathouse Loon's Nest. It now shelters a 1929 Ditchburn, *Mowitza*; a fibreglass inboard/ outboard; a kayak; an aluminum runabout; a paddle boat; and a Florida-style 18 1/2-foot Wahoo fishing boat. The 650 square feet of living space upstairs is temporarily being used as storage.

With its sage-grey exterior, cedar roof and blue trim, the boathouse has already mellowed into its surroundings. In the evening, lights beam down from the soffits to create a pleasant glow. Below the deck, quartz-halogen underwater lights illuminate the water like a swimming pool. "These underwater lights are ideal for swimming at night," says Barry Needler. "And for guiding boats home in the dark."

The frozen lake is used as a building platform for installing the boathouse foundation. Steel beams were used instead of conventional cribs in the construction of Loon's Nest.

The spacious interior now houses the Needler fleet. The flagship, seen on the left, is the *Mowitza*, a 1929 Ditchburn.

At night the new boathouse is ablaze in light. Special quartz-halogen underwater lights illuminate the lake water as well.

The afterglow of sunset on Lake Joseph.

One of these two boathouses was built circa 1920 and the other only two years ago. The new, larger boathouse has two slips. The living quarters above are insulated for winter use.

2

KUSKINOOK

LAKE MUSKOKA

An old boathouse once stood leaning lakeward on this narrow channel on Lake Muskoka. It had been there for decades and was on such a slant that just one shove was all it took to knock it down. According to its owner, Arthur Angus, "It was always difficult to land in that boat slip because it faced south and the boats were battered by the wind. When we designed the new boathouse in 1991, we were able to turn it around so the entrance is in the lee of the wind."

Arthur and his wife, Marilyn, wanted their new boathouse to blend into the surroundings, just like the stone-and-shingle cottage up the hill. The cottage and a smaller boathouse, both built in 1923, had been in the Angus family since the 1950s, and Arthur had fond memories of his childhood summers here. For their new boathouse, the Anguses first chose mullioned windows with the same arched lintels and window boxes as the small boathouse. The shed roof dormers are typically Old Muskoka, as is the brown-and-white colour scheme. When the old boathouse came down, about all that could be salvaged was some basswood panelling, which they used to line the new cupboards.

As Marilyn says, "We put a little of the old place back into the new." Even though basswood is soft and scratches easily, the Anguses chose it for the boathouse's interior walls because they liked its light honey colour and because it matched the basswood in the cottage. This was a favourite wood for interior walls back in the busy cottage-building era of the 1920s, and unlike pine, basswood tends to stay light as it ages.

Many years ago the cottage was given the name Kuskinook, an Assiniboine word meaning "west wind." Like many of Muskoka's grand old cottages, Kuskinook was not built for winter use, so the Anguses planned to use the new boathouse as their snowy retreat. For their floor-to-ceiling fireplace in the living room, they gathered 2,000 pounds of rock from the property. The cozy living space also has a kitchen, two bedrooms, a bathroom and a walk-out balcony. In the summer it is used as guest quarters, and in

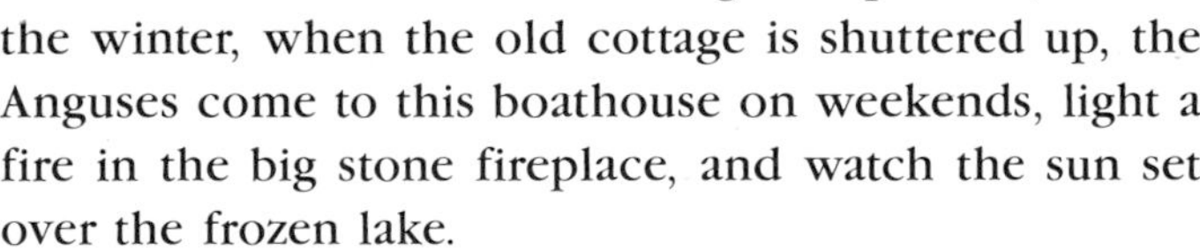

the winter, when the old cottage is shuttered up, the Anguses come to this boathouse on weekends, light a fire in the big stone fireplace, and watch the sun set over the frozen lake.

The hallway leads to the two bedrooms and bathroom. In the left corner is the massive Muskoka stone fireplace. The rugs are vintage Navajo, part of a collection of about sixty that was found in the old cottage.

A beamed cathedral ceiling lined with basswood makes the small space seem light and airy. Much of the furniture, like the spool daybed in the corner, came from the attic of the old cottage. New pieces, like the milk-painted coffee table, blend nicely with the old.

The spool bed, which the Anguses stripped and painted, was part of a collection of treasures in the cottage's attic. Through the window you can see the small boathouse built in 1923.

This boathouse emulates Old Muskoka style. The antique iron lanterns made by The Smithy at Glen Orchard have yellow light bulbs that cast a golden glow at night.

Jomar, one of the last Duke mahogany launches (built in 1966) occupies the downstairs of the smaller boathouse. Upstairs is a rustic sitting room and a tiny balcony with two Muskoka chairs. When Arthur Angus was a teenager, this was his favourite hideaway.

The two boathouses at Old Woman Island as viewed from *Marie*, a 27-foot Minett launch.

3

OLD WOMAN ISLAND

LAKE MUSKOKA

Several native myths have been told to explain the name of Old Woman Island on Lake Muskoka. The most enduring is that a native brave left his wife on the island in order to run off with a younger woman. The island was deserted until Richard Grand bought its 15 acres in 1987. There was nothing on it except neat circles of stones, firepits left by visitors who had used the island for cookouts and blueberry picking. Today the landscaped property has a newly built five-bedroom cottage and, at the water's edge, two boathouses that look as if they have been there forever.

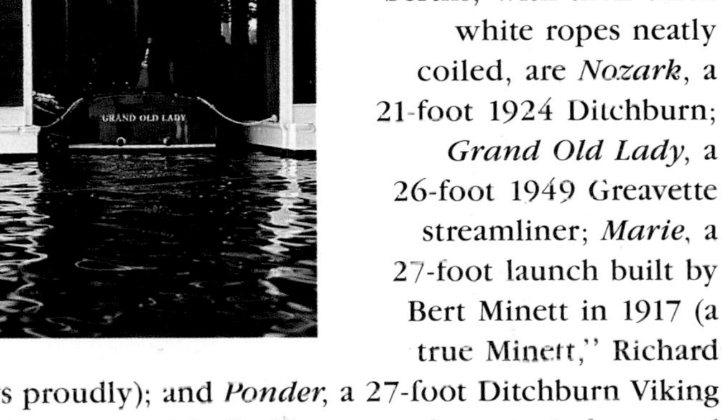

"We wanted them to look like Old Muskoka in architectural style," says Richard, "and then we stained them charcoal-black to make them appear older." Richard, whose family has been summering in Muskoka for generations, lives in Ottawa with his wife, Karen. It was on their car journeys from Ottawa to Muskoka that they had the idea to use black stain instead of the more common grey, brown or green. "We saw black farmhouses in Simcoe County," says Karen, "and they looked so attractive that we decided to copy the idea." The painter who tackled the four-month job lived on the island and worked every day. The finished result is a duo of handsome boathouses. Fine craftsmanship can be seen in details like the arched windows, the modified gambrel roof and the bevelled edges of the dock planks.

The larger boathouse was designed specially for Richard's collection of antique boats. Bobbing side by side in their berths, with their thick white ropes neatly coiled, are *Nozark*, a 21-foot 1924 Ditchburn; *Grand Old Lady*, a 26-foot 1949 Greavette streamliner; *Marie*, a 27-foot launch built by Bert Minett in 1917 (a true Minett," Richard says proudly); and *Ponder*, a 27-foot Ditchburn Viking with a stepped hull. The second storey is huge and "would make a great dance hall," but for now it has a large unfinished room and two bedrooms.

The smaller boathouse, with living quarters for Karen's parents, is decorated in summery colours. The compact space has a small kitchen, a bathroom and a cozy bed/sitting room that overlooks the lake. "It's an ideal getaway when my parents want to escape from the grandchildren," says Karen.

The large boathouse was built a few feet offshore and two ramps connect it to the island. The hanging lanterns look suitably nautical.

The pine interior of the small boathouse was designed by Karen as a retreat for her parents. Custom-made windows can be pulled up and hooked open to allow the lake breezes in.

AT RIGHT:
Sun streams in through the French doors, which have custom-made wrought-iron fittings. The floor planks are 12-inch-wide pine.

Richard Grand had the four-slip boathouse designed specially to house his collection of antique boats.

A 1939 Duke Playmate stored in the boat port of the small boathouse belongs to Karen's father and is known by the children as "Bumpa's Boat."

The boathouse now named Chadimar was built in 1903 by Toronto industrialist E.R. Wood. A cottage many times the boathouse's size but of similar style was built atop the hill at the same time. The gabled projection at the front of the boathouse was originally twice as long and was built to allow a 70-foot steam yacht to enter. Now there is a boat port for a pontoon and an upper-level sundeck.

4

CHADIMAR

LAKE ROSSEAU

In the summer of 1903 the cocktail chatter on Lake Rosseau centred on the building of a cottage show-place on Mazengah Island. Neighbours around the lake watched with interest as Toronto industrialist E.R. Wood erected his hilltop summer mansion. He insisted on the finest of everything for the fourteen-room cottage and hired swarms of builders. He constructed an equally grand boat-house with the same barn roof, cupola and gables as the lavish cottage. Jutting from the front of the boathouse was a pitch-roofed boat slip, long and tall enough to house the 70-foot *Mildred*, his fabled forty-passenger steam yacht.

The property was bought in the early thirties by Mr. and Mrs. Charles Houson. They eventually passed it on to their only child, Marjorie, who married J.E. Frowde Seagram, of Seagram liquor fame. By this time the *Mildred* was long gone, and the Seagrams decided to alter the boathouse. The long, covered boat slip was divided in half and a floor added to increase upper-level living space. In the upstairs sitting room, you can still see the original fireproof tin ceiling. The outside deck and boat port are more recent additions.

Marjorie and J.E. Frowde Seagram raised their two children, Charles Geoffrey and Diane, here and named the cottage Chadimar, an acronym formed from the names *Cha*rles, *Di*ane and *Mar*jorie. The boathouse has three bedrooms, a living room with stone fireplace, a kitchen and the tin-roofed sitting room, which has a long banquet table for feeding large groups. Downstairs, the dry-slip area has been converted to a playroom. It has been painted in bold blue and white stripes and sports a mounted sailfish on one wall and cabinets full of board games.

Today the cottage is owned by Dr. Geoffrey Seagram, and although his parents are no longer alive, their presence lives on. "Grandma came up here until her late eighties," says Geoffrey's daughter Kim, "and every afternoon her friends came for cocktails, clambering into the inclinater that would hoist them up the steep hill to the cottage." Grandma is most vividly remembered for her shocking pink, a colour that is found everywhere, on deck chairs, tables and towels. The Seagram daughters, Kim and Tracy, refer to it, with a slight roll of their eyes, as "Grandma's favourite colour."

The fireproof tin ceiling was originally installed when this was a boat port for a steam yacht, the ***Mildred***, sister ship to the ***Rambler***, which still plies the Muskoka Lakes. In those days the boathouse roof had a chimney because the steam engines were fired up while the boat was still in its slip. The Seagrams had the tin ceiling sandblasted and repainted.

This room was built as a dry-slip area for storage but is now used as a party room.

Guests first signed this wooden-covered guest book in 1946.

Eclectically furnished, the living room of Chadimar has sundry old pieces of pine and wicker mixed with 1960s rattan. In the background a small bat clings to the screen.

Tracy Seagram takes the inclinater up the steep hill from the boathouse to the cottage.

***The Gold Fawn*, a 21-foot Minett-Shields built in 1933, occupies some of the space formerly used by the *Mildred*.**

The five changing rooms at dock level have been used by many generations. In one, there is a hole drilled in the rear wall. Now plugged by a cork, the hole was drilled from the workroom next door so that young Geoffrey Seagram could spy on the girls. Directly in front of the changing rooms are stairs leading into the water. These were originally built so that young women could slip into the lake without being seen in their bathing costumes.

5

THE PINES

LAKE MUSKOKA

Newly built but somewhat Edwardian in style, this fanciful boathouse on Lake Muskoka is in fact made up of an eclectic combination of architectural features. "The basic precept was that everything would look old," explains the builder, Bill Stokes, who designed the boathouse in co-operation with the owners, architecture enthusiasts who paid close attention to the finishing details. They travelled the Ontario countryside, taking photographs of favourite structures with interesting windows and unique trim and mouldings. They chose the colour scheme of yellow and green because it was popular when Muskoka cottages evolved from unfinished board-and-batten and were first painted. One of the owners also had a fondness for the colour combination because of childhood memories of a cottage north of Temagami.

The deep, gabled roof line and cupola were copied from an old boathouse on a nearby island called the Isle of Skye. Some of the wooden trim detail was inspired by Penryn Park, a Victorian Gothic mansion in Port Hope, Ontario. The railing design and oval windows are similar to the Cedar Island boathouse on Lake Rosseau. This combination of design influences blends together to create a handsome structure.

The boathouse sits at the base of a steep cliff. At the top of the cliff is a similarly styled two-storey cottage with a wonderful view of the north end of Lake Muskoka. Landscaped from top to bottom with tiered flower beds and a winding flagstone stairway, the property was named The Pines because of its rare stand of first-growth pine trees. The boathouse's interior, completed in 1991, consists of a spacious sitting room with an open kitchen and bathroom, a total of 650 square feet. Gingerbread trimmed screen doors open onto the veranda on three sides. Diamond-shaped windows centred beneath the roof peaks draw attention to the unique herringbone ceiling design made of tongue-and-groove pine. "Even this ceiling pattern is a copy," admits Bill Stokes. "It's similar to the ceiling at Edenvale Inn, an old hotel in Port Carling."

A variety of windows add to this boathouse's interesting appearance. The multipaned windows on the boat-slip level were copied from those in a vintage Beaumaris boathouse. Three oval windows across the front balance the boat doors.

A small but well-equipped kitchen allows guests to cook their own breakfasts.

Victorian-style screen doors lead from this cozy sitting room (used as guest quarters). The tongue-and-groove pine patterns on the walls and ceiling add to the room's appeal.

The fairy-tale appearance of this boathouse is due to such architectural whimsy as turned finials, chamfered spindles beneath the balustrade, an ornate cupola topped with a flying-goose weathervane, and plenty of ornamental bric-a-brac.

The gazebo built on the dock beside the boathouse has the same chamfered spindles, railing design and herringbone roof pattern as the boathouse. It faces west and is an ideal place to watch the sun set on Lake Muskoka.

Tucked into a bay on Lake Rosseau, this boathouse at Windy Ridge has been enlarged twice over the years. Now with six bedrooms, it is the summer home for a family of four and shelter for several boats, including two vintage mahogany launches.

6

WINDY RIDGE

LAKE ROSSEAU

When Michael and Gwen Wilmott were married twenty-five years ago, they inherited this boathouse, part of a family compound on Lake Rosseau. Today, after being enlarged twice, it is the place they and their two children feel most at home, the place where they spend every summer. Michael's parents bought the property named Windy Ridge in the early 1950s. The original large cottage and various outbuildings were built in 1936 by Milton Cork, founder of the Loblaws grocery chain. Back then, the boathouse had just three slips and a small living quarters for the boatman that the family hired to take care of their mahogany launches.

Over the years there have been two major additions to the boathouse. About fifteen years ago the Wilmotts doubled the size of the living quarters, adding a fourth boat slip and a second gabled doorway on the east side of the building. A few years later, because, as Gwen Wilmott says, "The guests were sleeping in tents," they expanded again. This time they added a family room and two bedrooms, all three backing onto the land behind the west-side deck. Now it is a spacious, rambling summer home with six bedrooms, a living/ dining room, kitchen, family room and two bathrooms.

The whole place is geared to summer living. Everyone in the sporty family of four prefers to be outside, and in good weather they practically live on the deck, where they eat breakfast, barbecue and relax with cocktails. "It's a bit of a roadhouse atmosphere," admits Gwen Wilmott. "We're close to the country club, so often the young people — our children and their friends — end up here instead of going home."

In decorating the interior, Gwen had just three goals: bright, cheerful and comfortable. Living on the water, she feels, has the psychological effect of making things more casual. At one point the family discussed getting rid of the picnic table that they use for indoor dining and replacing it with a more formal table and chairs, but somehow a regular dining table just didn't suit their Muskoka lifestyle. The picnic table remains.

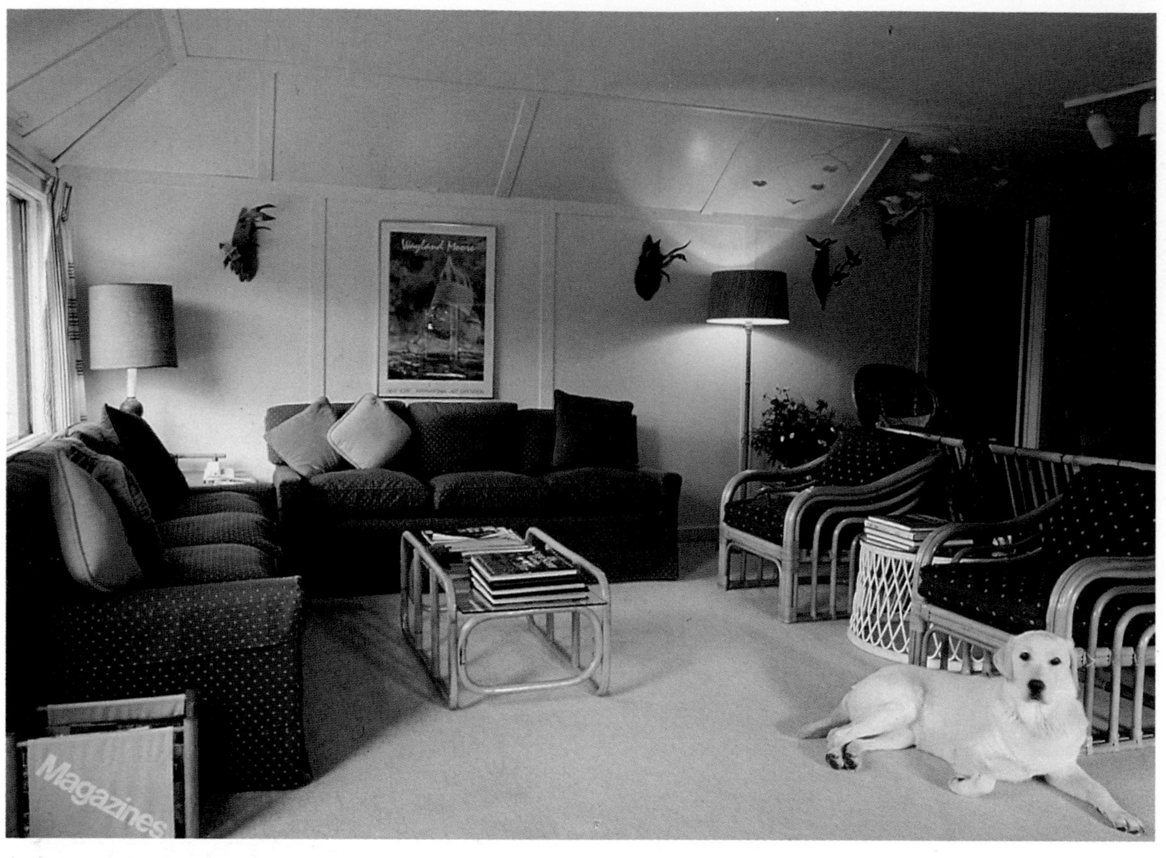

Jasmine, the family's golden Labrador, is at home in the boathouse's bright, cheery living room. Old wallboards, given a fresh coat of white paint, form the backdrop for a collection of handcarved birds by local artisans Walter and Beth Ruch.

A young girl's bedroom with view of trees and water.

The family's two launches. *Curlew*, a 33-foot Greavette with a V-12 Scripps engine, was the fastest boat on the lakes back in the late 1930s. The *Pippit*, a 24-foot Ditchburn, was built in 1925.

The unusual design of this two-slip boathouse features a single-door entrance at opposite ends and a dry-slip area, as well.

7

SULLIVAN ISLAND

LAKE JOSEPH

Proudly displayed on the cottage wall at Sullivan Island is a framed property deed. Tattered and yellowed, it is dated October 1900, when the property sold for $800. Like other cottagers, Laurence and Caroline Wight are fascinated by the history of their summer home. When they bought the island with its vintage cottage and boathouse in 1978, the contents were included — a windfall for these two avid collectors. Cupboards and drawers stuffed with linens and china, and rooms filled with antique wicker furniture, helped them unearth the cottage's past.

Their collections, in both cottage and boathouse, continue to grow: hutches full of tinware, shelves stacked with cut-glass carafes, walls lined with cast-iron grates, and perhaps most fascinating of all, a collection of stuffed birds. "We got to know a taxidermist who did birds," explains Laurence, "and we particularly liked his choice of mounting materials, all very natural-looking pieces of driftwood or rail fence." Upon entering the sitting room of the boathouse, one is greeted by a large white swan, a flying mallard, a barn owl and a great blue heron.

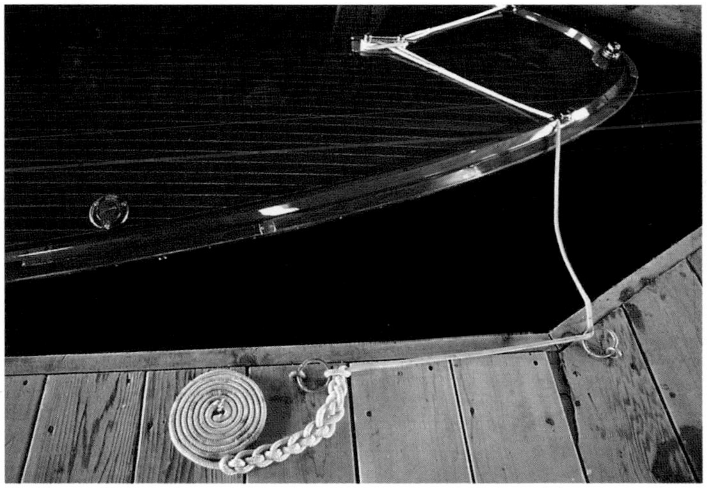

The white two-storey boathouse, still clad in its original set of asbestos shingles, is nestled in the leeward side of the island. The two boat slips house a sleek Canadian-built Kavalk and a fourteen-year-old Century launch. Everything is shipshape. For people who never throw anything out, the Wights manage to keep things in amazing order. And artfully arranged. Hanging above the boats, for example, is a neat line of old boat pennants. Rather than toss them out when they get faded and frayed, the Wights hang them from the overhead beams. Upstairs, the boathouse has a large, sunny sitting room with a Muskoka-stone fireplace, three airy bedrooms and a bathroom. The Wights painted the wicker glossy white and removed old varnish from tables and dressers. They lightened the basswood walls with a semi-transparent white stain and sanded the pine floors, which they plan to stencil. The comfortable space, used mainly by weekend guests, has the serene atmosphere of an earlier time. And, as is often the case in collectors' homes, in every corner there is something for the eye to linger over.

Stuffed birds occupy corners of the vast sitting room. The Wights painted all the old wicker white and chose bright yellow cotton for the cushions and the built-in window seats beside the stone fireplace. Six pairs of curtainless casement windows surround the room, allowing plenty of light to filter in, and the basswood has been lightened with a translucent white stain.

The bedrooms are spare and evoke another era. The furniture all came with the cottage, some of it already had handpainted designs done by its American former owners. All three bedrooms have huge closets designed for the steamer trunks that were rolled into them in the days when cottagers arrived by steamboat and stayed for the summer.

The Wights have a knack for turning clutter into artistic displays. Every corner has a designed look, from the firewood gathered in a wicker basket (with chewed beaver sticks in among the odd pieces of lumber), to pine-cone arrangements, to walls covered with fishing lures. "You never have to bathe alone," says Laurence Wight of the whimsical boathouse bathroom where walls are filled with panoramic group shots. Included on the wall of sepia photographs are army divisions from World War I, hospital staff, and a group shot of Ontario Provincial Police at Kitchener.

The circa 1900 boathouse was originally board-and-batten, which was later covered with asbestos shingles. "Not my choice," says Laurence Wight, "but they're fireproof and amazingly durable. We just keep painting them over and over." Sometime in the early seventies, sliding glass doors were put in the two bedrooms as walk-outs to the balcony.

The Kavalk is a 1986 Canadian-built gentleman's racer designed to resemble the Italian Riva speedboats.

A place for everything and everything in its place.

The lower half of this log boathouse was constructed of thick pine logs, some of them 50 feet long and almost 2 feet in diameter. The notched logs, piled one on top of the other, have no chinking and rely on the weight of the upper building to hold them in place. The upper storey, with its three steep gables, is a 2,000-square-foot living space used as year-round guest quarters.

8

MONTCALM POINT

LAKE MUSKOKA

This property is a sweeping headland that was once owned by a French-Canadian hotelkeeper back in 1900. He built a small resort and named it after his idol, French General Montcalm, who died fighting for New France. Montcalm House operated as a resort until 1942, when, like so many Muskoka hotels, it burned to the ground.

On the same height of land where the hotel once stood, current owners Patrick and Michele Brigham built their glamorous log-and-stone cottage. The boathouse, made from the same hefty pine logs, was constructed in two phases. The lower level, with three slips for boat storage, was built in 1986. Three years later a second level was added, with 2,000 square feet of living space designed as a luxurious winterized guest cottage. "This was an interesting project," claims Ernie Taylor, who collaborated with a log builder in the construction of the Brigham boathouse. "It's the only round log boathouse in Muskoka that I know of." The building process began in the winter, when a dozen 6-foot-by-12-foot cribs were sunk through the ice and filled with stone. "We laid the cedar decking after the spring break-up," explains Taylor, "and then the logs arrived, all pre-cut, tagged and notched to fit. They were assembled using a crane right on the site."

The logs are green at the time of construction, and they dry and shrink over a period of five years. Allowance must be made for this shrinkage around windows and doors. Because moisture was emitted by the logs while they were curing, the Brighams air-conditioned their living quarters. Guests visiting the Brigham boathouse find not only air-conditioning, but other amenities rivalling those of a five-star hotel. The decor is opulent, the lake views unparalleled, and the closets hold terry robes. Two lavish bedroom suites, each with an adjoining bathroom, feature bay windows and walk-outs to the balcony. Sunlight slants in through the white louvered shutters, and fans spin slowly overhead, giving the rooms a California ambience. The main living area has a cathedral ceiling and plenty of natural light from ceiling-high windows and skylights. Dominating the room is a 25-foot copper fireplace with a hearth of green slate. This fireplace opens into both the kitchen and living room. In the daytime, sunlight bounces off the fireplace's shiny copper, and at night tiny halogen spotlights beam down from the ceiling. "I wanted to create a romantic atmosphere in this boathouse," claims Michele Brigham, "so the feeling in this room is just like being outside on a starry night."

The kitchen's centre island has a built-in Japanese grill, a trio of copper-shaded lights, and cushioned metal stools.

A California flavour permeates the two guest bedrooms. Bleached oak trim, brass beds, potted palms and white louvered shutters create a sun-soaked atmosphere.

The freestanding zero-clearance fireplace has a copper chimney that rises 25 feet to the peak of the roof. The green slate on the hearth is repeated in the kitchen and bathrooms, and both the floor and ceiling of the living room are bleached oak.

At the back of the boathouse, behind the slip housing *Spatz*, the Brighams' 12-foot Sheppard roadster, built in 1943, there is a two-piece washroom and a built-in bar.

Seen here from inside the boathouse, a large cedar deck wraps around the shoreline. The flowers seen through the glass are in window boxes made from hollowed-out logs.

The Boys' (right) and Girls' Boathouses at Gibraltar Island were built at the entrance to a protected bay, with a crescent of beach and calm, shallow water.

9

GIBRALTAR ISLAND

LAKE MUSKOKA

The original owners of this rocky point on Gibraltar Island in Lake Muskoka were actors who toured Muskoka theatres at the turn of the century. They built a small cabin on a crest of land facing east towards Beaumaris. A grand two-storey brown frame cottage now occupies the same site. Down at the water's edge are two look-alike boathouses. In 1913, after the theatre folk had moved on, John H. Hillman of Pittsburgh bought the property and built the existing cottage and boathouses. Hillman, his wife and their seven children summered here for many years. Today the property is owned by grandson Henry L. Hillman Jr. and his wife, Kiki, of Portland, Oregon.

The Hillman boathouses resonate with family memories. One boathouse is called the Boys' Boathouse, as the male children slept in its large, open dormitory. Just off the balcony is a secret door known as a Lindbergh door because of its popularity following the kidnapping of Charles and Anne Lindbergh's son. These hidden doors locked from the inside and were built to allow children to escape. The other boathouse is called the Girls' Boathouse. It is a more private, feminine suite with a sitting room and separate bedrooms. Both the cottage and the boathouses were designed by Brendan Smith, a Pittsburgh architect who was hired to design several of the American summer homes in the Beaumaris area. One of the striking differences in the two boathouses is the step-out Juliet balconies at either end of the Boys' Boathouse. "It's still a mystery in our family," says Henry Hillman Jr. "In the original photographs, the Girls' Boathouse had balconies. We wonder if there was a fire at some time and it had to be rebuilt. But we have no record of it."

There's no shortage of boats to fill the slips. In the double boat slip of the Girls' Boathouse is the dazzling *Silver King*, a Gold Cup racer originally built for the Ringling Brothers in 1927. Propped up on stilts at the end of the slip is another prized craft, the *Walnut Diamond*, a wonderful rowing boat built around 1915 that Henry claims "skims across the water like a feather." The deep double slips in the Boys' Boathouse shelter four mahogany boats. Upstairs, where the boys spent many rough-and-tumble nights as children, Henry now has an office. He comes to this quiet place to read and work and no doubt think back to his childhood summers in this very same boathouse.

The large dormitory room in the Boys' Boathouse hasn't changed in years. Old hospital beds have been used by several generations of young Hillman boys. The same furniture was here when its owner, Henry Hillman Jr., was a boy. He now uses it as an office.

The bedrooms in the Girls' Boathouse are private, small and simply decorated. When built in 1913, the bedrooms were for the nannies and servants. Furniture in these old island boathouses rarely changes, because it is so difficult to haul away.

OVERLEAF:
Every year the family has a 10-inch sailboat race, and all the boats must be handmade. The "Christmas Island 10-inch Sailboat Regatta" is a treasured family event for both adults and children. "Everyone gets in the water with their boats," says Henry Hillman Jr., "and there's always lots of cheating."

The *Ramatola*, built in 1904, drops the grandchildren off for a visit. It is owned by Tom Hilliard, a relative of the Hillmans whose summer cottage is nearby.

The *Silver King* was built as a Gold Cup racer just before the stock market crash of 1929. As a result, it never raced. The boat was restored in 1936 after sitting in dry dock for seven years.

Curved ornamental lintels grace the doorway of the Boys' Boathouse. The more spartan doorway of the Girls' Boathouse can be seen through the door.

There is a generous dock complete with water slide for the children at this Lake of Bays boathouse, built in 1926. The covered veranda overlooks what remains of Bigwin Inn on the island across the bay.

10

The Boathouse

LAKE OF BAYS

In the days when Bigwin Inn was the glamorous hub of social activity on Lake of Bays, this boathouse was a busy place, famed for its parties. It sits on the mainland, directly across from the renowned Bigwin resort, and its location was no accident. The cottage and boathouse were built in 1926 by Gordon Finch, who made a fortune in mining and wanted to own the largest boathouse on Lake of Bays. He chose this location so he could follow the action at Bigwin Inn just by sitting on his boathouse balcony, telescope at hand. To keep in touch, he installed a direct telephone line to the resort, connected by underground cable.

No expense was spared in construction. Finch imported British Columbia cedar for the boathouse's exterior, Douglas fir for its interior walls and ceilings, and installed a large stone fireplace in its living-room. Because he was an avid sailor, he added nautical flavour to the decor. In the centre of the living-room floor is a compass fashioned from inlaid coloured tiles. On the walls are maps, mariners' charts and model schooners. The porthole windows are still intact, and there has always been a green door on one side of the boathouse and a red door on the other.

When John and Helen Scott bought the boathouse in 1949, they hardly changed a thing. "It's pretty much the way it always was," says Helen Scott. "Maybe there are some curtains that weren't always here. We regard this boathouse as a place to enjoy." As a young couple, they found the boathouse just as conducive to good times as did its former owners. Helen's children remember their parents' crowded parties when their father would stand by the fireplace and never move. Years later he confessed, "I thought the fireplace would be the only thing left standing when the boathouse fell in." Three Scott family weddings have been held in the boathouse over the years, including that of Helen Scott's granddaughter Lindsey Connell, who was married here at Thanksgiving in 1991. Even though Bigwin Inn now sits vacant and sadly neglected across the lake, the Scott boathouse remains a lively place, well used by family and friends all summer long.

A houseguest of the original owner, Gordon Finch, a.k.a. Captain "Skinch" Finch, had this poster made for one of Finch's famous parties. The mock newspaper page portrays the antics of the boathouse owner and his friends.

The interior walls and ceilings are lined with Douglas fir imported from British Columbia.

The large stone fireplace can be seen on the outside wall. "I sometimes think this fireplace is holding the whole place together," says owner Helen Scott.

The Deluce boathouse sits on a pristine section of Lake Rosseau shoreline. With three boat slips and two covered boat ports, there is plenty of space for boats. Along one side is a specially designed dock for Bob Deluce's Cessna 185 float plane.

11

DRIFTWOOD

LAKE ROSSEAU

When Bob and Catherine Deluce built this boathouse in 1988, they intended to build a cottage as well, knowing that a two-bedroom boathouse would be too small for their family of six. But after a summer in this bright, sun-washed place, they loved it so much that they still haven't built the cottage. The four children settled into the lower-level bedroom, which has bunk beds to sleep six. The main living space is spacious and airy, with six sliding glass doors that lead to a wraparound deck. With the help of designer Kate Zeidler, the Deluces have created a summer house of elegant simplicity.

"We wanted the feeling of being at the seaside, where the light is so bright that everything looks a little washed out," says Catherine. On the outside, the boathouse is beached-driftwood grey, and inside, the palette of pink, mauve and blue is reminiscent of a summer sunrise. The printed fabrics were specially chosen to improve as they fade. "Only certain prints fade well," adds Catherine, "and we didn't use any solid colours."

In keeping with the simple summery look of the boathouse, the pine V-joint walls were stained translucent white to let the knots show through. The pine floors were washed with a non-yellowing white stain. A design of swags and flowers was handpainted on the floors in the same colour scheme. In fact, there is barely a thing in this boathouse that isn't pink, white, blue or mauve. Even the open-plan kitchen has rose-pink and periwinkle-blue tiles. And the newly installed zero-clearance fireplace has blue and white tiles on the surround and the hearth.

From the water the boathouse has a commanding presence, with distinctive trim details and many window shapes — trademarks of architect Tony Marsh. It resembles the grey-shingled seaside houses built along the New England coast in the late 1800s. But here the backdrop is thickly wooded shoreline and, out front, a sparkling northeast view of Lake Rosseau. "The tall trees on the shoreline cast long shadows at certain times of day," explains Marsh, "so we positioned the boathouse and the decks to receive the maximum amount of sunlight."

A painted "peace dove" frieze by Stacey Lancaster surrounds the master bedroom. On the bed is a vintage Lone Star quilt in all the right colours. The bedroom has windows with lake views on two sides.

Inside the sun-washed boathouse is a large open space with a living room at one end and a kitchen and dining area at the other. The extra-long sofas are covered in a blue-and-white cotton print chosen to fade nicely in the bright light.

The beams and arches are all stained the same translucent white as the walls. None of the windows or sliding doors are covered, so when daylight pours in, the boathouse feels like a seaside cottage.

Toronto artist Stacey Lancaster handpainted the floors, which were first given a coat of non-yellowing white stain. The milk-painted dry sink was also washed with a white stain to soften the blue and make it look a little more worn.

Catherine Deluce painted an antique brass baker's rack in white enamel and then filled it with favourite pieces of blue-and-white pottery.

The trio of boathouses. On the left, in the distance, is the new one. The middle boathouse has had upstairs living quarters added to it. The one on the right is the old original built in 1908, that was spruced up but not altered.

KINLOCH

LAKE MUSKOKA

Squirrel Island, the 17 1/2-acre island near Beaumaris on Lake Muskoka, has long been associated with the wealthy group of Pennsylvanians who built cottages here in the early years of the century. One end of Squirrel was purchased in 1910 by W.L. Mellon, founder of Gulf Oil Corporation, and Camp Vagabondia, his vast cottage, is still the summer home of his daughter, Mrs. Thomas Hitchcock of New York. The southeast half of the island was originally owned by Mellon's friend William Donner but has changed hands several times over the years. Named Kinloch by former owners, it is now owned by Peter and Jennifer Gilgan of Oakville, Ontario. Gilgan, father of eight, explains, "We kept the name because it means something like 'gathering of the family at the lake,' and it seemed to suit."

Since purchasing the property in 1988 the couple has thoroughly renovated the large cottage and boathouses. One boathouse was altered to include a second-storey living quarters; another was restored; and a third was newly built with five slips for the family's boat collection, which ranges from a pontoon to the *Dolphin II*, a 31-foot Ditchburn. This stunning trio of boathouses, all decked out in mint-grey siding with white trim, is much admired and photographed. Boaters passing by invariably slow down, intrigued by architectural details and the spectacular window boxes spilling over with flowers.

The boathouses are on Millionaires' Row, the aptly named channel between Squirrel Island and Tondern Island. Once a week during the season, the restored steamboat RMS *Segwun* takes passengers along this route for a look at the palatial cottages, lavish gardens and immense boathouses that line the shore on either side. "If there's one thing that is uniquely Muskoka, it's boathouses like these," says noted Muskoka architect Tony Marsh. "They're much more visible than the cottages, which are often hidden in the trees."

The Gilgans hired Tony Marsh to draw up plans for their new five-slip boathouse and for the restructuring of one that had been built around 1908 by one of Muskoka's master builders, Peter Curtis. "Boathouses are really just garages for boats," adds Tony Marsh. "It's details like trellises, cupolas and window boxes that make them so interesting."

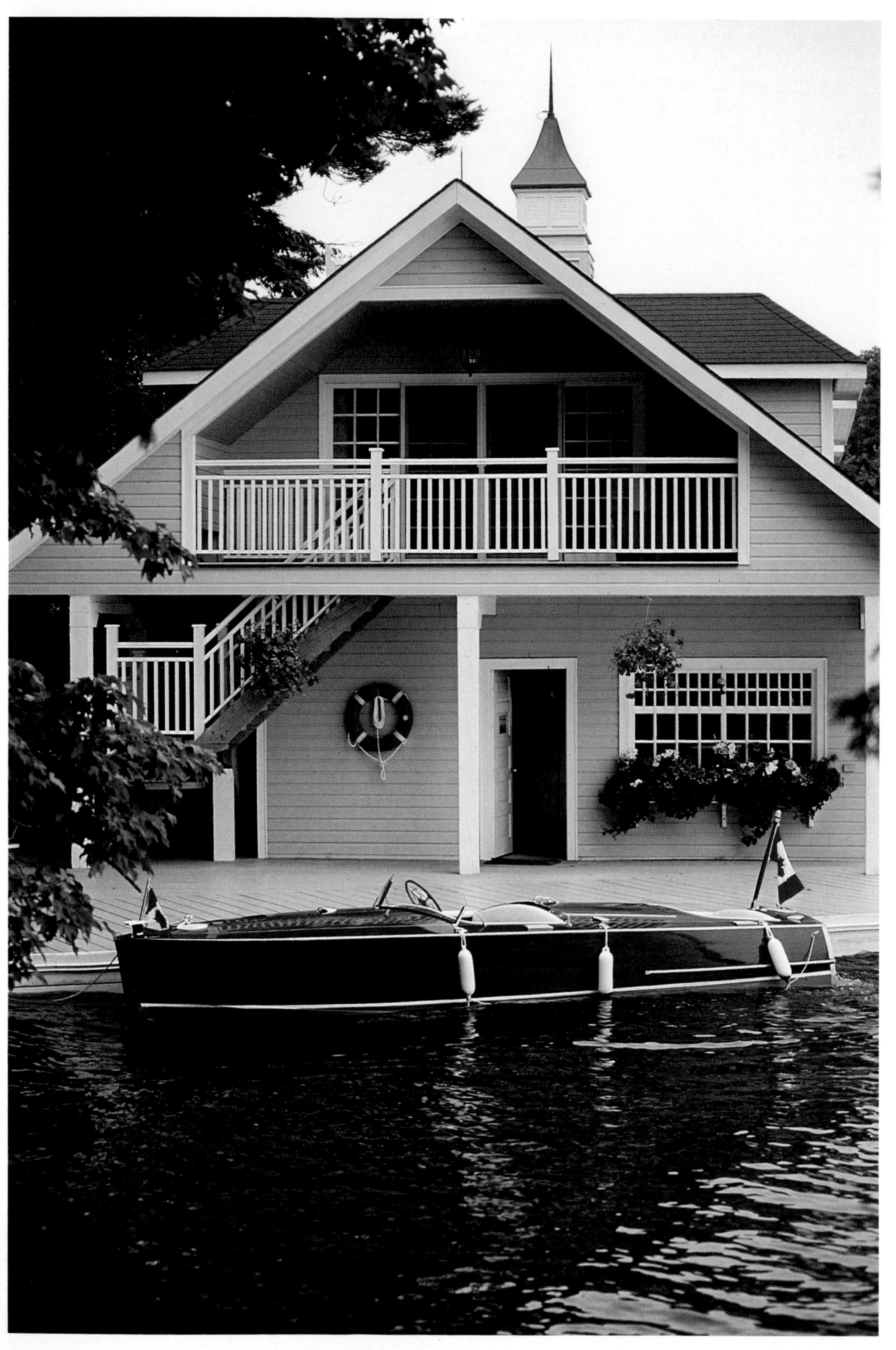

Architect Tony Marsh likes to use traditional Muskoka forms like pitched roofs, gables and cupolas in his boathouse designs. The roof extension here allowed for a covered balcony. Tied at the dock is *Uncle Henry Too*, a 1955 Chris Craft Gentleman's Racer.

The new boathouse was designed with five 22-foot-long slips. Stairs lead to a second level that is currently used as storage space.

Two classic Ditchburns occupy the restored boathouse. *Jesamy*, in the foreground, was built in 1924. Only 19 feet long, she is reportedly the smallest Ditchburn on the lake. *Dolphin II*, with flaps up, is a 31-foot launch built in 1929. Against the wall are two totem poles bought for the island's mini-golf course.

13

LLANLAR

L A K E R O S S E A U

On midsummer days, when the gardens are in full bloom and the window boxes at their luxuriant best, there is no more colourful sight in Muskoka than the boathouses of Llanlar. Set in a sheltered bay between two rocky promontories, this property has been in the same family since 1908, when American Joseph Irwin bought it from Reverend Elmore Harris.

There are splendid gardens throughout the property, a legacy of Irwin's granddaugher, Elsie Sweeney, who was once the grande dame and gardener extraordinaire of Llanlar. The gardens were planned and planted during her time here, from 1926 until she died in 1972. And sometimes they were opened to the public to raise funds for the Windermere churches. Today the gardens are maintained exactly as she would have wanted them by Miss Sweeney's nephew, J. Irwin Miller, and his wife, Xenia. The Millers and their five children and ten grandchildren share the property at Llanlar every summer.

The whole place is beautifully cared for and kept freshly painted in sunny yellow with white trim and rusty red docks. A perennial rock garden climbs the hill behind the smaller dry-slip boathouse. The lower level of this boathouse is used to store canoes and sailboards, and upstairs there is a sitting room that leads to the flower-filled balcony. Built in 1920, the large boathouse has four slips, one of which houses the *Llano*, the Millers' classic 30-foot Ditchburn cabin cruiser. Upstairs there is one huge room, about 50 feet long, with scrubbed maple floors, basswood walls and a stone fireplace. In Miss Sweeney's heyday, this was a well-used party room and decorated in her favourite Italian style, with blue damask sofas and plenty of colourful ceramics. After she died in 1972, Llanlar sat empty until 1976, when it was reopened for the August wedding of Irwin and Xenia Miller's daughter Margaret. The vast woody room above the boathouse was filled with flowers for the occasion, and the structure shook from the enthusiastic dancing of a hundred wedding guests. ''My husband was nervous that the floor would fall in,'' Xenia Miller recalls, ''but it survived the wedding. The next year, though, we had to prop up the whole place.''

The room has since been redone in more contemporary style and is used by the Miller grandchildren as a rainy-day playroom. Still in place is the original old wicker, the framed British Railway travel posters collected in the 1930s, and Elsie Sweeney's practise piano, which miraculously stays in perfect tune.

Though now used as a rainy-day playroom by the Millers' ten grandchildren, in its heyday in the late 1920s this immense room was popular for parties. The wicker furniture is all original to the cottage.

Japanese footbridges, waterfalls, fountains and thick carpets of flowers distinguish the property. For more active fun, there is a water slide and a diving tower.

Red gravel paths wend down the hill through the perennial rock garden to the docks and boathouses of Llanlar. The hilltop gazebo provides a lovely view of Lake Rosseau.

The *Llano*, a 30-foot Ditchburn cabin cruiser, snug in its berth in the large boathouse.

From the balcony of the small boathouse one can see Llanrwst, the cottage built in the 1950s by the famous American architect Eero Saarinen. It too is part of the Miller property and offers an unusual contrast to the Victorian-style boathouses.

Viewed from the cottage deck at dusk, the log boathouse appears to float on Lake Muskoka.

14

THE LOG HOUSE

LAKE MUSKOKA

George and Barbara Kiddell wanted their new boathouse to blend with their cottage on Lake Muskoka, which had been constructed many years earlier from a 150-year-old log cabin. Since Muskoka boathouses are not traditionally made from 10-inch square-cut timbers, this was not an easy task. However, they were able to find logs north of Huntsville that closely matched the old logs, and construction began in the winter of 1989. Family photo albums proudly document the building's progress: sinking the cribs through the ice in winter; cutting and assembling the logs on land; bringing the logs across the lake by barge in the spring; and then, with two barges and cranes, putting up the entire structure in one day. Barbara Kiddell remarks, ''Modern technology makes log building a lot easier than it used to be.'' Midway through the construction, though, they ran into a problem. A neighbour's objection interrupted their progress and forced them to move the boathouse 10 feet further from a shared lot line. Rather than abandon the project altogether (as the neighbours had hoped), they hoisted the building and moved it the required distance.

Today the boathouse presents a pretty picture from the land and from the lake. Every detail has been carefully considered. The large deck, which can be partially covered by a retractable green-and-white awning, is an ideal playground for the Kiddells' seven grandchildren. Inset in the railing is a latched gate that opens so the children can jump off the deck into the water. The upper-level living quarters, 500 well-planned square feet, includes two bedrooms, a kitchenette and a tiny bathroom. The rooms are decorated in log-cabin style with white country curtains and Canadiana pine furniture. Other authentic touches include wide floorboards from an old house and weathered ceiling beams that Barbara Kiddell rescued from a nearby barn.

To the Kiddells' delight, the logs are weathering quickly and in just a few years have almost matched the silver tones of the original old cottage. From their master bedroom in the boathouse, the Kiddells enjoy a sunrise view with Pine Island across the way and Lake Muskoka in all directions. According to Barbara, ''It's a perfect place to wake up on a summer morning.''

In keeping with its log-cabin style, the interior is filled with quilts, ruffled curtains and Canadiana pine antiques.

The compact kitchen is at the end of a long hallway and contains a bar fridge behind the blue cabinet door, a small corner sink and a micro-convection oven. "Everything we need to cook our own breakfast is down here," says Barbara Kiddell. The antique Welsh dresser on the left houses a collection of blue-and-yellow Italian pottery.

Approaching the boathouse at dusk. A wooden walkway links the deck to the shore.

15

WINGBERRY COTTAGE

LAKE MUSKOKA

When Harry and Lynda Littler bought Wingberry Cottage on Lake Muskoka eighteen years ago, the property consisted of a rambling 1920s cottage and a one-slip boathouse. But that was before Harry started collecting boats. Now spreading across the shoreline are three forest-green boathouses, the newest of which is an immense home designed specially to shelter six gleaming antique mahogany boats. People call it ''Harry's Museum,'' and it is a monument to Muskoka's boatbuilders. Displayed inside with the boats is an assortment of boating paraphernalia: framed Ditchburn drawings are mounted on one wall beside boat-show posters and sepia photographs of vintage craft; restored wicker chairs from old cabin cruisers surround tables stacked with boating magazines; and just inside the door is a hand-engraved wooden sign listing the names and vital statistics of every boat in the Littler collection.

Four 60-foot slips house the boats, all built between 1919 and 1938. In slip one, there's *Wingberry*, a 32-foot Ditchburn; in slip two, *Nika*, a 36-foot Minett; in slip three, a Duke Playmate and a 1935 Greavette; and slip four houses a 1919 Gentleman Racer and a 22-foot W.J. Johnson launch. A seventh, newly acquired treasure is *The Barnes*, stored in a separate boathouse. In all, a dazzling display of soft leather, highly polished wood and spotless chrome.

The 2,400-square-foot interior is immaculate. The walls are panelled in tongue-and-groove pine; the windows have dark green venetian blinds to keep out the sun and heat; and fans whir slowly overhead. Beside each boat lies a custom-made mat with the boat's name embroidered on it. These prize craft lie almost motionless, tightly tethered with thick white ropes.

Down the shore from Harry's Museum is another boathouse, with a two-slip boat port, a sauna, change room, tool room and a built-in bar at water level. Upstairs is a self-contained guest cottage. Living space in a third boathouse is used by one of the Littler children. With its array of green-and-white cottages and boathouses spread along the shore, and the perpetual coming and going of boats, it is not surprising that, as Lynda Littler says, ''People sometimes mistake our place for a summer resort.''

Lynda and Harry Littler both worked on the design of their guest-cottage boathouse. They chose barnwood, antique pine and a pink stone fireplace to create a cozy atmosphere for their numerous weekend guests.

The back wall of Harry's Museum, a boathouse specially designed to house antique boats and a shipshape display of boating memorabilia.

OVERLEAF:
The 1927 gas pump is still used to fuel the family's fleet of boats.

The 1992 Antique and Classic Boat Association Summer Rendezvous was held on a cloudy August afternoon at Wingberry Cottage.

The interior of the 2,400-square-foot four-slip boathouse that shelters the Littler collection of vintage Muskoka boats.

Two of the trio of Littler boathouses on Lake Muskoka. On the right is "Harry's Museum," which houses the family's antique boat collection. The boathouse on the left is the guest cottage.

The boathouse at Langton House on Lake of Bays is almost a hundred years old and once had a large dock area where steamboats would land.

16

LANGTON HOUSE

LAKE OF BAYS

There is a certain magic connected to a cottage that has had a former life as a summer lodge. The happy memories almost seem to be held within its walls. When Viki Mansell and Kevin Keeley bought Langton House on Lake of Bays in 1985, it had long ceased to be a hotel but was still in remarkably good condition. There wasn't one piece of rotted wood, even though the main house and boathouse were both built in 1895. It had been a farm property first, then the farmhouse was turned into a summer lodge. This was a common transformation in the early years of the century, when farm families saw the opportunity to earn extra income from the growing tourist trade.

Langton House sat on a grassy slope that dipped down to a curve of sandy beach on Lake of Bays, an ideal setting for vacationing families. In its heyday, in the twenties and thirties, Langton House had a separate dance hall that drew crowds from around the lake. The boathouse was used as a dormitory for the musicians. Some of their names and the instruments they played are still scribbled in pencil on the wooden bedroom wall.

But Viki and Kevin and their two young children use Langton House as a summer cottage. There is plenty of room for weekend guests and extended family—and plenty of work to keep everyone occupied. Their first task was to return the buildings to their simple rustic charm.

The boathouse, where steamboats full of hotel guests once landed, had been neglected. The cribs needed shoring up and a new dock had to be built along one side. Inside the boathouse, the old cedar tongue-and-groove walls were in good shape, and the pocket windows, which slide up and down, only required new screens to let in the fresh lake air. The pine floors were scraped, to rid them of a brown oily varnish, and left bare. "Viki and I like things untouched," says Kevin, "so we try to bring a place back to its origins." In late afternoon the boathouse takes on an amber glow. Sun slants into the main bedroom through the windows that face west down the lake towards Baysville. "The light in this boathouse is magical," enthuses Viki. "It's wavy and sparkling, and you do have the sensation of being on an unmoving boat."

Two doors lead from the living room into the master bedroom, which was originally two rooms. All the pine floors were scraped clean of varnish, but no planks needed to be replaced. The walls are all double-sided tongue-and-groove cedar and don't reach the ceiling. "There's not a lot of privacy in these bedrooms," comments owner Kevin Keeley.

Viki Mansell loves this blue-and-white fabric for its fresh, summery look against the weathered cedar walls.

The rustic bathroom has a sink with running water but no toilet. The fresh flowers in every room come from Viki's large cutting garden behind the cottage.

The slap-slap of water and the sweet scent of cedar make this boathouse bedroom a wonderful place to sleep. There were no cupboards in any of the rooms, so antique armoires and travelling trunks like this one are used for storage.

17

SUNSET ISLAND

LAKE JOSEPH

Sprawled along the shoreline of Sunset Island on Lake Joseph is an immense boathouse, possibly the last of its size to be built in Muskoka. Just like the original shingle-and-stone cottage built in the early 1900s, the new boathouse has Old Muskoka style. Manicured gardens and immaculately raked walkways encircle the island, which also has two smaller boathouses and a sleeping cabin, all stained deep chocolate-brown with bright white trim.

The permit to build the boathouse was granted in 1985, before new by-laws controlled the amount of allowable living space in boathouses. Because of deep water and engineering complications, it took five years to build. With four slips, 3,300 square feet of living space and fourteen underwater cribs for support, the boathouse rivals extravagant structures built at the turn of the century.

Elizabeth deJong, an interior designer, took over after the construction and transformed the second storey into a comfortable retreat. Despite the boathouse's size, its interior seems cozy, full of homey pine and overstuffed chairs. Two dormered rooms occupy opposite ends of the boathouse, joined by a long, narrow corridor. At one end is the master bedroom with a sitting area and French doors leading to a private covered balcony. At the other end is a gathering room with two conversation groupings, a compact wet-bar and built-in hutch, and another balcony. In the master bathroom, a jacuzzi bathtub is tucked into the window dormer, and there is still room for a generous glassed-in shower and a double-sink vanity along one wall. With allusion to the family's other full-time residence, in Switzerland, the pine valance in the bathroom has a Swiss design of cutout hearts.

To take full advantage of the interesting dormers in the two main rooms, Elizabeth deJong designed window benches with drawer space built in below. Port Carling cabinetmaker Rob McKee custom-built all the pine cabinets and trim details. Summery prints in pink, green and blue blend with the mellowing pine and the background of trees and blue water seen through every window.

There is no real kitchen in this boathouse, just this built-in hutch with a bar sink, a microwave and small refrigerator inside the cabinet. The cushioned window seats have storage drawers beneath them. They are lovely places to curl up and read on a summer afternoon.

Angular roof lines created by the gables add to this interesting master bedroom. Fabrics were chosen to blend with the outdoors, and windows on three sides allow cross breezes to drift through the room.

The two gables have deep roof projections that cover an outside deck. To keep the rooms from being darkened by this feature, the designer filled the triangle with glass, using three sets of French windows and doors, and a fanlight in the peak of the gable.

A perfect summer day on Lake Joseph as viewed from the boathouse deck.

The new boathouse (right) was designed to complement the island's two other boathouses (left).

The newly restored boathouse on Black Forest Island was built in the 1890s.

18

Black Forest Island

LAKE JOSEPH

Black Forest Island, with its fine old buildings, is regarded as one of Muskoka's heritage treasures. Many of the neighbours have fond memories of the place and were pleased when its new owners undertook the restoration of the island property. The lumber baron who built the cottage and boathouse in the 1890s used the finest of materials and employed the most talented craftsmen of the day. By 1909 the property had been sold to Clarence Black, an American who named the island Black Forest, alluding to his name and to his favourite region in Germany. It was in his time that the boathouse acquired its fairy-tale reputation. Black used to hide lollipops around the boathouse for the children, and so it became known as Uncle Lollipop's boathouse. The room upstairs also intrigued the children. It was a barbershop where Black kept a barber's chair, in which he was given his daily shave by one of the male servants.

By 1990 the two-storey shingled cottage and the boathouse, had fallen into disrepair. The boathouse had suffered rain damage, and the living quarters had long since become unlivable and been relegated to storage space. ''We decided to fully restore the property to the way it had been originally,'' explains the new owner. ''It was a massive undertaking, but now I think it was well worth it.''

The boathouse was lifted so that all the cribs and docks could be replaced. New windows were handmade to match the diamond-shaped originals on the lower level and the multipaned ones in the living quarters. A new V-joint ceiling was installed and a new pine floor. Duradeck was put on the floor of the large covered porch, and pot lights were installed in the new ceiling.

The owner felt lucky to have ''a lot of very fussy people working on this project. Every detail had to be perfect.'' Now the big, old cottage is in pristine condition, and there is a tiny treehouse for the grandchildren, a guest cabin, and a sauna on the property, all miniature versions of the cottage. The upstairs of the boathouse, once Uncle Lollipop's barbershop, is now a sun-filled party room complete with a reproduction Wurlitzer jukebox. ''It's like a dream room for me,'' says the owner. ''I love every corner of it.''

The covered porch doubles the living space of the boathouse's upper level. At night, tiny pot lights in the ceiling make it a romantic spot for dancing. Viewed from the porch is the new party room with its reproduction Wurlitzer jukebox. Special bracing was installed under the jukebox to keep the floor from shaking while the music is playing. Green-and-white canvas cushions cover the handcrafted pine furniture made by Parry Sound carpenter Wayne Brownlee.

A panoramic view of Lake Joseph from the boathouse. Gallons of forest-green paint were used in the restoration of Black Forest Island, some of it on this antique wicker porch set.

OVERLEAF:
The scale model of the *Sagamo*, one of the last of the fleet of Muskoka steamships, was made by Captain John Dionne, a retired Great Lakes seaman.

Along the shore from the boathouse is a sauna that was designed by contractor Jamie Blair as a miniature replica of the cottage. Both a water slide and a set of wooden stairs lead into the lake. The cedar-lined interior has a shower and washroom, as well.

With its half-timbered facade and mullioned windows, Calypso looks more like an English manor house than a Muskoka boathouse. "We're always shoring it up and it's still lopsided," complains Tannis Malabar.

19

CALYPSO

L A K E   J O S E P H

One doesn't expect to see a half-timbered Tudor house anchored to the shore of a Muskoka lake, but this is not a usual sort of place. From a distance it looks as though it might even be slipping into the lake. It dips and slants and creaks the way an English manor house might, and inside, the dark panelled rooms smell of cedar and wood smoke. This unusual boathouse is called Calypso, because it is on Calypso Point on Lake Joseph.

"It looks very British because it was built in 1917 by someone who was homesick for England," explains Tannis Malabar, whose uncle Tom L. Hay bought the property from the original owners in 1929. There had been a large cottage, too, but it burned down in 1919 and was never rebuilt. Since then the sprawling boathouse has served as the property's cottage. At water level there are two boat slips full of nesting swallows, and next to them, a small bedroom — "The one we all fight over," says Tannis. Upstairs there is a panelled dining room with a stone fireplace, an old-fashioned kitchen and pantry, a living room with another fireplace, a small screened porch that juts out over the water, and six more bedrooms.

A guest cabin that now sits near the old cottage foundation adds to the bed count. Often, on long summer weekends, as many as twenty-four people stay on the Calypso property. The attitude here is "the more the merrier," particularly on Saturday night, when most everyone gets into costume. The name Malabar is almost synonymous with costumes in Toronto because the family operated a costume-rental store there for decades. Now many of these outfits, from flapper gowns to clown suits, are crammed across coat racks at the far end of the boat slips.

Every summer the Calypso boathouse is shared among three families, the Malabars, the Brooks, and the Farquharsons, all of them involved in the ongoing task of upkeep. Calypso is a labour of love for all concerned. And everyone agrees that it's the best place in Muskoka on a Saturday night!

The living room is 40 feet long and 20 feet wide, large enough for two sitting areas including this one full of comfy old furniture.

The long, dark corridors in the Calypso boathouse are reminiscent of an old country inn. At the end of the hallway is a dining room where guests gather at the large oak table before a roaring fire.

OPPOSITE:
Gourmet meals are produced in this kitchen every summer. Cupboard doors were removed in the kitchen to open up the space and brighten the dark hallway. To the right of the kitchen is a pantry connected to the dining room.

In the long wood-panelled corridor, a stag's head serves as a hatrack.

Mementos of another era: in the living room, a well-used piano, stacks of board games and jigsaw puzzles, and a vintage wicker plant stand.

The costume department is down where the boats are stored, with dozens of outfits to choose from. Boxes of costume jewellery and other accessories lie scattered on top of the polar bear rug.

Cedar Island from the air, with its two unique boathouses. The smaller one was originally the laundry and the servants' quarters. The slip beside it was for a "dippy" (disappearing-propellor boat).

20

CEDAR ISLAND

LAKE ROSSEAU

Few boaters can resist slowing down as they pass this picturesque boathouse on Lake Rosseau. Its architectural features are so appealing that an exact copy was built by a Toronto designer at his cottage property on Lake Simcoe and photographed for the cover of a home-decorating magazine. Many of its features have been copied on other recently built boathouses around the Muskoka Lakes. This Cedar Island boathouse probably dates back to 1895, when Mrs. Lillian Massey owned the island and maintained a large farm on the mainland, now the site of the Muskoka Lakes Golf and Country Club.

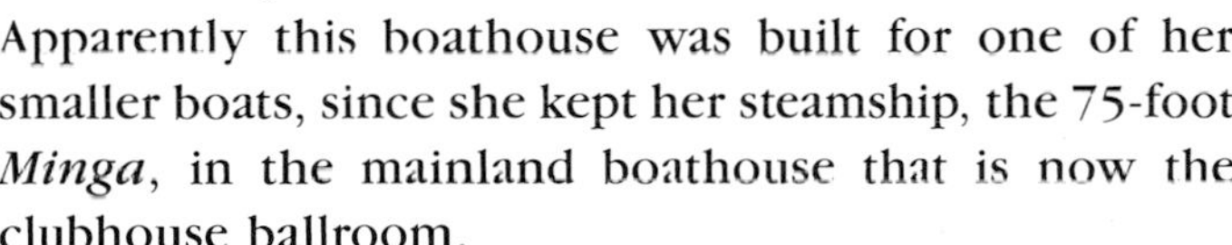

Apparently this boathouse was built for one of her smaller boats, since she kept her steamship, the 75-foot *Minga*, in the mainland boathouse that is now the clubhouse ballroom.

Tiny Cedar Island is edged with lush cedar trees and a stone wall. It has a quaint dry-slip boathouse and a rambling cottage built in 1885. The Pollock family of Cambridge, Ontario, have owned the property since 1918, and baby Taylor is the fifth generation of Pollocks to summer here. John Pollock proudly claims to have spent part of every summer of his fifty-six years at the island.

The one-slip boathouse, painted slate grey with white trim, presents a pleasing symmetrical picture, with exposed outriggers, wide eaves and a wraparound balcony. Upstairs are two bedrooms, a sitting room with fireplace, and a kitchen. The living space was originally intended for staff but is now used by members of the extended family. All the interior walls, ceilings and floors are clad in the original fir planks, and a large brick fireplace still dominates the living room, though it no longer functions. "With four fireplaces in the main cottage, we decided we could do without this one," says John Pollock, "especially since things were starting to sag beneath the weight of it. We ended up having the chimney taken off."

The old boathouse requires constant upkeep. The docks and cribs have been replaced twice and there have been several new roofs. Keeping their boathouse looking attractive is important to the Pollocks. This special care is appreciated by the Lake Rosseau boaters who pause to admire the old boathouse each time they pass by.

John Pollock was just a boy when he build this model sailboat with his father. Now John's grandchild occupies the portable crib at left.

On the bedroom wall in the background is a collection of old black-and-white sailing photographs that belonged to John Pollock's grandfather when he was Secretary of the New York Sailing Club. The boathouse interior has barely changed since his time.

The much copied and admired main boathouse at Cedar Island was built around 1895. The architectural details have been copied on many newer boathouses around the Muskoka Lakes.

21

CHARING CROSS

LAKE MUSKOKA

When Leslie Willis was a child, her father used to arrive at the cottage by train on summer weekends, pulling into the Bala station on Friday night. He was a travelling salesman, and the family had a cottage on the Moon River. Leslie can still remember the excitement of hearing that train arrive, so it is not surprising that she and husband Ron, a train buff, bought cottage property next to the railway bridge at Bala. Several trains cross the bridge every day, including the *Canadian* on its way across Canada. The Willises both love to listen to it rumble by.

The construction of their Lake Muskoka boathouse, with its bell-curved roof, porthole windows and interesting gingerbread trim, was a two-year labour of love. They wanted the boathouse to match the cottage that had been built a few years earlier and yet to look a little like a vintage train station, the kind with wide, overhanging eaves and sharply peaked gables. And just for fun, they named their place Charing Cross, after the old London train station.

Collaborating with two Bala builders, Kevin Dick and Dan Goforth of Design and Renovation Co., the Willises almost invented the boathouse as they went along. Neither they nor the builders had ever built a boathouse before. The building was designed to cantilever out from the shore, with part of the structure anchored to the land. Also unusual is the third storey, which was not part of the original plan. When the Willises saw how much space there was beneath the steeply pitched roof, they decided to add a loft and dormer windows. A spacious screen porch, large enough for a hot tub, was one design requirement. They also wanted the living room to be bright and to offer a view of the lake despite the overhanging roof on the adjoining screen porch. This was solved by installing floor-to-ceiling windows at two ends of the living room and a skylight in the roof.

There was a firm construction deadline. The Willises had promised the boathouse to friends for their wedding in August 1991. It was finished just in time. The bride arrived in an antique launch and eighty guests poured into the new boathouse to attend the ceremony. They spread out onto the wraparound deck and filled the spacious screen porch. It was a grand celebration and a fitting inauguration for the boathouse called Charing Cross.

Even the bathroom is bright and breezy, with a large domed window overlooking the lake.

Viewed from the loft, the living room is anchored by two leather sofas and a Muskoka rock table. The granite slab was left over from the stone walkway. Rather than let the landscapers crack it into pieces, the owners built a wooden base and turned it into a coffee table.

The deep eaves and carved wooden rafter ends are balanced by a turned railing on four sides of the boathouse. Some of the gingerbread trim came from an old porch that was being removed from Cranberry House, a vintage Bala hotel.

Afternoon sun warms the swimming dock (viewed from the boathouse deck).

An unusual perspective. This photograph, taken through the rear window of the boathouse, shows the interior as well as a reflection (from the glass) of the shoreline behind it.

22

THE WALKER COLLECTION

LAKE MUSKOKA

There are boaters and there are boat collectors. In the small and exclusive latter group, Murray Walker is well known. His huge boathouse on Lake Muskoka shelters a bevy of antique boats ranging from *Floss*, a 19-foot Minett built in 1909, to a Gold Cup racing boat, the *Rainbow IX*, that once belonged to Howard Hughes. Walker likes to collect boats that represent a decade — the oldest, best or most distinctive boats of a particular time. As a result, the inside of his boathouse is a sort of history of boat evolution. He has a wonderfully preserved birchbark canoe; the oldest disappearing-propellor ("dippy") boat afloat; and The *Clarie II*, a stiletto-hulled racing boat that he first saw at Lake Simcoe when he was eight years old (he waited until he was thirty-six to buy it). "I look for a long time before I buy," says Walker, "because I like to have variety in the collection. I think it would be boring to have only runabouts, for instance, from every era."

Walker's boathouse is designed for winter storage of his collection. Some of the slips are equipped with automatic hoists that pull the boats up in slings; others are hoisted manually and placed on big timbers. The engines are drained and winterized, and all chrome is coated with a thin film of motor oil. Soft cotton towels are used to clean the shiny wood. A bubbler system, with four or five bubblers, or propellors, keeps the water around the boathouse circulating and free of ice through the winter. Even hanging in their slings the Walker collection is a delight to see. "People always want to touch these boats — almost as if they're testing to see if the varnish is wet," says Murray. Perhaps that's why on one wall of his boathouse there is a sign that reads: "Please do not caress."

In preparation for winter, the Walker collection is either hoisted in automatic slings or raised up on timbers inside the boathouse.

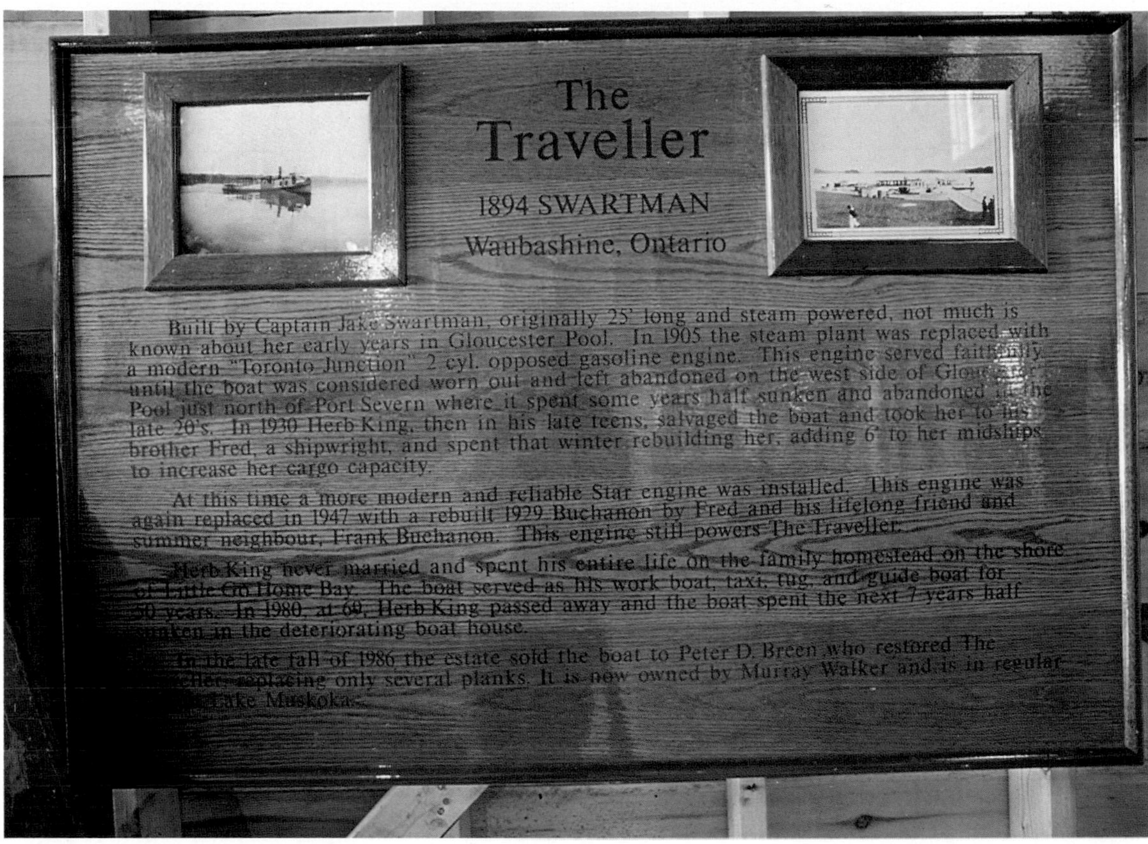

Murray Walker's wonderful old steamboat the *Traveller* was built in 1894 and converted to gas in 1905. Next to a birchbark canoe, the *Traveller* is the oldest boat in his vast collection. A carefully inscribed wooden plaque mounted on the boathouse wall depicts the *Traveller's* history. Walker uses all his boats, including the *Traveller*, which is perfect for taking large groups out on lake tours.

23

WILLARDBY

LAKE MUSKOKA

In the early 1880s, when Dr. Lewis Willard, a family physician from Pittsburgh, came to Muskoka on a fishing expedition, he fell in love with the Beaumaris area on Lake Muskoka. Because the air was so clean and free of pollen, he began to prescribe the resort area to his patients who suffered from hay fever. Before long Beaumaris became so crowded with these Americans that it was dubbed "Little Pittsburgh."

Dr. Willard spent several years as a guest at the Beaumaris Hotel before purchasing a lot on Tondern Island in 1889. He then built a two-story board-and-batten cottage on the brow of a hill and soon after, a boathouse. Both are still standing today — the property all recently restored and beautified by new owners and called Willardby in honor of the original owner.

The restoration was done by contractor Wayne Judges, a specialist in Muskoka heritage properties. Although the buildings were in very poor shape, they hadn't been altered in any way, which was a blessing. In reconstructing the boathouse, they were restricted by the small size of the original and the proximity of the next-door neighbor's boathouse. "Wayne is very good at finding solutions," says the owner. "We wanted to maximize the space but still maintain the look of an old boathouse. Some of the new ones seem to me to be far too playful and have little to do with early boathouse architecture."

Today the restored boathouse is a lemony yellow with graceful white trim. What had been a sort of plain Jane building is now rather fanciful. The screen porch is new, constructed above what had been an open flat roof. Now it's a favorite place to lounge in comfortable old wicker chairs. "If you move to the very end of the screen porch," says the owner, who comes from Switzerland to spend the summer at his Muskoka retreat, "you can watch the sunset over the lake." Details such as trim, window styles and lighting were chosen to tie together the boathouse and the vintage cottage. The gingerbread around the boathouse porch screens replicates the trim that surrounds the cottage porches. At night, when the lights glow from within and old-fashioned outdoor lamps spill gentle pools of light along the dock, the boathouse is especially pretty.

The upper level has a small bathroom and one large bedroom furnished with only the barest necessities. New windows slide across on gliders and sport fresh white curtains on simple iron rods. Basswood-lined walls replaced the original pine boards. "We wanted to save the old wood paneling," says the owner, "but animals had been nesting in the roof and the smell was impossible." The room seems spartan compared to the more lavish interior of the cottage but it's still a favorite with guests. Even the owners admit, "We sometimes go down and sleep in the boathouse just for fun."

Willardby, one of Muskoka's classic old properties. There's a rambling cottage on a hillside with a spill of sunny garden out front. At the water's edge a pair of boathouses sit side by side. One is a 1960s addition, built to house two boats; the other, which dates back to the late 1800s, was altered to include a fanciful screen porch and a covered deck.

As protection from gusty lake winds, one end of the screen porch has glass windows that pull up and hook onto chains.

The boathouse bedroom is refreshingly simple. The wooden floors were restored and new basswood lines the walls.

“All our guests want to sleep here instead of the cottage,” says the owner of this boathouse, built in 1885.

The newer boathouse, constructed in 1960, accommodates only boats.

Dusk descends at Willardby.

The Rookery boathouse from the dock.

24

THE ROOKERY

LAKE MUSKOKA

It's known in the neighborhood as the yellow place with the neat row of red Muskoka chairs on the dock. When gusts of wind sweep across the point and carry away the red chairs, they always get returned, because people know where they came from.

The Rookery is one of Muskoka's great old cottages, built in the days of sleeping porches, deep gables and wraparound verandahs. The century-old cottage sits on a breezy point facing west across the lake. Now painted a sunny yellow, it was crumbling into ruin when Craig and Didi Hind bought the property in 1991. Working with builder Wayne Judges, they completely restored it, recapturing its traditional charm.

Between the cottage and a sleeping cabin, there was a single-story, flat-roofed boathouse settled in a protected cove. When Craig and Didi learned that three grandbabies were toarrive within six months of each other, they realized they needed more space. Adding a second story to the boathouse with room for the new parents and babies seemed like the best solution.

The Hinds worked together on the plans, poring over graph-paper sketches. The boathouse interior reflects their shared design ethic of spare simplicity. Both are firm believers that cottages should stay cottagey. "Why have a duplicate of a city home on the water?" they ask. And limited by the 650 square feet allowed in the boathouse, they wanted to use every morsel of space. "I was inspired by being on a boat last summer," says Didi, "and the space-saving measures I saw there." Work began in January, and by June they were ready to move in, baby cribs and all.

The boathouse interior has the feel of a sea-washed beach house, with rough-sawn plank walls painted white, and cherry-stained floorboards that can be easily swept clean. A screened porch spans the back of the building for al fresco dining in the treetops. And open decks surrounding two sides have plexiglass panels in the railings for child safety. In the sitting room, a ship's ladder pulls away from the wall to provide access to an overhead loft, a clever way to add extra sleeping space.

"I consider practicality first," says Didi, "and then style." Indeed, the ingenious use of space in the two bedrooms is a testament to her philosophy. The rooms are small but not cramped, with windows framing watery views. The bases of the built-in queen-size beds feature drawers on castors. Closets hidden behind a curtain panel are spacious enough to store baby gear. And each bedroom has a crib tucked against one wall.

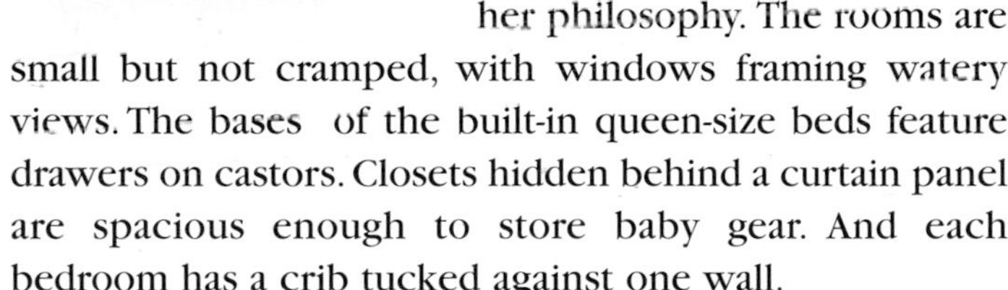

Working with Wayne Judges on both the cottage restoration and the boathouse addition has been a successful collaboration. "It's really important," says Didi, "to get a good builder like Wayne who can understand your ideas — and improve on them."

Both bedrooms are compact but comfortable, with built-in queen-size beds. Didi Hind made mobiles for over the baby cribs with twigs and starfish painted bright blue.

For the kitchen, Didi chose the unfitted look of open shelves and simple wooden cabinetry. Instead of filling space with a large refrigerator, she bought two bar fridges to fit beneath the cherrywood counter. Because the family is tall, the counters are higher than usual. The round cutout in the countertop is the lid for a garbage bin. Heavy chrome handles add to the cottagey appeal.

A ship's ladder pulls out from the wall and leads to the loft.

The walls are rough-sawn pine sheeting painted white. Builder Wayne Judges puts black felt paper behind the boards so that when they shrink, the cracks will show black instead of revealing the pink insulation. Even though boathouses are generally not used in winter, he insulates them to keep them cooler in summer and warmer in the off-season.

View of the living room from the loft.

The original boathouse consisted of this space for boats and, above it, a deck on the flat roof.

The view from the boathouse porch, facing west across Lake Muskoka. The Hinds' eye for style and symmetry is seen in the orderly arrangement of dock chairs.

25

MONTANA LAGO

LAKE JOSEPH

One hundred and twenty-eight cedar stairs lead from the hilltop cottage down to the water at this Lake Joseph property. The cottage was built in 1987, the boathouse ten years later. "Building the boathouse was the best thing we ever did — it added a huge dimension of enjoyment," says Ewing Rae, who shares the waterfront retreat with his partner, Faye Clack. Before the boathouse, the trek down to the water for a swim seemed insurmountable at times. In fun, they named their property Montana Lago — Spanish for "mountain lake."

Ewing worked with Toronto architect Andrew Clark on the conceptual drawings of the boathouse and then handed them over to local builder Heath Billington of Lake to Lake Construction and Design. "We spent a couple of years in the planning stages," says Heath, "and the boathouse changed form and position a few times." Priorities were to site it for the best view and privacy from the neighbors and to blend it with the cedar cottage on the hilltop. Another goal was to make it look substantial.

They chose one-by-eight rough-cut cedar for the siding and bulky two-by-four cedar for the trim. The dropped roofline with soffits just above the windows keeps the profile low, and the protruding deck breaks up the verticality. Heath's favorite term is "beefiness," and the sturdy design reflects that. He believes in punching up the details by using, for instance, thicker than normal trim around doors and windows. He also put up four columns instead of two on the outside deck canopy and chose pine roof shakes were chosen because they're thicker than the traditional cedar ones.

Faye spent a summer planning the interior in a sunny combination of yellows and blues. An enthusiastic cook, she put a lot of thought into the small kitchen, which is restricted by the boathouse building codes. She chose a propane stove, the quietest dishwasher on the market, and custom-made yellow and blue cabinetry. "We tend to entertain here at lunchtime when we can eat out on the covered deck," says Faye, "and for dinner we cook up at the cottage."

For Ewing and Faye, living on the water in a bedroom that faces east to the rising sun is pure pleasure. They both agree that the boathouse has changed their cottage existence. For one thing, they get far more sun down at the water's edge. "We positioned the building to make the most of a northeastern exposure," says Ewing, "I guess you could say we've made the best of a bad lot."

At the end of day when the sun is hitting the far shore, the setting is especially beautiful. "I love to sit out on the covered deck between five and seven on a summer evening," says Faye, "and just gaze across and watch the sunset colors on the far shore."

Small but efficient, the kitchen has a propane stove, dishwasher and microwave.

On sunny days, light bounces off the water into the cheerful living room. "Living on the water has given us a new perspective on cottage life," says Ewing Rae.

A contemporary take on traditional mullion windows allows for a clearer view.

The kick deck surrounding the building breaks up the verticality. Builder Heath Billington believes that "if you're going to show a detail, then punch it out — make it attract the eyes."

Outcroppings of granite plunge into the lake at Ewing Rae's property. A cedar stairway scales the cliff between cottage and boathouse.

It's a long way from the cottage down to the boathouse, but worth the trip for the ever-changing views of lake waters.

Bob and Gert Wharton's cedar-clad boathouse was built specifically to house their antique boat collection.

26

The Shallows

LAKE ROSSEAU

The boathouse is huge, with six slips, each one housing an incredible antique boat. But somehow, despite its size, it blends into a quiet cove on the great swath of Lake Rosseau shoreline owned by Bob and Gert Wharton. They bought the 1,600-foot property in 1996 so that all four of their grown children could have their own cottage. Now that they have nine grandchildren as well, the property, with its sandy beach, tennis court and stone and cedar cottages tucked in the trees, could be mistaken for a summer resort.

In order to build a home for their antique boat collection, they first had to tear down an existing boathouse of the same size. Once the demolition was complete, the new building could begin. Working from a barge with a drill rig, builder Peter Ernst and his crew drove fifty six-inch-round steel beams into the bedrock at the bottom of the lake. Then the timber framing was laid according to the size and shape of the boat slips. Each slip was custom built to accommodate a particular boat.

This boathouse is strictly for boats. Clad in low-maintenance cedar shingles, it has no living quarters; the two fake dormers in the roof are strictly for appearance, to break up the massiveness of the roof. The tongue-and-groove (one-by-six-inch V-joint) pine interior is pristine, free of the clutter, not to mention cobwebs, usually found inside boathouses. Simple fluorescent tubes mounted on the pine ceiling provide lighting, and white ropes drop from ceiling rings and attach to chrome cleats to steady the boats in the water. Each boat is polished to perfection.

Usually, boats are pulled up in winter by pulley systems rigged to the posts and beams of the boathouse. But in the Wharton boathouse clearspan trusses hold up the roof without any support posts. Another solution had to be found to hoist the boats for winter storage. Bob and the builders devised a steel gurney system on wheels, which can be moved from one slip to another. The Whartons claim it's easier to pull boats out this way. When not in use, the rig is moved to the back wall of the boathouse.

Building this boathouse with clearspan roof trusses provided an added benefit that Bob Wharton didn't anticipate. He has the cleanest boathouse in Muskoka. Without posts and beams, there's nowhere for swallows to nest. "This was the best surprise," enthuses Bob. "We can leave the doors open and not worry about the birds — and there's never any bird dirt to clean up."

Inside the pristine building are some of Muskoka's finest boats: the *EL-MAR,* a thirty-two-foot Minett built in 1925 that won Best Boat in Show at the 1999 Antique & Classic Boat Show in Gravenhurst; a twenty-foot 1952 Shepherd that has been in the family since the 1950s; a twenty-nine-foot Greavette Streamliner, the *Blueboy*, built in 1936; and Bob Wharton's most recent purchase — "I waited ten years for this one," he says — *Little Miss Canada II*, an eighteen-foot Greavette Gentleman's Racer originally built in 1933 for racing boat champion Harold Wilson.

The *Severn King* is the oldest boat in the Wharton collection. Built around 1900, it was used as a fishing boat on Georgian Bay. Her registration number, 25E82, means she was the eighty-second boat registered in the province of Ontario.

The Holiday House boathouse was completely rebuilt following a fire in 1999. Architect Tony Marsh worked from old photos to duplicate the original structure. "He understands the integrity of Muskoka architecture," says owner Lloyd Ross.

27

HOLIDAY HOUSE

LAKE MUSKOKA

The classic green and brown boathouse is a familiar sight on Millionaire's Row, the channel near Beaumaris most famous for its opulent cottages and boathouses built a century ago by wealthy Americans. Holiday House, with its sprawling cottage, hillside gardens, swimming dock and double boathouse, has been a focus of cocktail cruises for decades. But a keen eye will notice something different. The profile of the boathouse is the same, the materials and colors are the same, but it is a completely new structure. This boathouse was built after the original burned down in the winter of 1999.

"We built within the footprint of the original," says owner Lloyd Ross, "and, at the same time, we were able to make some subtle changes and improvements to the interior without altering the exterior envelope." The major change was creating one large boathouse out of what had been two buildings, circa 1905 and 1920. The two were separated at water level but joined by an upper-story enclosed walkway The exterior facade still appears as two buildings, but inside, at water level, it's one vast space completely lined in cedar, with five boat slips instead of three. The orientation was changed so that all the doors face the lake, and the entire structure is supported now by one hundred and twenty steel beams drilled into four feet of bedrock.

Architect Tony Marsh, who has designed and restored many of the Beaumaris boathouses, approached this project with one main thought — "What more can I put above the footprint?" Working with the Kaye brothers, builders from Milford Bay, he created living quarters that seem more airy and spacious, with peaks and beams in the ceiling and more elbow room in the hallways. "Instead of flat ceilings in the two main bedrooms, we put cathedral ceilings," says Tony, "and we expanded the dormers, which gives the illusion of extra space and light."

Furnishings were chosen to replicate the old wicker and Mission-style pieces that were lost in the fire. "I wanted to keep the old Muskoka look," says designer Margot Jarrett, who worked with Lloyd and Susan Ross on the basswood interior, "but with a fresher, lighter appearance.

The main cottage is warm and textured with rich colors, so we wanted the boathouse to be a refreshing change." Margot blended reproduction wicker in natural dark colors with some old wicker pieces from the main cottage. She chose sun-faded fabrics for the "loose but not baggy" slip-covered sofas and chairs in the living room. The Mission-style dining-room furniture, made by Stephen Strand, a local cabinetmaker, is an exact copy of the original, which had been made by caretakers during the winter months. Even the kitchen looks as if it was created by local craftsmen back in the 1920s.

For the Rosses, working with Tony Marsh on the rebirth of the boathouse was a wonderful experience. "I still get goose pimples when I look at it," claims Lloyd. "It's as if nothing has changed."

Details such as the brass binhandles in the kitchen are typical of the 1920s style. Back then, everything inside a boathouse was built on site by local talent. The dining-room furniture lost in the fire replicated by local craftsman Stephen Strand.

Two of the bedrooms have sleeping porches — an ideal place to enjoy cooling lake breezes. The "politically correct" moosehead is made of willow.

Antique binoculars and game boards occupy space in the country cupboard, which also houses a more modern diversion — a television set.

All the interior walls are lined in basswood, just as they were in the original building.

The reproduction wicker in the sleeping porch looks old. "I've gone back to dark natural wicker," says designer Margo Jarrett, "away from all white."

On hot summer days there's no better place than this screen porch off the boathouse living room.

The shingles and floor in the screen porch were painted yellow to keep everything light and airy. Electrically controlled translucent roll-down plastic shades protect the porch from rain and the prevailing west wind.

Completely lined in cedar, the interior has five slips and plenty of wall space for collections like this display of boat steering wheels.

The porcelain ceiling lights date back to the 1930s and came from a Pennsylvania factory. "I found fourteen of them at a flea market," says Lloyd Ross. "They were a great buy."

A hillside elevator built in the 1920s is still used to get from the boathouse to the large two-story cottage.

Builder Gary Kaye devised an underwater inertia baffle system to break the waves and protect the wooden boats. The *Vagabond*, a thirty-foot cabin cruiser, occupies one berth alongside the Rosses' 1928 Ditchburn, the *Princess*. "These boats are toys," says Lloyd Ross, "but we are preserving history. I hope, a hundred years from now, someone will be sitting in one of these and say, 'Thank goodness some old fool restored this thing.'"

An eighty-year-old boathouse finds protection on the leeward side of the island.

28

OWL ISLAND

LAKE MUSKOKA

"Owl Island is a great escape and everything we love about summer," reads an entry in the guest book of this boathouse. Indeed, it is a charming spot.

There is no main cottage, just this three-bedroom boathouse and a small bathhouse. Both were built eighty years ago by the Saunders brothers from Bracebridge. They lived in a ramshackle miners' cabin on the island while the construction took place. Both talented builders, the brothers added architectural details such as bell-curved rooflines, angled rafters, and a unique stone fireplace that anchors the building. Their grandmother spent time on the island, too. She laid the wonderfully curved flagstone stairs and planted lily of the valley and peonies that still bloom every summer. At some point, the brothers feuded and the property went to one of their sons, a man who spent little time here.

Directly across the bay in a mainland cottage, Bev and Ann Collombin and their four sons had been summering for thirty years, looking longingly across at Owl Island and its brown and white boathouse. They considered it a treasure, a place unknown to many other cottagers on the lake, hidden as it is on the island's leeward side. They knew if it ever came up for sale they would want to buy it. In 1990, they did just that.

"We knew it would need some work," says Ann, "but it was in remarkably good shape considering its age." The first major job was to raise the level of the boathouse docks, which were all below water. They didn't want to mess with the stonework — the fireplace and archway connected to the island — so had to find a way to raise the dock level without also raising the boathouse. Ken Kaye, of Kaye Brothers in Milford Bay, first supported the building with jacks, then chain-sawed two feet off the base all the way around, creating an open skirt. Then, while the building was held steady on jacks, he added two feet to the height of the docks. Now, the only telltale signs are the doorways into the lower level of the boathouse, which have less headroom.

The Collombins went to work on the island as well. Bev cleared away debris, took down seven dead oaks, limbed other trees, and built a tent platform on a gentle rise behind the boathouse. Ann tackled the interior. "Everything in the kitchen was a ghastly pea green and yellow," she says, "so I stripped it all down and painted everything a cornflower blue." There was no bathroom inside the boathouse, so after installing a septic system, the Collombins added a small washroom in what had been the entrance hall. The new entrance is through a kitchen door off the back deck.

Today, friends and family use the boathouse. It's a remarkably peaceful place where light dances in the windows and the woody scent of an old cottage permeates the air. After a night's sleep on Owl Island, visitors will often leave sweet thoughts written in the boathouse guest book.

Henry David Thoreau once wrote: "Even the tamest nearest island has a distinct character, unique, a place apart, existing in a state of grace outside the world." Owl Island is a window to such a place.

When Bev and Ann Collombin bought the island and boathouse, they painted the high-ceilinged kitchen in bold cornflower blue.

Sleep comes easily in bedrooms on the lake.

Framed black-and-white photographs in the living room show early days at Owl Island in summer and winter.

Almost yearly coats of Oxford brown stain are required to keep the old clapboard from weathering.

A bathhouse in the woods has a shower, sink and toilet and a dreamy lake view from the clawfoot bathtub.

The Ferguson boathouse viewed from the gazebo on Norway Point. In the foreground, the antique fourteen-foot dinghy built by Aykroyd Brothers in Toronto was a gift from the neighbors. The flagship of Graeme and Phyllis Ferguson's fleet is the *Heather Belle,* tied at the dock.

29

NORWAY POINT

LAKE OF BAYS

Two hanging geraniums are the only attempts to fancy up the exterior of this dark half-log boathouse on Lake of Bays. It stands, protected from the prevailing west wind, in a bay at Norway Point. The property was once the site of the WaWa Hotel, a three-hundred-guest wooden-frame building that burned down in the summer of 1923. Across the bay is Bigwin Island and the eerily decaying remains of another famous resort, Bigwin Inn.

The boathouse, which is strictly for boats, was built in the 1930s in a subdued half-log design. In contrast, the sprawling stone cottage, which resembles a Scottish hunting lodge, was designed as a grand statement by Bigwin Inn architect John Wilson. It became the summer home of Frank S. Leslie, who owned Bigwin Inn from 1949 until the early 1960s. A lovely swath of green lawn spills down to the boathouse, expanded a few years ago from four to five slips. Inside is a bevy of beautiful boats.

Today, Graeme and Phyllis Ferguson, who own this historic property, live here year round. The boathouse shelters their treasured boat collection. As with any vintage boathouse, repairs and renovations are ongoing. The doors, for instance, were all crooked and had to be replaced. New lifts were installed by Ace Boat Lifts of Bracebridge for all the boats — even the thirty-six-foot *Heather Belle,* which required an industrial-size lift. "We wanted to be able to do it all ourselves," says Graeme. "With this system, even Phyllis can put up all the boats on her own."

Their first purchase was the *Marie,* a twenty-six-foot Minett built in 1917, and that was when they "caught the bug." They have to stop now, say the Fergusons, because there's no more room in the boathouse. Their collection ranges from the sleek little Butson rowboat to the awesome *Heather Belle,* a generously sized cabin launch that was built in 1898 and came to Canada in 1902. At one time, she was licensed to carry twenty-two passengers on picnic outings from Thorel House on Lake Rosseau. She then spent some time at Santa's Village near Bracebridge, taking children on cruises up and down the river. The Fergusons bought her from the actor Donald Davis, who kept her at his Lake Muskoka cottage from 1971 to 1997.

"We love taking guests for cruises on the *Heather Belle,*" says Phyllis, "and everyone feels as if they're in an old movie, with the lace tablecloths and red velvet seat cushions." The interior, lined with mahogany paneling and furnished with the original wicker chairs, is like a Victorian drawing room. You might expect tea to be served on a silver tea service.

"No other cabin launch of this vintage has been in continuous use like this one," adds Graeme proudly. "The *Heather Belle* has never been unloved."

Heather Belle, a thirty-six-foot picnic boat, with its polished mahogany interior. An eight-horsepower electric system drives her at hull speed of eight knots.

The original 1930s boathouse is home to a gleaming collection of antique boats. When Graeme bought *Heather Belle* he added an extra slip to accommodate her.

OVERLEAF:
Graeme Ferguson in Marie, a twenty-six-foot Minett built in 1917 and restored in 1985 by Butson Boats. Almost all the woodwork above the waterline is original.

Naiad, the Ferguson's black lab, was named for the famous Lake of Bays steamer once owned by Chicago milk magnate Cameron Peck.

Golden rays of light spill from the boathouse onto the lake at dusk.

30

MONYCA ISLAND

LAKE ROSSEAU

For most island cottagers, the trip from mainland to island on a rainy day is a wet slog complete with soggy grocery bags. Few islanders have the luxury of a mainland boathouse where they can keep boats covered and ready to hop into when they arrive at the lake. That's what makes the mainland boathouse for Monyca Island so rare. Not only are the boats dry but you can drive a car right into the boathouse and step into the waiting boat. A garage door on the land side opens to the middle slip, which has a reinforced dock section for parking cars. On either side are boat slips, one holding a pontoon barge, the other a Shepherd cruiser. This is the unique welcome to Monyca Island.

Monyca was first settled in the late 1800s by the Watkins family. Their original log cabin, built in 1898, is still on the island, used now by owner Don Jackson as an office. The Watkins also built the huge turreted Victorian cottage just after the turn of the century. "I bought the island from the fifth generation of that family," says Don, "and ever since, I've been trying to restore it to how it might have been at the time of their ancestors."

From the mainland, it's a short boat hop to the fifteen-acre island. When you round a corner, you catch the first glimpse of the island boathouse, an enchanting structure afloat in a protected bay. It looks like something out of a fairytale. The original boathouse was falling into the lake and had to be torn down when Don bought the island in 1993. The new one, designed by architect D'Arcy Dunal and built by Bill Stokes of Windycrest Construction, is a more fanciful structure.

Back in the early 1900s, the island was a hub of social activity. The supply boats stopped here and dropped mail for all the surrounding islands. Cottagers would row across to Monyca to pick up their mail and catch up on local gossip. "We tried to preserve some of the history," says Don, "so we kept the old wooden mailboxes from the original boathouse and put them into the back wall of the new building. They still have names penciled on the little doors."

The Victorian whimsy of the cottage is repeated in design elements of the boathouse. Canary yellow board-and-batten is offset by plenty of white trim and fanciful fretwork. Perhaps the most striking feature is the rooftop cupola. From across the lake on a sunny day, it glitters like a sunburst. Bill Stokes wanted to try something different, so he designed the cupola with diamond-shaped windows and a cube of mirrors hanging inside. When the sun heats the windows, the cube moves and creates a glinting effect.

At night, the boathouse is even more spectacular, bathed in golden beams of light. Joe Macdonald, the caretaker, who lives with his wife year-round on the island, sums it up when he says, "There isn't any place quite like Monyca Island. It's magical."

A wooden corner cabinet houses a television and audio equipment. The handcarved doors feature scenes of Muskoka wildlife.

Decorator Scott MacDonald chose historical colors for the interior, warm tones of coral, yellow and green. Friends handpainted the table in the same colors during a weekend visit.

Don Jackson planned the boathouse as a gathering place for his teenage daughters. Instead of a separate bedroom, there's a daybed for napping. The quilt-covered bed is tucked in an alcove with its own window overlooking pine trees and water. Tongue-and-groove pine wallboards were washed with sea green stain followed by three coats of satin finish Varathane. Like the bed nook, the kitchen tucks into an alcove. Matching fretwork unifies the two spaces.

The outside deck offers sun, shade and a long lake view.

A side view of the Monyca Island boathouse shows the living room's window alcove.

Diamonds of brightly colored glass are copied from the vintage window design in the main cottage. The mainland boathouse, which stores both boats and cars, also has glass diamonds in the windows in these same primary colors.

A trio of crayon-colored chairs looks out on a tiny perfect island. Less poetic is its name — Garbage Island — bestowed when people used to dump their garbage on it.

Although it looks like an old Muskoka classic, this boathouse was built in 1992 by Grant Williamson. The architectural details — shed dormers, multipaned windows and exposed rafters — were popular boathouse features at the turn of the century, as was the hillside elevator that hoists supplies from the boathouse up the hill to the main cottage.

31

Brigadoon Island

LAKE MUSKOKA

When the R.M.S. *Segwun* and the *Wanda III,* Muskoka's lovely old steam cruisers, set off from Gravenhurst on a sunset jaunt, they head north up Lake Muskoka until they reach Brigadoon Island. Here they turn, just in time to watch the sun dropping down between Grandview and Cinderwood Islands. Then, as twilight descends, they head back to home port, bidding farewell to Brigadoon.

"Sitting on the screened portico of the boathouse and watching the steamboats cruise by was a great delight," says the former owner of this enchanting isle. "The boathouse is perfectly sited to watch the lake activity." Recently, Brigadoon changed hands. The new owners bought the island with its eight-bedroom wood-lined cottage and spacious guesthouse mainly because of the boathouse. They needed a slip long enough to berth their newly acquired thirty-six-foot Ditchburn.

Brigadoon was first purchased from the Crown in 1881. Thereafter many owners came and went. In the early days islands changed hands frequently: as one cottager observed, "Muskoka islands were like penny candy back then — you could buy two or three of them at a time." The original Brigadoon boathouse had been built at the turn of the century by a Pittsburgh architect. In 1960, it burned down and the same architectural firm returned to rebuild it. This time, a smaller, more modest building took its place.

Then in 1992 the owner needed a larger boathouse for his collection of antique boats. He tore down the 1960s boathouse and hired Grant Williamson of Elmo Starr Construction, a builder known for his talent at replicating the old Muskoka style. Without any existing photographs of the original boathouse, they used a neighbor's Beaumaris boathouse built in the same era by the same architect as a guide. They relied on the existing cribs to position and size the building. Some modifications were made, such as leaving an open boat port instead of closing it all in. And the handsome screen portico was included in the new blueprint. This way the entire place can be jacked up when the cribs need replacing. It also prevents rotting where the wood siding meets the wooden deck.

The upper level is larger than it appears from the water. There's one vast L-shaped room with a sitting area, kitchen, pantry, washroom and bedroom with a master bed as well as single iron beds tucked into nooks and draped in mosquito netting. The wall planking of the post-and-beam interior is laid in a V-pattern in order to appear more nautical. The painted wooden floor is dark green and all the walls are white, with tiny lights beaming up to the exposed rafters of the vaulted ceiling. It's a comforting place to be, especially as the sun goes down and the haunting toot of the steam whistle means the Segwun will soon sail by.

Old wicker freshened with white paint adds to the summery appeal.

A dreamy canopy of mosquito netting on the beds is "more for effect." Lake breezes blow in from all directions, keeping the rooms bug-free.

Exposed trusses and rafters add interest to the generous interior.

Extra-long slips provide room for antique boats. The *Brigadoon*, a 1941 MacCraft, holds pride of place. Built as an offshore patrol boat on Lake Huron, she has been passed on to each successive owner of the island.

A tree grows through it.

A more primitive form of the classic wooden boat, miniature style.

The *Liberty* motors away from Brigadoon toward the north end of Lake Muskoka.

The cliff that gave the island its name provides a dramatic backdrop to the cluster of boathouses and sheds at the water's edge.

32

CLIFF ISLAND

LAKE JOSEPH

There's a certain area about midway up Lake Joseph where it's easy to believe that you've stepped back in time. Many of the boathouses look just as they did in the Micklethwaite photographs taken at the turn of the century. These classic wooden structures were erected to shelter boats and house staff in the days when households were run by servants. Lacking architectural pretension, they offer a decided contrast to the immense new designer boathouses sprouting elsewhere on the lakes.

Cliff Island is one place with a clutch of these vintage boathouses. They huddle, all dark brown and somewhat decrepit, in a bay next to the famous cliff. The sixty-four-acre island is the largest private island in Muskoka, owned by the same family since the late 1800s and never divided. Jerry Hamlin shares Cliff Island with his sister, Lucile, and an uncle, George Forman Jr. It was Jerry's great-grandfather who came to Muskoka from Buffalo before the turn of the century. "He cruised all over the lakes in a house-boat," says Jerry. "He had the pick of the lakes then, and this is what he chose."

The main cottage, a rambling Adirondack-style place hidden in the woods, was designed by Buffalo architect Edward Green and completed by 1898. The launch boathouse was built then too, with a boat chauffeur's room in the upper level. Today, there is no boat chauffeur and the upstairs room is boarded up, its back staircase rotting away. Jerry says wryly, "Our boathouse is developing character — it's sinking and rising in different places."

At the water level, the boathouse is like a musty old museum with antique vessels piled in corners and heaped on rafters. There's a dugout canoe, rowing skiffs and Jerry's California Drag Boat, a 1965 Rayson Craft that was once the fastest boat on the lake. Propped in one corner is an old Peterborough Aqua Board that they used as kids. Nothing, it seems, is ever thrown away at Cliff Island.

The boathouse was built originally to house the Forman's steam yacht, the *Iagara* (it was to be named Niagara but the letter "N" never arrived). Used by the family for many years, it ultimately met an unfortunate demise as a hotdog stand named "Steamers" on Highway 69. All that remains now at Cliff Island is the *Iagara*'s propeller, which hangs over the boathouse door, and her steering wheel, now in Jerry's 1890 steamboat, the *Wendingo* — which is, he says, "the oldest working boat on the lakes."

In the 1920s, a canoe house was put up in the bay alongside the main boathouse. Tucked in the lee of the prevailing west wind, it was used to store boats in winter. In summer, the woodsy room with a stuffed deer head looming over the brick fireplace became the main hangout for the whole family. "This was the swim dock, the fishing dock, the makeout dock. Everything happened here," says Jerry. "As a matter of fact, of all the places on the island, it's still my favorite place to hang out."

The interior of the old canoe house is a favorite place to relax on summer afternoons. Built in the 1920s in a protected cove, it has developed character over the years. Porcupines have chewed away railings and doors — as Jerry says, "It's a well-chewed establishment."

When the Cliff Islanders were children in the '40s and '50s, fishing was a prime activity. Whenever they caught a large fish, they would paint an outline of it on a wooden board. These were hung with pride on the walls of the canoe house. They're all still there.

***Wendingo*, being paddled into the boathouse. According to Jerry Hamlin, who admits to being "a steam nut," she's the oldest working steamboat on the lakes.**

33

BLUEBERRY HILL

LAKE ROSSEAU

When Carol and Michael Nedham bought the steeply sloped lot on Lake Rosseau, it was covered in blueberries. Then the blasting began. In order to build the cottage, they had to blast away some of the rock. Today the moss green cottage is tucked snugly into the hillside, a long, narrow building with a projecting prow. Flagstone steps lead to the water and a boathouse. Now that the blasting dust has settled, the blueberries are taking root again, creeping across the rocky landscape — hence the name of this handsome summer property. "I was so pleased to see the blueberries," says Carol, "that now I always serve blueberry dessert when we have guests."

Both the cottage and boathouse were designed by Jamie Wright, a Toronto architect who first spent some time boating on the lakes, collecting ideas. "I discovered," he says, "that most boathouses built from the 1950s to the 1970s looked like suburban houses. And many of the new ones, I thought were too ornate." For the Nedhams, he designed an unassuming building with exposed structural elements and woodworking details more in keeping with Muskoka boathouse architecture of the 1920s. Great swooping eaves extend four feet over the surrounding decking to provide shade on all sides and effectively lower the scale of the building. The angular support brackets beneath the eaves are aesthetically pleasing and, according to the Nedhams, don't seem to appeal to nesting swallows — a decided bonus.

An outside staircase leads to the upper level, which has two bedrooms, a sitting area, a small kitchen and bathroom. High ceilings soar over the sitting area, a great expanse of window lets in plenty of light, and glass doors lead to a French balcony with space for two chairs.

Bill Stokes of Windycrest Construction built the boathouse, taking Jamie Wright's architectural concepts and "fancying things up a bit." "We like to create an older look," says Bill, "with details like chamfered posts and fish-scale shingles." He always leaves a trademark design element too — like the custom wooden finials in the dormer peaks. But it was his practical ideas that the Nedhams appreciated most — such as the inset back door, which created a little entrance nook at the top of the staircase. He suggested the removable section of railing opposite the back door; the railing lifts right out to allow furniture such as the large blue armoire to be hauled inside. And he built generous shelves over every window inside to provide extra display space.

The resulting boathouse was the product of a successful collaboration. "We were lucky," says Carol, "to have both a good architect and a good builder."

Finishing the interior in tongue-and-groove pine was going to be Michael Nedham's summer project, but time ran out after he did the ceiling. Now cozy and complete, the room has French doors that open onto a balcony.

OVERLEAF:
The underside of the swooping eaves is ribbed like a cedar-strip canoe. On one side the deck extends to accommodate a circle of primary-colored Muskoka chairs.

The boathouse, with its deeply sloped roof and wide eaves, was designed by Toronto architect Jamie Wright. "The idea is to bring the scale of the building down," he explains, "and to have it fit with boathouse architecture of the past." The exterior is clad in prefinished wood siding.

One of two boathouses on Christmas Island.
This one was built in 1988.
AT RIGHT: The restored canoe house on Fawn Island.

34

CHRISTMAS ISLAND

LAKE JOSEPH

When old established islands get new owners, the neighbors usually wonder what changes will take place. Will the character of the heritage cottages be destroyed? In the case of Christmas Island and Fawn Island, both on Lake Joseph, the worries have subsided. New owners, a couple with family roots in Muskoka, are transforming the islands into classic summer retreats with all of the old Muskoka character intact.

Both admit they keep gravitating to the tiny canoe house that perches on the shore of Fawn Island. "It's so romantic," says the owner of her hideaway. "It's a real water house. The bed faces east and the sunrise is literally blinding. Last summer when I was nursing our baby, it was just a great place to be. Very grounding and calming — for me and for the baby too."

When they bought Fawn, they wanted to restore the canoe house, which had been built by the original owners of the island in 1894. It had been lived in then but in later years was used merely to store canoes and other boating paraphernalia. The upper level, accessed by a back staircase, had a tiny airless bedroom with small windows. Jamie Blair, a period designer and builder, worked with the owners on the restoration using the footprint of the original. It was taken apart and reassembled joist by joist, piece by piece. "Basically," says Jamie, "we took an old utilitarian structure and beautified it."

To accomplish this, the exterior was shingled in cedar with flared edges at the base to give it the appearance of melting into the decking. New windows and doors on all sides offer spectacular views of the ever-changing lake waters. Stone walls were shored up and a flagstone patio fans out around the base. The upper level is a light-filled bedroom and downstairs there's a sitting room that the owner, a photographic artist, plans to use as her studio. In winter the canoe house still functions as a dryland boathouse when canoes and skiffs are hauled in through the wide doorway.

At Christmas Island the couple are reviving two boathouses. One, a flat-topped utilitarian structure built in the 1940s, has been made more attractive with the addition of French doors at the dock level. The second, a three-slip boathouse, was built for the former island owners in 1988. The half-log siding was chosen to complement the Adirondack-style cottage. In the upper level there's a guest bedroom, bathroom, large exercise and games room and a his-and-hers office space. At water level, a pair of classic boats occupy two of the slips. There's already a workroom in this area, and the owner plans to make his office here and create a lounge with comfortable armchairs. "After all," he says, "guys just want to hang out in boathouses."

The second story of this boathouse at Christmas Island was built before the regulation allowed only 650 square feet of living space. It has a large sitting room, a bathroom and two bedrooms, one used as an office. Some of the battered painted furniture was found in the old cottage and recycled.

The sitting room on the lower level of the canoe house was once a cluttered storage room. The style of the new windows and glass doors were inspired by a villa in Tuscany.

The box bed in the canoe house is built into a windowed alcove. Beneath it are storage drawers; above, skylights look into the pine trees.

One of two boathouses on Christmas Island, this three-slip one, built in 1988 to house a thirty-six-foot Minett, was recently repainted in sage green with lighter trim. Inside is the *Rascal*, a 1926 Gold Cup racer, and *Taipan*, a cigar boat with an S-formation cockpit. On the back dock is the family's homemade outdoor ping-pong table.

Jamie Blair, a specialist in Muskoka architecture, restored this canoe house tucked in a cove on Fawn Island. The stone patio forms part of the inside floor and fans out from the base outside as well. The upper balcony railings have childproof plexiglass panels.

"Experience the true essence of Muskoka," says the brochure for TamLwood, a bed-and-breakfast on Lake Joseph. Most guests arrive by boat to stay in this boathouse.

35

TAMLWOOD

LAKE JOSEPH

When Ted and Anne Grove built this boathouse in 1998, they planned to use it for family and friends. But Anne had given up a busy career to spend the summer at her cottage and was worried that she would find it lonely — or not have enough to do. A friend suggested that she turn the boathouse into a bed-and-breakfast. "It was a great idea," says Anne. "I have had such fun with it and met so many interesting people. I just hated the idea of the boathouse sitting empty and nobody enjoying it."

The setting is lovely, a pristine lot forested in red and white pines with a natural sandy beach in a protected cove. On one side the land rises in a steep ridge of granite, on the other the boathouse is angled to capture the long view down Lake Joseph. The Groves bought the property in 1991 and kept as many pine trees as possible during cottage construction in 1994. Those that had to be removed were milled on the property and made into the wall and floorboards for the cottage.

The board-and-batten boathouse is stained in a soft putty color with white trim. It has angled rooflines, and four sturdy columns beneath the deck overhang on both sides and wide trim on the multi-paned windows. Ted did a lot of the building himself, choosing elements that would blend with the cottage. The named their summer home TamLwood, an acronym for the family names: Ted, Anne, and their three daughters, Meredith, Lindsay, and Whitney — plus Wood for the woods on the property.

Anne runs the bed-and-breakfast from Monday to Thursday, mid-May to mid-October. On weekends she makes it available for family. It's the only b-and-b on Lake Joseph, and as far as she knows, the only boathouse b-and-b in Muskoka. Many of her guests arrive by boat. During the day they enjoy cruising the three lakes and then at night they return to this comfortable abode.

There are two large bedrooms, a bathroom and a sitting area with a small kitchen. Furnished in country-style décor, with all the cottage comforts, it also has a deck that wraps around three sides. Breakfast is served at the main cottage or at the umbrella table on the sunny deck.

After its first season as a b-and-b, TamLwood has proven a success. "Everyone who stays here has been wonderful," says Anne, who enjoys it as much as the guests. "They all seem to be thrilled that we would share this place with them."

A choice of dreamy bedrooms for guests at this Lake Joseph bed-and-breakfast.

The twenty-one-foot day sailer tied at the dock is the *Fifth Lady*. Ted Grove chose the name because he has a wife and three daughters. The Groves use the boathouse for family on summer weekends and run it as a b-and-b during the week.

Marmilwood, the boathouse cottage of Jack and Dolena Hurst, was once used as a convalescent hospital by the Royal Canadian Air Force.

Jack Hurst's 1938 Greavette Streamliner at home.

Traditional Muskoka chairs are stained to preserve the warm color of cedar.

37

POINT WILLIAM

LAKE MUSKOKA

Designing a Muskoka boathouse was a new experience for the award-winning Toronto architect firm of Shim-Sutcliffe. "We'd never done one before," says Howard Sutcliffe, who worked on the project with his partner, Brigitte Shim, over a two-year period. "The challenge came from combining such different spaces — a boat garage and sleeping accommodation." The pair, known for their ability to blend buildings into the landscape, wanted to capture a feeling of Muskoka, of Adirondack lodges, of woods and lake and luxury yachts — all abstractions that are imbedded in the design.

When the boathouse was still on paper, it won a Progressive Architecture Award, the American judges calling it "a sophisticated hut in the Canadian wilderness." It may not be exactly wilderness, this point of land on the south-western shore of Lake Muskoka, but the building is more sophisticated than the average boathouse. Elegant wooden walls and cabinetry lend a rustic sophistication to the interior. There's a pleasing mix of British Columbia fir, mahogany, birch, oak and jatoba, a Brazilian cherry.

"The main idea," Howard continues, "was to create an outer wrapper with those heavy timbers of salvaged Douglas fir. They're actually an extension of the under-water crib system and they form a shell, like the exterior of a boat, that protects the finely crafted interior." The inspired 650 square feet of interior space includes a small vestibule, a main bed-sitting room with its own private deck, a compact kitchen built into the mahogany cabinetry of the hall corridor, and a Japanese-style bath and dressing area with double ceramic sinks, a double shower, a deep tub, and windows that face both woods and water.

At the dock level are two covered slips and one open slip protected by the deck overhang. The boat doors are made of opaque fiberglass that recalls the look of Japanese lanterns when light glows from inside at night.

Wooden door panels close off the outdoor bar kitchenette when they're not in use. Two sets of stair-cases lead to the second story, one to the main entrance flanked by a roof garden, and the other to a rear back deck, a protected nook to hide away and read.

The decks, designed to capture the sun and block the wind, meld seamlessly with the interior space.

Drawings of the countless design details fill a thick binder that the architects presented to the owners, Gerald and Shanitha Sheff, when the project was completed. They both appreciate the exacting workmanship and take great delight in their boathouse, which they use all year round. It has the sensuous quality of a luxury yacht, but with extra comforts such as a big soaking tub, a wood-burning fireplace, and a television that disappears out of sight inside a mahogany cabinet. And everywhere they enjoy a view of water or woods. "I love the intimacy of the space," says Gerald. "It's wonderful in all seasons — even in winter it's the ultimate escape."

A compact kitchen with custom cabinetry forms part of the corridor. Oak floors painted a mustard yellow provide contrast.

The bedroom furniture fits into the walls, creating a feeling of spaciousness. A curved wooden ceiling keeps the space snug like a yacht interior, and a curved fireplace warms the space in winter.

OVERLEAF:
All the bronzework — custom boat cleats, lights and door pulls — was handcrafted by Takashi Sakamoto from Prince Edward County.

Custom mahogany windows frame two views in the bathing and dressing area.

Ceramic Japanese bowls turned into sink basins are built into the teak countertop.

The bedroom terrace looks down on the dock, enclosed by a low stone wall. Beyond it, a sweep of granite shoreline.

The Toronto architectural firm of Shim-Sutcliffe designed the boathouse for Gerald and Shanitha Sheff. They used a variety of woods, including reclaimed Douglas fir timbers for the boathouse exterior. Exposed wooden joists allow sunlight to filter through to the deck below.

At dock level, the bar area can be accessed from inside the boathouse as well. Doors fold across to close it off when not in use.

Every year, in May, barges full of annuals are brought to Woodmere Island for planting.

38

WOODMERE

LAKE ROSSEAU

It's something of a miracle that the old boathouse on Woodmere Island is still standing. Two devastating fires, one in 1939 and then another in 1998, destroyed several buildings on this seven-acre island — but somehow the boathouse, built in 1898, survived both times. As a result, it's a favorite hideaway for the island residents. Understandably, they're nervous about fires and nobody dares to light the hearth in the boathouse sitting room.

"We're very careful," says owner Pat Dalton, "especially in this boathouse, which is the oldest building on the island." The middle section of the wood-clad structure was the original dry-slip boathouse for storing rowboats and canoes and is now used as storage space. In the 1920s, the boathouse was expanded, with two slips added on either side and living quarters above.

The owners at that time were Lady Annie and Sir Thomas White; he was a cabinet minister in the government of Prime Minister Robert Laird Borden. The Whites sold the island in 1933 to the Hausermann family from Cleveland, Ohio, who owned it for fifty years before selling to Peter and Pat Dalton in 1983.

"This is our family gathering place," says Pat, who spends most of the summer on the island. "We have three families living here with six grandchildren and six dogs — it's the perfect island because we can all have our own space and privacy." For children, Woodmere Island is like a fantasy playground, with pine-needle paths, a stone wishing well and waterfall, a totem pole, sleeping cabins right out of Snow White and the Seven Dwarfs, and a playhouse fashioned from an old chicken coop.

Everything on the island is built to blend into the environment or to look as if it's always been there. Such is the case with the second boathouse, built in 1993 by Port Carling builder Wayne Dempsey. This two-slip boathouse is simple but elegant with decorative wrought-iron accents made by Wayne Church, a local artisan. It also houses a pair of exceptional boats. One is the *Tango*, a 1927 Ditchburn that Pat bought for Peter's sixty-fifth birthday. The other is the *Cameo*, originally a "tender" for the *Parthenia*, a cruise-ship-sized yacht belonging to the F. W. Woolworth family in New York. The tender, a twenty-foot coupe, ferried the Woolworth clan from the yacht to the New York harbor. In 1968 she came to Muskoka, where Pat Dalton first spotted her up on wooden blocks in a parking lot at Port Sandfield. Today she is well used for family outings.

With an island full of cabins and cottages to accommodate all the family members, the vintage boathouse, with its three bedrooms, kitchen, sitting room, bathroom and screened verandah, is used primarily for guests. "And for napping," adds Pat. "When people go missing we usually find them asleep in the boathouse."

Peter and Pat Dalton collect old tin advertising signs. The basswood walls have darkened since the boathouse was built in 1898.

The wood-lined bedrooms all have porcelain sinks typical of the period in which the boathouse was constructed.

The covered porch, furnished with white-painted wicker, offers a breezy retreat on summer afternoons.

The distinctive curved roof of the boathouse, the oldest building on this private seven-acre island. Beneath the enclosed porch are double doors that open to the dry-slip area, now used for storage.

Two classic boats — the *Parthenia* and the *Woodmere*, a 1928 Ditchburn — occupy the new boathouse at Woodmere, built in 1993 by Port Carling contractor Wayne Dempsey.

SUNNYSIDES

LAKE MUSKOKA

Chris Vandergrift and his wife, Jane Armstrong, had been looking for a cottage with a boathouse large enough to store their thirty-foot Duke cabin cruiser. In August 1997, when they pulled up to the dock at Keewaydin Island, the real estate sign was just being nailed up on a property with a classic old cottage and a boathouse with a thirty-four-foot slip. That was on Friday. By Monday they had bought the place. It was just what they were looking for.

"The nicest thing about it," says Chris, "is nothing had been done to alter the original cottage or boathouse. And both were built about 1927." The cottage has basswood-lined rooms, plenty of nooks and crannies, and every bedroom has a porcelain sink. The only necessary renovation was the cottage kitchen, which was original and charming with old wooden counters, but full of wood rot, so it had to be torn out.

In the boathouse, which also has the warm, woody smell of old cottages, only the bathroom needed redoing. It had been renovated in the 1950s and Chris wanted to return it to its original character. The porcelain sink was found under the cottage, probably discarded during the 1950s renovation. Everything else is exactly as it was when they moved in — the white-painted spool beds, the nautical touches such as boat lanterns turned into bedside lamps, the framed Muskoka maps on the wall.

They call their summer home Sunnysides because the property is at a narrow part of the large island, giving them frontage on both shores and sun all day long. The cottage faces east and the boathouse west. Two other identical boathouses were built on Keewaydin Island, all at the same time by a father for his three daughters. The other two have since enclosed the front balconies but otherwise maintain their classic character.

Keewaydin is the largest of a cluster of islands in northern Lake Muskoka known as the Seven Sisters. At one time, it was a port of call for the lake steamers and there was a summer post office here called Port Keewaydin. The island history is well documented in the photographs taken by Ed Hugil in the 1880s. Boaters cruising around the island today can still see many of the old boathouses captured in his photos.

For Chris and Jane, the island home is an ongoing pleasure. There is lots of space to store the antique boats that Chris has been collecting since 1986, including the wonderful *Crusoe*, the thirty-foot cabin cruiser built by Duke in Port Carling in 1952. And they still find treasures hidden in cupboards all over the cottage. Maybe it's not surprising when you buy a place with everything intact — "even peanut butter and jam still on the kitchen shelves."

When the Vandergrifts bought the property, they acquired everything that was left behind, including the furniture, bedding and artifacts in the boathouse bedroom.

A peaceful view of neighboring islands from the covered verandah.

OVERLEAF:
Chris found the old porcelain sink under the cottage when he restored the boathouse bathroom. The antique toy car belonged to his wife, Jane.

Chris Vandergrift bought the property on Keewaydin Island in 1997 mainly because the boathouse could accommodate *Crusoe*, his 1952 thirty-foot Duke cabin cruiser. The classic boathouse hasn't changed since it was built in 1927. Shed dormers in the hip roof feature the shaped rafters typical of Muskoka architecture at that time. A back staircase leads to the upper level and a double Dutch door.

Early morning light at Chaynemac Island.

40

CHAYNEMAC

LAKE MUSKOKA

You can still see the charred ceiling beams in the two-story boathouse at Chaynemac. Back in the days when wood-burning engines fired the family steamboat *inside* the boathouse, such burn marks were common. It's no surprise that many of these buildings didn't survive the steamboat era.

The name Chaynemac originated in the early 1900s when the first owners of this five-acre island called each other by the nicknames "Chay" and "Mac." The new owners, Bill and Ann Deluce, have kept the name and the spirit of the vintage property. Since buying the island in 1994, they have worked hard to restore the serene character of the place, which was known for forty years as the Nelson Davis island. "When ninety-year-old Mrs. Davis came for tea last summer," says Ann, "I was pleased that she really liked what we had done."

Nelson and Eloise Davis bought the property in 1941 and owned it until 1981. Davis was a business tycoon who hobnobbed with the wealthy, including members of the Royal family. The Queen Mother reportedly was a guest on the island one summer, and her bedroom in a woodsy cabin near the water is preserved much as it was when she visited. Davis collected nautical and marine artifacts, and many of these are still intact, including old brass ship lanterns that light the wooded paths and antique marine charts rolled up in boathouse cupboards.

In the heyday of this picturesque island estate, Davis had sixteen boats housed in three separate boathouses. One of them, the *Chaynemac V,* was custom built for Davis by Greavette in 1947. The Deluces were able to buy it when they bought the island. The classic wooden launch still occupies a berth in one of the immense island boathouses.

Nelson Davis had a full-time boat captain to attend to and operate his fleet. He lived above the boats in compact space still known as the captain's quarters. Today, the chart room still has the captain's old oak desk. Across the hallway is the bathroom, all freshly painted white but with the original light fixtures, sink, toilet and cast-iron tub on claw feet. In the bedroom, Mission-style twin beds are tucked beneath the sloping ceiling. The beds were made in the room during the winter months by the island caretaker. "They weigh so much they'll likely never be moved," says Ann. From the bedroom, doors open to a Juliette balcony with a wonderful view of Lake Muskoka.

The island is now an active, busy place in summer when Bill and Ann and their four children are in residence. Down at the boathouses, little has changed. The captain's quarters may look just as they did when Nelson Davis's boat chauffeur lived here, but now they're the summer digs of the Deluce's fifteen-year-old son.

The bedroom in the second story of the boathouse has twin beds that were built there and will probably never leave.

The swimming house is well used by members of this family who gather for a daily swim around the five-acre island. This quaint little building is beside the old steamer dock. Stairs that allowed bathers to discreetly slide into the lake in the days when modesty was in fashion pull up when not in use. There's a sauna and changing room inside as well. The steamer dock is now used to tie up the Deluce's 1947 Beaver float plane.

Old marine charts date back to the days when the estate's boat captain lived in the boathouse.

A complex hoist system of pulleys and chains makes opening and closing for the season a less daunting task.

When the Deluce family go cruising in *Chaynemac V*, Ann's brother-in-law often sits in the "mother-in-law seat" and plays the bagpipes.

View from the boathouse deck at Chaynemac.

The graceful lines of the boathouse on Lyford Island evoke the Quaker aesthetic — spare but visually strong. Owner Sherry Eaton worked with local builder Brian Humphrey on the design.

41

LYFORD ISLAND

LAKE JOSEPH

It was only a few years ago that the pretty blue boathouse on Lyford Island was transformed from a plain, two-slip boathouse to this handsome structure with its wraparound verandah and jaunty white trim. The balance and symmetry of the style is reminiscent of a seaside house in New England. "I love the island of Nantucket and the homes there," says owner Sherry Eaton, "and perhaps that was in my mind when we were designing the boathouse."

Lyford Island was named after a Welsh colonel, possibly a relative of the original American owner who bought the two-acre island in 1903 for one dollar. It remained in his family until Sherry bought it in 1989. The name Lyford didn't catch on with the locals, though — they called it Goat Island because, years ago, a mainland farmer used to bring his goat herd here to graze. It may be that the goats are the reason for the lovely swaths of exposed granite that now define the island landscape.

"I spent many years in Georgian Bay," says Sherry, "and this island reminded me of that area with its flat rock and low profile. I liked the fact that there were no steep hills, no bad sides or dark views. And all the bedrooms in the cottage have a view of water." She admits, though, that none are as luminous as the light-filled boathouse. Some day, she contends, she may move out of the cottage and into the boathouse herself.

For now, it's a soothing space for guests, as welcoming as any luxurious country inn with its freshly cut flowers, fine toiletries and soft bed-linens. The king-size bed is positioned to take advantage of the sparkling views of lake water. Two walls are composed of oversized multipaned glass doors that slide open to the covered porch. Overhead, in the vaulted ceiling, there are glass panels in the gables that offer a glimpse into the treetops. Wicker chairs on the porch face a tiny island inhabited only by birds residing in a twig birdhouse.

Sherry consulted decorating contractor David Bermann of Scandinavian Painting Inc. in Toronto for advice on the boathouse interior. Both agreed that the interior should be kept neutral — that there's no sense in competing with nature in such a setting. The wide plank pine walls (smooth side facing out) were treated with layers of knot sealer and primer to prevent the knots and resin from bleeding through, and then painted in a creamy off-white. "The idea was to keep everything light and airy," says David, "so that all the color comes from the lake and the trees."

Birdhouses — seen here in the form of bedside lamps — are a recurrent theme on this island. Toby Schertzer of DIN Studios made the headboard, and many of the interior finishing ideas came from decorating contractor David Bermann.

Splashes of red, blue and yellow brighten the mostly neutral interior. Watered-down white stain was applied to the pine wallboards to lighten the wood color.

A covered porch wraps around two sides, offering protection from wind and sun all day long.

Ouno Island's eyecatching sailboat boathouse, built in 1915, as seen from the steamer dock.

42

OUNO ISLAND

LAKE ROSSEAU

Every weekend for fifteen months, Valerie and Eric Grundy scoured the lakes of Muskoka and the Kawarthas with real estate agents looking for a cottage property. When they landed at Ouno Island on Lake Rosseau, they both knew immediately that their search had ended. "It just felt good," says Eric simply.

The property, which they bought in 1994, sprawls across a lovely low sweep of shoreline on the twenty-two-acre island. On a gentle hilltop sits the classic two-story cottage with gabled sleeping porches and wood-lined rooms. Its stone walkways lead to the large steamer dock and the boathouses. One two-story boathouse, built around 1900, was the first building on the island. At the time, it was used to store the canoes and rowboats that were the only means of water transportation. The upper level is now one large bedroom that opens onto a covered verandah. The other Ouno Island boathouse is something of a landmark on the lake.

Boats slow as they pass by the green and yellow sailboat boathouse — a unique structure attached at a ninety-degree angle to the three-slip launch house. It was built in 1915 by James Hardy, the island owner of the time and a founder of the Muskoka Lakes Golf and Country Club. He wanted to shelter his thirty-foot sloop, which was designed and built by Bert Minett, a famous Muskoka boatbuilder.

The building rises torpedo-like to a narrow peak with clearance for a thirty-five-foot mast. The door consists of three sections that open inward, but opening them is not easy. The two upper sections open on a pulley system. However, each of the three sections is kept shut by a wooden crossbar. So someone has to climb the ladder that spans one curving wall and, using a long pole for leverage, remove the crossbars from their latches. The boat that now occupies the single slip is the *Trillium,* the Grundys' twenty-foot Niad daysailer. "We love to sail, so we usually leave these doors open all summer," Eric explains, "just because it's such a difficult chore."

Over at the century-old dry-slip boathouse, the Grundys have converted storage space into a sparkling fitness room with polished wooden floors, a sound system and bar fridge. They love being able to slide open the barn doors, work out on the treadmill and gaze out at the lake. The doors open to a floating platform, where once rowboats and canoes would have been pulled out of the water on wooden rollers. It now supports two Thai lounge chairs where Eric and Valerie relax after their workouts and remind themselves that, despite "seven years of hard labor," Ouno Island with its quaint old buildings is still a great place to be.

Valerie Grundy's window boxes and planters earned high praise at the Muskoka Heritage Foundation's Garden Tour.

The Grundys turned the downstairs of the dryland boathouse into a fitness room. Being right on the water makes it ideal for post-workout dips in the lake.

OVERLEAF:
The interior is an intricate latticework of beams and rafters with pulleys for opening the three door sections.

This sailboat boathouse is an unusual sight in Muskoka. It was built in 1915 to accommodate a thirty-foot sloop. Two other sailboat boathouses exist on Lake Rosseau, both of them built in 1935 for the Osler family.

Donald and Margaret Hewgill's boathouse cottage basks in the glow of sunset.

43

HORSESHOE ISLAND

LAKE MUSKOKA

In the tenets of Japanese architecture, it is important to live lightly on the land. At Horseshoe Island, Donald and Margaret Hewgill do just that. Their cottage is a small boathouse tucked in a bay on this most northerly of Lake Muskoka's islands. It is quite unlike other Muskoka boathouses. There are no cupolas, no broad decks, no fancy fretwork, not even a boat slip, because it originated as a dry boathouse. This simple clapboard structure with its peak roof and small balcony sits gently on cribs at the shore. Only the back kitchen is on land, occupying a tiny chunk of waterfront. Little has changed here in almost a hundred years.

The boathouse was originally built in 1905 to store canoes and rowboats. When Don's uncle bought Horseshoe Island in 1949, it was the only building, apart from an icehouse out back. Rather than construct something new, he merely converted the boathouse into living quarters, with one large bedroom in the upper level. Later, he added a den with a fireplace on the building's north side. Where double wooden doors once opened onto the boat ramp, he put in a large picture window facing west toward the Indian River.

Don inherited the property from his uncle in 1965 — "a very pleasant surprise," he adds — and continues to maintain the boathouse much as it always was. A few years back he had to jack the whole place up and replace the cribbing. He also built a fanciful gazebo on the point where he and Marg sit and watch the setting sun. But like his uncle, he has resisted expansion, adding only the back kitchen in 1968. When more space was required, he worked within the framework and chopped up the existing interior. The upstairs bedroom was subdivided over and over again. Marg laughs as she meanders through the rabbit warren of rooms. "Now we have four bedrooms and two bathrooms up here. We use every inch of space." Even the tin-lined closet built originally to keep bed linens and blankets free from mice has been converted to a room with bunk beds for the grandchildren.

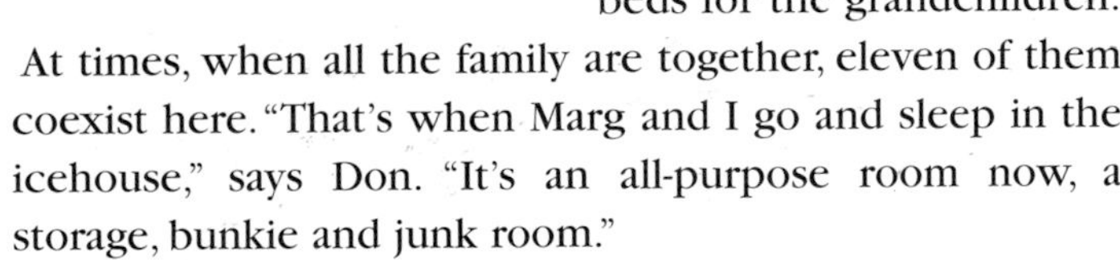

At times, when all the family are together, eleven of them coexist here. "That's when Marg and I go and sleep in the icehouse," says Don. "It's an all-purpose room now, a storage, bunkie and junk room."

Today, the Hewgill's boathouse has the casual affectionate atmosphere of a well-used family cottage. Surrounding it are untouched swaths of Muskoka landscape and beautiful pristine shoreline. From the water, when the long rays of the setting sun bathe the boathouse in golden light, it seems to float there — as lightly on the land as humanly possible.

The pine-paneled kitchen was added to the back of the original building.

A tin-lined closet becomes a bunk bedroom for the grandchildren.

Stairs lead to the second story and a maze of tiny bedrooms.

The boat doors of the dryland boathouse were removed and a large picture window has taken their place.

New docks wrap around the shoreline.

Built in 1905 as a dryland boathouse, the original structure has been maintained with just a few modern additions over the years.

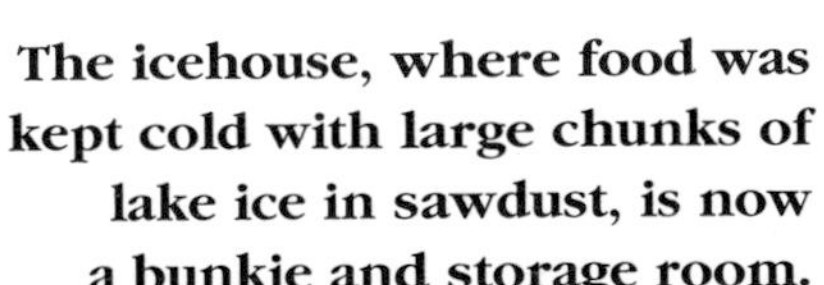

The icehouse, where food was kept cold with large chunks of lake ice in sawdust, is now a bunkie and storage room.

The two side-by-side boathouses and vintage cottage on Hideaway Island were restored by builder Wayne Judges. "This is my favorite kind of work," he says. "Sometimes it would be easier to tear down the old structures and build new, but you never get the same feeling. Also, you'd never be able to build this way again. The cottage is closer to the water than allowed today — and each boathouse has about a thousand square feet of living space."

44

HIDEAWAY ISLAND

LAKE ROSSEAU

When the current owners bought Hideaway Island in 1998, with its vast old cottage and twin boathouses, they were taking over a much-loved retreat that had been in the same family for almost thirty years. It had fallen sadly into disrepair. When the scrupulous restoration was almost complete, the son of the former owners returned. He wrote a moving letter describing his family's emotional ties to the island and his pleasure at seeing such "a beautiful and thoughtful restoration." His framed letter hangs in the kitchen of the turn-of-the-century cottage.

This is just one indication of the care that went into the revival of this lovely Muskoka property. Working with builder Wayne Judges, the new owners wanted to update everything without destroying the integrity of the original structures. "We believe that the first building on the island was constructed in 1876," says the new owner. " We know for sure that the main cottage was here in 1887 because that date and the owner's name, 'Mildred Cartwright,' are etched in a window pane. We think she did it with her diamond ring."

The renovation has been an all-consuming task. Even the legendary perennial gardens, tended for decades by the former owner, were preserved. All the plant material was moved to the far side of the island during the construction and then replanted in its original bed. The fun part has been finding treasures in cupboards (old woolen blankets, table linens and monogrammed bed sheets) and piecing together the island history from old newspapers found inside the walls. A 1905 copy of the *Mail and Empire* (an early version of the *Globe and Mail*) was found in one boathouse when the builders were tearing out the fiberboard walls. There are two matching three-slip boathouses at Hideaway. One is divided upstairs into two dormitory-style bedrooms (a green room for girls and a blue room for boys). Both have separate entrances up a back staircase and doors at the lake end that open onto a common verandah. The upper level of the second boathouse is a party room for the family's three teenage daughters. Neither boathouse has plumbing. Instead, hand-painted signs point the way to the Ladies and Gents washrooms and a shower house (his and hers also) tucked away in the woods.

Whenever possible, old furniture has been freshened with new paint, cabinet hardware cleaned up and reused, and bathroom fixtures restored or replaced with antique fittings from the same era. All in all, it feels and looks very much the way it did in the summer of 1887 when Mildred Cartwright decided to leave her permanent imprint.

Bathrobes are supplied
for the trek to the shower house.

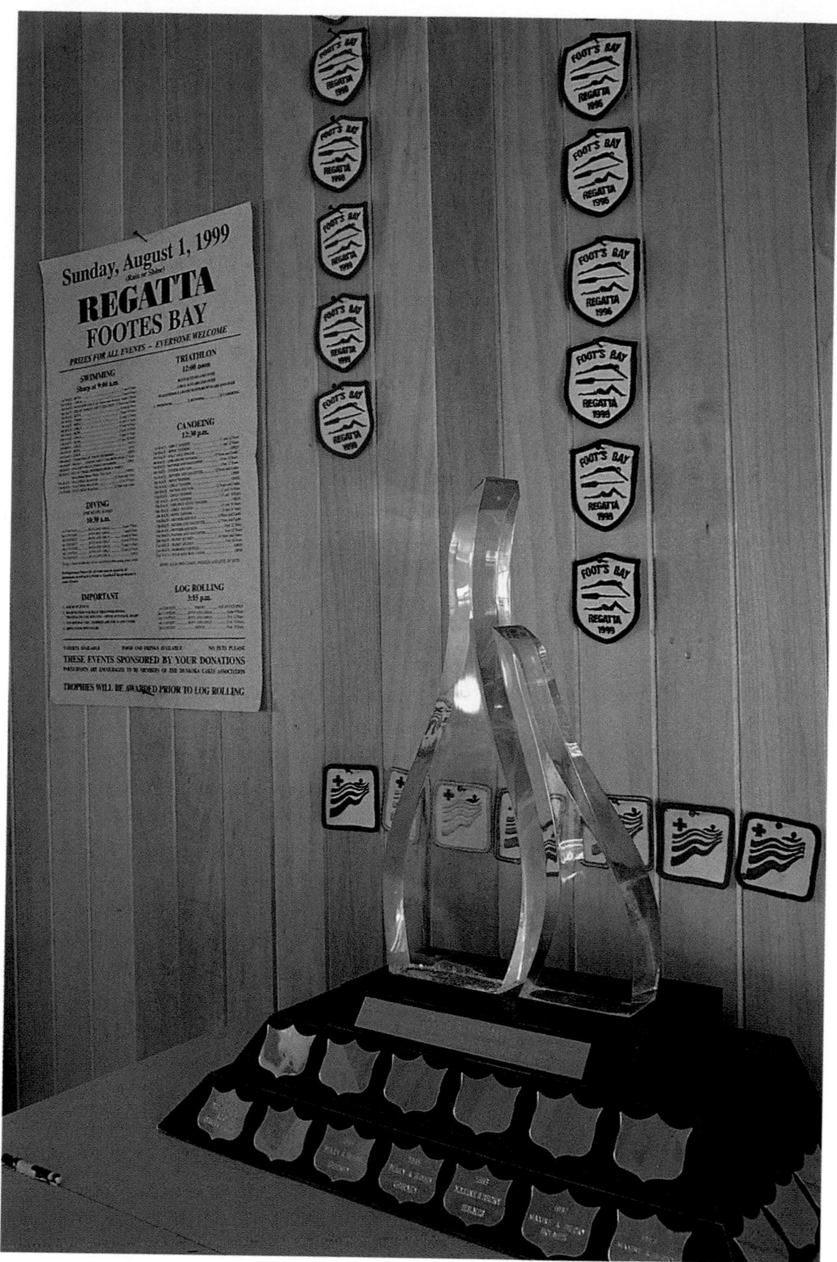

Regatta prowess displayed
on the basswood walls.

The girls' bedroom, built for the family's three teenage daughters. Upstairs in the second boathouse there's a party room — "just for hanging out."

The boys' bedroom, with its neat row of beds. Most of the furniture was in the boathouse or cottage and required just a fresh coat of paint.

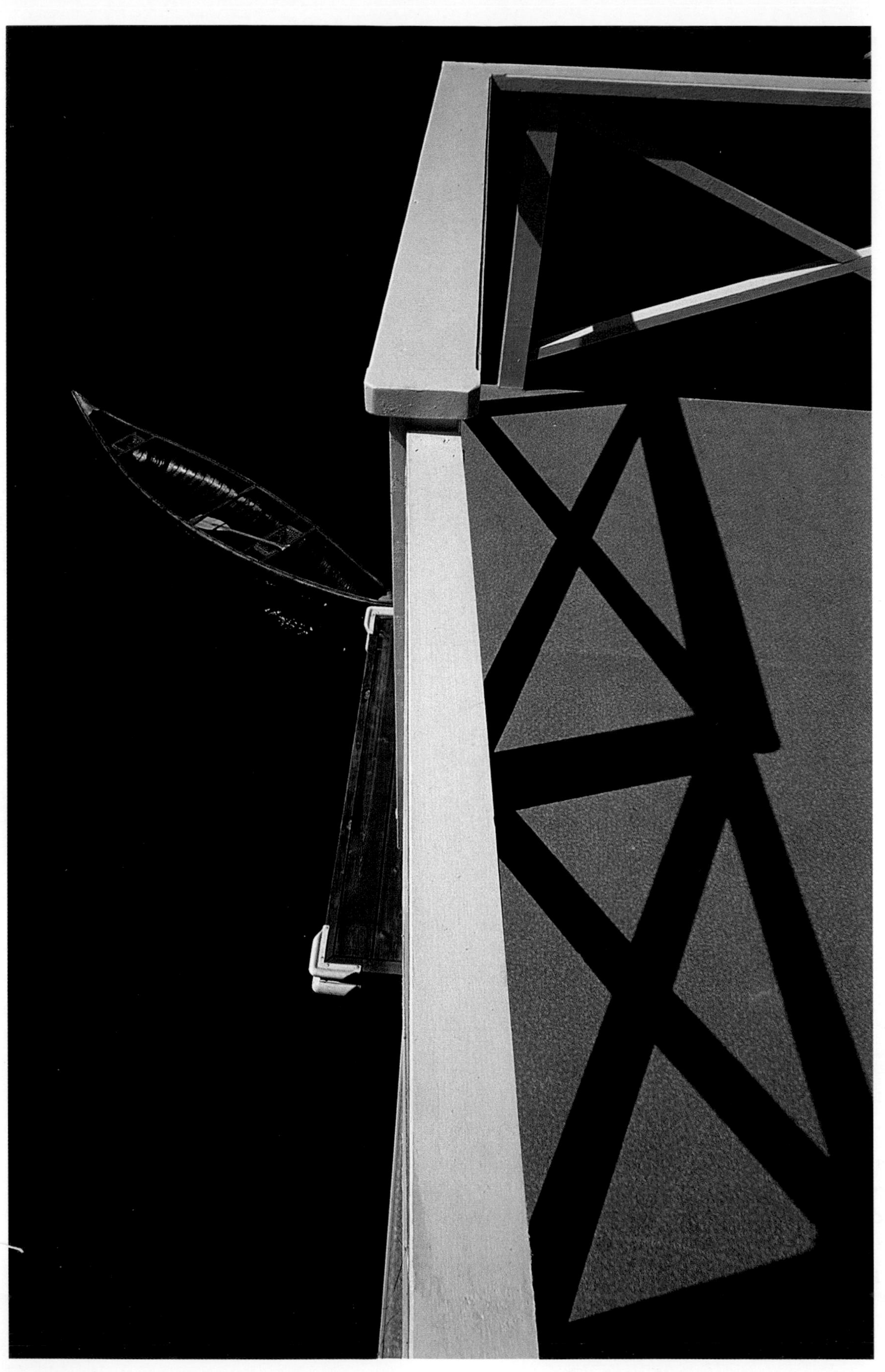

The old cedar-strip canoe, *Hideaway*, was a house gift from friends. The biggest challenge with the boat-houses was tearing out and replacing the old docks. They were interconnected, originally built as one big dock, so both buildings had to be raised at the same time.

Who can resist a swing on the old-fashioned porch sofa that glides on metal runners? From the covered verandah, doors open into the two separate bedrooms. In the distance, a wooden bridge leads to the half-acre island where the original cottage was built. An automatic sprinkler system snakes its way through the lushly planted window boxes, containers and flower beds on the island.

The Willowood boathouse used to be a single-story building with a flat, pea-gravel roof. Inside were massive squared-off ceiling beams used for hauling up boats before freeze-up. These were left intact. The exterior, however, has been totally changed. Architect David Gillett took advantage of the lovely setting to design a handsome boathouse in keeping with the 1920s cottage. He added verandahs, columns and overhangs but avoided any excess ornamentation.

45

WILLOWOOD

L A K E   R O S S E A U

"I wanted to capture summertime," says Michele Young. "Whenever I walk into this boathouse, I want it to feel like July twentieth."

Michele, her husband, Gordon, and their three children moved into this wooded property on Lake Rosseau in 1998. It had been the summer home of Gordon's parents for thirty years — the name "Willowood" a compilation of their names, William and Lois, and Wood for the street where they lived in Toronto. Michele and Gordon are still in the process of making it a place of their own.

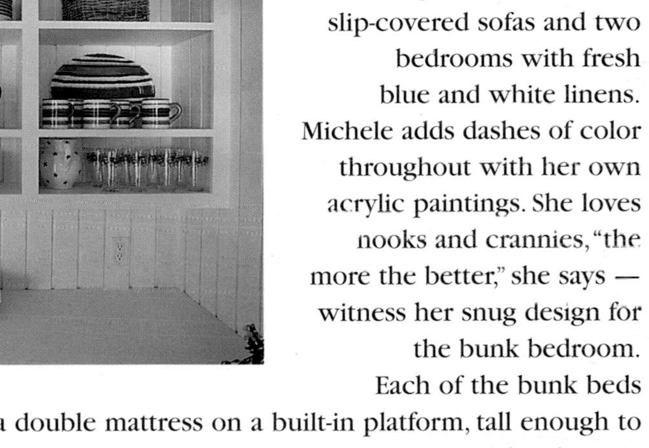

When they decided to add living quarters to the boathouse, they chose to complement the style of the 1920s cottage, with its verandahs, columns and mullioned windows. The boathouse had been simply a flat-topped garage for boats with two enclosed slips and a boat port. Architect David Gillett was hired to convert it to a two-story, three-slip boathouse.

"The boathouse setting is somewhat unique," says David. "The shore side is clearly visible from the cottage, so we had to make it as attractive as the lake side."

A wide flagstone path and stairway lead down a gentle slope to the boathouse. An arched canopy and elaborate woodworking details add interest, and the entry door, designed by Michele, is more welcoming than an ordinary utility door. The second story has mullioned windows on all sides. For the water view, the architect's goal was to keep the boathouse from looking like a three-car garage. To achieve this, he recessed the middle boat door to effectively lessen the bulk of the structure.

The interior has a breezy barefoot comfort. Rough-sawn plank walls are painted white and light dances in from all sides. Although it measures only the maximum 650 square feet, it gives the illusion of more space. There's an ample country-style kitchen and sitting room with white slip-covered sofas and two bedrooms with fresh blue and white linens. Michele adds dashes of color throughout with her own acrylic paintings. She loves nooks and crannies, "the more the better," she says — witness her snug design for the bunk bedroom.

Each of the bunk beds has a double mattress on a built-in platform, tall enough to sit down and not hit your head. The design, with cabinetry by local craftsman Chris Goneau, includes some space-saving measures perfected by boatwrights. Cubbyholes at the headboard lift up for storing books, a reading light hangs overhead, and each bed has its own tiny window with curtains that pull across for privacy. But unlike portholes on ships, these windows open to let in the fresh lake breezes.

Guests who stay in the boathouse fall in love with the sunwashed space that is luminous even on gray days. Just as Michele had hoped, it always feels like summertime.

White interior walls of rough-sawn pine are a key element in the summery beach house look that Michele Young prefers. Cottage blues and splashes of bright red add color. The floors are easy-care prefinished Brazilian mahogany. White slipcovers on the sofas may seem foolhardy with three children, but Michele claims, "They're easy because they can be washed."

OVERLEAF: The kitchen was designed to look old-fashioned, with painted wooden cabinets, chrome fittings and open shelves. A collection of blue-and-white china adds color to the white plank walls.

The design for the bunk bedroom was created with a ship in mind. Everything is built-in, compact and well crafted.

A generous helping of white keeps the interior sunny even on overcast days. One of Michele's acrylic paintings is propped on the headboard.

The boat port provides extra moorage and the stairway leads to the spacious deck.

The land side of the boathouse received equal attention because of its visibility from the cottage. A wide flagstone path leads to an entranceway with an arched canopy and wooden columns.

The middle boat door was recessed to keep the boathouse from looking like a three-car garage.

The middle boat door was recessed to keep the boathouse from looking like a three-car garage.

AT THE WATER'S EDGE

Located on Lake Rosseau, Bracken Island is joined to its smaller neighbouring island by a breakwater and walkway. The original peaked section of the boathouse was built in 1906 to house two Minett-Shields boats, the *Sea-Horse* and the *Blue Streak*. New owners added four more slips to the boathouse, as well as a second floor. Today the upper storey is a large recreation area with a slippery-floored broomball court and a ping-pong table. The long roof, which stretches almost 100 feet out from the shore, has two shed dormers enlivened by multipaned windows and flower boxes brimming with pink impatiens. A handsome rowing skiff fits perfectly into the narrow slip closest to shore.

Tucked into a bay near Beaumaris, this boathouse has a screened veranda at water level.

Festooned with ornate gingerbread, this newly-built boathouse sits snugly in a bay on Lake Joseph.

Amber light shining through leaded windows at John and Madeline Fielding's whimsical boathouse, Todmorden, near Mortimer's Point on Lake Muskoka.

Boathouses line the shore near Beaumaris on Lake Muskoka.

Bobbing in its Beaumaris berth is the *Robin Adair*, a 1927 Ditchburn.

Autumn turns to winter near Milford Bay, Lake Muskoka.

Boat storage at the Penney lumbermill, Lake Rosseau.